ANIMAL LAW

ANIMAL LAW

Challenges and Themes

Dr Simon Brooman, Dr Deborah Legge,
Dr Deborah Rook and Dr Rachel Dunn

5m Books

First published 2025

Published by
5M Books Ltd
Lings, Great Easton
Essex CM6 2HH, UK
Tel: +44 (0)330 1333 580
www.5mbooks.com

A Catalogue record for this book is available from the British Library

ISBN 9781789183702
eISBN 9781789183764
DOI 10.52517/9781789183764

EU GPSR Authorised Representative
LOGOS EUROPE, 9 rue Nicolas Poussin, 17000, LA ROCHELLE, France
E-mail: Contact@logoseurope.eu

Cover photo: pexels-yaroslav-shuraev-6889088

Book layout by Toynbee Editorial Services Ltd
Printed and bound by CPI Group (UK) Ltd, Croydon CR0 4YY

Contents

Acknowledgements

This book is about the issues that arise from our relationship with animals. It began as an update to Law Relating to Animals (1997) by Brooman and Legge, but it quickly became apparent that after leaving it for a number of decades, more than an update was needed. Brooman and Legge became Brooman, Legge, Rook and Dunn and has become a greatly enriched writing project as a result. The process has been a relatively long one, and we are grateful to Sarah Hulbert at 5m Books for her understanding.

There are so many great organisations working within Animal Law, but we would particularly like to thank Paula Sparks and all at A-LAW who brought us together at conferences on Animal Law and provided a great platform for research and discussion.

In terms of Environmental Law, the UK Environmental Law Association also provides a platform for research and discussion around environmental issues, including those affecting animals.

Closer to home, we would like to thank our friends and families who have heard us talking about the book for too long and must have wondered if it would ever be a reality.

We would like to dedicate this book to the memory of Steven Wise, prolific author and founder of the Nonhuman Rights Project, who sought to bring Animal Law into court as well as the international conscience. Steven helped to support claims in several countries, and he was an inspiration to all of us through his writing and direct legal action. We would also like to dedicate the book to the new 'breed' of pressure groups for animals across the globe, which seems to increase by the day – sometimes in areas hitherto considered well beyond the reach of such vociferous energy in support of animals. They are far too numerous to mention, but their work shines a light on poor practice and continues to advance the cause of better protection and less suffering for animals literally everywhere. We are in awe of your dedication and the spirit of justice that you exude on behalf of our cohabiters on planet Earth. You are a credit to human animals.

Simon, Debbie, Deborah and Rachel
May 2024

Introduction

Animal Law is a unique and relatively new area of study and research in the lexicon of legal disciplines. The first Animal Law course to be taught in a university in the United Kingdom (UK) was started by Mike Radford in the early 1990s, and the second, taught by Simon Brooman and Debbie Legge, began in 1994. Deborah Rook and Rachel Dunn have since taken up the reins and continue to teach the subject at their respective universities. The merits, or otherwise, of the emergence of new disciplines in law are not for detailed discussion here, but as committed researchers and experienced teachers in the area, we felt the need to put our cards on the table that we regard Animal Law as a distinct area of study and research and not as a junior partner of other areas of law. The number of academics publishing in Animal Law alongside courses offered across the globe is witness to a phenomenal surge in interest amongst the legal scholarship community.

Animal Law has clear roots in many areas; for example, there is a clear synergy of concern with Environmental Law but, put simply, the sentience of 'creatures' means that the considerations involved in determining the law that affects them are quite different – often interrelated, but requiring different considerations. In law, animals can be considered property, making them relevant to the study of Property Law. They can also be involved in trespassing cases, which brings them under Tort Law. Additionally, numerous crimes are associated with our use of animals, which falls within the scope of Criminal Law. These examples show the breadth of reach in the legal framework governing the interrelationship between animals and humans.

In recent years, a growing number of excellent Animal Law books have been published, including Knight, Phillips and Sparks' *Routledge Handbook of Animal Welfare* in 2022 and Fasel and Butler's *Animal Rights Law* in 2023. So why the need for a new book? Academics such as Steven Wise and David Favre in the United States, Mike Radford, Angus Nurse and, dare we say, ourselves in the UK, have written about a diverse range of approaches to the subject, from philosophical and rights-based analysis to public (e.g. how such laws can be challenged by judicial review), or black-letter law-based (examining how the law is applied, not its philosophical basis) approaches and how to teach it . However, no matter how diverse the approaches are, there are clear themes that emerge from the ether between them. This is where we hope this book fits into the overall status of publications in Animal Law – the identification of themes and challenges.

Choosing a title for this book was challenging in itself. We take no particular philosophical stance as some have done in terms of basing their contributions on animal rights and law, for example, although we certainly respect and appreciate the work of fellow academics such as Sean Butler and Raffael Fasel at the Cambridge Centre for Animal Rights Law. The Oxford Centre for Animal Ethics also has a long-standing track record for promoting legal theories in the area through its annual conference and the *Journal of Animal Ethics*. The UK Centre for Animal Law (A-LAW), along with their *UK Journal of Animal Law*, continues to be our 'home' community of Animal Law scholars and has an established conference to which we have all contributed large parts of our energy in recent years as organisers and contributors. This overall growth of dedicated and organised approaches to research and dissemination of ideas in Animal Law is one of the key pointers to the evolution of Animal Law as a separate discipline. The move to challenge existing law in court by groups such as the Nonhuman Rights Project in the United States and Advocates for Animals in the UK is a particularly interesting development of the 21st century, which adds context to claiming change for animals.

But where does this book fit in? Our approach to presenting a book about Animal Law takes no particular legal or philosophical standpoint upon which to discuss the various areas of concern. Rather, we observe that most of the various theories are useful for identifying themes, challenges and reasons for change that stretch across those areas. We have found that the numerous historical and contemporary contributions as to why there should be changes to laws protecting animals all have their value – the contributions from the Roman philosopher Plutarch to 21st century Peter Singer are pillars of learning in Animal Law – they teach us to ask why the law is as it is and how it should change. Some of the greatest minds in the history of humankind have looked at the similarities and differences between 'them' and 'us' – often finding that 'they' are much closer to 'us' than was generally accepted at the time. Add scientific evidence to the mix, and the cause for change was born.

To choose one theory seemed to us an impossible task – like choosing a favourite child or favourite animal when all have value and are deserving in their own right. Therefore, we have adopted a more practical approach for this book by identifying the major areas of concern and discussion, such as the treatment of wildlife, animals in experimentation, farmed animals and domesticated animals. We then explore those areas to uncover the themes that emerge to create a wider notion of the general themes of animal welfare. We have also revealed our perspectives on the main challenges facing these individual areas of human interaction with animals.

We have mentioned the major themes in this introduction to guide readers in approaching this book. Animal Law involves not only a lot of diverse laws themselves but also numerous different approaches by various jurisdictions worldwide. It is impossible to cover all of these, so we have focused on how the jurisdictions of the UK and the European Union reveal the themes and challenges of Animal Law. The practical reasoning behind this decision is also simple, as these are the jurisdictions with which we are familiar and have experience.

If we were to name one overarching theme that drew us to Animal Law, it would be our shared concerns for the treatment of animals and how the law could address this concern. Several sub-themes emerge from this focus, each presenting its own challenges:

- **Philosophical theories**: Understanding the philosophical theories that shape our relationship with animals is crucial for advocating legal changes. What key ideas have been proposed, and how can we use them to push for meaningful reform in animal law?
- **Cruelty vs. welfare-based approaches**: Is preventing cruelty still the main driver for legal change, or should we shift focus toward animal welfare and sentience? Should laws set only minimal standards to prevent cruelty, or should they require positive steps to meet the needs of each species based on their natural behaviour? How should growing scientific evidence of animal sentience, such as with farmed fish and lab animals, influence legal regulations?
- **Animals as property**: The legal status of animals as property allows owners significant control over them, within the bounds of the law. Should this paradigm shift? How does treating animals as property affect how laws are written and interpreted?
- **Criminal responsibility**: Over time, the law has increasingly criminalised certain human actions against animals. However, who determines what is considered criminal, and are current protections sufficient?
- **Challenges in enforcing the law**: Even when laws exist, enforcing them can be problematic due to limited resources or political will. Examples include the destruction of animals' habitats for profit, long-distance transportation of farmed animals, and questionable

practices in laboratories. How can these enforcement challenges be addressed?

- **Strategies for legal change**: What are the best approaches to changing animal-related laws? If judicial attitudes are changing in relation to those who transgress the law in their campaigns for animals does this make in-court challenges more or less likely to be successful?

Discussions around the themes and challenges emerge organically in each chapter, and the overall impression of the status of Animal Law is drawn together in the conclusion.

The first three chapters of this book identify the historical, scientific and philosophical contributions that have brought us to where we are today.

Chapters 1–3 form the core of our underpinning position on why changing the law in relation to animals is often desirable, necessary and supported by evidence. Chapter 1 examines how human attitudes – shaping the content of the law – have emerged and evolved. Chapter 2 examines how law developed at first through laws that dealt with observed cruelty, then created legislation which imposed an anthropocentric vision of animal use then more recently began to draw on science in terms of sentience, which competes with the protection of property interests. Chapter 3 examines some of the more modern approaches to why we need to change the law, drawing on the explosion in 'animal rights' contributions that have emerged towards the end of the 20th century.

The following chapters look in detail at specific areas of the law in the context of the themes and challenges they pose for those campaigning to change the law.

Chapter 4 examines the area of animal experimentation – often seen as the most difficult area to tackle because of the claims to scientific progress that emerge from the pro-experimentation lobby. It also attracts a good deal of public support, even though many experiments performed on animals provoke shock and condemnation when they are exposed to the public gaze. This area carries with it many of the themes listed above, such as what we are prepared to accept as necessary cruel practices in the name of scientific discovery. It is also an area where undercover operations are common, bringing with it questions as to the how and why of protest in this area.

Chapter 5 explores some of the legal themes and challenges arising from our unique relationship with companion animals. The human-companion animal relationship can exist as a close, dynamic, socially supportive bond perceived as akin to family that is characterised by a lifelong dependency of the animal on its human carer. The relationship is therefore one of vulnerability and dependence on the part of the animal. Due to living in an enclosed home environment with no free access to the outside world, the companion animal depends on its human carer to provide for all its basic needs, such as food, water, medical care and social interaction. Cats are less dependent on humans because many are allowed to roam freely outside and can therefore independently meet some of their needs. This vulnerability and dependence require the law to move beyond protection from cruelty and abuse as a minimum baseline for a sentient being and instead impose positive duties on those responsible for a companion animal to meet their wider welfare needs.

The chapter examines the legislation in England as a case study to demonstrate how legislation can seek to achieve this whilst also identifying some of the challenges in terms of the need for effective drafting, interpretation and enforcement of animal welfare legislation. A key theme in Animal Law explored in this chapter is the legal status of companion animals as property. This status is at odds with the perception of many people that their pet is a family member or close friend. This incongruity can create challenges for courts and those involved in policy and lawmaking. The chapter uses three case studies: pet custody disputes, pets in rental housing, and the abduction of pets, to examine some of the wider implications of the property status of pets and consider if there are alternative ways to legally classify the human-companion animal relationship that better reflect its unique nature.

Chapter 6 identifies some of the themes and challenges in using legislation to protect farmed animals and meet their welfare needs. It mainly focuses on animals reared and slaughtered for food (including fish) but also looks briefly at animals farmed for their fur. The chapter examines the growth of intensive farming practices in the West and asks whether farmed animals suffer in intensive farms. The key legal concept of unnecessary suffering is examined and applied to farmed animals. It is a concept that is used in different countries across the world, so understanding its limitations, especially the subjective nature of assessing necessity, is important. The vested interest many humans have in continuing the meat industry on a large commercial scale and cheaply can make law reform to improve protection for farmed animals challenging.

There is a need for legislation to keep pace with advances in science, for example, to protect sentient invertebrates, and legislation needs to be adequately interpreted by the courts and enforced by enforcement agencies to ensure the best protection for farmed animals. The legal status of farmed animals as property and their low moral status as resources for our use means their individual interests may not be prioritised in society and politics, meaning they do not receive the moral consideration they deserve as sentient beings. The chapter also looks at how farmed animal health and welfare interconnect with human health and welfare, including wider environmental concerns such as the climate crisis. To illustrate the point that eating meat is a moral dilemma and should not be done without thought to the lives of the animals being eaten, a leading ethical theory is applied to the question of whether it is ethical to eat meat. This illustrates the vital link between Animal Law and ethics.

Chapters 7 and 8 look at the challenges faced by wildlife law. Chapter 7 examines how wildlife is protected from cruelty, which in law is seen as unnecessary suffering, whilst Chapter 8 considers wildlife extinctions and biodiversity loss. These chapters, although split up for ease of understanding, are really one issue and need to be read together as they overlap. There is an argument that the cruel treatment of individual wildlife is a different issue from wildlife extinction and biodiversity loss, but it is important to consider both issues. We need to ensure the humane treatment of the individual animal but also ensure that wildlife survives. Both chapters address the status of animals as sentient beings. However, for wild animals, their protection is often limited to preventing unnecessary suffering, unlike the welfare approach applied to domestic and captive animals that focuses on meeting their broader welfare needs.

Chapter 7 looks at how the law has viewed wildlife historically and, in particular, how animals became categorised in law as property, and how this, along with the view of the land as property, has shaped the law. The chapter considers the law protecting wildlife from cruelty and then some of the related issues, particularly in relation to agriculture, hunting, shooting, fishing and keeping wildlife in captivity in zoos, as well as a brief look at other activities that wild animals may be used for.

Chapter 8 examines the adequacy of wildlife law and the challenges it faces to halt extinctions and protect biodiversity. It looks at the history and causes of extinctions, biodiversity loss and the development of international law. The severe impact that habitat loss and fragmentation is having on the efforts to conserve and save endangered species is also briefly looked at. The chapter considers how to protect migrating species along with the issue of invasive non-native or alien species. It explores trade in endangered species and the role of zoos in conservation. It then goes on to consider the human-wildlife conflicts that have arisen due to rewilding, fortress conservation and ecotourism. It considers the marine environment with a case study on the protection of whales. The impact of the climate emergency is a theme that runs through the chapter, as well as a discussion of how people and wildlife may coexist and the role of the law in facilitating this and dealing with conflicts.

Both chapters consider where the balance lies between human and animal interests and what the law can do to improve their lives. The chapters also examine issues around enforcement and provide suggestions for reform. Throughout the book, the UK is used as a case study as this is the legal system we know best and, in the past, has often been at the forefront of legal protections. However, we will also look at the regional approaches of the European Union and international controls as they provide a framework for domestic legislation.

Some of the content in the first three chapters first appeared in *Law Relating to Animals* (Cavendish Publishing, 1997) by Brooman and Legge, and we are grateful to Routledge for allowing us to use some of those chapters, which have been greatly reworked and rewritten. The other chapters are entirely new and original, reflecting the new team of writers. We have all contributed to lesser and greater extents to all the chapters, although each has taken a lead role for different chapters. It has been a team effort to cover such an expansive subject. The views given are, in the great majority of cases, those of all of us, but we had dynamic discussions about some of the issues, and the narrative sometimes reflects our best efforts at consensus.

There are now around 15 Animal Law or similar such courses offered at UK universities, but this should be seen in the context of the approximately 150 such courses available in the United States. Animal Law also has strongholds in Brazil, Australia, France, South Africa and elsewhere. Those teaching, studying and researching Animal Law are undeniably challenging modern legal orthodoxy regarding the treatment of animals. Changes in the law are frequent and ongoing. In this book, we have chosen to capitalise 'Animal Law' as we view it as a distinct field, comparable to Contract Law, Environmental Law and Land Law.

Whilst we have aimed to be entirely up to date at the time of publication, such is the momentum of change with new governments and the evolving legal agenda for animals that we may have missed something during the publication process. For example, as we write in November 2024, a Private Members Bill (a suggested change in UK law from a member of parliament outside the government), had been introduced with the intention of banning experiments on animals. It is unlikely to make it into law, but it illustrates the continued appetite for change not only amongst pressure groups, but also amongst legislators. Animal Law often moves faster than the pen.

We also admit our credentials as animal lovers in searching for meaning in our own lives through writing in support of animals. We hope this book will convince you that the law that protects animals needs reform – much has been done but there is still much to do and good reason for it.

CHAPTER ONE

Philosophy, science and the historical recognition of animal sentience

The thought of a world with no consideration for animals and no laws to protect them seems irrational, uncivilised, cruel and somehow inhuman. But how did we arrive at this view? What led humankind to regard animals as significant and deserving of protection? Who were the prime movers in our change of attitudes from the hunter-gatherer of pre-history to the intellectual and philosophical legislator-protector of today? This chapter gives an overview of the main philosophical contributions that, since the Ancient Greeks, have provided the foundations upon which the legal treatment of animals has been built. It also examines the scientific contributions since the work of Charles Darwin, which have increasingly provided evidence for legislators. It is not a chapter about law; rather, it is a chapter about the essential philosophical and moral basis of how we should regard animals, which has developed across the centuries and has sometimes, but not always, had an influence on the creation of specific laws. In short – it is about how humans began to recognise non-human animal sentience and how some appreciated that this required us to question how we should treat them. Our treatment of animals is dependent on a how humans view animals and, since Darwin, what we have discovered about them (Clark, 2011).

The contemporary philosophical and scientific status of animals is discussed in Chapter 3, but here we look at the main historical influences. The treatment of animals in law has been the subject of conjecture ever since the ancient Greeks. However, 'modern' legal protection of animals originated in early 19th century England in the form of agitation by a small group of concerned individuals. Two abortive attempts to form animal welfare societies occurred in 1809 in Liverpool and 1822 in London. Lasting success came with the formation of the 'society instituted for the purpose of preventing cruelty to animals' inaugurated on 16 June 1824 which eventually became the RSPCA with the support of Queen Victoria in 1840. Areas of concern, such as anti-vivisection, were soon drawn into the net of moral concern (Stone, 2023). Ultimately, this has become a global movement represented by diverse interest groups and supported by a considerable body of philosophical contributions. For the moment, 'animal rights' is the term that will be used here, but, as we shall see later, terms such as animal 'welfare' or 'personhood' have had a place in discussions about protecting animals since the turn of the 21st century. The term 'animal rights' was adopted in the 1970s, and although the term certainly has its flaws, in terms of what is being claimed for animals in law, it has been adopted as a practical and historically significant shorthand. Barely a day passes by without issues of animal abuse hitting the headlines in the media across the globe. Whether it is whaling or the transportation of animals farmed for food in the international sphere, or the more local issues such as the badger cull in the UK or puppy farming in Ireland, abuse of animals is rarely out of the headlines.

Those wishing to see better protection of animals are drawn from right across the social strata. The period 1994–95, for example, saw enhanced coverage of the animal rights issue resulting from the practice of transporting live animals from British airfields and ports to continental Europe. A lot of attention was given to the fact that the protestors not only included the traditional, recognisable radicals who had previously been associated with the so-called 'animal rights movement', but also a new militant middle class of individuals showing that concern for animals is widespread in all corners of the social strata. The animal rights debate has seen a significant increase in global participation, with a corresponding rise in animal welfare organisations even in previously untouched regions like China and Africa. Why has there been such a growth in the number of concerned individuals? Has there been a sudden change in the collective consciousness of millions of individuals in the 20th century, or can we trace historical evidence that concern for animals has always been embedded in human consciousness?

Perhaps the most compelling motivating force behind the comparatively recent surge in the number of people attaching themselves to animal rights issues is the wealth of detailed and reasoned philosophical analysis that started to appear on a large scale from the mid-1970s onwards. These were part of the emergence of zoocentric (human and animal-focused) notions of moral consideration, which expanded human moral concern to animals rather than maintaining anthropocentric (human-centred) versions of moral reality. Such moral discourse now includes consideration for animals in other moral discussions relating to biocentrism (expanding moral consideration to all species) and ecocentrism (concern for all of nature) (Hanlon & Magalhães-Sant'Ana, 2016). We will return to this in Chapter 3 when we consider modern approaches to moral consideration of animals and how these fit into wider concerns about the environment and damage to our climate and the global ecosphere.

Peter Singer's *Animal Liberation* (2015), first published in 1975, was a turning point in gaining academic and public recognition for the philosophical case to improve the treatment of animals. The quantity of philosophical material produced about our treatment of animals has grown exponentially, as has the number of laws and treaties giving protection to animals. Animal Law has become recognised as a discipline for legal study across the globe, and philosophical/ethical elements form part of the great majority of university disciplines related to the use of animals in biomedical science and husbandry (Dunn et al., 2023). The profound influence of moral discussion and its resulting growth in focused political pressure on the development of the law in this area cannot be doubted. It would, however, be a mistake to assume that the discussion of the moral basis for how we treat animals and the way that should be recognised in law has been the preserve of the 20th century. The most notable philosophers in history have asked questions about the moral status of animals sometimes as a way of examining and contrasting the morality that underpins human interaction and development.

A good deal of the early writing on this subject is based upon Judaeo-Christian religious traditions, which saw humans as created in the image of God and having dominion over all other species. Humans were accorded the divine commission to exercise 'dominion over the fish of the sea, and over the birds of the air, and over the cattle, and over all the earth, and over every creeping thing which creeps upon the earth'; Noah was 'given' the animals and plants (Genesis 1:26–28 and Genesis 9:3). Most of the early writing in the part of the world dominated by European/Judaeo-Christian attitudes concentrates on distinguishing humans from the 'beasts' to justify our treatment of them, which is based on our 'dominion' over them. The literature also illustrates the wider search for the 'essence of mankind' as humans struggled to find reasons for their own existence, including a blueprint of how they should treat each other, quite apart from how we should treat animals. When science was still in its embryonic stages, there was a lack of detailed knowledge of human/non-human physiology and 'sentience'. It is, therefore, not at all surprising that some of the best known writers and philosophers contributing to historical analysis of the status of animals sought to find their answers in religion.

The Bible, although widely interpreted as giving humans dominion over animals, contains many references to how this dominion should be exercised in a compassionate and kind manner (Deuteronomy 25:4; Proverbs 12:10). In the later texts of the Old Testament, humans are directed on several occasions to show kindness. For example: 'You shall not muzzle an ox when he treadeth out the corn' (Deuteronomy 25:4), and 'a righteous man has regard for the beast' (Proverbs 10:10). In contrast, the ancient religious doctrines of the Orient were reluctant to draw sharp distinctions between humans and animals. This, along with the belief that the immortal soul passed from one body to another, led to a different attitude towards animals and a predominantly vegetarian diet.

Theological analysis of the treatment of animals has continued down the centuries, although there are considerable differences in the status and treatment that different theologians and religions have argued should be accorded to animals. Theological approaches to the treatment of animals vary considerably depending on the scriptures of the various religions and how they have been interpreted. The emphasis changes over time; for example, 20th century theological discussions about according rights to animals have given way to 21st century religion-based arguments for a vegan diet (Simonds, 2023). This is also now heavily influenced by wider concerns about the environment and the part played in climate change by farming animals for human consumption.

As noted above, interpretation of the Christian doctrines of the *Bible* in terms of animals being provided by God to be the tools of humankind has been the key source of societal attitudes and corresponding legal approaches to animals for centuries. Chief amongst the antiquarian scholars of Christian doctrine was St. Augustine of Hippo (AD 354–430), who laid the foundations for those who followed by declaring animals to be subject to human use on account of their lack of reason and community of rights. However, the broad critique of his negative contribution in terms of animal welfare has been challenged (Hoenig, 2023).

Despite the limited status accorded to animals by most theologians, others have read the Bible differently to encompass a wider duty placed on humans to care for animals and avoid cruelty towards them. One of the many theological contributions to the animal rights debate over the centuries, published around the same time as Jeremy Bentham, was developing arguments that would shape the debate until the present day. Humphry Primatt (1776) presented a different interpretation of biblical teachings. He suggested that just as the difference in intelligence, wealth and physical attributes of humans does not lead to a conclusion that the more powerful can behave badly towards them, the same applies to the relationship between humans and animals. The crucial thing for Primatt was the similarity between humans and animals in terms of their physical ability to feel pain via nerves or organs and the fact that their suffering is exhibited in cries and groans, not speech. This different method of communicating pain, he argued, gave rise to the conclusion that to ignore it exhibited our lack of understanding of animal communications rather than an excuse to inflict it.

Primatt's concern for animals and his recognition of pain as a significant interest to be protected against in animals, as well as ourselves, presaged many of the arguments used by the animal rights lobby today. Even though Jeremy Bentham receives much credit for being the 'grandfather' of the animal rights movement, Primatt probably deserves greater status in this regard, as he recognised the similarities between humans and animals, which would later be confirmed and strengthened by Charles Darwin. He also recognised the significance of animal suffering and the philosophical links between what Richard Ryder and Peter Singer would later call 'speciesism', and racism. Primatt's name and his reasoning that resonates today should, perhaps, be more familiar to those who campaign for animals.

One of the most notable contemporary theologians to re-examine the traditional notion that gave humans absolute dominion over animals is Reverend Professor Andrew Linzey, who strongly refutes the contention that the Bible gives such unfettered dominion to humans. He stresses this is at odds with what we can discern from our own moral sense. He summarises that '…if we believe our capacity as moral beings is a gift from God freely bestowed upon us as an inherent part of our being made in the image of God, then we need to regard our moral responsibility towards animals with a degree of seriousness and urgency which hitherto has eluded us' (Linzey, 1979, p. 42).

For 2000 years or more, assumptions about what the Bible told us remained one of the key influences on philosophers as they endeavoured to identify the key differences between humans and animals that would justify our different treatment of them. However, before we assume that sentience-based approaches are a 'new' development, it should be noted that non-theological approaches have been prevalent since the 18th century and particularly since the work of Charles Darwin in the 19th century – they are far from being a contemporary modern approach. Many scholars from other disciplines have followed the approach taken by those such as Primatt and Linzey in emphasising the physiological, intellectual, self-awareness, reasoning and linguistic capacities of different species as more appropriate and significant influences on how we should treat them. These capabilities of animals may have now found their modern voice through the term animal 'sentience,' which currently supports claims for changes in 21st century approaches to Animal Law, however, the moral claim for the adequate consideration of animal sentience has its roots far deeper in history.

Plato (427–347 BC) and Aristotle (384–322 BC) both examined the status of animals. Aristotle considered humans to be the 'most excellent of all beings'. While not directly addressing the duties or rights that should be extended to animals, he set the tone of the debate for centuries to come. He distinguished humans because of, for example, their government, society, 'gift of speech' and perceptions of good and evil. However, the ancient Greeks, despite paving the way for centuries of philosophical discussion in this area, never reached a coherent view of human interaction with animals, which is evidenced by their treatment of animals 'accused' of murder (see Chapter 2).

The fate of the animals during the Roman period, whose philosophy predominated until the 6th century AD, has been well documented. For example, our understanding of the uses of the great amphitheatres of the Roman Empire (Turner, 1992), highlights how animals were considered playthings for entertainment. In an era when human rights were granted based on status, it is easy to see why animals and humans alike suffered immeasurably. The opening of the Colosseum in Rome was 'celebrated' by the killing of some 5,000 animals and an additional 9,000 were killed over the following three months (Turner, 1992). Any concern shown by the more thoughtful philosophers would have been drowned out by the constant craving for excitement, despite the suffering inflicted on both human and non-human participants (Brumbaugh, 1978). Despite the public slaughter and apparent lack of compassion for animals, the more humanitarian philosophers of the Roman Empire advocated for a different attitude. Seneca, Plutarch and Porphyry preached the ideas of universal benevolence, which incorporated a concern for the welfare of animals. Plutarch (AD 46–120) was a Greek tutor to the Emperor Hadrian, and his teachings provide a stark contrast to the slaughters that occurred in the amphitheatres (excerpt taken from Turner, 1992):

> Law and justice we cannot in the nature of things employ on others than men; but we may extend our goodness and charity even to irrational creatures; and such acts flow from a gentle nature as water from an abundant stream ... [An animal is entitled to cry] "Kill me for thy feeding but do not take me for thy better feeding." ... Yet for the sake of some little mouthful of flesh, we deprive a soul of the sun and light and of that proportion of life and time it had been born into the world to enjoy ... Let us kill an animal; but let us do it with sorrow and pity and not abusing or tormenting it, as many nowadays are wont to do.

Porphyry (AD c.232–c.305) was born in Phoenicia and moved to Rome at the age of 30. Being a vegetarian, he wrote at length on the moral case for avoiding animal flesh. He believed not only that this is an essential part of having a purified soul but that the exploitation of the animal kingdom, in general, is a denial of justice to animals and might have a negative influence on how humans treat each other. He argued that non-human animals communicate with each other (Clarke, 2011) and dismissed arguments claiming that humans are the only beings with reason and language, which is often used to justify their different moral treatment (Wynne-Tyson, 1965):

> The difference, indeed, between our reason and theirs appears to consist, as Aristotle somewhere says, not in essence, but in the more and the less; just as many are of [the] opinion, that the difference between the Gods and us is not essential, but consists in this, that in them there is a greater, and in us a less accuracy, of the reasoning power. And, indeed, so far as pertains to sense and the remaining organisation, according to the sensoria and the flesh, everyone will grant that these are similarly disposed in us, as they are in brutes. For they not only similarly participate with us of natural passions, and the motions produced through these, but we may also survey in them such affections as are preternatural and morbid. No one, however, of sound mind, will say that brutes are unreceptive of the reasoning power, on account of the difference between their habit of body and ours, when he sees that there is a great variety of habit in men, according to their race, and the nations to which they belong and yet, at the same time, it is granted that all of them are rational.

These pleas for compassionate treatment were, however, lost in the bloodlust of the Empire. The spectacles preferred by much of Roman society were those involving barbarity and slaughter on an enormous and bloody scale. The effects of this on the Roman public were far-reaching, as evidenced by the link identified between the spectacle and the sexual practices that followed driven by the high levels of excitement that were exhibited in amphitheatre crowds (Turner 1992). It has been suggested that the mass killing of animals was part of the Romans' need to prove they controlled the world (Clark, 2011, p. 45).

Changes in the prevailing attitudes towards animals may well have come about partly because of the decline of the Roman Empire as a major military power. The ritualistic slaughter in the amphitheatres was lost over time, apart from bullfighting, which remains in Spain and elsewhere, but so too were the thoughtful contributions of Rome's more humanitarian philosophers.

The ambivalence and lack of published work that prevailed over the following centuries was only ended by the revival of Aristotelian thinking in the 13th century by St Thomas Aquinas (1225–74). He ascribed to humans the right to treat animals as slaves and considered that everything on earth was placed there by God for the benefit of humans. He described humans as the 'intellectual species' with the right to do as they please with animals (Aquinas, 13th century):

> Hereby is refuted the error of those who said it is sinful for a man to kill brute animals; for by the divine providence they are intended for man's use according to the order of nature. Hence, it is not wrong for man to make use of them, either by killing or in any other way whatever. For this reason, the Lord said to Noah (Genesis 9:3): 'As the green herbs I have delivered all flesh to you.'

It is a large chronological jump from the Romans to the Reformation, pausing only to examine the views of St Thomas Aquinas, but very little of note was published about animals in the intervening period as the Dark Ages emerged. The Reformation and the revival of learning, which accompanied it, led to the beginning of the 'modern' history of philosophy including thoughts on the difference between humans and animals. Debate can be found in discussions between the 'rationalists' of the European continent and the 'empiricists' of Great Britain, which began in the 17th century. One of the most notorious rationalist statements came from René Descartes (1596–1650). His views led to widespread abuse of animals, particularly at the hands of scientists striving for invention and the advancement of medicine. He considered animals to be the same as machines, and, just as cruelty to a machine is impossible, so too, he argued, it is with animals, as they do not feel pain. True to his roots in the continental European rationalist tradition, he described animals as 'automata', showing the same qualities as machines because of an absence of intellect (Descartes, 1637):

> ... there are no men so dull and stupid, not even idiots, as to be incapable of joining together different words, and thereby constructing a declaration by which to make their thoughts understood; and that on the other hand, there is no other animal, however perfect or happily circumstanced, which can do the like.

According to Cartesian thinking, animals are 'thoughtless brutes', unaware of the sensations of pain, suffering, heat and cold. Descartes asserted that the fact that animals appear to react to these stimuli does not indicate a conscious reaction but merely indicates the same reaction as a machine being turned on, thereby denying any complex sentience. Any reactions to external stimuli could be attributed to the same response as a plant turning towards the sunlight: the response should not be seen as evidence of thought or intellect but merely of reflexive mechanical action.

Another rationalist who took up the reins of denying consideration for animals was Gottfried Liebniz (1646–1716). His views were also based upon the concept of man having been created in God's image and being the sole possessor of intelligence. His notion of man as the unique animal capable of harbouring the essential sentience, or 'spirit', added to the rationalist view of animals being created merely to serve humankind (Liebniz, 1710):

> The difference between intelligent (entities) and those which are not intelligent is quite as great as between a mirror and one who sees. As God is himself the greatest and wisest of spirits, it is easy to understand that the spirits with which he can, so to speak, enter into conversation and even into social relations by communicating to them in particular ways his feelings and his will so that they are able to know and love their benefactor, must be much nearer to him than the rest of created things which may be regarded as the instruments of spirits.

The views of Descartes in particular received criticism at the time, which continued for several decades after his death and into the next century as scientists and philosophers debated the validity of his theories. In the 18th century, La Mettrie argued that Descartes' reasoning, in terms of reflexive behaviour, could be taken a step further to explain human behaviour, thereby highlighting similarities rather than differences (La Mettrie, 1747). Descartes denied this by stressing the existence of linguistic capabilities of humans as showing that they are unique in being 'conscious'. In a twist of retribution, La Mettrie had to flee, first, to Leiden and then to Berlin to escape the theological response to this assertion, eventually finding sanctuary in the Court of Frederick the Great of Prussia. The strength of feeling that was aroused by these arguments was caused by their relationship with the very nature of mankind and our relationship with God.

Following Descartes' influential statement, experimenters and commercial agriculturalists used his theories to deny even the most minimal of humane considerations to non-human animals. The concern of 'over-sentimentality' was given Papal support by Pope Pius XII, who considered that the cries of animals should not arouse 'unreasonable compassion'. The predominance and legacy of this Catholic view of animals goes some way to explaining the different legal and moral status accorded to non-human animals in the southern States of Europe, which has caused modern-day difficulties in framing European legislation concerning animals.

Thomas Hobbes (1588–1679), although in no way as unsympathetic in his views as Descartes, found many differences between 'man and the beasts'. He used the absence of language in animals to distinguish them from humans and found differences in the fact that humans use language to name things (and even each other), to number and measure, to pass on knowledge – sometimes to even deceive themselves (Molesworth, 1994). He found that 'brute creatures' lack complex qualities of describing good and evil, and do not innovate to make themselves stand out in the crowd. In short, he found that animals lack the complexities of the minds of humans, which could give support to our treatment of them.

Despite the weight of post-Descartes discussion centring on the superiority of humans over animals, many philosophers became concerned about the treatment of animals in developing societies. British philosophers such as John Locke (1632–1704) and David Hume (1711–76), using their direct, empirical observations of animals as opposed to the 'rationality'-based arguments of the continental Europeans such as Descartes and, later, Kant, focused on the similarities that animals exhibit in relation to humans, as well as the differences. Locke did not doubt that there are certain sentient capabilities, such as memory, shared by both humans and animals, with further capabilities such as abstract thinking and comparison, which are better developed in humans: '… if [animals] have any ideas at all and are not bare machines (as some would have them), we cannot deny them to have some reason. It seems as evident to me that they do some of them in certain instances reason, as that they have sense, but it is only in particular ideas, just as they received them from their senses … and have not (as I think) the faculty to enlarge them by any kind of abstraction' (Nidditch, 1975).

Locke's chief concern was that mistreating animals might affect humans, particularly children: 'the custom of tormenting and killing beasts will, by degree, harden their minds even towards men; and they who delight in the suffering and destruction of inferior creatures will not be apt to be very compassionate or benign to those of their own kind.' (Johnson, 1801, p. 112).

Immanuel Kant (1724–1804) returned to the theme of the damage done to humans by the heartless and brutal treatment of animals. Kant appears to have had anti-cruelty tendencies, but to call him an 'animal liberationist' would be wide of the mark. To Kant, even though he stated that having encountered animals it would be difficult to harbour cruel thoughts against them, the primary reasoning against cruelty is to be found in the effect it has on humanity, not in the inherent sentient qualities of animals. He stated (Infield, 1963, p. 240):

> Tender feelings towards animals develop humane feelings towards mankind. In England, butchers and doctors do not sit on a jury because they are accustomed to the sight of death and hardened. Vivisectionists, who use living animals for their experiments, certainly act cruelly, although their aim is praiseworthy, and they can justify their cruelty since animals must be regarded as man's instruments; but any such cruelty for sport cannot be justified. A master who turns out his ass or his dog because the animal can no longer earn its keep manifests a small mind … Our duties towards animals, then, are indirect duties towards mankind.

Therefore, Kant's contention is that the primary duty to protect animals arises from an anthropocentric wish to protect human interests – a view that carries little support in the 21st century. Even in Kant's work, there is a hint of recognition of suffering and cruelty in the treatment of animals he witnessed in the 18th century. Kant was primarily concerned with protecting the autonomy and interests of humankind as the basis for much of his philosophical discussion of animals. His thinking does stretch into the modern-day treatment of animals – the call to protect human interests through, for example, the right to eat meat, the right to keep domestic animals for the benefit of owners, the right to research for medical advancement using animals in research, and the right to hunt animals for pleasure. These all have echoes of Kant's view of the relationship between humans and animals and the dominance of human interests. One wonders what Kant would have made of modern attempts to extend the notion of human autonomy to animals in the claims for personhood status to be granted to animals by The Nonhuman Rights Project in the United States (see Chapter 3 on personhood) by attempting to convince courts that certain animals are sufficiently sentient to be deserving of autonomy and therefore greater protection?

David Hume, writing in the generation after Locke in the mid-18th century, disagreed with his distinction between the species on the basis of rationality, 'Next to the ridicule of denying an evident truth is that of taking much pains to defend it, and no truth appears to me to be more evident than that beasts are endowed with thought and reason as well as men. The arguments are in this so obvious that they never escape the most stupid and ignorant.' He proposed that the depth of human reasoning goes beyond that of animals but does so merely by virtue of evolution, indicating that the differences can be explained in terms of degree rather than in kind.

Throughout the 18th and 19th centuries, the debate about the moral status of animals continued apace and would eventually lead to legislation in the UK and elsewhere seeking to protect animals from the appalling treatment that was meted out to them in relation to the production of food, transportation, medical experimentation, sport and recreation. Despite concern about the sentient capability of animals to experience pain and suffering and whether it could be equated with human suffering, the Cartesian view prevailed as the basis for supporting experimentation on live animal subjects during that period without the use of anaesthetics. Legislation regulating this practice would not be passed until the end of the 19th century, leaving dogs in particular to be the subjects of extreme cruelty due to their trusting and friendly nature even while being vivisected. They were often simply nailed to a board, and vivisection began, despite the cries of agony from the animals. Experimentation on animals became more and more widespread as scientists strived to make medical advances by any method at their disposal.

The end of the 18th century saw many philosophers and members of the privileged classes, particularly in England, becoming ever more critical of the practices being carried out in the name of scientific progress and of the treatment of animals in other areas such as farming and human 'sport and recreational pastimes' such as bull-baiting (French, 1975). The most notable of these is considered to be the utilitarian, Jeremy Bentham (1748–1832). In one of the most famous contributions to the historical development of arguments used by the animal welfare movement, he asserted that the immovable lines that had traditionally been drawn between humans and animals had been drawn in error. There is a moral basis to the eating of animals and some experimentation, he concluded, as long as there is a speedy death. But, in 1789, he came out firmly against 'torment' (Burns & Hart, 1970, p. 36):

> [A] full-grown horse or dog is beyond comparison a more rational, as well as a more conversable animal, than an infant of a day, or a week, or even a month, old. But suppose the case were otherwise, what would it avail? The question is not, Can they reason? nor, Can they talk? but, Can they suffer?

Bentham's contribution still resonates today and is often quoted by modern philosophers when discussing the status of animals. Bentham identified the central issue that emerges in modern discussions about animal sentience – that the complex qualities of human thought should not be the defining comparative factor in determining how to treat animals. The key question is their capacity to suffer. This core principle finds its place in much modern legislation – the legislative reasoning behind introducing or improving legal protection is knowledge about animals' capacity to suffer. The modern question is how far that protection actually protects the capacity for suffering. With this landmark statement, Bentham heralded the dawn of protection for animals in their own right rather than their anthropocentric value to humans (Francione & Charlton, 2017).

From this point, discussion of animal protection moved on to debates around ensuring justice for animals and the specific use of the term 'rights', a concept normally reserved for humans, as illustrated by Herman Daggett (1791, p. 7), who may well have been the unwitting nomenclator of the animal rights movement:

> If we judge impartially, we shall acknowledge that there are the rights of a beast as well as the rights of a man. And because man is considered as the Lord of this lower creation, he is not thereby licensed to infringe on the rights of those below him, any more than a king, or magistrate, is licensed to infringe on the rights of his subjects. If the Governor of the universe has given us liberty to prepare animal food, or if the rights of these creatures, in certain instances, interfere with the rights of others or with the rights of men, so as thereby to become forfeited, we may, in such cases, take away their lives or deprive them of their privileges, without the imputation of blame. And I know of nothing in nature, in reason, or in revelation, which obliges us to suppose that the unalienated rights of a beast are not as sacred and inviolable as those of a man …

In Germany, Artur Schopenhauer (1788–1860) asserted that animals could suffer pain and was critical of the traditional Christian and the human-centred Kantian positions, which had denied direct duties towards animals. He did, however, think that animals suffer less than humans, and it could therefore be justifiable to use them in 'the chase' (hunting), but not in vivisection. Just as Bentham became an idol of the animal welfare lobby in early 19th century England, so did Artur Schopenhauer in Germany (Schopenhauer, 1819, p. 480):

> The right of man over the life and powers of the brutes rests on the fact that, because with the growing clearness of consciousness suffering increases in like measure; the pain which the brute suffers through death or work is not so great as man would suffer… [The] limit, however, which is often transgressed, especially in the case of burden and dogs used in the chase; to which the activity of societies for the prevention of cruelty to

> animals is principally devoted. In my opinion, that right does not extend to vivisection, particularly of the higher animals.

Accordingly, Schopenhauer appears to give his support to the farming of animals but not to animal experimentation involving higher animals. Whether this extends beyond the term often used in this context today, higher primates, is unclear. One also wonders whether his attitude might have changed in light of the 20th century advent of factory farming or the advancements of human health claimed by the pro-animal experimentation lobby. Clearly, at the time of his statement, the focus was on animals being used for carriage of goods and people, as well as concern for hunting dogs and increased use of animals in experimentation. Two hundred or more years may have elapsed, but the issues of concern often show remarkable similarity to those of modern times.

There is, however, a strong case that can be made to support the view that it was not just philosophy that brought arguments regarding the treatment of animals into the area of public debate but the work of one man, Charles Darwin (1809–1882). Darwin was not the first to notice and record similarities between the species. In 1661, Samuel Pepys noted in his diary that he had seen a 'strange creature', believed to have been a chimpanzee or a gorilla, from Guinea and commented that it was 'so much like a man in most things ... I cannot believe but that it is a monster got of a man and a she-baboon. I do believe it already understands much English; and I am of a mind it might be taught to speak and make signs' (Pepys, 1661).

Darwin provided scientific reasoning to support intuitive observation. He explained that there are evident similarities between people and animals not only in terms of physical characteristics such as muscles, bones and reproductive systems but also in terms of 'higher mental powers' such as memory, attention, curiosity, limitation and reason, which are seen in animals to varying degrees. Darwin (1871, pp. 34–35) added the voice of science to those of philosophers, which together started humans on the path to using 'sentience' as the pre-cursor of animal protection:

> If no organic being excepting man had possessed any mental power, or if his powers had been of wholly different nature from those of the lower animals, then we should never have been able to convince ourselves that our high faculties had been gradually developed. But it can be clearly shown that there is no fundamental difference of this kind. We must also admit that there is a much wider interval in mental power between one of the lowest fishes, as a lamprey or lancelet, and one of the higher apes than between an ape and man; yet this immense interval is filled up by

> numberless gradations ... there is no fundamental difference between man and the higher mammals in their mental faculties.

One attribute of humans that Darwin accepted as being a fundamental difference between the species is what he referred to as 'the moral sense'. He believed 'any' animal that had progressed intellectually would eventually have developed a sense of morality or conscience to the same extent as humans. Darwin's findings opened a new era in science, attempting to prove, using empirical evidence, the existence of significant differences or similarities between the species that would affect our treatment of animals.

Darwin's discoveries created a revolution in science, and no less can be said of the animal rights movement. The extent of similarity – in this context, animal sentience is the keystone of 21st century developments in Animal Law and philosophy. It reaches to the heart of legislation and forms an essential component of new developments in thinking. Studies continue to reveal the complexity of animal sentience beyond their capacity to suffer, as first alluded to by Bentham and confirmed in science by Darwin. Some challenge the notion of similarity begun by Darwin, but the majority are in accord with his evidence of notable similarities with humans in terms of physiology and the ability to experience the pain, suffering and pleasure also associated with sentient capabilities.

Ironically, Darwin's theories are sometimes used as evidence to deny the claim for improved animal protection. Some argue that Darwin's discoveries highlighted differences to justify different treatment to legitimise the use of animals for human benefit and the 'survival of the fittest', running counter to the argument of protecting like with like (Rachels, 1991). It is submitted here that the crucial contribution of Darwin was that he clearly recognised the 'similarities', not the 'differences', between organisms, which should influence drawing them closer together in terms of protection. In addition, he saw the development of the moral sense of humans as being part of this evolutionary process. Just as humans were slow to recognise other races as fellow creatures, Darwin saw attitudes towards animals as evidence of the evolutionary development of humankind in recognising the similarities between species. He stated, 'sympathy beyond the confines of man, that is humanity to the lower animals, seems to be one of the latest moral acquisitions ... This virtue, one of the noblest with which man is endowed, seems to arise incidentally from our sympathies becoming more tender and more widely diffused until they are extended to all sentient beings.' (Darwin, 1871, p. 41).

Jeremy Bentham and Charles Darwin together provided, perhaps, the two most historically significant milestones on the road to modify the relationship between animals and humans. Darwin gave us the science about similar sentient qualities to back up what Bentham had found through observation encapsulated in his statement, 'Can they suffer'? Darwin's discoveries placed humans alongside animals in terms of many characteristics and informed a moral approach to our decision-making based on scientific evidence. The historical view of dominance through difference to moderate the human–non-human animal relationship gave way to notions of similarities and common bonds. To treat 'brute creation' in ways beneficial purely to our own species became more morally questionable and began the move towards a new era of animal justice through protective legislation.

The impact of Darwin's science on the animal rights movement is beyond comparison. Many previous contributions had been caught in a loop with theological teaching, and this might not have carried forward to the modern animal rights movement. However, the thoughtful historical references to the sentience of animals from Porphyry and Plutarch through to Bentham and Schopenhauer laid the foundations of respect for animals being as they were, primarily based on observation and intuition. Darwin handed to the modern movement the evidential support of science, bringing with it a new approach to campaigns for better treatment of animals. Previously, justification of our use of animals was predominately based upon humankind being unique and made in the image of God, with absolute dominion over the animals, or arguments that concentrated on driving an immovable wedge between the sentient capacities of humans and animals based on intelligence, language and capacities for pain and suffering were now the subjects of both philosophical *and* scientific challenge. Science, after Darwin, gave evidential support to philosophers such as Peter Singer and Tom Regan that there are similarities between the suffering of animals and humans and that animals are also the experiencers of life like ourselves.

Within 50 years of the publication of Darwin's findings, philosophical contributions began to use Darwin's discoveries to create a new vision of our relationship with 'the beasts'. The following extract from the 1906 work of J Howard Moore (1906, p. 323) illustrates this as he compares Darwin's discovery to that of Galileo and Copernicus. He also introduces us to the term anthropocentricism, whereby humans create a relationship with the animals and the rest of the environment based purely on the possibilities for human gain:

> The doctrine of organic evolution, which forever established the common genesis of all animals, sealed the doom of anthropocentricism. Whatever

> the inhabitants of this world were before the publication of The Origin of the Species, they never could be anything since but a family. The doctrine of evolution is probably the most important revelation that has come to the world since the illuminations of Galileo and Copernicus. The authors of the Copernican theory enlarged and corrected human understanding by disclosing to man the comparative littleness of his world – by discovering that the earth, which had up to that time been supposed to be the centre and capital of [the] cosmos, is in reality a satellite of the sun. This heliocentric discovery was hard on human conceit, for it was the first broad hint man had thus far received of his true dimensions. The doctrine of evolution has had, and is having, and is destined to continue to have, a similarly correcting effect on the naturally narrow conceptions of men. [Darwin] correctly predicted that the way in which animals were treated in his time would come to be regarded as purely anthropocentric exercises of human dominion to be replaced, in large part, by a new philosophy which recognises the 'unity and consanguinity' of all organic life.

Moore estimated a timescale of perhaps one to two centuries for the impact of Darwin's theories to have taken their full course. As we look back on the achievements of those who have campaigned for better treatment of animals since Darwin published *On the Origin of the Species*, we can see numerous advances in animal welfare that implicitly recognise animals as having sentient qualities in many ways similar to our own. However, as we shall see in later chapters, there are troubling areas where animal abuse appears to be accepted as a morally justifiable cost of our use of animals. Moore's hope of a new human morality in treating animals has some way to go to fulfil his projections of our own evolutionary development. This is partly based on the anomaly that emerged from the science after Darwin's discovery: that animals are seen as both similar to humans to support our use of them and sufficiently different to allow treatment of them that would not be tolerated or legal for humans. For example, in relation to animal experimentation, animals are sufficiently similar to support testing on them rather than humans, but sufficiently different that the same protection granted to humans is not required (Robertson, 2015, p. 236).

Similarities are the main reason for continuing the use of primates (although now banned in Europe – with a possible waiver – and in the UK) and other animals in research. Animal welfare groups argue that the similarities should be interpreted as a reason to ensure that animals are not used, on the grounds that their experience may be so like ours as to raise moral concern over their suffering. One of the foremost scientists to continue the work started by Darwin in the search for the origins of the human species was paleoanthropologist Richard Leaky (1944–2022). He was in no doubt that the distance between animals and humans is not as great as some would have us believe. As he analysed fossil evidence, particularly in Africa, he became convinced that the differences between animals and the higher primates are no more than 'an accident of history'. He stated that the differences have been consistently exaggerated because we were blinded by our own accomplishments, which appear to go beyond those of animals (Leaky & Lewin, 1992, p. 352).

Leaky presented evidence that fossil records show a complex picture of the development of *homo sapiens* from other species of apes. The qualities that some regard as being unique to humans – consciousness, emotions, language and morality, for example – would be very unlikely to emerge in a single genetic leap. This leads to the inevitable conclusion that aspects of our 'unique claims' are extremely likely present in other species. Humans have been shown to differ by less than 2% from chimpanzees in their genetic makeup, whereas horses and zebras – species that can also mate and produce offspring like humans and chimpanzees – show greater genetic differences. He concluded that chimpanzees are very close to us in evolutionary terms. Unless the 2% difference can be shown to account for 'all' the different characteristics claimed to be in the sole possession of human beings, then there is strong scientific evidence that some characteristics are possessed by animals other than ourselves. Just how far down the 'evolutionary ladder' these attributes might be found continues to be the subject of modern-day research.

In recent times, particularly since 1970, animal studies have investigated the attributes of animals that were traditionally considered to be unique to humans, such as the use of language, emotional experiences and their individual requirements according to sentience. Scientists ask questions such as 'What is it actually like to be an animal? Can they use language or make friends?' in order to determine how we should behave towards them. Such studies have overcome difficulties in the interpretation of behaviour that prevented the scientific community as a whole from taking such research seriously. The weight of evidence is now so compelling on the question of animal sentience that it leads to a conclusion which requires that the moral implications be taken seriously (Brooman, 2018). However, vested interests in agriculture, animal experimentation, exploitation of wildlife and other areas of human use of animals are powerful and deeply entrenched based on human benefits that protagonists are reluctant to give up that protagonists are reluctant to give up. Challenging the status quo is very difficult where it requires humans to sacrifice their interests.

The place of emotions in the experience of pain and suffering has been dismissed by the scientific community in general as a clear case of anthropomorphism – that is, projecting the thoughts and behaviour of humans into our interpretation of animal behaviour. This is one of the central arguments of those scientists who deny the need for a change in our relationship with animals, suggesting that we are in danger of attributing human characteristics to non-human animals and of misinterpreting what they refer to as 'response behaviour' as evidence of a higher level of sentience than actually exists. Darwin (1872), however, found no difficulty in ascribing emotions to animals, having observed their facial expressions and body language.

Many scientists have traditionally sought to avoid describing animal responses in terms of emotions such as fear, mood, excitement and loneliness. Emotions are difficult enough to judge in our own species, even though we have a complex language to communicate with each other. Identifying and describing emotions in animals, whether the same as ours or not, is a task the scientific community has yet to come to terms with. However, those working with animals, animal owners and observers regularly observe that animals have emotions, which may put them at odds with some in the scientific community: 'It is clear that animals form lasting friendships, are frightened of being hunted, have [a] horror of dismemberment, wish they were back in the safety of their den, despair for their mates, [and] look out for and protect their children whom they love.' (Masson & McCarthy, 1996, p. 220). The general acceptance of emotions in animals might have considerable consequences for our relationship with them and, therefore, our legal provision for them.

If there is one human attribute that is used to encapsulate the 'difference' between the species more than any other, it is the use of human language. The existence of language as a primary distinguishing feature of humans from non-human animals has been the centre of controversy and debate to the present day, with dolphins and primates the subject of intense study. Studies such as those by Gardner et al. (1989) with Washoe, and Duane Rumbaugh with Kanzi, explored the development of language by chimpanzees and attempted to demonstrate the linguistic capacities of 'higher' animals. Gardner's research showed that their chimpanzee, Washoe, could use a complex symbol system to communicate what he wanted to eat, play with or where he wanted to go, showing evidence of a rudimentary understanding of language in chimpanzees. Washoe was shown to be capable of listening and responding to complex verbal commands. In one of the experiments, for example, he was asked to 'point to the picture of the orange' or 'point to the picture of the umbrella' and could do this repeatedly, without difficulty. These studies showed how chimpanzees can learn, be taught and acquire by observation the use of spoken words. The attribute the ancient philosophers considered exclusive to humans as the most significant element of 'difference' is not so exclusive after all (Byrne, 1985).

These studies have failed to convince everyone that animals have the competence for a complex linguistic system like humans (Frey, 1980). If studies such as this are recognised as proving the existence of a highly developed linguistic capability in higher-order animals, then many of the arguments used by the philosophical opponents of the animal rights lobby would, at the very least, have to be rewritten. Language, in the sense that it enables us to communicate with each other and highlights our own individuality, has been a crucial factor in ascribing the level of sentient capabilities of different species and has been the basis of the intellectual development of the human race (Leaky & Lewin, 1992, p. 239). Without it, we would still be a comparatively undeveloped species; with it, we have gone as far as beginning to explore space. The importance of language as a vehicle for sentient development cannot be underestimated. If higher-order animals show an ability to learn and use language, evidencing their possession of higher sentient capabilities similar to our own, it raises more fundamental questions about the human practices of using them as tools and subjecting them to suffering, such as experimentation and farming. Such use rests upon the assumption that they are not the same as us, but this may not be the case, as Leaky and Lewin (1992, p. 224) explain:

> [Ape-language studies] tell us that in ape brains, which are the same size and organisation as the brains of Homo ancestors, the cognitive foundations on which human language could be built were already present. This does not prove that those same foundations were present in our ancestors, but to me it is highly suggestive. It tells me that the 'vastness of the gulf between ... man and the brutes' is not as great as many people believe. The sentiment of the 'specialness' of Homo sapiens derives, I'm sure, from the sense of wonder that emanates from human consciousness and self-awareness. But we are in danger of being tricked by its cogency. The evidence from primate language studies suggests that we are not as special as we would like to believe. For me the issue of community is clear: our language skills are firmly rooted in the cognitive abilities of ape brains.

However, other studies conducting research into aspects of non-human animal sentience have produced less conclusive results in relation to other species with less developed sentient capabilities than the primates. A study carried out with baboons in Kenya by Robert Siforth and Dorothy Cheyney led the latter to comment on their sentient capacities: 'They don't know what they know' (Channel 4, 1995). Dr Gerald Williamson, a biologist at the University of Maryland, conducted a five-year study into whether bats shared food with fellow non-related bats. He found that young bats returned without food approximately 20% of the time and that they were able to 'beg' food from other bats. Describing this as 'friendly' behaviour is possible yet refutable, as it is difficult to say that the bats are actually 'aware' of what they are doing.

However, we know from the work of Freud that humans engage in many activities without actually thinking consciously about them. Scientists such as Dr Celia Hayes have described this type of behaviour as 'robotic' in that it does not give any real evidence of an 'internal light' being on (Channel 4, 1995). Other animals show a variety of complex, 'clever' behaviour: squirrels store food for long periods and know where to find it; some species of birds can adopt ingenious methods to get at concealed food; insects use remarkable techniques to conceal themselves or to catch prey; monkeys, birds and otters, for example, use various forms of tools to catch or consume prey. But all these instances could be attributed to the process of natural selection over the millennia, trial and error learning, or just luck.

The implications of the studies presently being carried out by scientists are potentially enormous. Are we prepared to see our legal codes based upon the sole criterion of species membership without any significant underpinning moral basis? Jared Diamond (1991, p. 24) suggests that if we manage to unlock the door to determining animal consciousness, then we might, at the very least, have to revise the basis of our laws governing the treatment of animals:

> If our ethical code makes a purely arbitrary distinction between humans and all other species, then we have a code based on naked selfishness devoid of any higher principle. If our code instead makes distinctions based on our superior intelligence, social relationships, and our capacity for feeling pain, then it becomes difficult to defend an all-or-nothing code that draws a line between all humans and all animals.

Herein lies the problem for the animal rights lobby: Those who defend or take part in current uses of animals have a built-in defence to those who argue for the enhanced status of animals enforceable by laws aimed at protecting animals in their own right. The question raised is: 'So you think they deserve better status because they possess sentient qualities deserving of protection? – Well prove it.' On the other hand, it has been argued by those such as Tom Regan, Peter Singer and Mary Midgely: 'Should we not at least give non-human animals the benefit of the doubt?'

This position aligns with those who argue that a 'precautionary principle' should be applied to changes in environmental policy (Kriebel et al., 2001). Considering the increasing weight of evidence about animal sentience, harm done to animals, and uncertainty in the area, should we not be taking preventative action and enhancing the protection of animals? (Sunstein & Nussbaum, 2004). We will return to how the law should treat animals in Chapter 3, but first, in Chapter 2, we look at how the law has developed in relation to animals.

CHAPTER TWO

How has the law treated animals?

Introduction

Humankind's use of animals stretches back into prehistory, but the protection of animals using law is only a relatively recent development. Contemporary legal approaches to animals primarily attempt to protect other species from some of the more morally questionable practices of humans in the form of abuse, neglect or mistreatment; however, a glance through the pages of history shows a far different picture. For centuries, animals had no legal protection, being treated merely as property, not deserving of welfare protection, and even, on occasion, the recipients of harsh treatment as the result of legal proceedings against them: 'Justice, indeed, so far as animals are concerned, seems in earlier days to have dispensed altogether with her scales and to have worn a permanent bandage over that eye, which should have been turned to the wrongs [against] dumb creatures' (Fairholme, 1924).

This chapter sheds light on how legislators have grappled with the moral imperatives that arising growing concern for animals. This is at the heart of a major theme in this book – the challenges that have been faced in putting into place laws to adequately protect and deal with moral concern for animals. Growing awareness of sentient qualities brings with it the potential problem of outdated or inadequately worded legislation. How have lawmakers responded to those concerns, and how did things change over time?

Why is it important to look at the history of Animal Law? This is a legitimate question, as the focus of those concerned with improving animal welfare is on the here and now, and there may seem to be little to gain from looking back. However, the development of law across time reveals a great deal about the here and now – it can tell us how the law came to be, and it often highlights the philosophical anomalies that underpinned it. It also demonstrates that present law was built on a misconception about animals, such as their level of sentience. The importance of viewing law as it developed in the context of human knowledge and presumptions at the time reveals an inherent weakness in its logicality, which is carried into the present.

The status of animals as property, for example, has led to current problems caused by international trade, as discussed in a case study later in this chapter. James Mason goes as far as calling this misplaced view of animals by a new term, 'misotheory', to express what he describes as the historical development of 'hate, contempt, loathing, fear, and all the other negative views that humans have about other animals' (Mason, 2017, p. 140). He suggests that this led to animals being viewed as inferior, ready for human exploitation. When investigating the misery of animals reared for human consumption in modern intensive agriculture, those used in painful scientific experiments, our disregard for wild animals or those transported great distances to be slaughtered, we can see the echoes of this historical development of human attitudes that led us here.

This chapter examines five notable periods in the history of the treatment of animals in law: Ancient Greece; the period of Roman domination of Europe; medieval Europe, mainly from the 13th century onwards; England in the 18th and 19th centuries; and the move to legislate for animal 'sentience' in the late 20th century/early 21st century. The legal status accorded to animals at these times is particularly interesting as each marks a significant point in human history where attitudes to, and protection of, animals appear to have undergone a major shift reflecting knowledge, awareness and developing human morality in relation to animals.

Historical attitudes to animals and early legislation

The first well-documented era that reveals a different attitude towards animals than we have today begins with the ancient Greeks. Plato (427–347 BC) produced works that put forward the ideal structure and functioning of the relationship between the state and the individual in *The Republic* and *Laws,* much of which was based upon the Athens which Plato knew. He described how the law treated animals 'accused' of murder (Plato, 4th century BC):

> If a draught animal or any other beast kill a person, unless it be in a combat authorised and instituted by the state, the kinsmen of the slain shall prosecute the said homicide for murder, and the overseers of the public lands, as many as may be commissioned by the said kinsmen, shall adjudicate upon the case and send the offender beyond the boundaries of the country.

These 'trials', along with trials where the person accused could not be traced and therefore the prosecution was of inanimate objects that had caused a death, took place outside the ancient Greek equivalent of a town hall cum community centre, the 'Prytaneum', in the open air so that the judges would not be tainted by 'contaminated air' emanating from the accused. Walter Woodburn Hyde (1916, p. 698) explains:

> [Regarding] the trial of animals, we know but little, only the fact that such trials were held here. They probably were based on the same principle as those of inanimate things. Not that the Greeks were obsessed, at least in the historical period, with the idea that animals any more than things were morally responsible for their acts – though this was probably at the bottom of such trials, as it certainly was in the case of things; but rather they held the general notion that the moral equilibrium of the community had been disturbed by the murder and that somebody must be punished or else dire misfortune in the form of plagues, droughts, and reverses in men's fortunes would overtake the land. So, the ideal legislation of Plato on this point was based upon the same idea which was at the bottom of all the murder laws of Athens – that the Erinys or avenging spirit of the dead man must be appeased. In substance this was merely another manifestation of the lex talionis [retribution and revenge], the oldest and deepest rooted of all human laws, axiomatic in all primitive societies, and traceable ... even in the most advanced. Greek literature furnishes many examples of the idea of 'blood for blood'. Whether the slaying was premeditated or not made no difference, for in either case a crime had been committed and a pollution had appeared in the community which must be removed.

The Greeks, Hyde suggests, were the only ancient civilisation to use such trials, but the ancient Persians punished animals by decree; for example, a dog would be punished by 'progressive mutilation corresponding with the number of persons or beasts bitten, beginning with the loss of the ears and ending with the amputation of the tail' (Hyde, 1916, p. 700).

Despite their harsh attitude towards their fellow creatures, the Greeks extended humanitarian attitudes between each other, firstly to barbarians and then to animals. The philosophers Empedocles and Pythagoras extended the notion of 'community' as existing not just between humans but also between humans and the animal world. Indeed, Pythagoras went further than any Western legal system has ever done by declaring the killing of an animal to be murder (Jones, 1956, p. 62). Despite this evidence of diverse attitudes towards animals in Ancient Greece, the principal application of the law to animals was in relation to their status as property. There is some dispute amongst contemporary commentators on the law of

Ancient Greece as to whether animals were considered as coming as part and parcel of the land upon which they were farmed (Harrison, 1968, p. 229).

In the second historical period, the Romans, whose influence dominated the period from 510 BC to AD 565, also regarded animals as being property, in a similar way to the Greeks. Animals were treated as 'things' in that they were classified as capable of being privately owned (Borkowski, 1994, p. 143). They were treated as *res mancipi,* described by Borkowski as 'things useful or essential to the household in early Roman society.' He goes on to describe the place of animals within this definition, which was important in determining how *dominium* (acquisition) was obtained, as property could only be transferred in the way appropriate to its classification (Borkowski, 1994, pp. 145–146):

> According to Gaius (Institutes, 2.14a) res mancipi comprised the following things: slaves, beasts of burden, Italic land, houses on such land and rustic praedial servitudes (i.e. easements and profits over land). As regards the animals, there was juristic dispute about the moment when the beasts became res mancipi – the Sabinians claimed it was at birth, whereas the Proulians held that it was when the animal was broken in. Gaius lists oxen, horses, mules and donkeys as examples of beasts of burden, but the list appears to be comprehensive – no other animals seem to have been regarded as res mancipi. Once the category of res mancipi was established in early law, it did not prove susceptible to amendment. For example, camels and elephants could be regarded as beasts of burden but were 'discovered' by the Romans after the list of res mancipi was established – so they did not qualify. The most probable reason for the reluctance to expand the list of res mancipi was that the formal modes of conveyancing necessary to transfer dominium in such things increasingly came to be seen as cumbersome and inconvenient.

Borkowski explains how acquisition of *res mancipi* could be obtained by the formal modes of conveyance – *mancipatio* and *cessio.* These modes of conveyance were indeed complicated: *mancipatio* was a mode of title transfer that, according to Gaius, required the presence of the transferor and transferee, at least five witnesses, a prescribed set of words and a set of scales; *Cessio,* although similarly cumbersome to *mancipatio,* differed in that it involved a magistrate, a different set of formal words and no scales (Borkowski, 1994, pp. 189–190). Acquisition of wild animals could also be obtained in Roman times, but in a different way (Buckland, 1932, pp. 205–206):

> [Occupatio] was acquisition by taking. It was not of great significance, its chief importance being in relation to wild animals captured for food or other purposes. These were acquired only when effectively seized, which was true of all occupatio, but there was in their case the further rule that the ownership lasted only while they were effectively held, subject to the modification that of certain things, e.g., bees and pigeons, the ownership lasted only so long as they retained the habit of returning to their quarters – animus revertendi. The question what amounted to such capture as gave effect to the intent to acquire is, in effect, what amounts to gaining possession. It was agreed after disputes that a wounded animal was not 'occupied' til seized. We are not told whether killing itself was enough, and, as to trapping, the matter seems to have depended somewhat on the position of the trap.

There were several consequences of the Romans' legal classifications of animals, some of which have echoes in law today. A significant separation runs throughout Roman law relating to animals defined as either 'wild' or 'domestic', so it was important to know into which group an animal naturally fell. 'Beasts of burden' – working animals – naturally fell within the domestic classification, whereas other animals with usefulness to humans, such as deer and bees, were ordinarily classified as wild animals with more difficult routes to gaining title over them.

Turning to the third historical period, the Middle Ages, records here reveal that, as early as the 9th century, animals were sometimes treated as morally culpable in the same way as people. Most of these cases appear to have been recorded from the 13th century, when animals were prosecuted for a wide range of criminal offences such as being noisy in church, murder and property damage, as well as being afforded protection normally reserved for people. Animals were prosecuted in the ecclesiastical courts with sentences including banishment, excommunication and the death penalty, with a separate approach for wild animals as opposed to domestic animals (Hill, 1961, p. 11):

> The reason for indicting wild animals before ecclesiastical courts was ... purely a practical one. They were anonymous sinners. It was difficult to arrest them, and impossible to bring a whole company of them, a swarm of locusts for example, into court, although occasionally representative members of the species were caught and compelled to sit – if sit is the right word – through the proceedings. As a rule, however, it was found difficult to exercise an ordinary sentence against a multiplicity of creatures, many of them very small, and therefore the divine judgment had to be invoked upon their sins by means of a sentence of excommunication, exactly as it

was invoked against human criminals whose identities were unknown. This difficulty of recognition did not, of course, occur in the case of domestic animals which committed crimes. They were in the same position as human criminals whose identity could not be established, and like human criminals they could, in many parts of Europe, be compelled to stand their trials in the lay courts of justice.

Gerald Carson has commented that 'It requires a considerable act of imagination for a person living in the culture of the 20th century to understand the involute thought of the medieval legal mind and the high seriousness of our ancestors in arraigning cabbage worms, he-goats, and indeed, all animal kind, domestic and wild, in a court of justice where to the solemn tolling of bells they were tried' (Carson, 1972, pp. 25–26). The following extract from a piece by Hampton L. Carson (1917, p. 410) illustrates what must indeed have been, by modern-day standards of animal welfare, a most bizarre scene of cruelty – a story with such notoriety that it is still often repeated at Animal Law lectures and conferences:

In the open square of the old Norman city of Falaise, in the year 1386, a vast and motley crowd had gathered to witness the execution of a criminal convicted of murder. Noblemen in armour, proud dames in velvet and feathers, priests in cassock and cowl, falconers with hawks upon their wrists, huntsmen with hounds in leash, aged men with their staves, withered hags with their baskets or reticules, children of all ages, and even babes in arms were among the spectators. The prisoner was dressed in a new suit of man's clothes and was attended by armed men on horseback, while the hangman, before mounting the scaffold, had provided himself with new gloves and a new rope. As the prisoner had caused the death of a child by mutilating the face and arms to such an extent as to cause a fatal haemorrhage, the town tribunal, or local court, had decreed that the head and legs of the prisoner should be mangled with a knife before the hanging. This was the medieval application of the lex talionis, or 'an eye for an eye and a tooth for a tooth.' To impress a recollection of the scene upon the memories of the bystanders, an artist was employed to paint a fresco on the west wall of the transept of the Church of the Holy Trinity in Falaise, and for more than 400 years that picture could be seen and studied until destroyed in 1820 by the carelessness of a whitewasher. The criminal was not a human being but a sow, which had indulged in the evil propensity of eating infants on the street.

Some churchmen believed it was wrong for the church to prosecute animals as it assumed that animals have some relationship with God. Despite these reservations, the proclamation by St Thomas Aquinas that animals were capable of being possessed by the devil was certainly an influential factor in the treatment of animals in the Middle Ages, which resulted in prosecution for 'grievous crimes' and criminal sanctions. This practice began to wane after the 16th century, when the focus came to rest on the owner, not the animal itself (Turner, 1992).

Animals were certainly assumed to understand the nature of what they were doing for a large period of the Middle Ages, which led one distraught pastor in Dresden in 1559 to appeal to the Elector of Saxony for help in bringing to justice sparrows for 'their incessant and extremely vexatious chatterings and scandalous acts of unchastity committed during the sermon' (Hill, 1961, p. 10). As a final example of the extent to which the full legal procedure was applied to animals, it is worth considering proceedings in a French ecclesiastical court, in Autun 1522. Local rats were summoned to appear before the court for having destroyed barley crops in the local area. When they failed to appear on the given day, their counsel, Bartholomew Chassenée, defended them by saying that the summons had not been circulated widely enough. In consequence, a further summons was circulated to all the parishes within the bishopric, but still not a single rat appeared on the given day. Chassenée explained it would take a considerable amount of time for the rats to spread the word and gather from their far-flung homes. The court accepted this and granted a delay in the proceedings, but not a single rat appeared. Chassenée had yet another explanation, in that the rats were disturbed by the plaintiffs' cats in the area and were scared to appear unless assured they would be protected. The court, naturally, accepted this, and, in consequence of a delay in further action by the plaintiffs, judgment was finally entered in default to the defendants (Carson, 1917, p. 31).

Records kept in churches across Europe show that the practice of prosecuting animals was not confined to any individual country but was widespread and persisted until as late as 1906 in one Swiss case (Hyde, 1916, p. 709). Most recorded cases were in France due to better record-keeping rather than a greater inclination to prosecute animals on their part. There are some 200 cases recorded in this curious chapter in the development of European Animal Law jurisprudence. E. P. Evans (1907, pp. 10–11) discusses why animals might have been involved in judicial proceedings:

> A Swiss jurist, Eduard Osenbrüggen (Studien zur Deutschen und Schweizerischen Rechtsgeschichte. Schaffhusen, 1868, pp. 139–149), endeavours to explain these judicial proceedings on the theory of the personification of animals. As only a human being can commit crime and thus render himself liable to punishment, he concludes that it is only by

> an act of personification that the brute can be placed in the same category as man and become subject to the same penalties. In support of this view, he refers to the fact that in ancient and medieval times, domestic animals were regarded as members of the household and entitled to the same legal protection as human vassals ... According to old Welsh law, atonement was made for killing a cat or dog belonging to another person by suspending the animal by the tail so that its nozzle touched the ground and then pouring wheat over it until its body was entirely covered ... Symbolism and personification, as applied to animals and inanimate objects, unquestionably played an important role in primitive legislation, but this principle does not account for the excommunication and anathematisation of noxious vermin or for the criminal prosecution and capital punishment of homicidal beasts, nor does it throw the faintest light upon the origin and purpose of such proceedings.

Eduard Osenbrüggen's explanation, therefore, is not entirely satisfactory to Evans, who regards the prosecution of animals and witches as having arisen from the same basic superstitions as a result of the aggressive spreading of the Christian faith in northern Europe. One of the tools inevitably used to convert the masses was fear, and this resulted in 'demons' being identified in people and animals, leading directly to their prosecution for all manner of 'offences'. This encouragement of superstitious beliefs combined with a peculiar sense of equity was a lethal combination that obliterated common sense. It was the product of a barbaric sense of justice in a society often ruled by brute force, together with an intention to retain control by fear on the part of the ecclesiastical leadership (Evans, 1907, p. 40).

Piers Beirnes (1994) also examines the medieval prosecution of animals in a 1994 article that re-examined Evans' observations made nearly 90 years earlier. He concluded that Evans underestimated the number of countries involved in such practices, citing other countries such as Belgium, Denmark, Portugal, Russia, Spain and Turkey as having been found to have evidence of such trials. Other, less numerous trials were found in the United States in 1662, and two in England in 1771 and 1861. It seems that the practice was widespread across many countries for a long period of time, although there appear to have been concentrations of dramatic trials directly against animals in France, Germany and Italy. However, Beirnes also points out that the killing of an animal was often the outcome of trials in medieval England against people for causing injury to others using an animal – which effectively amounts to the same outcome for the animal. Beirnes is critical of the academic credence of Evans' work and suggests that his accounts are not entirely accurate. He suggests that one likely explanation for the trials is to deter those in control of animals from letting their animals roam free and dangerously for the damage and injury they might cause. Finally, Beirnes reflects on the fact that, far from being replaced, proceedings or practices leading to animal deaths have increased through, for example, lawful destruction in experimentation and for 'crimes' such as homelessness and aggression. All these lawful methods of euthanasia continue today.

Whether the medieval prosecution of animals was due to the church wishing to enhance its influence, a barbaric form of retribution and revenge, personification of animals by way of an illustration of punishment, or to instil obedience and moral behaviour in people, may never become clear. It was probably due to a combination of these factors (Slabbert, 2004). It should come as no great surprise that non-human animals were subject to harsh and disproportionate treatment when humans were also the subjects of barbaric treatment. However, if we are of a mind to consign these incidences of inhumane or illogical treatment of animals to anomalies of distant history, it is sobering to remember, as mentioned earlier, that a dog was sentenced to death by a court as late as 1906 in Switzerland. In current, more 'normal' times, the destruction of animals, most usually dogs that have attacked people, is common even where there is no more than evidence of natural behaviour. Justification for such action is normally based upon considerations of human safety rather than the moral culpability of the animal itself. However, it still represents a form of 'capital punishment' for animals that the animals themselves could never properly contemplate or understand.

In the final period of history examined in this chapter, we witness the beginnings of protection for the welfare of animals. This more recent phenomenon has flourished alongside maintaining the status of animals as property in law. Early indication of the perceived need to protect animals from unnecessary suffering is illustrated in early 17th-century regulations. These regulations limited the speed of postal services out of respect for the horses and the owners and included attempts in Ireland to regulate the practice of yoking horses to the plough by their tails (Thomas, 1983, p. 189). But the first substantial early attempt to secure some kind of protection for animals occurred in the US, albeit on a small scale, when the Puritans of the Massachusetts Bay Colony passed their 'Body of Liberties'. This was the work of an Englishman, Nathanial Ward, a barrister educated in Cambridge who emigrated to New England in 1634. Accepted by the General Court of Massachusetts in 1641, the Body of Liberties included a section on animals: 'No man shall exercise any tirranny or crueltie towards any bruite creature which are usuallie kept for man's use'. There was also a section protecting animals in transit, outlining that animals should be fit before travelling and should be cared for during transit: 'If any man shall have occasion to leade or drive Cattel from place to place that is far of, so that they be weary, or hungry, or fall sick, or lambe, it shall be lawful to rest or refresh them, for a competent time, in any open place that is not Corne, meadow, or enclosed for some peculiar use' (Leavitt, 1978, p. 11).

Some writers and philosophers had shown concern about the treatment of animals in the centuries before anything was formalised in law (see Chapter 1). Specific legislation came about due to significant pressure group politics. Keith Thomas (1983, pp. 181–182) suggests that one of the chief reasons for this climate of social change was the growth of towns and cities and the distance created between people and their exposure to the means of rearing and slaughtering animals on farms:

> As a result of this growing concern, a significant historical root of modern animal welfare legislation developed in the UK, where the long line of legislative protection of animals began with an unsuccessful battle to secure legal protection for bulls as a result of bull-baiting in the 19th century. This activity had grown in popularity along with bear-baiting and cock-fighting and could occur at almost any major public gathering. These dubious practices had become entrenched aspects of English life as the general population sought entertainment: 'The bastard sport of baiting ... afforded pleasure to princes and ruffians alike. For no discernible reason, the English were more addicted to this pastime than other nations' ... (Turner, 1992, p.33)

The campaign to improve the legal protection of animals came in the late 18th century and early 19th century when the educated classes of England became concerned about human attitudes towards each other in terms of welfare and, in a similar vein, more concerned about the treatment of animals. Welfare for animals became caught up in the debates concerning the welfare of children, the sick, needy, old and mentally infirm (French, 1975, p. 23). The writing of people such as Jeremy Bentham played an influential part in this revolution in attitudes, serving as a focus for widespread concern. As English tourists went abroad in the late 18th century, they were often shocked at the treatment of animals. After witnessing 15 or 16 bulls die at a Portuguese bullfight, William Beckford commented, 'I was highly disgusted with the spectacle' (Thomas, 1983, p. 143).

Men had been severely punished for apparently cruel acts before the turn of the 19th century, but the perpetrators had been punished for malicious destruction or deprecation of another man's property, not because of any legal rights enjoyed by the animal itself. In 1793, for example, John Cornish was found not guilty of maliciously maiming a horse, even though he had ripped its tongue out. This followed a ruling by the judge that he could only be guilty if it showed the wounding occurred because of 'malice shown towards the owner of it', an attitude which continued into the early years of the 19th century (Turner, 1992, p. 104). This is an extreme example of the effects of law historically defining animals as property.

In some ways, the choice of bull-baiting as the first attempt at wholesale legislative change was a strange one, and Table 2.1 shows its journey through parliament. At the time, the suffering of many other animals, such as horses used for transport purposes, was recognised as being of much greater magnitude in terms of the number of animals involved (Evans, 1907, p. 105). But the bull-baiting issue took on significance because of the distaste shown towards it as an exercise undertaken purely for human 'enjoyment and pleasure' at fairs and wakes. Indeed, many similarities can be seen with modern-day arguments against hunting, which maintains a high public profile even though more animals suffer in the production of food and in scientific experimentation. Table 2.1 shows the events leading to the passing of the first major piece of animal welfare legislation in the world and was the first move towards that '*jus animalium*' (meaning animal rights or animal liberation) for which Bentham had pleaded.

The text of the 1822 Act was as follows:

> An Act to prevent the cruel and improper Treatment of Cattle.
> [22 July 1822 – D 1822, 3 Geo 4, C 70.]
>
> Whereas it is expedient to prevent the cruel and improper Treatment of Horses, Mares, Geldings, Mules, Asses, Cows, Heifers, Steers, Oxen, Sheep and other Cattle: May it therefore please Your Majesty that it may be enacted: And be it enacted by the King's most Excellent Majesty, by and with the Advice and Consent of the Lords Spiritual and Temporal, and Commons, in this present Parliament assembled, and by the Authority of the same, That if any Person or Persons shall wantonly and cruelly beat, abuse or ill-treat any Horse, Mare, Gelding, Mule, Ass, Ox, Cow, Heifer, Steer, Sheep or other Cattle, and Complaint on Oath thereof be made to any Justice of the Peace or other Magistrate within whose Jurisdiction such Offence shall be committed, it shall be lawful for such Justice of the Peace or other Magistrate to issue his Summons or Warrant, at his Discretion, to bring the Party or Parties so complained of before him, or any other Justice of the Peace or other Magistrate of the County, City or Place within which such Justice of the Peace or other Magistrate has Jurisdiction, who shall examine upon Oath any Witness or Witnesses who shall appear or be produced to give information touching such Offence ...

Table 2.1 Events leading to the passing of the first major piece of animal welfare legislation.

Year	**Legislative event**	**Comments**
1800	First Bill to put down bull-baiting	Introduced by Sir William Pulteney and opposed by the then Secretary of War, William Windham, on the grounds that the Bill was anti-working class. Bill failed by 43 votes to 41.
1802	Second Bill to put down bull-baiting	Introduced by William Wilberforce and opposed again by Windham who now claimed that the bulls derived satisfaction from the baiting. He also claimed that the attempt to deny the working class their pleasures was unconstitutional and that the upper-class reformers should look at their own 'rich sports' such as hunting and racing first. Bill lost by 64 votes to 51.
1809	Bill to introduce 'rights' for animals	Introduced by former Lord Chancellor, Lord Erskine, to protect 'domesticated' animals such as cattle and horses. The Bill was aimed at proscribing malicious wounding, wanton cruelty, beating and other abuse of horses and cattle. Opposed by Windham on the grounds that it might prejudice the rights of property, that men should be trusted to regulate their own behaviour and that the legislation would be too difficult and arbitrary to enforce. Bill lost after much indecision before the committee stage.
1821	Ill Treatment of horses Bill	Introduced by the new champion in Parliament of the animal-welfare movement, Richard Martin, MP for Galway in Ireland where he was known as a 'benevolent despot' and was a follower of field sports himself. When another MP suggested it should be extended to asses, the House erupted with laughter, suggesting that dogs, then cats, would be next! Bill lost.
1822	Ill treatment of Horses and Cattle Bill introduced. Royal Assent given 22 June 1822	Introduced, once again, by Martin, this Bill became the first notable legislative success of the animal welfare lobby in the world. The Act, now referred to as 'Martin's Act,' made it an offence to 'beat, abuse, or ill-treat any horse, mare, gelding, mule, ass, ox, cow, heifer, steer, sheep or other cattle.' Infringements of the Act were penalised by a minimum fine of 10 shillings and a maximum of two months' imprisonment. The Act proved difficult to enforce, with Martin taking to the streets himself and bringing offenders to the attention of the authorities in court.

Richard Martin – 'Humanity Dick', as he was known to George IV – is a significant figure in the development of the law relating to animals. As Member of Parliament for Galway, he deflected the ridicule aimed at him in the House of Commons because he wanted to protect animals using the law and succeeded where Lord Erskine had earlier failed. Known as a benevolent character, Martin was a knowledgeable and astute parliamentarian with a sense of humour and an ability to hold the attention of the House. These 'winning ways', along with a steely character illustrated by his brushes with *The Times* over their misquoting of him (Turner, 1992, p. 126) helped him accomplish what some had thought impossible and others thought ridiculous. He brought the first case under his Act himself when he had two men, Samuel Clarke and David Hyde, arrested for beating horses at Smithfield Market in London. Both were convicted and fined 20 shillings each. Despite his championing the cause of animals and actively seeking out offenders, he was noted for his kindness of heart in relation to the treatment of offenders. He is known to have offered to pay the fines imposed on offenders himself, happy that they had learnt their lesson, scared to death by Martin's formidable reputation. He addressed the first annual meeting of the Society for the Prevention of Cruelty to Animals (the precursor to the Royal Society for the Prevention of Cruelty to Animals) in 1825. Martin defended the direction of his earlier attempts at reform, which focussed on the sports of the masses, namely bull-baiting. In the following extract from the speech he gave in 1825, one can sense the essential essence of the man (Fairholme, 1924, p. 38):

> Now, although it is true enough that there is much cruelty in those gentlemanly sports (hear, hear), yet it is no reason to reject the attempt to put down a few acknowledged barbarities, because we can't put them all down. (Applause.) For my own part, I could wish to get rid of every one of them, good or bad. (Hear, hear.) But if I can't get 100%, why, then, I must be satisfied to take 50 or 25%. (Much laughter.)
>
> But I must say that it makes me blush, as a Member of Parliament, to be obliged to confess that the great indisposition to put an end to cruelty to animals exists in the House of Parliament itself. (Hear, hear.) I may truly say, that a greater love for, or, at least, adherence to, the principle of cruelty exists in St Stephen's Chapel than in the Bear garden itself. (Laughter.) In the House of Commons, containing six or 700 members, I am sure there are ten to one against any measure to diminish the sufferings of the brute creation. (Hear, hear.)

Martin's hope that his Act might prevent bull-baiting and the baiting of other animals was short-lived. In a classic example of statutory interpretation, defining the word 'cattle' was the problem, with only some magistrates allowing the Act to be used to prosecute *bull* baiters. Mr Adolphus, who represented the accused in an 1825 case, argued that the meaning of the word 'cattle' should not be extended to include the superior bull, as it was not the custom of statutory interpretation to extend the specific mention of the inferior rank to the higher.

In the summer of 1825, two lions by the names of 'Nero' and 'Wallace' were baited by dogs in Warwick, an event that was criticised in the national press by *The Times* and the *Morning Post.* The reaction of *The Times,* in particular, shows how feelings were beginning to run against the baiters when they criticised 'the torture of a noble lion with the full consent and for the profit of a mercenary being who had gained large sums of money by hawking the poor animal about the world and exhibiting him. It is vain, however, to make any appeal to humanity where none exists or to expatiate on mercy, justice and retribution hereafter when those whom we strive to influence have never learned that language in which alone we can address them.' (Turner, 1992, p. 136).

In 1835, the practice of baiting was finally declared illegal. Joseph Pease's amendment to the 1822 Act created several new penalties:

> An Act to consolidate and amend the several Laws relating to the cruel and improper Treatment of Animals, and the Mischiefs arising from the driving of Cattle, and to make other Provisions in regard thereto. [9 September 1835. AD 1835, 5 and 6 Will 4, C 59.]
>
> ... any Person who shall, within Five Miles of temple bar, keep or use or shall act in the Management or conducting of any Premises or Place whatsoever for the Purpose of fighting or baiting of Bears, cock-fighting, baiting or fighting of Badgers or other Animals, shall ... forfeit any Sum not exceeding Five Pounds, and in default of immediate Payment shall be liable to be imprisoned and kept to hard Labour for any Time not exceeding Two Months ...
>
> ... if any Person shall ... wantonly and cruelly beat, ill-treat, abuse, or torture any Horse, Mare, Gelding, Bull, Ox, Cow, Heifer, Steer, Calf, Mule, Ass, Sheep, Lamb, Dog, or any other Cattle or domestic Animal, or if any Person who shall drive any Cattle or other Animal shall, by Negligence or ill Usage in the driving thereof, be the Means whereby any Mischief, Damage, or Injury shall be done by any such Cattle or other Animal ... shall [pay for the damage caused and] such a Sum of Money,

> not exceeding 40 Shillings nor less than Five Shillings with Costs, as to such Justice shall seem meet ...
>
> ... from the passing of this Act, if any Person shall keep or use any House, Room, Pit, Ground or other Place for the Purpose of running, baiting or fighting any Bull, Bear, Badger, Dog or other Animal (whether of domestic or wild Nature of Kind), or for Cock-fighting, ... shall be liable to a Penalty not exceeding Five Pounds ...

Despite the passing of this Act, its implementation had to overcome some entrenched attitudes. Some were less willing than others to give up part of their heritage. Stamford in Lincolnshire was the scene of escalating yearly confrontations between inhabitants and authorities over the continued practice of bull-baiting. It was something they were not prepared to give up without a fight, despite the new legislation. In 1836, eight arrests were made, and funds raised in the town helped the defendants prepare their case. A London police officer, sent to witness what was happening, was given short shrift by the inhabitants and threatened. He saw a bull covered in blood but was kept away from the bull-run by threats. Five of the defendants were acquitted, which locals saw as a victory. The following November, in 1837, another bull-run was planned. The escalating situation led to the home secretary reminding the mayor of his duties, and 200 special constables were drafted in by central government. But the run still took place, as they were reluctant to intervene. In yet further escalation, in 1838, the army was drafted in alongside 12 London police officers, and local magistrates felt obliged to make it clear that they would apply the law in full. However, as the date of the planned bull-run approached, a bull was introduced into the town, resulting in a spontaneous bull-run, which was put down by the dragoons. A serious confrontation took place, and the intentions of the authorities were clear – the tradition would not be allowed to persist. In 1839, a similarly strong presence of the authorities at the appointed time was surprised by another bull-run. A confrontation with a crowd of some 4000 people took place, and the bull was recovered and 'escorted to a hotel yard between two columns of cavalrymen'. The Home Secretary presented the mayor with a bill for £600 to cover the cost of outside forces that were being drafted in each year. Hitting the inhabitants in the pocket seemed to do the trick, and the mayor promised that the tradition would end (Turner, 1992, p. 137).

It is possible to hear echoes from the Stamford tale in more recent confrontations by drawing parallels with the continuation of fox-hunting in the UK. Similar claims to 'tradition' and resistance to outside interference by 'townies' are often made, and the introduction of the Hunting Act

2004 has been beset by difficulties (Nurse, 2017). Confrontations, sometimes violent, continue to occur between hunt followers and anti-hunting protestors, although they do not reach the apparent seriousness of those in Stamford in the 1830s. The call to respect tradition illustrates many of the problems faced by animal welfare protestors and lobbyists – cruel practices involving animals are seen as a human right or as part of historic tradition, and 'outsider' interference is unwelcome. Some humans are extremely reluctant to give up traditions, even in practices known to involve animal cruelty.

The 1849 Cruelty to Animals Act strengthened the law protecting animals (AD 1849, 12 and 13 Vict, C 92):

> ... if any Person shall ... beat, ill-treat, over-drive, abuse or torture, or cause or procure to be cruelly beaten, ill-treated, over-driven, abused, or tortured, any Animal, every such Offender shall for every such Offence forfeit and pay a Penalty not exceeding Five Pounds.
>
> ... every Person who shall keep or use or act in the Management of any place for the Purpose of fighting or baiting any Bull, Bear, Badger, Cock, or other Kind of Animal, whether of domestic or wild Nature, or shall permit or suffer any Place to be so used, shall be liable to a Penalty not exceeding Five Pounds ...

By this Act, it became possible to prosecute both the perpetrator of the acts in question and those causing or procuring such acts, thus making it possible to prosecute the master as well as the servant. Provisions were also introduced to provide for animals going to slaughter, such as the requirement to feed and water them properly.

After 1850, the emphasis of proposed reform shifted from openly cruel practices to the relatively new and growing practice of experimentation involving animals behind closed doors (examined in detail in Chapter 4). Scientists began to see animals as useful tools that could open the gateway to discoveries to alleviate human suffering. This brought with it concerns about the violation of fundamental moral principles concerning our relationship with animals (French, 1975). In the UK, concerted and well-organised protests against animal experimentation led to the Cruelty to Animals Act 1876. In continental Europe, where the use of animals for experimental purposes had always been much more common, control came later.

The 19th century remains a period that witnessed radical changes to the law relating to animals, which led Queen Victoria to comment that during her reign, she had noticed, in particular, 'with real pleasure, the growth of more humane feelings towards the lower animals' (Thomas, 1983, p. 149). However, continued unease in relation to practices *outside* the laboratory led in the early 20th century to the passing of the principal Act, which protected animals in the UK for nearly 100 years, the Protection of Animals Act 1911. It was largely repealed by the Animal Welfare Act 2006 – more of that Act later. The 1911 Act finally gave significant protection to 'any animal', but broadly excluded wild animals, animals used as 'food for mankind' in their preparation or destruction unless there was accompanying unnecessary suffering, and completely excluded animals used in experimentation except in certain instances, which are now mainly protected by the Animals (Scientific Procedures) Act 1986 (see Chapter 4). The various 19th-century cruelty to animals acts had certainly changed cruel practices, including 'leisure and sporting pursuits', but it was the 1911 Act that finally made these practices illegal, which broadened the scope of protection to more animals. The Act became a blueprint for protection across the globe as more countries began to enact protection legislation for animals, particularly those in the British Empire (Robertson, 2015, p. 82).

The 1911 Act made it unlawful to mistreat *any* animal other than those particularly excluded. The types of mistreatments identified were quite broad, including definitions such as 'beating' and less obvious ones such as 'infuriating'. A duty was placed on owners to protect their animals. Animals could be removed from their owners and destroyed if this would be kinder to the animal in the circumstances. The 1911 Act was also notable in that it recognised elements of animal sentience through provisions that regulated causing the animal 'unnecessary suffering' – this could be read quite widely to include the ability to exhibit natural behaviours. It is therefore a significant milestone in worldwide animal protection, despite its real function being merely to clarify and consolidate existing UK law at the time.

France was the first to follow the British lead in respect of animal welfare legislation when, in 1850, after much work by Jaques-Phillipe Delmas de Grammont, it passed the 'Loi Grammont', an Act that was similar in its aims to the British legislation regarding cruelty. The dawn of animal legislative protection had begun in earnest, led by the UK and France, but other countries took time to follow suit, even to this day (Brooman & Legge, 2023). In the US, for example, there are large discrepancies regarding the date of introduction of the first anti-cruelty laws, ranging from, for example, 1828 in New York, 1859 in Washington, and 1868 in California to 1889 in Florida.

The development of laws to protect the 'sentience' of animals

The final milestone period is the late 20th/early 21st century, where moves began to protect more than direct maltreatment of animals by adding to what should not be done 'to' animals and regulating what should be done 'for' them. This type of legislation reflects much of the emerging philosophy and science of the time, which provided more evidence of the sentience (defined in detail below) qualities of animals. Discussion is often centred on rights, personhood and sentience – all of which recognise animals' desires, emotions and needs beyond food and other basic requirements. This period built on another significant development – the concept of protecting the sentience of animals (The Brambell Report, 1965). This report provided definitions of the 'sentient qualities' of farmed animals, though not explicitly calling it sentience, appreciating that they can suffer and feel stress, as well as other emotions such as frustration, fear and pleasure. The Brambell Report outlined the following requirements for the protection of farm animals:

- Freedom from thirst, hunger and malnutrition.
- Freedom from discomfort.
- Freedom from pain, injury and disease.
- Freedom to express normal behaviour and,
- Freedom from fear and distress.

The recognition of normal behaviour, fear and distress, which were then protected in legislation, marked a significant step for animals kept and slaughtered in food production in the UK. Along with the Protection of Animals Act 1911, it became a blueprint for legislation elsewhere. In terms of moves towards protecting the sentient qualities of animals, it marked a point of recognising there is more to animals than the desire for basic needs and more going on inside their heads than merely basic instincts, which carries with it moral implication for human use of animals.

The importance of recognising sentience has gained popularity around the world, not only through law but also, as will be highlighted in Chapter 3, through philosophical and political arguments to grant animals rights or greater protection. Bentham's famous statement, 'The question is not, Can they reason? Nor, Can they talk? But, Can they suffer?' has been frequently cited when outlining the protection animals receive (Bentham, 1789). The importance of the sentient qualities of animals is implicit within all the leading theories, as will be explained in Chapter 3. Peter Singer uses sentience as the basis in his theory, using Bentham's work to argue for his utilitarian concept of equal consideration of interests. Regan's rights theory applies inherent value because, he suggests, animals are the subject of a life. Although he does not say so explicitly, the concept of sentience is apparent in Regan's application of this, which is why not all live beings, such as plants, are included. Like Regan, Francione uses sentience as an argument to grant animals legal rights, and we have political arguments emerging from those such as Donaldson, Kymlicka and Cochrane, who use sentience as a starting point in their arguments for political rights and citizenship. In 2012, a collection of prominent natural scientists came together to sign the Cambridge Declaration on Consciousness, recognising that all mammals and birds, and other species, including octopuses, are 'conscious beings', which is a euphemism for 'sentient'. A similar Declaration was signed by experts in New York in 2024, which highlighted the indication of consciousness in all vertebrates and many invertebrates, including insects. In law, sentience has become a baseline for protecting animals, and the scientific significance of proving sentience in different animals has grown. It is now difficult to discuss Animal Law and welfare without a working understanding of how animals' sentience will be affected by changes in practice.

Almost a century after the significant milestone of the 1911 Act, the Animal Welfare Act 2006 was introduced in England and Wales, which implicitly recognised sentience in s.62, stating that 'suffering' incorporates both physical and mental suffering of animals. In the explanatory notes for s.1, it is stated that the animals to which the Act applies are limited to vertebrates other than man, as 'these are currently the only demonstrably sentient animals'. It can be argued that this is now scientifically outdated (Rowan et al., 2021). Elsewhere, several countries have recognised sentience explicitly in law: Austria in 1988, Germany in 1990, New Zealand in 1999 and 2015, Tanzania in 2009, Chile in 2009, The Netherlands in 2011, Colombia in 2016 and Switzerland in 2022.

Until 2022, the UK did not explicitly recognise sentience in law, but this was done indirectly through our membership of the EU in the 1997 Treaty of Amsterdam, now Article 13 of the Treaty on the Functioning of the European Union, which provides (European Union, 1997):

> In formulating and implementing the Union's agriculture, fisheries, transport, internal market, research and technological development and space policies, the Union and the Member States shall, since animals are sentient beings, pay full regard to the welfare requirements of animals, while respecting the legislative or administrative provisions and customs

of the Member States relating in particular to religious rites, cultural traditions and regional heritage.

On leaving the EU, the UK Parliament had lengthy debates to decide which laws to retain under the European Union (Withdrawal) Act 2018. Article 13 was discussed at length and, to the dismay of many, was not retained, with the government arguing the Withdrawal Act was not the right place to enshrine sentience into our law, highlighting the 'sufficient protection' provided by the Animal Welfare Act 2006 (Brooman, 2018). This caused criticism from many interest groups and the public, causing the government to introduce a bill in 2018 that would provide for longer prison sentences for animal cruelty offences, something that had been advocated for many years, and the need for ministers to have regard to the welfare needs of animals as sentient beings in formulating and implementing government policy. After consultation, however, it was decided that the enshrining of sentience into the law needed further consideration and was separated from the bill. At the time, this felt like a loss for animal welfare, but when considering the impact of Article 13, the mere recognition of animal sentience in law seems to make little difference in the EU (Dunn & Jowitt, 2024). For example, though Article 13 stipulates that the Union and Member States must pay full regard to the welfare of animals as sentient beings, some animals still receive poor protection in light of their sentient qualities – the plight of farmed wild animals such as mink is a notable example, which is still allowed under EU law. In addition, the welfare of farmed animals in the UK remains poor in terms of animal sentience in areas such as large-scale overcrowding, access to outside environments, slaughter without stunning and more (see Chapter 6). There are also concerns that post-Brexit trade deals may allow the introduction of animal products from countries with poor animal welfare standards (Animal Protection Index, 2023). In the EU, in addition to poor conditions similar to the UK, live export of animals still occurs on a large scale, even though it has been continuously demonstrated it creates extremely stressful and sometimes fatal situations for the animals (Compassion in World Farming, 2017).

If Article 13 were being applied properly, would we not be witnessing more significant changes in the treatment of farmed animals than is the case? A significant issue with Article 13 is its wording – governing bodies merely need to show that they have 'paid full regard' to the welfare of animals during the creation of their policies, which does not prevent them from continuing with the policy if poor welfare is demonstrated. An example is the plan in Spain to build the world's first octopus farm, with the proposed slaughter method being submersion in ice water, even though scientists and welfare groups have outlined how cruel the intensive farming of octopuses will be (Rook et al., 2023). Octopuses are highly intelligent problem solvers with high-order sentient capacity, which at least raises questions as to how they experience such inhumane slaughter techniques. It was perhaps right that the UK government decided to devote more time to the sentience of cephalopods and decide a way to proceed that was more than merely recognising sentience as a symbolic gesture (Radford, EFRAC oral evidence 2018).

After four years of discussion, awareness raising and consultation, the Animal Welfare (Sentience) Act 2022 was passed in the UK. It is a short Act, with only six sections, but it goes further than merely recognising sentience. Firstly, s.1 (s.1(2)(1)) establishes the Animal Sentience Committee, whose role is to review government policy that is being or has been formulated. This is like other committees established to advise the government on specific matters, such as the Climate Change Committee, established under the Climate Change Act 2008, to advise on emissions targets and prepare for the impacts of climate change. The Animal Sentience Committee can choose to produce a report under s.2, questioning:

> (2) … whether, or to what extent, the government is having, or has had, all due regard to the ways in which the policy might have an adverse effect on the welfare of animals as sentient beings.
>
> (3) The report may also contain recommendations as to the steps the Committee considers the government should take for the purpose in subsection (4).
>
> (4) The purpose is that of ensuring that, in any further formulation or implementation of the policy, the government has all due regard to the ways in which the policy might have an adverse effect on the welfare of animals as sentient beings.

Once a report has been published by the committee, under s.3, the Secretary of State must lay a response to the report before parliament within three months from the day the report is published. During the passing of the Act, Lord Benyon commented:

> It is important to understand what the Bill is and what it is not. It is intended to embed consideration of animal welfare into the policy decision-making process. It does not change existing laws, nor does it dictate to ministers which decisions they should ultimately make. It is for ministers to make those calls, taking all relevant considerations into

> account, and for Parliament to hold them to account. The Bill is designed to support Parliament in doing so. (House of Commons, 2021)

Some observations can be made on these powers and reporting systems. Ministers need only to demonstrate that they have paid 'due regard' to the welfare of sentient beings, not 'full regard' as was required under Article 13. The committee does not have a duty to provide a report on 'all' policies and therefore can choose when to produce reports, which may lead to inadequate supervision. It can decide how to publish the reports but cannot address issues relating to devolved competencies, as it can only review the policies of the government of the United Kingdom and not policies relating to legislative provisions falling within devolved competence, such as from the Welsh and Scottish Parliament. This is important as a significant set of devolved powers lie within Animal Law and regulation. The government does not have to follow committee recommendations, and the UK Parliament does not have to set aside time to discuss them or the government's response to them. Time will reveal the effectiveness of the Animal Sentience Committee in light of these loose supervisory and advisory structures.

Finally, judicial review has become a new tool in the animal welfare and rights toolbox when authorities act outside or beyond their powers (Thomas, 2022). It has been used in cases concerning animal experimentation, such as *BUAV* v. *Newcastle University* (2010) to challenge the legality of project licences and in cases concerning farming, such as *The King (on the application of The Humane League UK)* v. *the Secretary of State for the Environment, Food and Rural Affairs* (2023). Although judicial review aims to ensure accountability, its success in Animal Law cases has been limited. Environmental Law utilises judicial review to challenge decisions made regarding the environment, and, though success rates are not particularly high, it is still viewed as a vital mechanism to ensure environmental protection (Day, 2023). However, the ambit of judicial review regarding the work of the Animal Sentience Committee will be minimal. The nature of judicial review excludes the possibility of the courts advancing the law on animal sentience, as they can only look at the legality of decisions made and potential errors of law, not the legal issues themselves and the finding of fact. Further, there is no option to judicially review the government should it decide not to adopt the recommendations made by the Animal Sentience Committee. The regulation of the law relating to animals may become static as a result, despite developing a scientific appreciation of animal sentience.

A case study in sentience and the development of new law: Cephalopods and decapods

The Animal Welfare (Sentience) Act 2022 makes a significant progressive step in animal welfare in the UK by expanding the definition of animals protected under the Act to include some invertebrates. Under s.5, an animal is defined as a) a vertebrate other than *homo sapiens*, b) any cephalopod mollusc and c) any decapod crustacean. This list can be added to by secondary legislation under s.5(2). The debate on the inclusion of cephalopods and decapods was one reason why the Act took some time to be drafted, as more evidence was gathered to provide scientific justification for their inclusion (Brooman, 2017). An important piece of work that helped substantiate the scientific justification for recognising cephalopods and decapods as sentient was carried out by a team at the London School of Economics led by Professor Jonathan Birch, which was funded by the UK Department for the Environment, Food and Rural Affairs (Birch et al., 2021). The team reviewed over 300 scientific studies to assess the evidence of sentience in cephalopods and decapods, and evaluated the welfare implications of current commercial practices on these animals. They used eight criteria to determine evidence of sentience to provide a level of confidence for each, stating whether they could confidently say the animals satisfied or failed each criterion. They found strong evidence of sentience in octopods, with slightly less evidence concerning squid and cuttlefish, although the evidence was still seen as substantial. For decapods, there was substantial evidence of sentience in lobsters and crayfish and strong evidence of sentience in true crabs, but less evidence for other decapods. This study shows the importance of scientific studies on the sentience of animals and the impact they can have on the formulation of policy, as without them, cephalopods and decapods may not have been included in the scope of the Act.

To what extent, if at all, does including cephalopods and decapods in the Animal Welfare (Sentience) Act 2022 better protect the sentience of these animals in practice? Chapter 6 outlines the current concerns with the farming and slaughter of cephalopods and decapods, with evidence of extreme suffering. Birch et al. (2021) also addressed this issue in their research, recommending the banning of certain practices, such as declawing and 'nicking' of crabs, selling live decapods to untrained handlers, slaughtering them by boiling them alive, or slowly raising the temperature of water, tailing and live dismemberment, and freshwater immersion. The report recommended electrical stunning at the time of killing and calls for further research to find more effective 'dispatch' (killing) techniques as there is, currently, no known slaughter method for these animals that is commercially viable and humane in large-scale operations.

There are still doubts about the overall clarity and consistency of UK law, even with the addition of the 2022 Act. The transport and slaughter techniques currently allowed in the UK are based on their exclusion from coverage under the Animal Welfare Act 2006. Since 2013, all cephalopods, specifically octopus, squid, cuttlefish and nautilus, are protected species under the Animals (Scientific Procedures) Act 1986, but decapods are not included. The varying protection these animals receive under the law presents a pressing need for consolidation and updating, especially in light of conclusive evidence of their sentience. The new sentience provisions and the work of the new committee in the UK provide an opportunity to develop new approaches and, potentially, change the law in this area following recommendations (Nurse, 2019). With specific recognition and consideration of sentience under the Act, it is hoped this will improve the protection of animals over time in all areas of use, particularly where there are major concerns, such as in the production of food.

Defining 'sentience'

Perhaps surprisingly, one crucial element omitted from the Animal Welfare (Sentience) Act 2022 is a definition of sentience. This may seem unusual, but it may be a sensible omission – there is no universal definition of sentience, and with the current state of knowledge, it continues to evolve with science. A specific definition would soon become outdated. For example, previous definitions focused on pain and pleasure, and negative feelings in particular, but new definitions are starting to include other states, such as distress, and place more emphasis on emotions as well as feelings. Defining sentience also requires expertise from multiple disciplines, such as animal behaviour and husbandry, philosophy and law, and the risk of developing inconsistencies makes it difficult to provide a one-size-fits-all definition (Brooman, 2017). The definition used by the London School of Economics' (LSE) Climate Change Laws team (2024) defines sentience as:

> Sentience (from the Latin sentire, to feel) is the capacity to have feelings. Feelings may include, for example, feelings of pain, distress, anxiety, boredom, hunger, thirst, pleasure, warmth, joy, comfort and excitement. We humans are sentient beings, and we are all familiar with such feelings from our own lives. A sentient being is 'conscious' in the most elemental, basic sense of the word. It need not be able to consciously reflect on its

feelings, as we do, or to understand the feelings of others: to be sentient is simply to have feelings.

This is more detailed than the definition developed by the Global Animal Law Project and later adopted by the British Veterinary Association 'Sentience shall be understood to mean the capacity to have feelings, including pain and pleasure, and implies a level of conscious awareness' (House of Commons, 2022). The LSE team's additions to the prior, less detailed definitions of sentience, such as those of the Global Animal Law Project, are vital, as research is emerging that shows animals most often experience the world differently to humans and do not experience their feelings in the same way as we do (Yong, 2022; de Vere & Kuczaj, 2016). By extension, a lack of understanding of how animals experience suffering need not prevent protecting their sentient qualities. The danger of anthropomorphising the feelings of animals (viewing them through the lens of human experience) is that we might unnecessarily exclude some from emerging definitions of sentience. The Animal Sentience Committee has been issued with terms of reference to help guide their work, which state that sentience may be defined by the committee for its own purposes but can only be applied to policies relating to animals defined as sentient under s.5. There is a potential benefit to this, as it will allow the committee to work with definitions as they develop with science, rather than confining them to a definition that may rapidly become outdated. It does, however, place a significant burden on the committee to achieve consensus in defining animals as sentient and may impact how effective they are in undertaking their duties – once definitions enter the public arena, they may be resistant to change.

Although there are concerns about the potential effectiveness of the Animal Welfare (Sentience) Act 2022 and the Animal Sentience Committee, it is nevertheless a significant step in the law, establishing the world's first committee devoted to animal sentience, and has great potential to impact legislative policy and protection for animals. What then, is the importance and significance of recognising sentience in law, and why has this movement gained traction worldwide? Could it really make a difference? It is certainly something that appears to be a central influence to be explored in the new age of 21st century animal welfare and protection.

Recognising sentience could protect animals previously excluded from animal protection and welfare legislation once a species is proven to be sentient according to the definitions adopted. This is a positive potential outcome and might provide a road to developing the overall protection given to animals. This assumes, however, that scientific evidence is continuously evolving and that those in key positions put evidence into practice building new legislative frameworks. Browning (2022, p. 310) suggests that the new age of defining sentience has such positive benefits:

> Animal sentience is a, if not the, key component of animal welfare. The recognition of this fact has led to a recent shift towards the inclusion of sentience within animal welfare legislation, which has had effects on their care and welfare, including in changing attitudes towards animals, improving their care, and strengthening the justification required for their use.

This view is supported by leaders in the field, such as Professor Donald Broom (2011, 2014, 2022), who has also noted that public concern for animal welfare has steadily increased in recent years, drawing the attention of policymakers and thereby promoting changes in the law (Broom, 2009). He suggests that the more the public knows and understands animal sentience, welfare and treatment, the more influence might be brought to bear on law reform.

Using sentience as the key indicator for protection may provide some objectivity in defining a species' worthiness of protection. Blattner (2019, p. 121–2), for example, suggests:

> Thus, if scientific findings show that an animal is sentient, this is sufficient to bring them directly under the purview of the law without getting the administration or legislature involved. This strategy seems to nullify all and any attempts to deny animals legal protection simply because they are not sufficiently appealing, emotionally close, or economically useful to us … The recognition of animal sentience seems to help Animal Law overcome cognitive biases – systematic patterns of deviation from norm or rationality in judgment (Ciccarelli & White, 2018, p. 324) – that most people have about animals.
>
> Despite the widespread avowal to sentience, the function and operability of the legal recognition of animal sentience are nebulous and lack scholarly conceptualization. It is, for instance, unknown if the concept has symbolic value only, or if it gives rise to moral, and potentially legal, duties owed to animals. Answering these questions may help us gain more certainty about the laws in place and bring to the fore new strategies for practicing lawyers, academics, and activists.

Blattner draws attention to the fact that the legal recognition of species needing protection may be unduly dependent on human feelings towards them, such as appears to be the case with fish. There are also issues with allocating research time and funding to specific animals, which means their sentience is more likely to be demonstrated and acted upon.

A systematic review of research conducted on animal sentience by Proctor, Carder and Cornish (2013) found that vertebrates were significantly studied more than invertebrates, and mammals were the most popular animals studied. Further, there was a tendency for studies to explore negative states, rather than positive states, in animals, even though the definition of sentience has moved on from considering it to be purely a function of pain and suffering. Their study also noted that, in light of the billions of farmed and wild-caught fish involved and their increasing use in scientific procedures, there were fewer than the expected numbers of studies centred on the sentience of fish and their capacity for suffering. They attributed this lack of research to a lack of consensus around the existence of suffering in fish (Proctor, Carder & Cornish, 2013).

Browning (2022) also comments on this but contends that there has been greater recognition of animal sentience, both publicly and officially, demonstrated by an increase in research into animal sentience. There is a wider recognition of fish sentience and a rise in related research, but this appears to be lacking in quantity. The wide variety of fish species leads to the possibility that science has not yet picked up the potential need to protect some species ahead of others. Blattner (2019) attributes this not just to a lack of studies but also to cognitive bias in science such as research results being favoured that allow for the continued use of animals (anthropocentric bias) and ascribing sentience to animals that have the most human-like traits (anthropomorphic bias). He asks for scientists to adopt the precautionary principle (where there are threats of serious or irreversible damage from an action, even where scientific evidence is inconclusive as to the result, they should be forestalled) to guide them when assessing whether animals are sentient (Blattner, 2019). It is clear that the recognition of sentience in animals often rests upon their usefulness or conceptions of attractiveness to humans – moral consistency between the species is far from being achieved.

A positive outcome of the enhanced view of the importance of sentience and its broader definition in modern discussions is how this has changed perceptions of animals' welfare and influenced legal developments. Scientific research in this area is increasing, and with it, Animal Law is moving into a new phase of development. We have come a long way in redefining our views of the cognitive and emotional states of animals from the time of the Ancient Greeks, which is where this chapter started. The trajectory of development still appears to be upwards, if at times slower than we might anticipate or desire. It is to be hoped that recognising animal sentience does not become merely symbolic, failing to find its way into legislative change, or for it to become an animal sentience version of 'human-washing', but rather that it provides the impetuous of better protection, and for more species.

Anomalies of present-day Animal Law

Property status

The basis for the introduction of legislation concerning animals has not always been a straightforward concern for animal welfare; indeed, a great deal of legislation regarding animals has been introduced to protect human property interests. Even where law has been developed to protect animals, it rarely goes so far as law protecting humans. For example, if one person inflicts pain upon another person, they are usually subject to criminal prosecution by the state, which might impose financial or more serious penalties. There might also be a civil action, which would result, possibly, in financial compensation being awarded to the victim. In the case of animals, however, the animal does not receive an award of compensation against the perpetrator, which highlights their property status. It is the owner who is the recipient of damages for the 'damage incurred to property'. In addition, an action may often be defeated simply by the cost of taking it up in the courts, preventing it from even getting off the ground, which further emphasises the lack of recognition for animal harm in law (Favre, 2021, p. 41).

The treatment of animals as property without rights is a common feature of the law relating to animals: abuse of an animal is abuse of the human interest in the animal concerned; over-fishing the Atlantic fish stocks is the loss of a public environmental resource; poaching results in the loss of possible financial gain through sale; the hunting of a species to near extinction raises concerns about the loss of rare species to be enjoyed by future generations, and so on. Therefore, it has been argued that animals do not have legal 'rights' as such, despite the appearance in much legislation that they do: they are the 'subjects' of protection in various laws, but they do not have the right to the benefits of legal action, merely the right to welfare protection because of it. Animals are not protected as independent entities deserving of intrinsic inviolable rights but as objects to be used by people within certain boundaries, which we term 'welfare', a notion that is bound up in the roots of our legal treatment of animals as property, as illustrated here by this 1690 contribution of John Locke (Laslett, 1988, pp. 287–278):

> Though the Earth, and all inferior creatures be common to all men, yet every man has a property in his own person. This nobody has any right to but himself. The labour of his body, and the work of his hands, we may say, are properly his. Whatsoever then he removes out of the state that nature hath provided, and left it in, he hath mixed his labour with, and joyned to it something that is his own, and thereby makes it his property. It being by him removed from the common state nature placed it in, it hath by his labour something annexed to it, that excludes the common right of other men. For this labour being the unquestionable property of the labourer, no man but he can have a right to what that is once joined to, at least where there is enough, and as good left in common for others.

In his historic contribution to the documentation on the development of English law, Sir William Blackstone, in the 1794 edition of *Commentaries on the Laws of England*, outlines the basis of the legal status of animals, which remains largely intact today (Blackstone, 1794, pp. 2–3):

> In the beginning of the world, we are informed by holy writ, the all-bountiful creator gave to man "dominion over all of the earth; and over the fish of the sea, and over the fowl of the air, and over every living thing that moveth upon the earth". This is the only true and solid foundation of man's dominion over external things, whatever airy metaphysical notions may have been started by fanciful writers upon this subject. The earth, therefore, and all things therein, are the general property of all mankind, exclusive of all other beings, form the immediate gift of the creator.

On the importance of the property status of animals in pre-history, he comments (Blackstone, 1794, p. 5):

> The article of food was a more immediate call, and therefore a more early consideration. Such, as were not contented with the spontaneous product of the earth, fought for a more solid refreshment in the flesh of beasts, which they obtained by hunting. But the frequent disappointments, incident to that method of provision, induced them to gather together such animals as were of a more-tame and fequacious nature; and to establish a permanent property in their flocks and herds, in order to sustain themselves in a less precarious manner, partly by the milk of the dams, and partly by the flesh of the young.

Finally, he justifies the treatment of animals as property in terms of it giving an incentive to farmers by giving them rights of ownership in the land and 'moveables,' including animals, upon it (Blackstone, 1794, p. 7):

> [T]he art of agriculture, by a regular connexion and consequence, introduced and established the idea of a more permanent property in the soil, than had hitherto been received and adopted. It was clear that the earth would not produce her fruits in sufficient quantities, without the assistance of tillage; but who would be at the pains of tilling it, if another might watch upon an opportunity to seize upon and enjoy the product of his industry, art, and labour? Had not therefore a separate property in lands, as well as moveables, been vested in some individuals, the world must have continued a forest, and men have been mere animals of prey; which, according to some philosophers, is the genuine fate of nature.

The term 'animal' for current laws usually covers any creature that is not a human being, but specific statutes, such as the Animals (Scientific procedures) Act 1986, may give a slightly amended definition of 'animal' in line with its purpose. Legislation relating to animals divides them into *domestic*, *captive* and *wild* animals for different levels of protection, with domestic animals being deemed as absolute property and the ability to treat wild animals as property being strictly limited. Subject to animal welfare laws, the treatment of domestic animals does not differ significantly from the treatment of other chattels in English law (Holdsworth, 1973, pp. 488–489).

Limited property rights in wild animals can arise by lawfully taking, taming or reclaiming them, as a result of their being born on a person's land until they can fly or run away or move onto the land from another's, as a right of an owner of land who has retained exclusive rights to hunt, take and kill animals on their own land or as a result of being granted those rights by the owner. These qualified rights are usually only important in relation to actions for trespass on property, and do not grant unlimited property rights. This branch of the law relating to wild animals presents more difficult problems than that of domestic animals, for several reasons (Holdsworth, 1973, p. 490):

> The law as to the original acquisition of the ownership and possession of animals ferae naturae has, at different periods, been affected by four different sets of influences. Those influences are the Roman rules as to the acquisition of such animals, the rights of the Crown, the rights of landowners, and the Game Laws enacted in the interest of larger landowners. All these influences have combined to make the history of this branch of law very complex.

A case in 2020 (*Borwick Development Solutions Limited* v. *Clear Water Fisheries Limited*) explored the property claims of wild animals concerning fish kept in nine enclosed lakes in Lancashire for anglers at a commercial fishery. When the fishery was sold, no rights to the fish were granted or reserved in the transfer. The sellers, Borwick, tried to claim that they retained proprietary interests over the fish and that they were not included in the sale of the land. The appeal judgment is an interesting read, exploring the proprietary rights of wild animals, citing Roman law from early English authors. The court affirmed previous case law that animals *ferae naturae* (wild animals) cannot be subject to absolute property rights, and there can be only qualified property rights. The proprietary rights discussed in this case were *ratione soli* (the exclusive right to hunt, take, keep and kill when animals are on the owner's freehold land) and rights acquired *per industriam* (when an animal is in someone's possession by way of some effort or industry to capture or tame the animal, and it lasts so long that the animal remains in that person's possession). The court had to decide whether the fish were wild and whether ownership rights were retained upon the sale of the land. The court held that fish are wild animals and cannot be subject to absolute ownership and that the proprietary rights to the fish were lost upon the sale of the land. The *ratione soli* depended on whether the right had been reserved or granted, which it had not and thus automatically passed with the sale of the land to Clear Water Fisheries Limited. *Per industriam* required retention of the animals, and when the land was sold, Borwick lost their right to enter the land or do anything with the fish. The law relating to the property status and ownership of wild animals is much more complex than that for domestic animals, and it can be much harder to establish property rights over wild animals.

Although extremely valuable to the progress of humankind, the treatment of animals as property has, arguably, been extremely damaging to the fate of animals. As 'property,' animal 'owners' have been able to dispose of their animals as they wish. Not only has it been difficult for the law to reach into areas of welfare concern where there were human property interests at stake, such as farming, but the continuing status of animals as property means that, as Gary Francione has noted, 'animals are regarded merely as means to human ends, which means that the law embodies the instrumentalist view of animals' (Francione, 1996, p. 25). He concludes that, as a society, our laws reject the notion of intrinsic value in animals in favour of allowing their owners to do as they please with their 'possessions'.

The courts of many countries have sometimes been asked to consider whether animals can be attributed with legal personality or status. Dolphins have attracted particular attention for centuries because of their apparent desire to actively seek out human contact and their obvious intelligence. Seafaring nations record many historical tales of dolphins coming to the aid of sailors in trouble. More recently, philosophers and, indeed, courts of law have been asked to consider whether a dolphin is a legal 'person'. In 1977, two men, Steve Sipman and Ken LeVasseur, were tried in the United States for releasing two bottle-nosed dolphins from the University of Hawaii's Institute of Marine Biology, where they were confined in concrete tanks for research purposes. Sipman and LeVasseur released the dolphins as they felt they were slaves and did not agree with the experiments being carried out on them. They argued an unsuccessful evils defence, or necessity, believing their actions were necessary to avoid an imminent harm or evil to another. It is a classic contemporary incidence of the philosophical questions being asked about the sentient status of higher-order animals, and it is particularly interesting because it was a crucial question asked in the case deciding on the continuing liberty of the two men. They attempted to raise the defence of necessity, which 'allows' the commission of an offence if the action is done for the avoidance of imminent and more serious harm to oneself or 'another'. The defence is common to most legal systems around the world. The question was whether a dolphin could be defined as 'another' for the purposes of the defence. Judge Doi declined to designate a dolphin as 'another' and defined them purely as property. He also decided that any possible cruelty to the animals in terms of isolation and behavioural change would not outweigh the more serious 'offence' in this case, namely theft, thus reinforcing the property status of animals. A further attempt to obtain leave to appeal in the Federal Court by claiming the Thirteenth Amendment in respect of involuntary servitude was also rejected by the judge (*State of Hawaii* v. *Le Vasseur* (1980)). A similar argument under the Thirteenth Amendment was also unsuccessful in the case of *Tilikum* v. *Sea World Parks and Entertainment* (2012), concluding that Tilikum the orca did not have sufficient standing to bring such a claim and that the Thirteenth Amendment only applied to persons. It will be seen in Chapter 3 that arguing legal personhood and extending constitutional rights to animals in the United States has proved to be difficult.

The philosophical basis of Judge Doi's decision was questioned by Mary Midgley, who pointed out that corporations can be termed 'legal persons' in law to sue and be sued. She compared the decision in this case to the difficulties women had in the United States in bringing themselves within the definition of 'person' to be able to practise law and to sit on a jury (Midgely, 1983). In summary, philosophical anomalies in legal systems across the globe allow a sentient animal such as a dolphin to be treated as having less legal status than a corporation, which benefits from the legal fiction of being treated as a 'legal person' with rights to act in court in their own name. The proposition that there is a need to grant animals an enhanced new legal status above and beyond their current status as property is discussed in detail in the next chapter.

Not only have animals been treated as property, but property interests relating to land ownership are often considered more important than animals. In the UK and elsewhere, there are several statutes giving wide discretionary powers to landowners or their employees to kill or injure animals where there is conflict with human interests. Even though the *indirect* effect of the Animals Act 1971 might be to protect livestock, Les Brown proposed that this is not the actual intention of the Act, which is in place to protect property interests in the animals (Brown, 1989, pp. 160–161):

> Property interests have long been protected in English and US law, sometimes in ways which do not consider the interests of all animals involved. For instance, the (UK) Animals Act 1971 gives the occupier of land, or the landowner, wide powers in protecting livestock from any dog found on his property, but excessive trust seems to be placed in both his rational powers and the morality of his motives and attitude… All the occupier or landowner needs is 'reasonable ground for believing that an attack on the livestock is imminent and no other reasonable means of dealing with the situation is available'. Under this Act, the dog would have little chance against a person who believed that all dogs found on properties are marauders, who ruled out the possibility of mistakes of judgement, who was malicious towards a dog known to belong to an unfriendly neighbour, and who acted without witnesses. In its protection of property rights, the Act leaves open the possibility of an infliction of unnecessary suffering on an animal.

Some apparently protective statutes, even though they cater for the welfare of animals, sometimes remove this protection if occupiers or landowners take action to protect their property. The Protection of Badgers Act 1992 prohibits the taking, injuring or killing of badgers (s.1), cruelty to badgers (s.2), interfering with their sets (s.3), and selling badgers (s.4). But (s.7) provides exceptions if the person shows that 'his action was necessary for the purpose of preventing serious damage to land, crops, poultry or any other form of property'. There are strict licensing provisions (s.10) to allow the killing or taking of badgers, and normally an occupier would have to comply with these. There is, however, an exception to this where it was not apparent before the time of the killing that such action was necessary. An occupier is thus protected if he can show that the action was immediately necessary to protect his property.

Therefore, although we have an array of legal protection for animals, their property status still governs the extent of this protection and how they are treated within law and society. The law still upholds the property status of animals, and though Chapter 3 outlines the modern challenges to this, it is still the prevalent determinant of how humans address issues relating to animals.

Case study in property status: The welfare of animals in international trade

The status of animals as property has had a large hand in the development of another significant problem in terms of animal welfare – the global trade and transportation of animals. Animals traded internationally, whether legal or illegal, are commodities, and the main purpose of their trade is the financial gain of those selling them. Due to their property status, they can be traded worldwide. In recent decades, many countries and legislative supranational areas, such as the European Union (EU), have introduced new or improved legislation to protect them (Brooman & Legge, 2023). However, one significant barrier to improved animal welfare is international trade. The EU introduced what was widely considered a potentially valuable tool in tacking animal welfare. Article 13 of the Treaty on the Functioning of the European Union 1997 (European Union 1997), outlined above, provides that member states should pay full regard to animals as sentient beings, including when formulating and implementing the Union's transport policies.

However, implementation has been dogged by accusations that the article has been loosely implemented and that practices such as fur farming and international trade in live animals have continued despite considerable evidence of wild animals suffering in captivity and the misery of animals enduring long-haul transportation. Animals are defined in the EU Treaties of Lisbon and Amsterdam as 'sentient beings', meaning they should be accorded protection as such – there is concern that the EU is not implementing legislation it has already passed. Creating legislation is an important step, but implementing it in a manner sufficient to satisfy legal interpretation and good conscience continues to be controversial, as it is often in conflict with the continued exploitation of animals as property and as a mere utility to owners for profit. EU law still shows its hand as a protector of trading animals as property above animal welfare considerations (Broom, 2017).

The protection of trade above animal welfare is a long-standing problem. In 1996, the European Court of Justice confirmed the lower status of moral concerns for animals in *R., ex parte Hedley Lomas (Ireland) Limited v. Ministry of Agriculture, Fisheries and Food* (1996). The court held that the temporary ban on the export of live sheep to Spain, between 1992 and 1994, because of fears over whether they were complying with rules regarding the stunning of animals before slaughter, was a breach of EC requirements regarding the free movement of goods. The Ministry was not allowed to invoke moral concern for the animals' welfare to support their action and was compelled to depend on the enforcement of regulations in the member state concerned. The case confirmed the supremacy of economics over animal welfare in the EU.

This situation has been repeated at the domestic level. In *R* v. *Coventry Airport, ex parte: Phoenix Aviation* (1995), the UK Court of Appeal was asked to consider whether it was lawful for public authorities operating airports and docks to ban the flights or shipments of livestock by exporters due to problems caused by public demonstrations. The court held that these authorities do not have the power to distinguish between these flights or shipments and other lawful trades. Even if they did, they would not be permitted to ban the export of live animals, as this practice is considered lawful. Simon Brown LJ (1995, p. 62), in a harsh rebuke of animal welfare protestors, stated with some vigour how the courts would protect lawful trade activities, even at the possible expense of animal welfare. He emphasised, 'Public authorities must beware of surrendering to the dictates of unlawful pressure groups. The implications of such surrender for the rule of law can hardly be exaggerated … Tempting though it may sometimes be for public authorities to yield too readily to threats of disruption, they must expect the courts to review any such decision with particular rigour – this is not an area where they can be permitted a wide measure of discretion.'

However, Sykes (2016) argues that the decision of the panel of the Dispute Settlement Body (part of the World Trade Organisation) in 2014 regarding the EU ban on the importation of seal products (EC–Seals Products case) may mark a subtle change in the policy direction of this important international trade organisation, which is often viewed with scepticism by animal welfare advocates. The panel upheld the EU's ban despite protests from Norway and Canada that the ban breached international trade rules. For the first time, they recognised the pursuit of animal welfare as a globally recognised ethical responsibility and said the ban was a legitimate action to protect public morals. Sykes argues that this may shift the direction of implementing international trade rules to allow the greater enhancement of countries' animal welfare protection and has the potential to facilitate it.

However, despite this optimistic view, the operating rules and implementation of treaties by the World Trade Organisation (WTO) continue to attract criticism from pressure groups and academics. For example, it is criticised for failing to incorporate widespread developments in world farming welfare standards (Hooton, 2019), which is possibly the area of greatest animal welfare concern due to the number of animals involved. It has also been suggested by McCulloch (2019) that WTO rules might feasibly be used to prevent Britain from banning, for example, fois gras or prohibiting live exports in the post-Brexit era, which would weaponise WTO rules against countries trying to improve welfare standards.

Iyan Offor (2020, p. 4) also noted the conflict between international trade legislation and improving animal welfare, describing it as being 'fundamentally incompatible with the ideology that supports animal trade'. Offor notes that this flies in the face of consumer awareness and public opinion, which continually shows evidence of support for enhanced animal welfare. He also highlights some of the future problems of attempting to use trade law as a mechanism for improving animal welfare – the vested interest groups and governments are reluctant to do so, eyeing the increased economic benefits of trade as more important. Despite the hopes of Sykes (2016) that reform of international trade law might have provided a way to enhance worldwide animal welfare, the lack of movement since the EC–Seals Products case casts doubt on whether recognising animal welfare as a legitimate public morality concern carries with it any inertial impact for animal welfare issues created by international trade.

Conclusion

The historical development of Animal Law shows a continued, if sometimes painfully slow, progress to implement improved animal welfare standards. Viewing Animal Law as it developed from ancient times, through medieval prosecution and on to the beginning of the reform era does leave the contemporary reader wondering what was in the minds of humans at the time and how or why they ignored the cruelty of what they could see with their own eyes. It has required considerable stamina, courage and flexibility of those seeking change in the face of such resistance to changing the accepted norms. It is possible to see the mistakes made in drafting that led to issues in interpreting legislation and how public awareness has often been the cause of changes in the law.

The ancient Greeks and Romans, credited with being the cradle of civilisation, are revealed as having had very mixed attitudes towards animals – contrast the legal process used against animals by the ancient Greeks or the Roman amphitheatres with the contributions of Pythagoras or Plutarch, for example. Certainly, the amphitheatres have gone, but their spirit lives on in bullfighting in southern Europe. The status of animals as property that we see today began with the Greeks and the Romans bringing the problems associated with allowing ownership to dictate our relationship with animals – although this is at least modified by animal welfare law and the continuing development of laws. Contrarily, the cruelty of many current practices is clear for us to see, as it is often done in plain sight. We may see progress, but the misplaced view of animals in the past has permeated into the present.

The madness of medieval prosecution of animals is a long way behind us, and as we view that from the present day, it seems unbelievable that humans could so mistake the role of intention in criminal law. However, when seen from the future, how will those looking back to our time view human use of billions of animals in modern agriculture, farming of wild animals for their fur, trophy hunting of animals, or the status of animals for the most part, as equivalent to the ownership of any inanimate object?

At the time of writing in 2024, the shifting sands of Animal Law appear to be moving again. At a supranational level, for example, three proposals for law reform have been brought forward by the European Commission (2023) that further recognise animal sentience and suffering – tackling the illegal pet trade, live transport of animals and potentially banning fur farming and sales in Europe. However, there are no guarantees that these proposals will come into being. The process of changing the law relating to animals, begun in the early 19th century, is ongoing and often repeats itself: concerns are frequently raised with confrontation, vested interests respond with ridicule or denial, philosophical and scientific support emerges for change, reform is still denied, and finally, recognition emerges leading to reform of the law. However, this may not go as far as lobby groups hoped, leaving them to carry on campaigning.

Issues remain in the law in terms of, firstly, recognising sentience in certain species, secondly, moving this into law, and thirdly, balancing the equation of animal sentience with their usefulness to humans. This leads to many contemporary anomalies, which are discussed in Chapter 3.

In Chapters 4–8, we discuss the various areas of Animal Law and the challenges faced in enforcing and reforming the law. Although there is much heartening progress to be seen, when observed from the perspective of developing awareness of sentience and suffering, there is much to be done. The role of humans, such as those on the Animal Sentience Committee in the UK, may be crucial, as they are now the moral gatekeepers of the development of Animal Law. As the late Steven Wise, champion of legal rights for animals and founder of the Nonhuman Rights Project in the United States, remarked (Wise, 2019, p. 393):

> Nothing of what I have written today could reasonably have been envisioned in 1995. What it took then, and what it takes today, is an unreasonable envisioning, firmly grounded in jurisprudence, science, and history, of the coming world in which many non-human animals will unthinkingly be seen as the subjects of justice. How that was done will be told in the 50th anniversary [edition] of Animal Law.

CHAPTER THREE

Leading theories on why and how the law should protect animals

Introduction

This chapter aims to draw together some of the leading and dominant philosophical and scientific contributions to the debate over the status of animals that seek to influence the development of Animal Law. Many of the historical contributions discussed in Chapter 1 remain as pertinent today as they were when first published. However, advancing knowledge continually adds new dimensions through which the philosophical basis of Animal Law can be critiqued. The philosophical implications of discovery, for example, related to animal sentience, have influenced legislators across the globe in some aspects of the treatment of animals by human societies. However, it is worth noting that despite welfare gains in many areas, it is still evident that the connection between humans and animals most often involves considerable suffering for a high number of species (Brooman, 2017). Steven Wise (2019, p. 393) notes that much of Animal Law is essentially grounded in Cartesian ethology and pre-Darwinian biology, which needs to be re-envisioned in jurisprudence, science and history. The question is, therefore, what should change in Animal Law, and why? Articulating this is one of the most dominant challenges for animal lawyers.

This chapter brings together many of the best-known contemporary theories that cross many of the themes in this book. Here we examine the challenges posed, such as understanding the arguments put forward for change, understanding the differences between those theories and whether this is important, defining how sentience fits in, recognising the inherent value of animals to challenge the predominance of property-based control of animals, and solving the puzzle of where claims for animals fit into overall environmental concerns.

This chapter will give an overview of the main philosophical and practical theories currently influencing the development of Animal Law. Firstly, we address the issue of what needs protection through changes in the law. Then, we move on to discuss recently dominant philosophical theories based on claims for 'animal rights' or utilitarianism. Furthermore, we explore claims for personhood and relatively new theories relating to citizenship for animals and redefining animals as living property. We discuss the 'push-back' theories from those more driven by maintaining the current philosophical order between humans and other species, which would deny major changes and certainly reject rights-based theories. Other notable philosophical positions are addressed before discussing the link between the growth of wider environmental damage and whether claims for animals should be refocused through action for global environmental initiatives. The key challenge addressed in this chapter is how those involved in claiming more for animals can articulate why this should be done. We appreciate that there are other relevant theories, such as Earth jurisprudence or ecofeminism, which can also provide for further protection and/or rights for animals. However, in this chapter, we are only focusing on those that we consider to be the dominant theories relating specifically to animals and have influenced Animal Law.

Many of the laws introduced over the last two centuries have been based on the notion of 'cruelty', which started to attract notable public concern in Europe at the end of the 18th century. Jeremy Bentham referred to 'cruelty towards animals', a notion that remains at the core of protective legislation. As science uncovers more about what causes animal pain and suffering, our definitions of 'cruelty' have evolved (Bentham, as quoted by Bowring, 1859, p. 562):

> The legislator ought to interdict everything which may serve to lead to cruelty. The barbarous spectacles of gladiators no doubt contributed to give the Romans that ferocity which they displayed in their civil wars. A people accustomed to despise human life in their games could not be expected to respect it amid the fury of their passions. It is proper for the same reason to forbid every kind of cruelty towards animals, whether by way of amusement, or to gratify gluttony. Cock-fights, bull- baiting, hunting hares and foxes, fishing, and other amusements of the same kind, necessarily suppose either the absence of reflection or a fund of inhumanity, since they produce the most acute sufferings to sensible beings, and the most painful and lingering death of which we can form any idea. Why should the law refuse its protection to any sensitive being? The time will come when humanity will extend its mantle over everything which breathes. We have begun by attending to the condition of slaves; we shall finish by softening that of all the animals which assist our labours or supply our wants.

The belief in the 'prevention of cruelty' advocated by Bentham still forms the main basis of current legislation and the incremental changes that are regularly introduced. The continuing debate regarding Animal Law centres on how far society should go in recognising and prohibiting 'cruelty', granting rights, personhood or enhanced status in some form, and enhancing an animal's right to a life according to its species. Not all philosophers contributing to the area are advocates of change. In the 1990s, English philosopher and advocate against animal rights Michael Leahy defended the status quo (1991, pp.176–178):

> That animals should be treated humanely, and with this proviso, that they may be killed, experimented upon, hunted, raced, or petted is both the legal, and perfectly defensible, position to hold. It is no accident that it seems to confirm the position of animals near the foot of our thumbnail hierarchy or 'order of obligation' ... Reformers and those with axes to grind will argue that much of this is all wrong despite its being the case. But my argument [is] that it is not difficult to defend something roughly resembling the *status quo* rather than being bludgeoned into a guilty conscience by accepting that one is a covert elitist or racist. The animal liberationists certainly think that the 'cruelty-kindness view'... is speciesist since it ignores the extent to which animal awareness is akin to that of human beings. But if this is a mistake and animals are properly to be understood as primitive beings, at least as different from us as they are similar, then their modest entitlement to humane treatment, accorded them by common sense and enshrined in the law, might well be vindicated.

However, it could be argued that Leahy's vision of maintaining the status quo has already become a victim of time – there have been significant advances across the globe with almost universal new legal provisions in favour of animals. Animal Law is far from static, although its pace of change can sometimes appear slow.

What needs protection? And which animals?

Two leading theories emerged in the 1970s and 1980s in relation to contemporary arguments for greater account to be taken of the moral position of animals, which still carry a great deal of theoretical weight in the animal welfare debate. The first is the inherent value theory, which was proposed by Tom Regan in his book *The Case for Animal Rights* (Regan, 1983). Regan's contribution was highly influential and claims that some animals possess 'inherent value' in that they have desires, an identity, a memory and a sense of the future in a similar way to humans. This, in turn, gives them moral standing, which should be taken into account by lawmakers. Thus, in relation to animal use in agriculture or experimentation, for example, animals should have their inherent value as the 'experiencers of life' considered, and it would be difficult to justify using them because of their inherent moral claim, or 'right', to certain treatment. Under Regan's theory, animals are accorded 'moral' rights, which could be reflected by giving them 'legal' rights. This 'strong animal rights position' is certainly the philosophical blueprint that would have the most far-reaching effect on the relationship of humans to animals. It has also given rise to claims for 'personhood', a term that has come to the fore in 21st century claims for animals and is discussed later in this chapter.

The second broad area of discussion occurs through the philosophical concept of utilitarianism, which rejects the notion of intrinsic moral rights held by animals and embraces the idea of considering the morally significant 'interests' of animals in the cost-benefit assessment instead. The utilitarian advocate for improved animal welfare argues that animals have an 'interest' in not suffering, which should be considered in our treatment of them. Both arguments agree that animals possess some qualities in common with humans that give rise to the need for better protection than we have been prepared to give. Proponents of both arguments use the cases of infants and severely mentally disabled or senile adults and find interests or inherent value in animals, which might be said to go beyond those of these particular humans. This is based on the apparently superior sentience of some animals over humans in those situations. It is argued that if we accord interests or inherent value to those humans, then it would be morally inconsistent not to do the same for the analogous qualities of animals (Singer, 1975, p. 18).

A critical difference between inherent value theory and the equal consideration theory of utilitarianism is that inherent value theory recognises that there is an inbuilt quality of the individual that should not be surrendered except in the most extreme of circumstances, whereas utilitarianism demands equal consideration but is willing to override this if the needs or desires of the many outweigh the needs or desires of the few. Therefore, according to inherent value theory, we should never allow the use of a sentient animal like a chimpanzee in experiments. Its apparent self-awareness and undoubted sentience would ascribe to its inherent value, which should not be sacrificed, in much the same way as we would not sacrifice individual humans for the sake of collective benefit, as inviolable 'rights' of the individual are not tradable in this way. In theory, utilitarianism might allow such sacrifice in circumstances where, in the cost-benefit assessment, the benefits greatly outweigh the detriments to the animals involved.

Utilitarianism, as it is applied to the animals' issue, proposes that as animals suffer and feel pain in much the same way as humans, their interests should be considered as part of the equation. To ignore them based on no more than membership of a species ignores comparable sentient qualities. This is illustrated by the demand that we should first consider using the insensate human in experimentation on account of their 'missing sentience', or we would be accused of 'speciesism'. For some in the animal welfare lobby, the main problem is that the theory might, in the final analysis, allow the interests of the chimpanzee (or human) to be overridden by the consequential benefits obtained by experimenting. Individuality would not carry the same weight as it does as a part of 'strong' animal rights theory.

The language of the animal welfare lobby is the source of continual debate as academics, politicians, lawmakers and interest groups find dissatisfaction with earlier theories. Searching for a single moral theory appears to be akin to searching for a true definition of human rights; there may be no single answer, and it will evolve with time. Despite the use of language as the primary historical tool to distinguish 'man from the beasts', ironically, we constantly come across the inadequacies of language in describing crucial moral concerns, emotional responses and intuitive responses of humankind in our interactions with each other and animals. Bear this inadequacy of language in mind when reading the following account of some of the leading moral theories underpinning the challenges to Animal Law.

Animal rights and inherent value

Gary Francione (1996, p. 31) suggests that 'What differentiates the modern animal protection movement from its predecessors is the acceptance by the former of the notion of animal rights.' The crucial feature of the 'inherent value' argument is that it is an uncompromising denial of the modern-day arguments regarding the benefits that we obtain from the use of animals. It is the ultimate argument in favour of the individual animal by replacing the notion that 'the needs of the many outweigh the needs of the one' with the notion that 'the needs of the one are equivalent to the needs of the many'. There is evidence of this notion in human attitudes towards 'the gift of life'. No one, it appears, feels such a burning desire to benefit the whole of mankind that they willingly allow themselves to be sacrificed in the cause of medical advancement. It is contended that animal rights-based approaches differ from animal 'welfarists' in that proponents seek to abolish exploitation rather than merely regulate it (Kotzmann & Pendergrast, 2019, p. 170).

It could be argued that Albert Schweitzer was one of the 'grandfathers' of the modern animal rights movement. Writing in the 1920s and 1930s, he coined the phrase 'reverence for life', which arose out of a search for a common theme in his pursuit of the 'ethic of universality' and his critical evaluation of previous attempts at defining morality (Schweitzer, 1923, p. 254):

> A man is really ethical only when he obeys the constraint laid on him to help all life, which he is able to [help in times of distress], and when he goes out of his way to avoid injuring anything living. He does not ask how far this or that life deserves sympathy as valuable in itself, nor how far it is capable of feeling. To him, life as such is sacred. He shatters no crystal that sparkles in the sun, tears no leaf from its tree, breaks off no flower, and is careful not to crush any insect as he walks.

There are elements of Schweitzer's appreciation of life approach and its recognition of the value of all life in much of the contemporary work on animal rights, although there are considerable differences in the substance of the respective arguments. Tom Regan has continued the theme into modern times, although he would not accept 'inherent moral value' for all forms of life as Schweitzer did, but only to those animals who are 'subjects of a life', which would exclude lower lifeforms. Regan regards at least some animals as having 'enhanced' moral status. Schweitzer (1923, p. 264) was critical of the use of animals in experimentation. However, he stopped short of condemning it outright by saying that those involved should 'care to alleviate as much as possible the pain which they cause'. Modern 'inherent value' proponents such as Regan go much further by calling for an end to 'all' animal experimentation. This applies particularly to experiments involving mammalian animals, which are 'subjects of a life' (Regan, 1983). Despite these differences, Schweitzer's argument constituted one of the stepping stones towards present-day rights-based discussion.

The attractive element of the inherent value argument, according to its proponents, is that it gives due weight to the interests of the individual animal. The chief problem for some proponents of animal rights is that any legislation passed, even regarding animal 'welfare', only protects animals in relation to allowing our continued use and disposal of them as property (Francione, 1997). Regan suggests that legislation is framed in terms of protecting human interests rather than those of animals. The central proposal in Regan's writing is that he sees inherent value in animals, specifically mammals of one year or older, which should accord them a moral 'right to life' and a right to be treated properly in our dealings with them. He sees them as possessing beliefs, desires, perceptions, memory, self-consciousness and a sense of future, which should be protected in the same way that we protect those moral claims for people. If it were accepted as the basis for future legislation, inherent value arguments would give animals the right to better fundamental treatment irrespective of their value as resources to humans, thus ending farming, experimentation involving animals, hunting and trapping. Intrinsic moral rights would become rights enshrined in law. He points to the basic moral discrepancies in our treatment of animals to support a radical remodelling of the law relating to them (Regan, 1982, pp. 159–160):

> On the one hand, human beings, of whatever colour, gender, or religious persuasion, are recognised as having interests; are understood to be subjects who can themselves be benefited or injured; are viewed as individuals who can themselves press their claims or have them pressed by others acting on their behalf; are acknowledged to be possessors of a life that is better or worse for them considered as individuals, logically independently of their value to others; and are not relegated to the legal status of property but themselves have legal rights. On the other hand, we have non-human animals, members of many species which are now known to be like humans in the relevant respects – for example, they have interests and can be benefited or injured – but who are relegated to the legal status of property and who are denied legal rights. And my question is: Is there any satisfactory way to explain this discrepancy that does not itself bespeak the very prejudice at issue? Not surprisingly, I think not.

Regan looks to protect animals in the sense that they are experiencers of life and deserving of protection in their own right. He rejects the positivist's view that the only real 'rights' are those given specifically by statute or a person's voluntary act. Regan appeals to us to base our legal protection of animals on the, presently, unquantifiable qualities of animals leading to moral rights. On a practical level, this would obviously have significant effects on the interpretation of current legislation. It would require the introduction of new legislation at both national and international levels. Currently, for example, one of the chief reasons we protect endangered species is to ensure that future generations see them. Using Regan's (1985, pp. 22–23) model would switch the emphasis of law from benefiting future generations to protecting animals in their own right:

> Animals, it is true, lack many of the abilities humans possess. They can't read, do higher mathematics, build a bookcase or make *baba ghanoush.*

> Neither can many human beings, however, and yet we don't (and shouldn't) say that they (these humans) therefore have less inherent value, less of a right to be treated with respect, than do others. It is the *similarities* between those human beings who most clearly, most non-controversially, have such value (the people reading this, for example), not our differences, that matter most. And the really crucial, the basic similarity is simply this: we are each of us the experiencing subject of a life, a conscious creature having an individual welfare that has importance to us whatever our usefulness to others ... Some there are who resist the idea that animals have inherent value. 'Only humans have such value,' they profess ... But there are many, many humans who will fail to meet these standards and yet are reasonably viewed as having value above and beyond their usefulness to others. Shall we claim that only humans belong to the right species, the species *Homo sapiens?* But this is blatant speciesism.

Some might argue that current laws relating to, for example, farming or experimentation already protect animals and give them 'rights' (Stucki, 2020). Still, Regan denies this and uses the example of a protected painting to illustrate why this is not necessarily the case: a law may protect a painting, but it would be ridiculous to state that the painting is the possessor of 'rights'. Regan sees the claim for the 'moral rights' of animals as a separate issue from the resulting 'legal rights' that might be introduced. Regan is of the view that morality will accept nothing short of the granting of legal rights to animals. This would not mean legislating for them to have the right to go to school or to have a bus pass but would recognise the inherent value and natural lives of animals distinct from our own prejudices towards them. In cases involving pain, suffering or other 'abuse,' a court would consider the situation from the animals' perspective, not from the perspective of any human benefits to be gained. For Regan (1982, p. 160), the importance of inherent value means that 'a legal system that excludes it, is blind'.

Francione's approach is based on a similar premise to Regan's: that the inherent value in the individual animal is deserving of protection in its own right. However, these two leading contributors to the development of the area differ in their belief of how such claims should be accomplished, with Regan favouring incremental changes to human practices and accomplishing gains through winnable campaigns. Francione, on the other hand, contends that this does not achieve enough, and he has constantly, strongly advocated veganism as a main tactic to draw out the philosophical discrepancies across the breadth of other areas of animal misuse and suffering. Comparing Regan and Francione, although they agree on much, shows the challenge faced in identifying a common philosophy to satisfy and unite the animal welfare, rights and advocacy constituencies. It could be argued that the lack of a coherent single philosophical position has prevented further development of law to protect animals, although discussion of this hypothesis is beyond the scope of this book.

Regan's theory has been criticised by other contributors who, broadly speaking, favour maintaining the current treatment of animals. They see the protection of animals as having gone far enough. Frey (1980) denies Regan's use of the word 'right', arguing that such a moral claim is only suitable for 'rational agents', namely humans. Other writers from within the animal rights movement itself, although agreeing with Regan's basic aim of improving the treatment of animals, find themselves unable to equate animal rights with human rights on the scale demanded by Regan. Most writers, it seems, are content to settle for the pragmatic view that the pain and suffering of animals needs further protection. The argument that a 'right to life' is comparable with a human's 'right to life' may have contributed to obscuring the core issues caused by trying to define 'human rights', let alone 'animal rights' in the 1980s and 1990s. Indeed, dominant figures in the broadly termed 'animal welfare movement' (it is difficult to even find a collective term for the whole movement without the possibility of complaint) have moved to claim 'personhood' (see later in this chapter) for animals, possibly in response to the philosophical baggage collected by claiming animal 'rights'.

Perhaps the greatest strength of a 'rights'-based argument is that, unlike the utilitarianist argument, it brings to the fore the importance of individuals by focusing on the fact that the needs of one may outweigh the needs of many. It is the philosophical starting point for findings around animal sentience – if sentience between species is similar, it seems odd not to protect both equally, despite the more superficial differences between species, such as their appearance. The notion of 'strong animal rights' as opposed to notions of interests or improved welfare has certainly attracted much interest, as is examined in the following section.

Can animals have rights?

Unfortunately, the word 'rights' has been 'hijacked' by some philosophers who have struggled to find a definition of what a moral 'right' actually is in relation to humans and whether 'rights' exist at all. The conflict between the definition of human rights as opposed to animal rights has resulted in some in the animal welfare movement abandoning an association with, or claim to, 'animal rights'. Therefore, when engaged in discussion about animal rights, the proponent of classical rights theories responds that 'animals can't have rights'. Why is there so much disagreement concerning the granting of 'rights' to non-human animals?

The first problem occurs with the everyday usage of the word 'right'. When we speak of 'rights', what are we actually referring to? 'Human rights' would probably be the first definition of 'rights' that would come to mind if one were asked, and these would encompass the classical 'rights' embodied in the European Convention on Human Rights, including, for example, the right to a fair trial, the freedom to express oneself, and the freedom to associate with others. In addition to this extremely important, fundamental protection of what we consider to be the qualities that make the living of life richer by keeping us free from oppression and retaining our liberty, there are less fundamental 'rights' that are also protected in various ways. These might include, for example, the 'right' to a free bus pass and the 'right' to a pension.

The 'fundamental moral rights' claimed for animals are different from these kinds of 'human rights', which, in most cases, would have no value to animals. The moral rights claimed for animals include those to protect their physiological, emotional and psychological attributes, which give us a moral reason for that protection, such as greater freedom to exhibit natural behaviours in agricultural environments. This lies at the heart of many arguments for improved animal protection. Some call this a 'right'; others refer to 'interests' or dismiss altogether any moral claim for enhanced or equal consideration. Other rights claimed by the animal welfare movement are more fundamental, such as the right to life and freedom from slavery. Therefore, identifying a universally acceptable term that fits the claim for animal 'rights' has proved to be frustratingly elusive.

The second problem occurs at a more fundamental philosophical level in the way that 'rights theory' has developed in relation to people. In classical philosophy, as espoused by Immanuel Kant, 'rights' cannot be granted unless the recipients of those rights have the will or capacity to enforce them and accept a duty not to infringe the rights of others. Rights are granted, therefore, only to those who can fulfil the 'social contract', which exclusively applies to humans. As animals have no concept of duties towards others and because they are incapable of exercising their will in relation to 'duties', the claim for animal rights has been dismissed by some legal/philosophical contributors. However, this view is itself challenged in that there is little logic in attaching rights to duties in an arbitrary manner. It is also pointed out that animals, given enhanced legal protection, would presumably have that law enforced by certain bodies, thereby creating something that, in all but name, has the attributes of a legal 'right'.

A third problem occurs when we try to equate human and non-human animal 'rights'. It is argued that when we talk of 'animal rights' we cannot ascribe to animals 'rights', which could be equated with 'human rights'. An animal's right to life, for example, would be lost if it came into conflict with the right to life of a human. An example of this is the 'lifeboat scenario', which has been used as the basis of theoretical discussion between philosophers to determine the nature of 'animal rights' (Regan & Singer, 1989). The scenario involves four humans and a dog in a lifeboat; one must be cast overboard to secure the safety of the others. If we ascribed to the dog the same right to life as the humans, then the decision as to which would be cast overboard would have to depend on drawing lots. Most humans would probably agree, however, that it would be the dog who should go first, illustrating that the right to life of a dog is not equivalent to that of humans.

This highly unlikely scenario gathered significance as it appeared to signify the dominant human position – in such an 'ultimate situation' the animal would likely lose out. Regan has since clarified his position to accept this ultimate moral conundrum in favour of humans but denies it affects the veracity of claims for rights in most other situations where animals are worthy of consideration, thus closing the gap between his rights theory and utilitarianism (Regan, 2008). The lifeboat scenario has even given rise to books to unpick its potential philosophical outcomes and pitfalls (Engel & Comstock, 2016).

To deny animals certain basic needs or enforceable 'rights' such as the right to adequate food and water when being raised to provide food for humans does appear to be morally illogical. We should not deny animals those rights because they do not have equivalent value on our imaginary lifeboat, as to do so would be an arbitrary decision based on speciesism.

What is clear is that the traditionalist argues that, for the sake of consistency of argument, animals might best be described as having 'interests' which need to be taken into account, rather than 'rights'. But this is not accepted by everyone, and there are authoritative arguments that 'rights' already attributed to animals by law (in relation to scientific experimentation, for example) do not need to give rise to corresponding duties or need to be claimed by individuals themselves, as they can be claimed by another on their behalf (Feinburg, 2017).

The foregoing discussion assumes that 'rights' are something that humans have, as yet, been unwilling to universally grant to all animals on account of their sentient capacities. Feinberg, on the other hand, argues that animals have 'rights' enshrined in the law already, to counter arguments by classical philosophers that animals do not have the necessary attributes to become right-holders (Feinberg, 2017, p. 373):

> Statutes making cruelty to animals a crime are now very common, and these, of course, impose legal duties on people not to mistreat animals; but

> that still leaves open the question whether the animals, as beneficiaries of those duties, possess rights correlative to them… Children start legal proceedings, not on their own direct initiative, but rather through the actions of proxies or attorneys who are empowered to speak in their names. If there is no conceptual absurdity in this situation, why should there be in the case where a proxy makes a claim on behalf of an animal? … the animal itself claims its rights through the vicarious actions of a human proxy speaking in its name and on its behalf. There appears to be no reason why we should require the animal to understand what is going on as a condition for regarding it as a possessor of rights.

It may be that the argument over the recognition of 'rights' for animals and whether animals can actually have them is a 'red herring'. 'Rights' have been ill-defined for humans, let alone animals, and to become embroiled in that argument may be distracting us from the essential issues. The rights granted to many animals have a remarkable resemblance to rights given to humans. Laws protecting animals, such as Martin's Act and the numerous laws introduced since, protect animals against their owners, which, Feinberg suggests, recognise that animals can be harmed and that there should be a reckoning for such behaviour in law. To deny that these are rights enforceable in law appears to be illogical. Fasel and Butler, from the Cambridge Centre for Animal Rights, separate rights into 'thick' and 'thin' rights. 'Thick rights' are those akin to human rights and are fundamental, including the right to life and freedom from torture. They highlight that thick rights are incompatible with an animal's current status as property, and since property traditionally cannot hold rights, animals currently lack thick rights. Thin rights are those already seen within our laws, such as protecting animals from unnecessary suffering or imposing welfare duties on humans. Thin rights may be easier to advance as they are already supported by the government and judiciary, though they are criticised by animal rights advocates as they do not provide sufficient protection for all animals and are basic in their approach (Fasel & Butler, 2023). These days when people are arguing for rights for animals, they are arguing for thick rights, which would include changing the property status of animals. Clark (1977) suggested that the use of the word 'right' has its problems for the proponents of animal welfare improvements. If this is so, perhaps it is the reason that claims for animal welfare appear to have changed around the year 2000 – 'personhood' and 'welfare' became much more prominent than 'rights'. However, the intention remains the same – the person who says 'animals can't have rights' should be judged on whether they mean classical 'rights' normally reserved for humans or that animals don't deserve any moral consideration at all. Animal welfare campaigners might agree with the technical problems encountered by the former but not the apparently inhumane motives of the latter.

Most campaigning organisations move within the language of 'welfare' with regular national or international campaigns to improve various aspects of Animal Law provisions, such as protecting wild animals, animals in experimentation, domestic animals or animals raised in farming. However, in the place of claims for rights has come the call for legal personhood for animals, which appears to be a very close cousin of its precursor 'animal rights'. In fact, personhood can probably be considered the same claim for animal rights under a different name, especially if we consider previous claims that argued for animal rights based on the individual intrinsic value of the animal itself.

In addition, certain areas of development relating to animal sentience cannot be assigned solely to developing animal protection based on improving welfare. The nomenclature of animal 'sentience' has gained a lot of traction in framing claims for enhanced protection, particularly regarding developments in the EU and the United Kingdom (UK) following the UK's departure from the EU in 2021 after the 2016. Broadly speaking, the movements for better protection divide into two camps – those claiming for better animal welfare while not challenging whether the fundamental use of animals is right per se, and those who contest whether the ways in which we use animals should continue at all. All proponents of improved animal protection fall somewhere between these fundamental goals, and they are generally able to be described as one general movement (Kotzmann & Pedergrast, 2019, p. 159).

Enhanced legal rights for animals: How far should we go?

The question of whether animals have intrinsic moral rights gives rise to the further question of how far we should accord them a status as 'persons'. Regan's theory of 'rights' only goes as far as making a case for prohibiting exploitative relations with animals. Should we go further by enabling them, for example, to instigate legal proceedings through 'another' and to become the sole beneficiaries of any financial awards? Aside from the conflict involving the very meaning of the word 'rights', many have argued that animals should have their inherent rights and interests recognised in the law beyond the current situation, which views them as property in common law, objects of interest for future generations in Environmental Law, and the recipients of limited protection in animal welfare law. Comparisons are drawn with the situation of ethnic minorities throughout the Western world who struggled for centuries to attain rights comparable with those of the white man. As an extreme example, the lack of legal recognition of those rights led to one American court finding that African Americans had no legal rights that a 'white man' need respect (*Dred Scott* v. *Sandford*, 1856). This now seems absurd and in violation of basic humanitarian philosophy. It is worth bearing this in mind in terms of where we are now in relation to claiming rights or welfare for animals – much of what we witness may seem absurd, wrong, and a violation of animals, but the language we use to instigate change may differ between various theories, leading to distracting conflict or debate. Change is likely to happen piece by piece rather than holistically.

The critical question the law has asked, when granting rights to individuals or groups of individuals, is whether those entities are 'persons' deserving of the granting of 'rights' – hence the emergence of the term 'personhood'. Despite numerous steps towards introducing these 'rights', animals have never been granted equal legal status or the corresponding rights that recognise their similarities to us. Yet the law has granted specific legal rights to entities that could in no way claim to have the equivalent sentience to even the lowest order animals. Corporations, partnerships, central and local government, clubs and societies all exercise their 'rights' through representatives or legal counsel to uphold their 'rights', for example, to seek damages for negligence and protect their business interests. It is suggested that to deny animals rights on the basis that they are different and lack the essential qualities necessary as 'persons' denies the fact that we have already bypassed this requirement in these instances.

In an article that examines the nature of 'rights' granted to 'legal persons' such as human beings or, indeed, corporations, Roger Galvin (1985, p. 252) argues that 'rights' should be granted to non-human animals:

> Logic dictates that if a species shares with us those attributes that we believe make us essentially human, we must conclude that we believe that the species in question is entitled to 'personhood'. The alternative is to discard the term altogether because it has no scientific, moral or legal justification; it is a term with no descriptive content. By clothing animals with the mantle of 'personhood' we recognise both their legal existence and the concurrent entitlement of legal protection, to the extent consistent with their nature. Such protection can only be effective if animals possess the right to have their interests judged independently of the subjective values that humans place upon them.

Galvin sees these rights in three forms: the right to live a life according to their nature, instincts and intelligence; the right to live in an ecologically sufficient habitat; and the right to be free from exploitation. This would create the corresponding duty upon humans not to infringe those rights and would lead where necessary to those rights being upheld by advocates for animals in a court of law – a strategy that has gathered pace since Galvin's article was published, particularly in the United States, through the work of the Nonhuman Rights Project, which was set up by Steven Wise in 1995 with the specific mission to create 'actual legal rights' for animals primarily through taking legal action in the United States.

Rosemary Rodd suggests a way in which enhancing legal rights for animals might work changing it from being seen as an unworkable abstract theory (Rodd, 1990, p. 254):

> The 'personhood' of some species need not mean that all animals would have to be granted equal status ... some species, such as sponges, are unlikely to have subjective experience. Nor need it mean that animal persons must necessarily have exactly the same legal rights as normal adult humans. In some instances, this might not be in the animal's own best interests, as in the case of euthanasia, where it is arguable that the animal's inability to comprehend his suffering is a crucial reason why it should be permissible to end his life painlessly if there is no reasonable hope of his recovery… However, we might no longer feel so easily justified in killing them, as the Nuer say, 'just for nothing' (i.e., merely to eat, not out of necessity).

Helena Silverstein describes why sentience becomes important in claiming animal rights and how it aligns with still unresolved claims for rights in sections of human society. (Silverstein, 1996, p. 231).

> Sentience becomes the crucial identifying characteristic that dissolves the gap between humans and non-humans. With sentience, activists maintain that animals gain an identity worthy of rights. Not only must humans be caring and considerate to animals, but they must also be restrained by the rights of animals. These alternative identity images contained within animal rights are noteworthy because they resist the dominant conception of rights and the identity images normally associated with rights … The movement to rights attempts to align the identity of the animal rights movement with the identities of movements for civil, women's, and gay and lesbian rights. Like these movements, the animal rights movement seeks to extend moral and legal rights to a group that has been excluded from consideration.

In light of this discussion, it is worth noting how various jurisdictions have begun to look at the challenges faced in relation to animals, rights and law. The granting of status, which seems to be strikingly similar to what we would ordinarily term 'rights', appears to be increasing in several areas of the world. Two examples are the recognition of animals as sentient beings and animals being recognised as more than mere property through enhanced constitutional status. Questions remain about how this would operate in practice. For example, how would a conflict between a licensed, yet damaging contractor tasked with taking out a portion of forest containing a protected mammal be adjudicated? How would the interests be weighed, and by whom? Many such questions as to animal rights in practice are yet to be determined (Chapron et al., 2019).

In 2000, Switzerland recognised the dignity of creatures in its constitution, and this new 'status' has been repeated in some form by several countries. In 2002, Germany included the protection of animals in its constitution. Most countries have some form of legislation that protects animals in some way, be it in agriculture, protection against abuse or more specific protection such as those subject to experimentation. This was illustrated by the legislative framework of the EU (Epstein & Kempers, 2023, p. 1344).

In 2009, the EU recognised animal sentience in Article 13 of the Lisbon Treaty. This, indirectly, created a path to an uproar amongst animal protection organisations in the UK when 52% of the population voted to leave the EU in 2016. During the process of leaving, the commutation of Article 13 into UK law was initially dropped by the UK government, arguing that there was already sufficient animal protection legislation in UK law. A significant public backlash, and the impression that the UK government had misread the signals that would be picked up by such a move, eventually led to the creation of an Animal Sentience Committee in the UK. This committee has the task of overseeing all new legislation and policy in terms of its potential impact on the sentience of animals (this is explored in detail in Chapter 2). This looks very much like a state-guaranteed right to have the impact of new legislation considered as far as it affects animals, though is it the choice of the Animal Sentience Committee as to what they decide to review. Despite the problems associated with the term, perhaps we have moved into a new era of rights for animals after all?

Utilitarianism and animals

Despite being regarded as one of the 'fathers' of the modern animal rights movement Peter Singer, as a utilitarian, does not in fact present an argument for 'animal rights' at all. This strange anomaly occurs because of the inherent confusion, left untouched, between a notion of 'rights' for animals as espoused by Tom Regan and the broad spectrum of philosophical ideals covered by the term 'animal rights movement'. This term is a misleading historical error that has never been rectified. Singer does not call for the recognition of moral 'rights' leading to the necessity for 'legal rights' but uses utilitarian principles, which would have the effect of creating enhanced protection for animals.

Utilitarianism, as applied to humans in the tradition of Jeremy Bentham, applies two basic criteria to moral decision-making. The first is that everybody's interests, whether black or white, male or female, European or African, carry the same significance. The second principle is that any act should be undertaken having given due consideration to all competing interests and recognising the best possible equilibrium between the satisfaction and frustration of the interests of those affected by the action. Utilitarianism is not, therefore, a philosophical tool that was devised purely to advocate the animal rights argument. The whole basis of our present moral attitude towards animals, and accordingly how the law protects them, is actually based upon the notion that society feels able to say that the benefits we gain from using animals for food, experimentation or whatever outweigh the disadvantages to the animals themselves. Utilitarianism can in some ways be regarded as the philosophical 'cause' of our treatment of animals, not just as one suggested route to a remedy for its perceived ills. For example, as seen in Chapter 4, the cost-benefit assessment for animals to be used in scientific experiments is very much a utilitarian position. Peter Singer is the foremost contemporary advocate of using the principles of utilitarianism to promote a different approach to our treatment of animals. He claims this would have the same effect as using a 'rights'-based approach by prohibiting many of our present uses of animals because the present ends do not justify the present means.

Utilitarianism, as applied to the animal welfare debate, claims that animals' interests, principally the interest in not suffering or being subjected to pain, should be given much greater weight by humans in deciding whether to proceed with a certain course of action, such as farming animals for food or using them as the subjects of experimentation. In the case of experimentation, for example, there are the competing interests of the animal not to suffer and the possible benefits to be obtained from the experiment. Utilitarianism imposes a degree of egalitarianism on all conflicts, in that 'all' competing interests must be considered to decide upon a course of action. The argument of the utilitarian in relation to animals is that animals have interests that should be considered where they are similar to our own – such as the interest in not suffering pain.

As will be discussed later, classical 'rationalist' theories hold that animals cannot be accorded 'rights' for a variety of reasons. Depending on how the term 'interest' is defined, utilitarian theories can remove the need for claiming 'rights' at all and assert the moral claim to have 'interests' taken into account instead. Of course, it is still a moot point whether an 'interest' protected by law might reasonably be interpreted as a legal right being accorded to the animal. The attraction of utilitarianism here is that it removes us, in part, from the need to consider whether animals can have rights and stops that area of uncertainty distracting us from the core issues of sentience, pain and suffering, leading to claims for equal consideration.

Utilitarianism, as it is applied to animals, is subject to much controversy and debate, with writers such as Frey (1980) arguing that animals cannot have interests because they have no desires or emotions that are based on thoughts as they are incapable of having such complex thoughts due to their lack of language.

However, the argument for the interests of animals from the utilitarian perspective has been most notably argued by Peter Singer in his highly respected book, *Animal Liberation*. Singer is regarded by many as starting a new era in the development of the law concerning animals (Rowan, 1984; Francione, 1996). He does not argue for the 'same' rights for animals as we give to humans, just for their interests in avoiding suffering to be adequately considered (Singer, 1995, p. 4):

> It is an implication of this principle of equality that our concern for others and our readiness to consider their interests ought not to depend on what they are like or on what abilities they may possess. Precisely what our concern or moral consideration requires us to do may vary according to the characteristics of those affected by what we do: concern for the well-being of children growing up in America would require that we teach them to read; concern for the wellbeing of pigs may require no more than that we leave them with other pigs in a place where there is adequate food and room to run freely. But the basic element – the taking into account of the interests of the being, whatever those interests may be – must, according to the principle of equality, be extended to all beings, black or white, masculine or feminine, human or non-human… If possessing a higher degree of intelligence does not entitle one human being to use another for his or her own ends, how can it entitle humans to exploit non-humans for the same purpose?

Utilitarianism, when applied to claims for 'animal rights', is unsatisfactory to some within the movement. Nozick (1974, p. 41), highlights a key concern with utilitarianism in any situation involving people or animals by introducing the concept of 'utility monsters', who gain disproportionately more utility from others' sacrifices. This scenario could lead to the acceptance of highly dubious practices. Tom Regan is also critical and has consistently questioned utilitarianism in that, in the final analysis, it allows any human or animal to be used where the benefits outweigh the costs, thereby sanctioning a 'good end' by 'evil means'. This, he argues, fails to accord the necessary value to 'individuality', which exists irrespective of that creature's value to other creatures, and amounts to a violation of individual rights (Regan, 1980, p. 21). In response to these claims that he would sanction experimentation on animals 'or humans', where the benefits were proved to lead to a cure for diseases, Singer responds that he is very doubtful as to whether this could ever be proven to a satisfactory level. He doubts whether any experiments would be valuable enough to warrant experiments involving humans or animals, and the application of the utilitarian animal rights theory would amount, in practice, to total prohibition. For Singer, the ethical answer is to ban animal experiments until we are ready to consider the use of human infants and brain-damaged humans who possess no more significant sentient qualities than some of the animal subjects of experimentation.

Utilitarianism is faced with challenges such as the difficulty in deciding what preferences or satisfaction of interests should be taken into account in given situations. Bentham suggested that accounting for the pleasure and pain outcomes of an action would be the best approach, but in recent times writers such as Singer have preferred to talk of the 'maximisation of preferences' or 'interest satisfaction'. However, it is very difficult to pick out all the potential benefits in a given situation. Do we look one week, one month or years ahead? Utilitarianism is dependent on being able to accurately compare the different experiences of different animals. But in relation to comparing the pain and suffering of animals, how do we go about identifying the 'nature' of this in different species to compare it?

Utilitarianism theory has trouble protecting the lives of certain animals for their own sake. In agriculture, for example, Singer explains how knowledge of the future is essential in making the taking of certain lives wrong. But if some animals cannot appreciate the future, then the painless taking of their lives and their replacement by another animal might be considered acceptable. For 'inherent rights' advocates, this capacity for sensing the future is only one indicator of 'sentience', which would not carry the significance that Singer applies to it in relation to farm animals. There are other capacities in being an 'experiencer of life', such as the ability of memory or perception, which are relevant to creating 'rights'. The possibility left by utilitarianism for experimentation or the use of animals in agriculture leaves the theory unacceptable to many within the animal welfare and rights movement, despite its historical significance in the creation of the movement itself (Višak & Garner, 2016).

Claiming 'personhood' for animals

Since around the year 2000, claims for 'animal rights' have largely been usurped by the language of claims for 'animal personhood', although there are notable exceptions (Kotzmann & Pendergrast, 2019). The reasons for this are not entirely clear, but it would be fair to say that those claiming animal rights were met with stiff opposition on the grounds that animals are incapable of having rights or that animals can't have rights without duties, amongst other arguments. However, it is possible to see that the area of human rights has also come under extreme pressure from the far right of politics, controversially suggesting that claims for human rights are abused by individuals of dubious repute, such as international criminals, terrorists and, more controversially, asylum seekers. Even the United Nations Declaration of Human Rights (UN General Assembly, 1948), framed following the Second World War in 1948, has come under pressure in some right quarters as not fit for purpose for the 21st century. Indeed, the United Kingdom Conservative Government in 2022 threatened to 'overhaul' the Human Rights Act 1998, which is largely based on the Universal Declaration (Siddique, 2022). This never came to pass, as the opposition was extremely vehement and effective in forcing ministers to back off from such radical attacks on universally accepted and respected international law. For reasons that are beyond the scope of this book, the manipulation of populist anti-human rights arguments illustrates the potentially treacherous waters for animal rights to enter. The timing of the move away from framing claims for rights to those of personhood is not easily identified. It was probably, at least in part, based on the human rights controversies concocted by right-wing politicians for reasons that are hotly disputed (Giannoulopoulos, 2020).

In this political climate, it is unsurprising that those claiming legal rights for animals shifted their terminology. The term 'personhood' has been used for some time in 'animal rights' literature, but the claims for animal 'personhood' are very closely aligned with claiming animal 'rights' as noted by Galvin (1985) and Rodd (1990) above. The personhood movement has been primarily based in the United States, with Stephen Wise and David Favre, amongst others, leading the way. This shift in emphasis has involved a significant change in tactics by making direct claims on behalf of animals in the courts. Their arguments are based on claims for a *writ of habeas corpus*, which protects people on the grounds that no one should be incarcerated without lawful reason and permission from the courts of the land. The legal personhood campaign in the United States seeks to extend this claim to animals because they possess similar cognitive (which is more than sentience) capabilities to be classed as autonomous beings deserving of freedom, which is an underpinning reason for the existence of a *writ of habeas corpus*. The first case in the United States concerned Tommy the Chimpanzee, who was being kept alone in a cage on a used trailer lot (*Nonhuman Rights Project v Lavery,* New York Supreme Court, Appellate Division, December 2014). The Nonhuman Rights Project argued for a *writ of habeas corpus*, but it was rejected by the court, which argued social contract theory, citing the work of Cupp (2013, pp. 38–39):

> Needless to say, unlike human beings, chimpanzees cannot bear any legal duties, submit to societal responsibilities or be held legally accountable for their actions. In our view, it is this incapability to bear any legal responsibilities and societal duties that renders it inappropriate to confer upon chimpanzees the legal rights – such as the fundamental right to liberty protected by the *writ of habeas corpus* – that have been afforded to human beings.

They further outlined that though Tommy is not a legal person, he does benefit from welfare protection from the legislature, and that they thought it more appropriate to appeal to the legislature to provide further welfare protection for chimpanzees rather than seek rights through the court.

There have been more successful cases outside of the United States, such as Cecelia the chimpanzee in Argentina (2016, File No. P-72.254/15), Kaavan the elephant in Pakistan (W.P. No.1155/2019) and Estrellita the woolly monkey in Ecuador (2022, Case No. 253–20-JH) all recognised as non-human legal persons and/or the holder of rights. Further, with Estrellita, the Ecuadorian Constitutional Court considered outlined rights that wild animals are entitled to, such as the right to exist, the right to habitat, the right not to be hunted, fished, captured, collected, extracted, detained, trafficked, traded or exchanged, and the right to demand their rights from the relevant authority. Though this relates to wild animals, lower courts have been using the list of rights in cases concerning companion animals (ReVista, Harvard University, 2023).

In the United States, there have not yet been any successful personhood cases. The case of Happy the Elephant in 2022 is the closest the Nonhuman Rights Project has come in the United States. Happy is an elephant kept in the Bronx Zoo without company for a number of years. In this case, though still not successful, the courts were less dismissive than in the Tommy case, and two judges accepted the arguments, with five rejecting. From the majority, it was stated that granting Happy legal personhood would 'have an enormous destabilising impact on modern society'. This is arguably not true, as the above-mentioned cases from other jurisdictions have had no known destabilising impact. The court again focused on contractual arguments maintaining that Happy could not bear social responsibilities and legal duties. However, those in the minority rejected this view, stating, 'But the holder of a right need not have a duty at all. Humans can create a legal system that confers rights on animals even if animals cannot bear duties, and even if animals are unaware of the rights they have been granted' (p. 13). They further highlighted arguments put forward by the Nonhuman Rights Project that the *writ of habeas corpus* has been used in the past for property, namely slaves, women and children, when they were not deemed to be persons under the law and instead chattels:

> The novelty of an issue does not doom it to failure: a novel habeas case freed an enslaved person; a novel habeas case removed a woman from the subjugation of her husband; a novel habeas case removed a child from her father's presumptive dominion and transferred her to the custody of another (see infra section II). More broadly, novel common law cases—of which habeas is a subset—have advanced the law in countless areas. (p. 10)

Though the case was ultimately unsuccessful, two judges accepting the arguments is encouraging and hopefully results in future success. There have been advances in the United States outside of the court system due to the work of the Nonhuman Rights Project, such as the city of Ojai in southern California passing an ordinance in 2023 recognising the legal right of liberty for elephants. This means that elephants in Ojai cannot be held captive unless the space is comparable to that of an accredited sanctuary. There are currently no zoos or sanctuaries in Ojai, so this may be merely symbolic, but it legally recognises the importance of rights for elephants.

The problem has been convincing the courts that this claim is valid and that it is not mere membership of a species, namely humans, that underpins the doctrine (Thompson, 2019). The movement has also been faced with the challenges posed by the structure of the United States legal system, with both national (federal) courts and local (state) court systems creating difficulties due to the sheer number of legal systems that have to be negotiated to achieve change. This is not such a prevalent problem where there is a simpler political structure as is the case in most other countries. For those claiming personhood for animals in the United States, there is a structural barrier to national legal acceptance of the arguments.

However, the new personhood movement, primarily the Nonhuman Rights Project, has taken its claims into court in several jurisdictions and has achieved success at times, such as in Columbia, where a court granted the *writ of habeas corpus* to an Andean bear supported by Stephen

Wise and the Nonhuman Rights Project, who gave evidence to the court (Franceschini, 2021). Though the Supreme Court of Justices later revoked the writ, stating it wasn't the appropriate mechanism, they did rule that animals feel and therefore are subjects of rights. There is also a move to court action in the UK with the establishment of lawyers' practices set up specifically to challenge corporations and the arms of government through public law remedies such as Judicial Review championed by Advocates for Animals (Thomas, 2022), as well as the Good Law Project, which extends to animals. This has yet to reach as far as personhood-based arguments, as UK courts still tend to follow the 'old' view of animals as legal chattels – not as rights holders or legal persons in their own right. This still bases legal recognition of animals partially on their value to humans, but it is perhaps indicative of emergent values, albeit that this was at a low level in the court system. As for the overall move to claim legal personhood for animals, it would certainly bridge the philosophical gap between the status of humans and non-human animals (Wills, 2020).

However, problems remain with the basis of claims for personhood. The reliance on establishing autonomy, favoured by the Nonhuman Rights Project, is questioned as being too narrow. Shapiro (2019), for example, outlines how personhood might be established through recognition as being part of a community, or cognitive capacity. Delon (2019) argues that the notion of autonomy works if you are talking about species, such as chimpanzees, with similar intelligence to our own but is less effective when addressing other species. Animals that are the subjects of unnecessary suffering, such as chickens, may fail to meet the criteria if autonomy is the most significant test for better treatment. This is echoed by Weisberg (2019), who argues that basing claims for animal protection on human attributes risks marginalising animals who have other capabilities and capacities that make them deserving of protection as of themselves without having to confirm capacities defined by human experience. Woodford (2019) suggests that the autonomy-based approach to claiming better protection for animals should be abandoned.

Defining animals as 'living property'

The status, or lack of it, accorded to animals as 'property' significantly held back the development of adequate protection for animals. An interesting idea that emerged in the early 21st century from academics such as David Favre was to create a new class of living property that might provide a compromise position to further the better protection of animals (Favre, 2021). It is an adjustment to the claim for personhood of animals discussed above and recognises the fact that humans appear to be reluctant to move on the position of animals as property, bound up as it is with serious economic consequences in relation to animals utilised for profit. The first caveat is that it does not apply to wild animals, only to those in some form of captivity. The main premise is to create a fourth category of property in addition to the existing ones – real, personal and intellectual property. It attempts to redress the anomalies created by defining animals as personal property, but it is limited on moral grounds as it does not address the problems associated with protecting animals of equivalent sentience, be they wild or domestic. In that respect, it is not a 'strong' animal rights position, as is the case with claims for rights by those such as Tom Regan, as it attempts to solve the problems associated with balancing animal rights against human interests (Favre, 2021, p. 54).

The theory tends to avoid complicated questions of comparative sentience – which animals deserve of protection? This has been a cornerstone of much legislation in giving protection to animals according to their sentient capacities, so for example, wild animals in captivity might be considered as deserving of enhanced treatment compared to domesticated agricultural animals according to their specific natural behaviours. This approach is a cornerstone in much law following the revolution of approach in 1960's UK law (The Brambell Report, 1965). However, that approach has been fraught with difficulties over time, as laws often fail to keep up with the developing evidence of animal sentience and carry the intrinsic baggage of allowing morally dubious care and treatment, such as scientifically discredited slaughter techniques (see Chapter 6). The advantage of developing a new theory of animals as living property, argue its proponents, is that it would give the animals enhanced status and protection without directly challenging their entrenched 'property' status – as is the case with animal 'rights' or personhood arguments, which place the intrinsic value of the animal above their property status.

In legal terms, Favre argues that the law provides an avenue for changing the status of animals through equitable aspects of property law. The specific scope of this in Property Law is beyond the scope of this book but suffice to say it transfers to the animal certain rights to better treatment, thus adjusting the pure legal interest of the human owner, which has tended to lead to maltreatment across the centuries. The animal is accorded self-ownership of certain factors that we recognise from existing conversations around the development of Animal Law – a duty of care owed by owners to their animals and the right to sufficient space according to species. However, Favre suggests this should extend to the right to due process and representation where fundamental aspects of their lives are being considered (Favre, 2021, p. 72). This would certainly be a new departure for legal systems worldwide. Favre also specifically aims the new theory at problems associated with the genetic engineering of animals by creating strong restrictive guidelines for the manipulation of animal genetics, which often have adverse consequences for animals in care and nurture, as well as poor welfare outcomes for members of many species.

Defining animals as living property presents a new social contract with them, potentially impacting domesticated animals and international trade. Favre also proposes a law to immediately ban product testing on live animals. Given the contentious nature of animal testing, this suggestion is likely to be met with resistance from both the scientific community and governments. A significant shift in public opinion would likely be the only force capable of driving such reform. Finally, the theory draws on early 21st century developments aimed at enhancing the protection of animals and non-sentient things such as rivers (see later in this chapter on the link with environmental concerns) in several jurisdictions. It asserts that courts can play a crucial role in enhancing animal protection – an approach dominant in the United States. However, whether this theory will gain traction or significantly improve the welfare or status of animals in practice remains to be seen.

Pragmatic theories supporting greater protection for animals

The problem encountered by the proponents of increased animal protection has been to fit their arguments to a single moral theory, such as inherent value theory or utilitarianism. This is illustrated by Tom Regan's 'lifeboat scenario', discussed earlier, within a theory based on the inherent value of all species of a certain level of sentience. Similarly, Singer's utilitarian stance has faced challenges in defining a moral code applicable to all situations and contexts.

This challenge has led other philosophers to approach the issue of a change in our relationship with animals in ways less dependent on a single moral theory. Stephen Clark (1977, p.186), sympathising with a hypothetical 'amoralist', embraces many different philosophical approaches to the consideration of the fate of animals in the search for a practical outcome rather than a single theoretical device:

> I have not offered any consistent moral system in the course of my explorations. The first reason for this is purely practical: I am very much more interested in achieving a practical issue than in the details of abstract philosophy, and am willing to argue on almost any basis to achieve that

> end. The second reason is Aristotelian: I doubt if there is any set of rules, any clear and compendious system, that does full justice to the vagaries and unformalisable sensitivities of our moral experience.

Clark accepts, for example, the Kantian notion that improving the human attitude towards animals might improve human attitudes towards our own species. He also concurs with the criticism of utilitarianism in that the doctrine, based as it is on the calculus of outcomes in terms of pleasures and desires, supposes that the pleasures and desires of different species are 'actually' comparable.

Mary Midgley (1983) also avoids using a single moral theory to underpin her claims for animals. She largely supports animal causes, but, while she dismantles the absolute denial theories of writers such as Descartes and Liebniz (see Chapter 1), she is wary of 'rights' claims for animals. She supports positivist theories that 'rights' might only exist as far as they are given to those who can understand and claim them. She also recognises the important part played by the proponents of utilitarianism, such as Bentham and Singer, but finds Singer's case for dropping species barriers in favour of considering the pain and suffering of animals and humans as morally unacceptable. Instead, she defends the notion of 'our tendency to respond differentially' as being a 'natural one' (Midgley, 1983, p. 105).

Midgley recognises that we treat animals in morally questionable ways but does not feel able to embrace a single moral theory to explain why. Her more pragmatic approach is certainly favoured by many of those in the animal rights movement, who often agree with the strands of several moral arguments against our present treatment of animals. Not everyone in the animal welfare movement has the time to examine the complexities of moral theory as applied to animals. Consequently, we work with our instincts that there is something wrong with how animals are treated and we may worry about the moral theories later. Empirical observation of animal suffering can be a powerful experience and explaining it in moral terms to those who may not understand can be frustrating. The ladies of London who witnessed Smithfield Market once it was drawn into the expanding suburbs knew instinctively that the treatment of animals going to slaughter was not right and no definitive theoretical argument was needed as proof. Midgley's pragmatic approach is reflected in her solution meeting the challenge of changing the treatment of animals in practice. For example, in the context of animals used in scientific procedures, Midgley (1983, p. 28) observes:

> Both sides now acknowledge the need to meet each other's arguments. It must emerge that some experiments are much more justifiable than

> others. The feat of justification cannot, in any case, be performed merely by raising an umbrella marked 'science'. It demands attention to the actual benefits which can reasonably be expected, and serious comparison of the conflicting values involved.

Citizenship theory and animals

So far, this chapter has explored ways in which we can award animals rights or greater moral significance, which will change how we relate to them. More recent theories have started to explore how we can award animals greater protection through rights while working more closely within our current paradigm. Donaldson and Kymlicka (2011, p. 1) summarise the problem:

> The animal advocacy movement is at an impasse. The familiar strategies and arguments for articulating issues and mobilizing public opinion around animal welfare, developed over the past 180 years, have had some success, on some issues. But the built-in limits of these strategies have increasingly become clear, leaving us unable to address, or even identify, some of the most serious ethical challenges in our relations with animals.

They argue that the three current paradigms, the 'welfarist' (that animal welfare should be provided for within their current property status and only prevents suffering deemed to be unnecessary), 'ecological holism' (this is not concerned with individual animals but rather the connectedness and welfare of the ecosystem as a whole), and the 'basic rights' (such as the right to life or freedom from torture) approach, have not generated enough change and so have developed a new framework operating within the political sphere. Further, as this chapter has demonstrated, the animal rights/welfare movement has been limited by focusing on negative rights, such as the right to life, i.e., not to be killed, confined or tortured. This contrasts with a more 'live and let live' approach to animals, such as that advocated by Francione (2015, pp. 224–228), who suggests that animals should not be used at all, including being kept as companion animals. However, these approaches, taken together, do not consider that we live in a shared society with animals, incorporating diverse relationships and interactions that are dependent upon co-existence. Viewing animals through this lens creates an opportunity to develop positive rights that people may owe to animals, which is explored below.

Donaldson and Kymlicka adopt a strong position of inviolable rights, which animals are given on account of their sentience or selfhood. This is based on their subjective experience of the world and not due to their cognitive abilities, thus rejecting the need for the argument in marginal cases. The case for inviolable rights is based on an individual's basic rights not being sacrificed for the means or good of others. This is inconsistent with the current welfarist paradigm, which suggests that an animal's welfare should be provided for and they should be subjected to humane treatment, until the point that their use becomes 'necessary'. For example, if the only way to advance medical treatment is through experimentation on animals, then the welfarist paradigm allows for this to be done, so long as it is as humane as possible. If animals are accorded inviolable rights, this would not be allowed, as those rights cannot be sacrificed for the greater good of humans. Though inviolable rights have now been widely accepted for humans, this is not the case for animals. Donaldson and Kymlicka recognise that our relationship with animals will differ depending on the type of membership they occupy in our human – animal communities. They categorise animals as follows:

- Co-citizens – these are domesticated animals, for example, our companion animals, farmed animals and animals used in scientific research.
- Denizens – these are animals who share our spaces and who have a right of residency to share our physical world with them, but they do not have the same interspecies sociability as co-citizen animals, such as pigeons, foxes and rats. The aim here is for a peaceful coexistence.
- Sovereignty – wild animals who are entitled to their own territory and the right to live their lives freely and apart from humans, such as beavers, elephants and lions. They have habitat rights and autonomy, and humans should not colonise or develop their space.

The application of the citizenship theory discussed here focuses on co-citizen domesticated animals. This is because 'citizenship' is the appropriate framework for conceptualising membership for domestic animals on account of their requisite capacities to be citizens: to have and express a subjective good, to participate, and to cooperate (Donaldson & Kymlicka, 2017, p.122).

At first sight, this may appear to be a radical theory. However, citizenship theory may not be too far removed from the existing situation in society today. There would likely be initial reluctance and scepticism in recognising the capacity for domestic animals to be co-citizens, due to how we view citizenship as a human experience. Usually, the concept is associated with allied activity such as political participation, voting and protest, which would obviously exclude animals. However, this exclusivity does not necessarily flow from citizenship theory for animals.

Domesticated animals can be political participants merely by their existence, such as the example of service dogs – specifically police dogs. Police dogs benefit society by assisting police officers in carrying out their duties, for example, helping to apprehend a suspect during arrest, which can carry the risk of serious injury for the animal concerned. This danger sparked a recent change in the law in England, namely the Animal Welfare (Service Animals) Act 2019, known as 'Finn's law'. This Act is the result of an attack on a police dog named Finn, who was stabbed in the chest and head when chasing a robbery suspect. A loophole in the law in England meant a charge of unnecessary suffering under Section 4 of the Animal Welfare Act (AWA) 2006 was not possible, so an alternative charge of criminal damage was brought as Finn is subject to the continuing definition of domestic animals as property under the law. The 2019 Act closed this loophole by providing that the harming of a service animal during an officer's duty could now lead to a charge under the AWA 2006. This Act, while being an incremental welfare reform, did more than just increase protection for service animals. It also recognised that service animals provide a unique contribution to society, and they are deserving of a more appropriate status than mere property, i.e., they contribute to society as citizens.

In addition, because of their service in the police, more benefits for police dogs become available, which also fits within the citizenship theory for animals. Some police forces, such as Nottinghamshire and Leicestershire, have introduced pensions of up to £500 per year for their police dogs so that when they retire, they can be allocated a home and receive medical expenses for work-related injuries or illnesses (Leicester Mercury, 2022). Therefore, citizenship theory accords much more positive rights for animals, and there is evidence that this approach is already taking root in society. A word of caution is also required here as Donaldson and Kymlicka counsel that citizenship rights should be accorded, as they are for humans, independently from their contribution to the overall good of society. This recognises citizenship rights should be given as a right and be extended to animals regardless of their cognitive abilities or contribution (Donaldson & Kymlicka, 2017, p. 22). Thus, we should be resistant to accepting that only animals who provide a service, such as police dogs, should be considered co-citizens and awarded rights, but rather that it is an example that is a witness to existing practice.

Kymlicka has written further on the subject and suggests that such instances provide an alternative path to animal rights, moving away from arguments centred on personhood, stating that domesticated animals should be included in other legal categories, such as 'workers' or 'family members' and treated accordingly. He suggests that the need for this new approach is simple: because we have domesticated some animals and created a unique relationship with them (Garfield, 2020), it is logical to accept that they share membership in our society. This, he states, carries social standing and rights for domesticated animals, some of which are already recognised in law and form part of the development of a 'social recognition strategy' (Kymlicka, 2017, p. 125). This approach does not replace the ultimate goal of personhood for all animals but provides a potentially viable avenue to achieve personhood for certain animals. There is a compelling element to this social recognition strategy in that it can already be seen as part of existing practice, such as the police dogs discussed above, who are granted recognition for their contribution and the associated financial and other benefits arising from that. Kymlicka suggests that the logical conclusion is that this should be taken a step further by recognising these animals as co-workers, which would give rise to the requirements associated with employment such as remuneration and pensions (Kymlicka, 2017, p. 147).

It is certainly the case that social recognition theory, while it may be initially challenging for some in appearance, is quietly and inexorably developing organically in society. Ladwig, in a strong attack on the theory, argues that it uses concepts appropriate to mediate relations between humans to those between humans and animals where animals have no understanding of those concepts (Ladwig, 2015). This critique echoes John Rawls' (1980) theory of denying animals rights based on contractualism, which is discussed later in this chapter. Alternatively, it has been argued that the theory is too narrow in that it provides less for wild animals than animals that exist in closer proximity to humans (Cochrane, 2013). In addition, Castello uses the theory to support a call for strong constitutional protection of wild animals through the granting of citizenship-type rights in Australia (Castello, 2022). He argues for wild animals' rights to political representation, recognition of self-sovereignty without outside interference, the right to live as communities or individuals as they see fit, and the right to protection of both their bodies and their ecosystem.

However, some jurisdictions, such as Germany, Switzerland and India, seem to have already accepted the enhanced status of animals constitutionally, in contrast to litigation-based attempts to have animals recognised as 'persons' in court. There is a long-standing judicial and political inertia to instant awards of personhood status. At the same time, the practical outcomes of animals being entrenched in human activities appear to be giving rise to providing animals with avenues for greater protection and care, such as pensions and medical costs than has even been achieved through claims for animals to be recognised as persons. As Castello summarises, it may be more palatable to the opposition to claim 'legal animalhood' rather than legal personhood. It may be that Donaldson and Kymlicka's approach provides an alternative theoretical method to improving animal welfare and protection rather than what has been achieved through claims based purely upon sentience and suffering or those based on adjusting the property status of animals (Favre, 2021).

Claims for animals in the context of wider environmental concerns

Recognition that humankind has severely damaged planet Earth, placing all species, including humans, at risk, has dominated environmental politics for some time. There is no doubt that human activities need to change, and this recognition has led to several theories to support and influence how that change comes about. Of particular interest here is the discussion concerning the relationship between claims for environmental protection and claims for animals. They may be inextricably linked at times, for example, where calls to reduce plastics finding their way into the oceans benefit both humans and other species in the food chain. However, there is a more philosophical aspect to this discussion, with many voices claiming that environmental destruction and damage is morally wrong and should be prevented. Schapper et al. (2022), for example, suggest that claims for the environment should be integrated with those for animals, as it might weaken dominant anthropocentric approaches to biodiversity governance. It has also been suggested that the international criminal court could be used to strengthen international action against both environmental and wildlife destruction with the development of the law on ecocide (Legge & Brooman, 2020). However, as attractive as this seems at first glance, the ability of the international community to control and protect the environment and its inhabitants via international criminal law is doubted because of the inherent acceptance of eco-damage in the international community as a precursor for economic development via commodification of resources. For example, is damaging deep sea mining likely to be banned if it proceeds with 'codes of practice' in place to give the façade of acceptability (Cusato & Jones, 2024)?

Animals are associated with claims for the environment in several ways. This is discussed in more practical detail in Chapter 8 but is worthy of mention here as the link between environmental and animal concerns creates some philosophical issues. Firstly, the contribution of human use of other animals is recognised as one direct cause of climate damage. For example, agriculture involving the rearing of animals is known to be a significant contributor to environmental damage through emissions of CO_2 into the atmosphere, thereby contributing to global warming. The world is littered with examples of how this damage has come about.

The second way that animals are associated with calls for change is through the benefits that might accrue to animal welfare through protecting habitats. It is difficult not to feel slightly desperate at the sight of the higher primates losing their habitats as the trees fall around them. Protection for these habitats as the 'lungs of the Earth' would carry a significant benefit for those species caught up in the destruction of habitats for logging, palm oil production and the hunt for bushmeat.

Therefore, claims for animal welfare and animal rights are tightly enmeshed in wider claims to protect the environment. One theory that underpins these concerns is the claim for 'Rights of Nature' (RoN). The connection is that the theory makes claims for non-human life, including animals and is grounded in rights theories for animals based on intrinsic value independent of any value to humankind. These claims move the debate away from basing protection on instrumental value to humans, to moving the solution to recognising intrinsic rights held by the entities themselves. We use the word 'entities' as the debate has stretched to protecting inanimate things such as rivers and national parks. For example, in New Zealand in 2017, the Whanganui River was recognised as a legal person to respect a Maori tribe's close spiritual connection with the river (Te Awa Tupua (Whanganui River Claims Settlement) Act 2017; Chapron et al., 2019). In 2018, the Supreme Court of Columbia ruled that the Amazon is a subject with rights and ordered the government to protect it. In 2008, Ecuador recognised the RoN in its constitution, with the resulting case law for Estrelitta the Woolly Monkey, and Bolivia adopted the 'Law of the Rights of Mother Earth' in 2010. The United Nations recognised the RoN in 2012. Panama introduced legislation (Law No. 371, 2023, Article 29) for the protection of the rights of turtles and their habitats, which included living and having free passage in a healthy environment free of pollution and other anthropocentric impacts that cause physical and health damage. These developments show an emerging approach to protecting the environment at both national and international levels. How effective these various proclamations become is yet to be seen.

Parallel to this has been the centuries-long struggle for the rights and welfare of animals and the development of protective legislation that has gone along with it. In modern times, the claims made for animals and those for the environment seem to be moving closer together – it is the case that Animal Law has often been seen as the younger sibling of environmental law, despite there being obvious differences in terms of sentience and the harm done to living creatures (Brooman, 2017). In addition, there have been environmental concerns for two thousand years, as discussed in Chapter 1. There is no doubt that the damage humans have done to the environment poses an existential threat to animals and humans – perhaps it is wise that the two movements coalesce where necessary. Protecting the environment brings the possibility of protecting every living creature, and it cannot be overstated how concerned we all should be.

It may seem unorthodox and unusual to grant rights to non-sentient things until it is considered against the accepted view regarding other non-corporeal entities. Corporations, businesses and trade unions have enjoyed separate legal status for many years – they can take people to court, be taken to court, enter contracts and have many other capabilities as if they were a living human. On practical and theoretical grounds, this supports the possibility of enhanced rights-based approaches to both the environment and animals. However, for both animals and the environment, the impact of these approaches has, so far, been limited (Schapper et al., 2022). Epstein and Kempers (2023) recognise the similarities between these claims for rights for animals and non-sentient entities in the environment, such as rivers, but the crucial difference remains the sentience of one against the other. This can lead to disagreements between the two lobbies; for example, protecting the environment might require the sacrifice of an invasive animal species. However, they argue that European law, as it stands, currently gives animals within the EU the status of rights holders with legal rights because of the obligations placed on humans to protect them. This, they contend, recognises that animal protection can be claimed separately from environmental concerns.

However, Platvoet argues that wild animals may effectively be rights holders under existing European law, but these are not based on developing individual rights for animals. Rather, such moves are born out of anthropocentric interests such as biodiversity. She argues that the underlying effect of passing legislation such as the Habitats Directive is not to provide rights for animals but to protect the elite position of humans against environmental concerns defined by humans. For example, 'nativeness' of species is favoured even where invasive species may enhance biodiversity (Platvoet, 2023). For those involved in claiming better animal protection through inherent value, sentience or personhood-type arguments, doing so via wider environmental concerns has a significant philosophical loophole into which such arguments may fall.

We can see this in practice, as it has been claimed that environmental law generally has failed to protect the decline of certain notable species, such as elephants, which have shown signs of evolving into a tuskless species as part of natural evolutionary protection (Du Toit & Kotzé, 2022). There remain issues, such as how these RoN will be claimed and what happens when they conflict with the rights and legally supported activities of corporations and businesses. Who will represent the RoN, and who will have the right to bring a case? These questions remain unanswered for the moment, despite the immediate appeal of granting RoN to non-human entities, including animals. Environmental protection may protect animals as a fortunate collateral benefit to protecting the environment but seeking to change the law to protect animals by recognising their inherent value as individuals remains a contested route to success (Epstein & Kempers, 2023). Linking environmental and animal rights concerns may be a shared concern that brings benefits to animals with it, but it may have its limits as a provider of rights attaching to animals as persons or rights holders or moving the 'development continuum' of animal protection legislation forward (Robertson, 2015).

The influence of science after Darwin – the birthplace of sentience arguments

The place of science in the moral argument concerning animals is currently changing. In the 18th and 19th centuries, scientists were seen as the opposition by animal welfare campaigners – ruthless pursuers of medical advances with little or no regard for the animals they used as the subjects of live experiments. However, the work of Charles Darwin brought about a radical change in the role of science in attributing new protection to animals. The ramifications of Darwin's revolution in science are increasingly becoming apparent. Darwin saw evidence for the clear relationship between humans and other species, but others have always denied how far these similarities extend. Scientific evidence is beginning to reveal more conscious awareness down the evolutionary ladder, evidenced by long and painstaking research involving close observation of animals over months and sometimes years. Without the aid of language, it is very difficult to reveal the thoughts of a monkey, cow, dog or rat without long-term observation.

As evidence of suffering comes to light, there are indications that legislation should change if it is to remain morally consistent. We have a choice whether to leave laws in place that protect purely based on species membership, as favoured by many such as Frey (1980) and Carruthers (1992). Or, as Masson and McCarthy (1996) suggest, the moral case for a change of approach is overwhelming:

> What are the implications of finding that animals lead emotional lives comparable to our own? Must we change our relationship with them? Have we obligations to them? Is animal testing defensible? Is experimentation on animals ethical? Can we confine them for our edification? Can we kill them to cover, sustain and adorn ourselves?

> Should we cease eating animals who have complex social lives, passionate relations with one another, and desperately love their children? ... Freedom from exploitation and abuse by humankind should be the inalienable right of every living being. Animals are not there for us to drill holes into, clamp down, dissect, pull apart, render helpless and subject to agonising experiments. They are, like us, endangered species on an endangered planet, and we are the ones who are endangering them, it and ourselves. They are innocent sufferers in a hell of our making. We owe it to them, at the very least, to refrain from harming them further. If no more, we could leave them be.

The rejection of moral rights and the interests of animals

Many contributors, some from the rationalist and contractualist traditions, seek to discount or reduce animals from various areas of moral consideration. Some rationalists, such as Descartes (see Chapter 1) and Spinoza writing in the 17th century, stressed a human's rationality as setting them apart from the rest of the animal kingdom. They sought to discount all consideration regarding animals. Spinoza went as far as seeing pity as evil because it is a feeling and causes pain (Rhys, 1913, pp. 175–176). The associated theory of contractualism, in the tradition of Locke, Rousseau and Kant, attempts to define how the fundamental underpinning moral values of society are to be decided. The contents of the 'contract' are described by John Rawls (1972, p. 11) as 'the principles that free and rational persons concerned to further their own interests would accept in an initial position of equality as defining the fundamental terms of their association.'

Contractualists tend to avoid ascribing moral rights to animals as the theory is aimed at governing the principles of the dealings – the rights and duties – that exist between articulate, self-interested 'rational agents', a term that, by its definition, excludes animals. Whereas some writers from these traditions deny that animals should be the subjects of our moral concern at all, Rawls uses these philosophical tools to distinguish humans and animals and the degree to which the laws of society should protect them but falls short of an absolute dismissal of their interests. In his eyes, the rules of society are to be decided upon by rational agents who would choose the rules to govern their interaction from behind a 'veil of ignorance'. This term refers to the need to make the rule-makers ignorant of some things, such as their relative intelligence, physical strength and personal desires. Otherwise, they would create rules that reflected their own strengths at the expense of other rational agents – strong people might have certain benefits bestowed upon them or only wealthy people might be entitled to a fair hearing in a dispute. They would, however, have to be aware of certain broad concepts, such as happiness and freedom, to be able to create a set of rights and duties that would be applicable and relevant to all those rational agents.

What then is the place of animals in this equation? Animals, lacking the necessary linguistic skills, could not take part in the fictitious 'discussion'. However, the question remains whether animals might be accorded any rights in this decision-making process occurring behind the 'veil of ignorance'. The rationalists have generally argued that animals should not be accorded rights for three main reasons: firstly, they cannot be accorded rights because they are not rational agents and therefore cannot contribute to the decision-making process; secondly, because they are not rational, they cannot recognise the duties they owe to other possessors of rights; and thirdly, according them the same status as humans would be against a 'common sense' rationale, which suggests we should accord greater status to our own species. This view of ascribing welfare or other legal rights to animals is often criticised because it fails to make adequate provision for animal suffering, and it perpetuates the damaging property status of animals through anthropocentric notions of those species considered as deserving of enhanced legal status and protection (Jowitt, 2022).

One of the first philosophers to look at the moral status of animals this way was Immanuel Kant (1724–1804), who regarded the 'rational bond' between humans as creating duties towards each other. He denied that similar duties are owed to animals but still managed to find a route to allowing them some consideration (Kant, 1780):

> So far as animals are concerned, we have no direct duties as animals are not self-conscious and are there merely as a means to an end. That end is man. We can ask, 'Why do animals exist?' But to ask, 'Why does man exist?' is a meaningless question. Thus, if a dog has served his master long and faithfully, his service, on the analogy of human service, deserves reward, and when the dog has grown too old to serve, his master ought to keep him till he dies ... If a man shoots his dog because the animal is no longer capable of service, he does not fail in his duty to the dog, for the dog cannot judge, but his act is inhuman and damages in himself that humanity which it is his duty to show towards mankind ... He who is cruel to animals becomes hard also in his dealings with men.

Thus, Kant explains why we owe no direct duties to animals but only indirect duties to those humans who might be upset, angry or merely affected financially by our actions. Such a philosophy certainly has no room for the ascription of rights to animals, which is argued by Regan, or the similar value placed upon the pain and suffering of animals in the utilitarian balancing act performed by Singer. In Kant's view, humans are the only beings who carry any inherent reason for direct moral concern. This view is criticised as protecting animals only so far as it affects humans, once again denying intrinsic value in animals and is therefore lacking adequate legal basis and rationality (Jowitt, 2022).

In response to the inability of animals to be at the imaginary bargaining table to emphasise their interests, many have argued that representatives could argue on their behalf for some recognition of the status of animals when the decisions are being made behind this 'veil of ignorance'. The idea of representation is a fundamental pillar of the legal system in relation to those who cannot represent themselves, such as the very young, the mentally subnormal and indeed all those who choose an advocate better equipped to state their argument than they are themselves. To philosophers in the rationalist tradition, it appears that the representation of animals behind the veil of ignorance is disallowed as the concept of 'rationality' denies other species the opportunity to have their case presented.

Rawls applies a general theory of contractualism to determine how the rules that govern the interaction of rational agents are to be created and enforced. His ideas appear much more sympathetic to the 'animal rights' movement than others writing within this tradition. He argues that the 'initial contractors' should be ignorant of 'accidental features' such as race, gender and intelligence to avoid bias or prejudice in determining the contract. In that case, it might only be a small step to include 'species' in the list of accidental features. However, Rawls argues that his notions of 'justice based upon fairness' are limited as they cannot embrace all moral relationships, including how humans conduct themselves towards animals. He goes on to explain why he feels that his theory does not allow for animals to be considered as the recipients of the right to 'justice' (Rawls, 1972, p. 504):

> The natural answer seems to be that it is precisely the moral persons who are entitled to equal justice. Moral persons are distinguished by two features: first they are capable of having (and are assumed to have) a conception of their good (as expressed by a rational plan of life); and second they are capable of having (and are assumed to acquire) a sense of justice, a normally effective desire to apply and act upon the principles of justice, at least to a certain minimum degree. We use the characterisation of the persons in the original position to single out the kinds of beings to whom the principles chosen apply. After all, the parties are thought of as adopting these criteria to regulate their common institutions and their conduct to one another; and the description of their nature enters into

> the reasoning by which these principles are selected. Thus equal justice is owed to those who have capacity to take part in and to act in accordance with the public understanding of the initial situation.

It is clear from what Rawls says that even though his arguments, based as they are upon the implicit acceptance that rationality is the essential quality necessary to be considered as a recipient of 'justice', he does not reject the claims of the animal rights movement for 'some' consideration for animals. He suggests that 'the capacity for feelings of pleasure and pain and for the forms of life of which animals are capable clearly impose duties of compassion and humanity in their case' (Rawls, 1980, p. 512). It is unclear whether this would leave animals with 'rights' that fall a long way short of those accorded to humans or of the nature of the rights advocated by Regan. This is highlighted by a contribution to the debate by Roger Scruton. He is unwilling to accord the status of 'personhood' to animals (Scruton, 1996, p. 66):

> Creatures who are by nature incapable of entering into this dialogue have neither rights nor duties nor personality. If animals had rights, then we should require their consent before taking them into captivity, training them, domesticating them or in any way putting them to our uses. But there is no conceivable process whereby this consent could be delivered or withheld. Furthermore, a creature with rights is duty bound to respect the rights of others. The fox would be duty-bound to respect the right to life of the chicken, and whole species would be condemned out of hand as criminal by nature. Any law which compelled persons to respect the rights of non-human species would weigh so heavily on the predators as to drive them to extinction in a short while. Any morality which really attributed rights to animals would therefore constitute a gross and callous abuse of them.

Like Rawls, Scruton does not deny that animals are without moral status – but denies them rights. He is willing to say that animals may be owed limited duties that protect them against some forms of ill-treatment but that the institutions of food production and scientific experimentation are defensible and necessary: 'Virtuous people may engage in activities like raising pigs for slaughter, eating meat, fishing with a line, wearing furs, or shooting crows and rabbits, which many observers of the human world have denounced as depraved' (Scruton, 1996, p. 99).

A similar theme is proposed by Finnis (1980, p. 194) on the basis that humans possess the fundamental capacities to be treated differently to animals, even if we protect, in relation to some humans, only their potential or previously existing fully sentient development:

> Those who propose that animals have rights have a deficient appreciation of the basic forms a human good. At the root of their contention is the conception that good consists essentially in sentience; for it is only sentience that is common to human beings and the animals which are said to have rights … And if the proponents of animal rights point to very young babies, or the very old and decayed or mentally defective persons (or to someone asleep?), and ask how their state differs empirically from that of a flourishing, friendly, and clever dog, and demand to know why the former are accorded the respect due to rights holders while the latter is not, we must reply that respect for human good reasonably extends as far as human being, and is not to be extinguished by the circumstance that the incidents or 'accidents' of affairs have deprived a particular human being of the opportunity of a full flourishing.

Other contributors are less willing than Rawls to accept that the theory can still leave room for more account to be taken of specific claims of the animal rights movement. Peter Carruthers stresses the claim that animals are not rational agents and cannot sign up to any 'social contract' based upon rights and duties. They have no appreciation of duties and, therefore, should have no rights, which was the main argument in cases against granting personhoods to animals, such as Tommy the chimpanzee and Happy the elephant, discussed earlier in this chapter. He argues that animals matter only when cruelty towards them exhibits a trait in us that may be manifested against humans, which would seem, at first glance, to be following the Kantian tradition. But the Kantian idea that we should not harm animals because it harms humans who care about animals is also rejected. It is only when the harm inflicted upon animals is of a 'trivial nature', such as wanton cruelty, that we should criticise the harmer. He goes to great lengths to show that humans are the rational agents, and therefore it is humans who should be our prime concern. If the animal rights lobby's activities disturb the interests of humans by, for example, affecting employment opportunities, then that would be morally wrong – he contests that humans are what matter in somewhat forthright terms (Carruthers, 1992, p. 168):

> There would be economic and social costs in placing further restrictions on our use of animals, particularly if factory farming and scientific experiments on animals were forbidden… the increasing cost of increasing concern for animal welfare is to distract attention from the needs of those

> who certainly do have moral standing – namely human beings. We live on a planet where millions of fellow humans starve, or are near starving, and where many millions more are undernourished. In addition, the twin perils of pollution and exhaustion of natural resources threaten the futures of ourselves and our descendants. It is here that moral attention should be focused … Our response to animal lovers should not be 'If it upsets you, don't think about it', but rather, 'If it upsets you, think about something more important'.

Frey (1980) argues against both the claim to accord animals with moral 'rights' and the claims that animals have interests. His theories reject any notion of 'natural rights'. He asserts that because people have widely differing views on what is morally right or wrong, to claim that one has a 'moral right' to something is merely stating one's own preference; there are no such things as underlying 'natural moral rights'. In that case, he argues that pointing to the divine 'moral right' to something is pointless, and we are better concentrating on the treatment of animals by working out 'principles of rightness and justification of treatment'. Unfortunately, Frey's arguments do not define what should be considered a moral right for humans or animals, as he merely rejects the notion of 'moral rights' altogether. Frey also attacks the second primary tool of the animal welfare movement, the claim for animal 'interests'. He denies Singer's claim that the interests of animals in not suffering pain are morally supportable. Frey suggests a 'ladder' to deny claims for animal rights and interests, which works like this:

- Animals cannot speak.
- Because they cannot speak, they cannot have thoughts.
- Because they cannot have thoughts, they cannot have desires or emotions.
- Because they cannot have desires or emotions, they cannot have interests.

His book appears, at first sight, to be an indictment of any attempt to consider the plight of animals from a moral standpoint. But despite subtitling the book *The Case Against Animals*, he concludes that one should look to other sources to justify animal welfare claims. He appears to cast doubt on the human moral right to confine animals in zoos or to use them for experimentation, but does not provide any positive framework around which legislation could be framed except for a reference to the 'higher' animals' ability to 'suffer unpleasant sensations'. His disdain for claims for the moral rights of animals is based upon his general dislike of any claim to a moral right, which he views as being open to abuse by anyone claiming them in their own interests (Frey, 1980, p. 168):

> My conclusion ... with respect to animal rights, then, may be seen as part of – certainly, it coheres with – my overall view about moral rights generally. The implications of this overall view, however, do not run merely to the denial of moral rights to animals: they extend also, and doubtless more unpalatably, to a denial of moral rights to human beings. And one important thing this means is that we have no moral right to an animal's confinement in zoos, to its ceaseless drudgery and labour on our behalf, to its persistent exploitation in the name of cosmetics, clothing, entertainment, and sport, to its blindness, dismemberment, and ultimate death in the name of science, and, to be sure, to its appearance on our dining tables … On the other hand, it is a nonsense to suppose, as many animal rightists do, that the denial of moral rights to animals leaves them utterly defenceless; it no more does this than the denial of a right to abortion on demand leaves a pregnant woman defenceless … On my view, then, questions can still be raised about our treatment of animals; but the answers cannot now consist in appeal to our reliance upon moral rights, claims to which have never really settled questions about our treatment of other creatures anyway.

In summary, the chief criticism of contractualist or rationalist theories as applied to animals is that they deny animals moral rights that could be bestowed upon them in light of their sentience. The influence of the contractualists, with their notion of the suffering of animals as being different and of substantially less moral concern than that of people, has meant that advances in the welfare of animals or the proposals to grant them distinct rights have been slow to develop. Historically, the claims of significant differences between the species, to the effect that humans can rule without significant interference from moral philosophy, find their roots in the theological teachings of the world's religions. The proponents of the denial of any significant cognisance of the claims of the animal rights lobby have constantly defined differences, which are being questioned as science makes discoveries about animals. There has been considerable movement in relation to the law protecting animals since 2000. But scientific evidence about the existence of pain and suffering or 'lifestyle' requirements of animals and their significant similarities to ourselves has only been partially recognised by the legislators, due to our traditional reliance on highlighting the differences between ourselves and animals, rather than the similarities. Contemporary proponents of the animal rights movement, most notably Regan and Singer, propose that similarities between humans and animals demand a re-evaluation of our laws relating to animals. Critics of these campaigns deny that animals have a moral status in any way approaching that of humans.

Conclusion

If there is one thing we can recognise, it is that there has been progress in passing legislation to protect animals. Animal welfare, rights, personhood, citizen and other animal protection movements are bound by a collective desire to further the protection of animals. What they appear to be less clear on, as shown in this chapter, is a single unifying philosophical reason for why this should be done. For some, the inherent value of animal life is paramount, giving rise to claims for animals as rights holders and persons. For those in the utilitarian tradition, what we gain from the exploitation of animals is not worth the cost borne by these individuals. For others, the arguments are tied up with wider environmental concerns that catch animals in the loop of fears about our own survival or notions of 'who' is a citizen in society. The challenge is how to navigate the numerous theories for change and placing them into a coherent and persuasive argument that can be articulated clearly.

The answer to changing the law may lie in the need to challenge it from different perspectives – both practical and forward-thinking, as well as theoretical and philosophical. For example, Amy Wilson (2019) argues in the South African context that the way forward lies in incremental steps to change areas of practice where there has been a clear failure to protect animals. There is less focus on the philosophical 'why', and Wilson relies on the willingness of authorities or courts to accept the moral case for animals alongside a practical need to educate those involved in the judicial system regarding the changes they should make. In a different way, Joe Wills (2018) argues for introducing a general offence of killing in the UK but does so from the philosophical perspectives of John Stuart Mill and Joel Feinberg under the 'Harm Principle'. This philosophical argument proposes that the state should only impose criminal sanctions where there is potential harm to others. Wills draws animals within this protection because of their potential to be seen as persons without being specific as to how and where this would be done but stresses the untenable position of UK law on the question of killing animals. Overall, it seems fair to say that the philosophical and practical approaches to changing Animal Law, both have their place in the overall picture.

In the era of global climate concerns, many argue that the greatest potential for change lies in linking claims for animals with claims for the environment, but even here, there are doubts as to whether this benefits animals. Although we can recognise the collective benefits of 'saving the planet', and so bringing about the ultimate protection of species survival, others doubt whether joining the two movements is sufficient for animals. It is a powerful argument but is currently disputed as the best philosophical and practical route to improving overall animal protection. It would seem strange to argue that we should dispense with direct action for animals and replace it with a global environmental movement – hoping for the best when it comes to animal protection. This would undermine arguments that criticise the current state of injustice done to animals. It would also be difficult to reconcile with the notions of the other philosophical positions discussed here, such as animals being worthy of protection in their own right. The two movements may coexist but are unlikely to coalesce into a single enviro-animal movement for change. Many of the aims and methods of change may be shared, but a single environmental movement might see much animal suffering slip through the net.

It is useful, if not essential, for those advocating challenges to existing legal protection to be able to elucidate their reasons for doing so. To claim without viable justification is likely to be met with short shrift by legislators – the inertia of Animal Law is clear to see, as change sometimes take decades to introduce and further years to modify. However, there is no single clear response that answers the question, 'On what basis is this claim for greater protection made'? Perhaps it is better to see the various philosophical contributions discussed in this chapter as the claimant's collection of wonderful thoughts and ideas – these are some of the finest, most recognisable and erudite contributions explaining why those of us claiming more for animals do what we do. Focusing light on the mistreatment of animals, explaining why it is wrong, and articulating how to prevent it, is essential in the process to reform Animal Law.

CHAPTER FOUR

Animal use in experimentation

Introduction

Across the globe, animal experiments are usually regulated but the number of animals used continues to increase. Continuing concern has led to the growth of social media platforms which have brought evidence of suffering in animal experimentation laboratories to a larger public audience. It is fair to say that we have found this the most challenging area to balance the moral, ethical and legal dilemmas posed by using animals in experimentation. The use of animals to bring about the rapid production of vaccines in 2020 due to the pandemic brought this into sharp focus. What would we have done without animals being used in the production of those vaccines? Or looking from an alternative viewpoint – were we ready? Was the pandemic made more likely by human inaction on both our interactions with animals, which caused the virus to jump species, or the failure over time to produce adequately funded alternative research? Both explanations seem to carry some validity. If the lifeboat dilemma was difficult to unpick (see Chapter 3), we appear to have lived through a live scenario in the pandemic that brought the competing interests of animals and humans into sharp focus.

The challenge to lawyers, philosophers, academics and others in the area of animal welfare is to bring developing recognition of animal sentience onto the legislative table to bring about significant change rather than piecemeal alterations. Those practising and supporting the continued use of animals in scientific research predominately argue from two main standpoints: the benefits gained, and that animals lack sufficient moral status to be protected against invasive use. However, both the basic argument over the benefits (Rollin, 2017) and the broad acceptance that animals can be mere scientific 'objects' (Michael, 2017) are frequently challenged. Favre (2021, p. 131) suggests there may be significant reasons to change animal testing, but the overall use of animals in some scientific pursuits may be justified if the harm is minimal. The issue appears to revolve around the types of use, which species are used, and whether there are alternatives available for research. However, no jurisdiction has managed to adequately balance the issues involved to create a satisfactory legislative position.

The chapter outlines the extent and types of animal use in experimentation, the moral issues raised, how legal change was accomplished in some jurisdictions, and the remaining challenges to be resolved on moral and legal grounds. The jurisdictions observed here are limited by the space available, and we have chosen to look at familiar jurisdictions, in the UK and EU, to examine the issues raised by using animals in experimentation. The arguments can be readily transposed into other jurisdictions, all of which have varying levels of control. This chapter also examines the evidence supporting suggestions that challenge existing practice and regulation. It is fair to say that it is one of the most challenging areas of concern for those in the animal welfare lobby because of the overall public support for the continuing use of animals in experimentation. The pandemic of 2020 saw vaccines hurriedly passed into common usage after testing on animals had been completed – further entrenching the view of the necessity of invasive research on animals.

In most other areas of Animal Law, there appear to be readily available alternatives. So, for example, in relation to farming, there are alternative food sources available; in the use of animals for clothing, such as fur, there are clearly alternative man-made garments available; and in relation to whaling or other types of wild animal hunting, there is no real need to hunt such animals. Animal research appears to present the added difficulty of attempting to change practices, as it has become the scientific norm to use animals in research and, as we will see, alternative models are not widely adopted. It should be borne in mind, as Rollin (2017) suggests, that there is a knowledge gap in what might have occurred in alternative testing development if animal use had been more regulated or banned some time ago.

Although the moral argument is contested, the practical effect of concerns over animal suffering has generally led to more careful oversight in many countries/jurisdictions rather than a wholesale reduction in the number of animals used. Animal use has continued to escalate in the 21st century, just as it did in the 20th century. Assessing the number of animals used is notoriously difficult, but Taylor and Alvarez (2019) estimated a worldwide total in 2015 to be around 115 million animals. As will be seen in this chapter, it can be difficult to know exactly what happens during scientific procedures, but information on the number and types of procedures is easier to access. Great Britain provides annual statistics on the number of animals used and the types of procedures carried out. The 2022 Home Office *Annual Statistics of Scientific Procedures on Living Animals in Great Britain* showed there were 2.76 million scientific procedures carried out on live animals, which was a decrease from most previous years. It is important to note that the number of procedures is not the number of animals used. Some animals may be reused in several experiments, so the number of procedures is higher than the number of animals used. Most of the procedures, around 96%, used mice, fish, birds or rats, and of these, 53% were used for basic research (to expand knowledge of living organisms in the environment), 24% were used for applied research (attempts to address diseases), 21% were used for regulatory use (to satisfy legal requirements, such as testing the safety and effectiveness of pharmaceutical substances, most of which are toxicity and safety testing) and 1% were used for other reasons, such as procedures in higher education settings or in relation to the preservation of species (Home Office, 2023).

Though the numbers are, on average, decreasing every year, there is still a substantial number of animals used in scientific procedures. Further, there is a lot of secrecy surrounding these procedures, which can cause alarm for animal welfare advocates and means they remain an area of concern in Animal Law. There appears to be a common perception, certainly in the most 'developed' nations, that animal experimentation is an uncomfortable necessity, despite concerns over the types of experimentation, limiting suffering in certain circumstances and performing experiments only where necessary. The notion of the Three Rs (replacement, reduction and refinement) emphasises the place of experimentation as an unfortunate necessity but modifying this is possible.

The advances claimed to have been brought about by the use of animals in experimentation are, at first sight, compelling (Paton, 1993). It is one thing to complain about the wearing of fur to serve human vanity: quite another when scientists claim they are saving or significantly improving the quality of human lives. If there is a change in prevailing attitudes towards animal experimentation, it might seem morally inconsistent to not also change attitudes towards agriculture, hunting and trade, where the claimed benefits to humans are less significant or cater merely to human lifestyle. However, the broad assumption that animal experimentation is an undesirable necessity is questioned by many. It continues to attract criticism regarding its overall value and whether the moral cost of animal suffering is sustainable (Lafollette, 2011).

The terms 'animal experimentation' and 'vivisection' are often used interchangeably despite the fact that each is, in fact, quite different. 'Vivisection' actually refers to experimentation by 'cutting' or 'wounding' a live animal, a graphic term that appealed to animal rights activists. 'Animal experimentation' in general uses many more techniques in addition to cutting or wounding, such as behavioural testing, genetic defect research, testing of drugs for human and animal use, surgical training, basic compound testing, cosmetic testing and many more. But the term has now assumed common usage and is a convenient shorthand for the somewhat clumsy term 'animals used in experimentation'.

The history of animal experimentation, welfare concerns and the influence of lobby groups

Despite the continuous interest in the anatomy of animals throughout history, it was only in the 17th and 18th centuries that animal research became widespread. There had been experiments carried out before, but they were comparatively modest affairs compared with what came later (Maeler & Tröhler, 1987). Alcmaeon of Croton (450 BC), Herophilos (330–250 BC) and Erasistratos (305–240 BC) are all recorded as having made discoveries about sight, tendons and nerves, and the difference between sensory and motor nerves, respectively, using experiments on animals. Galen of Pergamon (circa. AD 130–210) records being uncomfortable with vivisecting some animals, such as apes, because of their reaction, yet he stated the research needed to continue. He made discoveries about the brain and heart and is credited with discovering that the veins contain blood, not air. Yet he made some startling errors that were supported for centuries, including women having two wombs – one for male and one for female embryos – and the eating of fruit being harmful (Maeler & Tröhler, 1987, pp. 15–16).

The scientific revolution that accompanied the Renaissance saw the birth of the modern era of animal experimentation. René Descartes' philosophical treatment of animals was a large contributory factor in the considerable increase in the number of animals being used in scientific discovery in the 18th and 19th centuries. Even though the number of animals used paled into insignificance compared with the explosion in use in the 20th century, considerable competition developed between the scientific communities of France, including Claude Bernard (1813–1878) and Francois Magendie (1783–1855), and England, including Marshall Hall (1790–1857) and Sir Charles Bell (1774–1847). Along with this, gathering pace throughout the 18th century, came the growth of the animal welfare lobby, particularly in England, which began to exert pressure on scientists to change their practice. This developed alongside philosophical concerns, notably from Jeremy Bentham (1748–1860). His simple yet compelling focus on the suffering of animals, rather than the differences between humans and animals, served as a rallying call to the anti-vivisection movement. Scientists were subjected to intense scrutiny of their practices, whereas in France and Germany, to the consternation of English scientists arguing that our science was being left behind, there was far greater use of animals (French, 1975). The move towards more animal experimentation was also criticised by those who viewed better sanitation and more effective health policies as a means of improving the health of the nation. This early historical backdrop led to the creation of laws relating to animal experimentation.

Early legal control

The UK led the way in developing laws to regulate the use of animals in experimentation following concerns raised about animal welfare. An examination of the history of the UK's legislation governing animals used in experiments demonstrates the development of how animals have been used in science, our changing feelings towards their suffering, the importance of animal organisations in generating legal change and, ultimately, the difficulties in protecting animal welfare in law when the suffering caused to them is predominately for the benefit of humans.

The continuous 19th century battle between the scientific and anti-vivisection lobbies eventually led to success for the animal rights lobby, when the Cruelty to Animals Act 1876 was passed, the first known legislation in the world to regulate the use of live animals in research. Previously, the RSPCA had tried, unsuccessfully, to prosecute people for cruelty in animal experimentation under the Cruelty to Animals Act 1849 (Eurogroup for Animal Welfare, 1994) for cruelty to domestic animals. The first attempted prosecution took place in 1874 when Eugene Mangan and three organisers were prosecuted for the methods used in inducing epilepsy in two dogs at the annual meeting of the British Medical Association in Norwich in August 1874. The prosecution was unsuccessful as Mangan had returned (or fled) to France, and the organisers had not taken part in the demonstration so could not be held accountable.

The main problem encountered in bringing a prosecution for the criminal offence of cruelty to domestic animals was the qualification 'unnecessary', which required an experiment to be proved to be completely unnecessary – an almost impossible task. Therefore, throughout the greater part of the 19th century, any alleged instances of cruelty in animal experimentation went entirely unpunished, serving merely to intensify the anger of anti-vivisectionists, frustrated that the law appeared to offer little, if any, protection to animals used in experimentation (Turner, 1992). Since the latter half of the 19th century, animals involved in experimentation in the UK have been protected, firstly, by the Cruelty to Animals Act

1876 and subsequently by the Animals (Scientific Procedures) Act 1986 (ASPA), whereby experimenters have been able to carry out experiments on animals by obtaining Home Office licences (discussed in more detail below). It is interesting to note that the effect of the introduction of legislation was not to 'reduce' the number of animals used in experimentation. In 1878, less than 300 experiments were being performed on animals; by 1970, there were more than five million (Ryder, 1983). The 1876 Cruelty to Animals Act had been widely criticised because of its ineffectiveness in dealing with the treatment of animals in relation to medical experimentation (Ryder, 1989). The introduction of the 1876 Act came about as a result of successful anti-vivisectionist lobbying in response to changes in policy by the scientific community. For example, in 1870, scientists from leading UK institutions decided to use animal experimentation to the same extent as their French and German counterparts. In the same year, the Royal College of Surgeons began a reform of examinations that required a greater use of animals in training, thus setting the scene for the intervention of parliament (French, 1975). In May 1875, there were two unsuccessful attempts at introducing legislation, but both were poorly worded and introduced into the parliamentary session too late (Ryder, 1981).

The Cruelty to Animals Bill introduced through the House of Lords on 20 March 1876 was a much stricter version than eventually reached the statute books. Effective lobbying and a Royal Commission report (HMSO, 1876) had created the potential for far-reaching reform of the law. Dr George Hoggan, an English physiologist, had been working in France with Claude Bernard, the notorious French scientist, and returned appalled by the experiments he had witnessed. In a letter to the *Morning Post* on 1 February 1875, he described dogs that would 'make friendly advances to each of the three or four present and as far as the eyes, ears and tail could make a mute appeal for mercy eloquent, they tried it in vain' (French, 1975, p. 414). The letter stirred up a groundswell of opinion against animal research, and an anti-vivisection league was founded, which came to be known as the Victoria Street Society. It had the support of leading public figures such as Tennyson, Ruskin, Victor Hugo and Lord Shaftesbury. In addition, Queen Victoria used her influence to persuade on Prime Minister Disraeli to instigate a Royal Commission, which set about cross-examining several notable scientists of the time, including Charles Darwin.

The Royal Commission Report of January 1876 noted the concern of the British public and recommended that animal experimentation should be subject to regulation and control because of possible abuse. The report supported the continued use of animals, which the Commission felt had already improved public health, but only within a framework to promote humane practice. This build-up of momentum led the following year to the introduction of a parliamentary bill, with the original aim of severely curtailing animal experimentation. But the effectiveness of the pro-animal research lobby was demonstrated by the last-minute lobbying of the Home Secretary by the General Medical Council whilst the Bill's sponsor, Lord Carnarvon, was away from London after the death of his mother. The science lobby proceeded to lobby the Commission chairman, Lord Cardwell, members of the Cabinet, and members of both Houses of Parliament, saying that the Bill was too restrictive to allow significant medical progress. The resulting one-month delay led to the introduction of a new Bill containing provisions that were to prove more favourable to the research community than the provisions of the original Bill, and difficult to enforce, receiving Royal Assent only five days later. Experiments to alleviate either human or animal suffering would now be allowed, and cats and dogs could be used, as could asses, horses or mules. It has been argued that this series of events marked the beginning of a new relationship between scientists and politicians, whereby the view that 'scientists know best' began to take hold (Ryder, 1989).

The 1876 Act introduced a licensing system to perform experiments on living vertebrates. This was issued after an application was made to the Home Secretary. Such licensing of animal experiments provided the blueprint for legislation across the globe. The location had to be registered, as did the proposed experiments, which had to be shown to be for the 'advancement by new discovery of physiological knowledge or of knowledge which will be useful for saving or prolonging life or alleviating suffering'. In addition, there was a controversial list of exemptions to the coverage provided by the Act that could be performed with specific certification, such as the use of cats and dogs, which caused concern because of their common domestication. The introduction of the Act may have been considered to have been a great victory for the anti-vivisection lobby in England, and for short time, up to 1882, it probably was (French, 1975, p. 191).

In 1883, the scientific lobby managed to obtain a significant foothold in the operation of the Act. The newly formed Association for the Advancement of Medicine by Research, composed entirely of scientists, had the principal objective of representing experimental medicine on the political front. They were invited by the then Home Secretary, Sir William Harcourt, to advise on the administration of the Act, which resulted in far more applications for Home Office licences being successful and radically transformed the Act's operation, helping to bring about a rapid growth in the use of animals in research. The number of licences increased from 42 in 1882 to 638 in 1913 as experimental medicine flourished. Anti-vivisectionists saw the Act as a scientist's charter but were unable to bring about significant change for 110 years. Despite attracting a committed and impassioned membership, the anti-vivisection lobby suffered from many problems, including conflict within its own ranks and an inability to attract public support for their tactics, which led the 1876 Act becoming entrenched in practice before united opposition could force a change.

Throughout its life, the animal rights lobby was concerned about several perceived flaws in the structure and operation of the 1876 Act (Ryder, 1981). For example, there were suspiciously few prosecutions under the Act, with Turner (1992, p. 218) commenting that 'humanitarian and sceptic alike join in wondering whether any Act in history has been so scrupulously observed' and Clarke (1977) observing that the Research Defence Society showed a 'startling lack of integrity' in basing their support on the Act and the lack of prosecutions under it. There were few investigations, and investigators, into the benefits of the proposed procedure, with scientists merely needing to show there was a purpose to it to be granted a licence, and some experiments, such as psychological ones, were not covered at all. Other issues were the species covered by the Act being too narrow, the rearing and housing of animals not being covered, and the requirements of euthanasia of an animal in pain being vague and contributing to further unnecessary suffering. In addition, there was inadequate reporting on the number of animals used and the purpose of the experiments was not made publicly available. A Home Office Advisory Group was set up following a second Royal Commission investigation of 1906–1912 but it did not fulfil its brief to reassure the public that adequate supervision of experimentation was taking place. It recommended an increase in the inspectorate, better provision for anaesthetising animals, and that the power of inspectors should be widened to order the death of animals suffering pain. It also recommended the replacement of the Association for the Advancement of Medicine by Research with a more independent advisory body, appointed by the Home Secretary, from a list of names not involved in scientific research. Since the amendments could be made within the current legislation, these recommendations were approved without requiring new legislation.

Animal experimentation activism and lobby groups: The influence on legal change

Despite the continuing work of the RSPCA, it was not until the 1960s and 1970s that the movement against the use of animals in experimentation found an effective voice through the work of an increasing number of organisations opposed to the use of animals in experimentation. Peter Singer outlined one type of experiment that tends to attract severe criticism (Singer, 1991, p.147):

> At a prestigious institute in the US, monkeys were trained to run in a cylindrical treadmill. The monkeys received electric shocks unless they kept the treadmill moving. Once the monkeys had received initial training at keeping the treadmill in motion, they were subjected to varying doses of radiation. Monkeys receiving the higher doses vomited repeatedly. They were then put back into the treadmill to measure the effect of the radiation on their ability to keep it moving. During this period, if the monkey did not move the treadmill for one minute, shock intensity was increased to 10 mA. (This is an intense electric shock, causing severe pain.) Some monkeys continued to vomit while in the treadmill. The irradiated monkeys took up to five days to die.

The exposure of such experiments caused some wide public outrage, and tighter controls were demanded to prevent the use of animals in research, and campaigns began for the use of alternative research methods or to at least bring down the number of animals used. The impetus for change was spurred on by the publication of the Littlewood Report (HMSO, 1965), which recommended 83 changes to the control of animal experimentation. However, by the 1979 general election, only 20 of these recommendations had been implemented (House of Lords, Hansard, 1979). The movement attracted increasing numbers of people, and the cause began to increase the momentum for change. In the 1970s, two incidents brought the issue back into the public arena. These were a *Sunday People* story about 'smoking beagles' in 1975 and the imprisonment of two animal rights activists from the Animal Liberation Front (ALF) (Ronnie Lee and Clifford Goodman) for damage to property used by animal experimenters (Monaghan & da Silva, 2023). The ALF in the US went to extreme and sometimes violent measures to send their message. For example, they liberated more than 100 animals used in medical research from 12 labs at the University of Minnesota, causing an estimated $1 million of damage in the process. In the UK, the ALF began more extreme, non-direct liberation techniques, such as contamination of Sunsilk shampoo supplies with bleach in 1984, forcing a recall of the brand of shampoo. Contamination techniques continued with products such as beef and turkey, and in November of that year caused a huge economic impact through the hoax that they had contaminated Mars Bars. During this time, the ALF in the US had moved away from liberation efforts and towards destruction of property and arson, such as setting fire to a lab at the University of California, causing millions of dollars in damage, and were finally placed on the FBI's domestic terrorism list (Nagtzaam, 2017). Bombs were sent to the homes of CEOs of businesses and scientists working on animals. It was a time of extreme activism, that did not achieve its end goal and contributed towards the greater secrecy of animal experimentation, as detailed in the later sections of this chapter. The anti-vivisection lobby might have managed to significantly shift the debate in their direction were it not for the fact that their pro-science opponents began to fight back by forming their own pro-experimentation groups, which managed to influence governments more effectively and gain political and public support.

Due to the negative associations with animal experimentation lobby groups, some began to change their tactics, which involved less activism and more political or peaceful measures. It has been suggested that because the anti-vivisection movement decided to compromise with the experimentation lobby after their limited successes in the late 19th century, they became less effective as radical proponents of change in the 20th century (Rodman, 1977). They sought to police the changes that had taken place rather than looking for further restrictions on the use of animals, which continued with relative ease. To this day, there is a considerable distance between the various degrees of acceptance of animal experimentation. The chief aim of many governments is to reduce, refine and replace experiments (the Three Rs) and all pro- and anti-experimentation groups are seen as forming an invaluable part of that process. These incidents, along with the plethora of a new wave of writing on the subject, which began to appear in the 1970s, helped to create a climate for change at a political level. The scientific community also appeared to recognise a groundswell of public opinion and academic arguments that needed addressing. On 16 July 1979, the Research Defence Society's President, Lord Halsbury, tried to head off criticism by introducing the Laboratory Animal Protection Bill into the House of Lords, which covered some of the criticisms of the animal welfare lobby (although it was still considered inadequate), but the Bill failed to become law.

During the general election campaign of 1979, the animal welfare movement succeeded in obtaining a commitment to new legislation from an incoming government when the Conservatives promised to 'update' the existing legal framework. The Home Secretary asked the Advisory Committee set up under the 1876 Act to consider a new legal framework. In 1985, the government introduced its Animals (Scientific Procedures) Bill. It contained many changes to the original version of the Bill produced in 1983, which had been secured by an alliance of the Committee for Reform of Animal Experimentation (CRAE), the Fund for the Replacement of Animals in Medical Experimentation (FRAME), and the British Veterinary Association (BVA) following several meetings (Hollands, 1986). These included the grading of experiments according to severity, to determine whether the experiment should go ahead, and the inclusion of a termination (the killing of the animals) requirement if animals were found to be in severe pain. Further, Hampson (1987) noted that a 300-page report by the RSPCA on the pain and suffering of animals used in experiments also influenced the government's thinking during deliberations. However, the animal welfare lobby was far less successful in securing further changes as the Bill proceeded through parliament. This was partly a result of considerable differences in internal opinion as to what they should accept in the legislation and because of a fear of alienation from proceedings if they were considered too 'radical'.

The Bill proceeded through parliament without the anti-vivisection movement being able to mount effective, united opposition against it, despite the reservations of many. The Bill was supported by the Labour Party, a factor that was critical in ensuring that its passage through parliament was a relatively straightforward affair. The Bill was, however, opposed by many, such as the Liberal/Social Democratic Alliance parties in parliament, most of the animal welfare organisations, some church leaders and many academics, on the grounds that it did not go far enough in restricting experiments on animals. The RSPCA was less vocal in its opposition to the Bill than the other welfare organisations, as it had decided quite early on to support the Bill as the best way of securing at least some improvement in the treatment of animals. But they were clearly hopeful throughout the passage of the Bill of securing more than the Bill finally delivered, with the RSPCA council chairman, Anelay Hart, writing to *The Times*, criticising the Bill, saying it would not have the RSPCA's full support unless changes were made to it. The Bill finally received Royal Assent and became the ASPA 1986, which is now the current legislation in the UK. It was amended in 2012 by the ASPA amendment regulations. The British Union for the Abolition of Vivisection (BUAV), now renamed Cruelty Free International (CFI), has been the most recognisable organisation advocating for the discontinuation of animal experimentation. CFI has been critical of the 1986 Act from its inception (BUAV, 1992). They were initially suspicious of the scientific community being given the power to implement the balancing of 'pain versus benefits' requirement – those carrying out experiments are required to assess the likely pain to be endured and to rank it according to the Act so that the Home Secretary can decide whether to grant a licence (more detail below). The lack of independent scrutiny in the absence of ethics committees added to their suspicions. BUAV at the time, in common with the Working Party of the Institute of Medical Ethics, questioned why there had been so few prosecutions under the Act, suggesting this was not evidence of compliance but rather of a lack of willingness to prosecute (BUAV, 1992, p. 3). They highlighted how almost three million experiments were carried out in Great Britain each year, with almost two-thirds using no anaesthetic. They brought to public attention the kinds of experiments being carried out, including the Draize eye test (instilling chemicals into the eyes of animals to test potential irritation or damages from the substances), the LD50 test (poisoning a group of animals to determine the dose of a test substance necessary to kill half of them), and for weapons research. At this time, cosmetic testing was still legal in Great Britain, and six project licences were issued, which applied to over 12,000 experiments, highlighting the lack of consideration of the pain of individual animals. Also highlighted was the lack of Home Office Inspectors, with only 19 inspectors in 1994, and a decline of inspections by 20% since the 1986 Act was passed (Statistics HMSO, 1994). The latest number of inspectors is, for 2022, around 20 inspectors. The number of inspectors remains controversially small.

At the inception of the 1986 Act, BUAV indicated that they felt that the Act could become workable with the inclusion of the following strategies: ending the cruellest, trivial and discredited experiments, such as cosmetic testing; creating a strategy to reduce the number of animals used in experimentation by 50% by the year 2000; and encouraging the development of alternatives and strengthening the institutions and guidelines set up under the Act. The Research Defence Society had a different view in their contributions to the review of the Act (Matfield, 1996):

> Regrettably, this review of the Act is certain to be used by the antivivisection groups as an opportunity to attempt to undermine public confidence in the legislation and the way it is implemented … it is difficult to see how they can avoid being entirely one-sided in their comments ... When the UK legislation is compared to that of other countries, it is clear that our system of regulation is more stringent than that of any other country in the world … The overwhelming impression of the scientists and technicians involved with animal research in the UK is that laboratory animal welfare has improved considerably over the last decade ... Since the 1986 Act is already the most stringent … one should question the idea of merely making it more stringent and more complex.

The 1986 Act also replaced the Advisory Committee established under the 1876 Act with the Animal Procedures Committee (APC), which had to issue a yearly report on matters of policy and practice or matters referred to it by the Home Secretary. This was replaced when it was renamed the Home Office's Animals in Science Committee in 2012. They originally described their role as being located 'between the changing attitudes of society to animal usage on the one hand and society's aspirations for increased health and safety on the other' (HMSO, 1996, p. 6, para. 36).

In other parts of the world, laws restricting animal experiments were practically non-existent and came much later than in the UK, well into the 20th century. Some European countries were finally forced to introduce legislation in the 1980s by Directive 86/609 of the European Union (see below). The unique history and development of legislation relating to animals used in experiments in the UK provide context for the current regulations and their influence on laws in other jurisdictions. By understanding the development of the law, which includes the influence of welfare lobby groups and opposition from the scientific communities, we can see how far we have come, but also why greater change continues to be a challenge.

Should experiments on animals be banned or regulated more tightly?

Whether we retain the use of animals in experiments, have tighter regulations, or ban their use altogether is a difficult argument that will most likely not have a consensus for some time. Experiments are carried out for a variety of reasons, such as for medical advances, behavioural studies, or toxicity testing, and there will be differing opinions about the necessity for them. Further, not all experiments are carried out for human gain, and some are for advances in veterinary science and medicine. This comes under the category of regulatory testing in the UK, and in 2022, of the approximate 325,000 regulatory procedures carried out, 26% of them were for veterinary use (Home Office, 2023). The majority, however, still benefit humans, which results in complex debates. We do not have the space here to go through all the arguments for and against in this section, and this is just a small outline of some of the main arguments.

Arguments for maintaining the status quo

The proponents of continued animal experimentation have become much more vociferous in recent times as a response to the increase in momentum built up against it by the 'animal rights' lobby since the 1970s. It is argued that experiments on animals have provided an important contribution to medical and surgical advances, bringing about major improvements to the health of humans and animals (Paton, 1993). Many examples are cited, such as the development of insulin for diabetes, the whooping cough vaccine, heart and lung surgery, kidney transplants, the polio vaccine, drugs to treat asthma, and anaesthetics for surgery. Dr Mark Matfield, prior Executive Director of the Research Defence Society, commented that:

> During this century, there have been tremendous advances in medical research, much of it dependent upon animal experimentation. The result has been enormous progress in our ability to diagnose, prevent and treat a wide range of diseases and injuries, both for humans, and, with veterinary medicine, for animals as well. The total amount of death and suffering which has been alleviated or prevented has never been calculated. However, one study measured this in terms of life expectancy and proposed that modern medical research had added twenty years on to the average western lifespan. That would be the approximate equivalent of saving 100 million human lives. (Matfield, 1991)

It is argued that research involving animals should continue in the future in order to combat, as yet unsolved, medical problems such as cancer, AIDS, and genetic, psychiatric and neurological conditions. The advocates of experimentation point to the possibilities for treatment to which animal-based studies will provide a large contribution, and often simplify it to an emotive argument to consider the impact of a lack of medical treatment on loved ones (White, 1991). In 1994, the British Association Promoting Science and Technology highlighted the benefits of research involving animals, such as vaccines, antiseptic surgery and anaesthetics, insulin for diabetes and developments in transplantation, and the arguments have remained broadly the same ever since. There have been moves in the area, such as the introduction of local ethics committees in the UK in 1999 and amended legislation in 2013 following an EU Directive in 2012, but the framework for countries with existing legislation has remained relatively static, as has the overall use of animals in terms of numbers and severity of procedures. Other areas of controversy, such as the farming of animals for their fur, the control of religious slaughter, and the legal status of animals in recognition of sentience, have seen far greater movement. It is generally accepted, for example, that animal fur used for fashion is completely unnecessary and not needed by humans to be able to live. The use of animals in experimentation, however, has a very strong establishment acceptance, as it is seen as necessary to maintain and further human health, and it is difficult to see much movement during the short to medium term.

One of the most detailed examinations of the cases for and against animal experimentation was the report produced by a Working Party of the Institute of Medical Ethics on *The Ethics of Using Animals in Biomedical Research* in 1991 (Smith & Boyd, 1991). The 16 members of the Working Party, including R.G. Frey and Clive Hollands (well-known adversaries in the animal experimentation debate), represented a cross-section of differing views mainly from the 'centre ground' of the debate but did not include any representatives from specifically 'absolute rejection' groups such as the British Union for the Abolition of Vivisection. Had it done so, agreement might have been more difficult to reach. The group examined the full range of moral arguments and highlighted the 'tragic conflict' involved in using undoubtedly sentient animals against the lack of viable alternatives at present. In light of this, and conscious of the need to come up with a workable conclusion in spite of their moral differences, the group supported the use of animals in experimentation, backed up by suitable legislative regulation. They supported the view that animal experimentation had 'proved worthwhile for human purposes' in terms of advanced health levels and doubted whether the advances in human health might all have been achieved without the use of animals. Therefore, they supported the use of animals as long as there are continued efforts to reduce, refine and replace the use of animals in experimentation (Smith & Boyd, 1991, pp. 310–313). Some of these arguments, whilst maybe valid at the time, have become more questionable with the advancement in technology and the greater promotion of the Three Rs, which will be explored in more detail below.

Over the last 30 years, there have been other more groundbreaking procedures on animals for scientific gain. For example, the cloning of Dolly the sheep in the 1990s, the first mammal cloned from another adult cell, was part of a research project to produce genetically modified livestock. The cloning techniques led to advances in stem cell research for humans (Liu et al., 2020). Cell-cultured meat, or lab-grown meat as it is also known, is in continuous development and a method of producing meat products without the need to slaughter animals. Though the cells are still extracted from live-farmed animals, fewer animals are needed to provide the meat, and techniques are becoming more refined that are better for animal welfare (Chriki, Ellies-Oury & Hocquette, 2022). This is also a way for scientists to carry out procedures on non-living animals, which is a technique some researchers use where possible.

Some arguments in favour of using animals in experiments are proposed from a moral perspective. Animals are not perceived to have an equal moral status to humans, mainly due to their lack of ability to reason and of cognitive abilities (Cohen, 1986), and to experiment on humans who have these qualities is not accepted. We can see this argument in history when unacceptable experiments were conducted using live humans. The Nazis carried out horrific experiments on Jewish people in concentration camps (Roelcke, 2004) and the Tuskegee experiments in the United States, where more than 100 people died as a result (Cuerda & Lopez-Munoz, 2013). Because of experiments such as this, there are strict requirements and ethical guidelines for research involving humans, but this is not matched in those for animals, as it is generally believed that it is better to use animals than it is to use, even willing, humans. If the benefit to humans is greater than the cost to the animals used when a cost-benefit assessment is carried out, it is deemed to be morally acceptable.

Public support has also remained relatively strong for animal experimentation. In 2018, Ipsos conducted a survey on behalf of the Office for Life Sciences, a repeat of a survey they did in 2016. They found similar levels of public acceptability of animal research, but that it was dependent on the purpose and context of the research. The respondents accepted the use of animals in medical research at 65% and for scientific purposes at 68%. Those who believed animals should not be used in research for welfare reasons had increased slightly from 35% in 2016 to 38% in 2018. The statistics also highlighted little knowledge or understanding of the law, with 38% believing that cosmetic testing on animals was still being used in the UK and 23% of respondents believing that research is only carried out on animals when there are no alternatives. In terms of the Three Rs, less than one in ten respondents knew more than a little about it, and 41% believed that scientists are actively working to find alternatives to live animal models, though in reality, it is lower than this. Lastly, 41% of respondents associated animal research organisations with secrecy. Certain illnesses can also impact public support. For example, at the onset of the COVID-19 pandemic, a UK survey found 73% of respondents considered it acceptable for researchers to use animals – such as mice, dogs and monkeys – to develop tests, treatments or vaccines if there was no alternative. Additionally, 11% of respondents stated their views towards animal testing had changed due to the COVID-19 outbreak and were more accepting of animal research (Understanding Animal Research, 2020). While support for animal testing appears to have increased at the onset of the pandemic, further research is needed to assess current public opinion. With public support remaining high, a ban is unlikely, however, the welfare of the animals used is firmly recognised. What is clear is there needs to be better education regarding how animals are used in experiments and why, for people to make an informed decision when considering the arguments for animal experimentation. Continued research into alternatives is also vital.

Arguments against animal experimentation

The anti-vivisection lobby has attracted many leading historical figures to the fold who have made contributions to the debate. The playwright George Bernard Shaw (1949) alluded to the advances in knowledge gained by animal experimentation but argued that we would, rightly, not allow such experiments on humans in the pursuit of knowledge. He went on to say that the 'attack on vivisection is not an attack on the pursuit of scientific knowledge' and the 'knowledge we lose by forbidding cruelty is knowledge at first hand of cruelty itself, which is precisely the knowledge we wish to be spared' (Shaw, 1949, pp. 29–31). He suggested that if we were to stop animal experimentation, we would not prohibit the advancement of knowledge because alternatives would be discovered instead. However, this would have the positive outcome of preventing cruelty to animals for the benefit of humans.

Despite the contribution to increased human and animal welfare claimed by the scientific lobby, Henry Salt wondered whether this would, were it possible, affect an animal's possible agreement to become the subject of experimentation: 'Can we doubt that the victims themselves, if once they could realise the noble object of their martyrdom, would vie each with the other in rushing eagerly on the knife? The only marvel is that, where the cause is so meritorious, no 'human' volunteer has as yet come forward to die under the hands of the vivisector!' (Salt, 1915, pp. 72–73).

One of the leading protagonists in the cause of animal welfare in the 1960s and 1970s was Brigid Brophy (1971), who was certain that the only way forward was to ban animal experimentation. Circumstances and regulations may have changed since 1971 when the piece was published, but her sentiments are still shared by many and remain just as relevant today, which shows how resilient animal experimentation has been to legal reform. Her primary sentiment was society's moral obligation to find alternatives to stop animal experimentation, and that by not doing this, scientists continue to 'mislead themselves' by thinking there is no other way.

One of the main justifications for the continued use of animals is the possibility of discovering significant benefits for mankind or animals. Defining 'significant benefit' is subject to controversy, as illustrated by the public outcry that arose in the United States in 1996 when the Bion Space Project, funded by Russia, France and the US, announced that it was going to send monkeys into space to study why spaceflight takes such a severe toll on humans. The effects of space travel are well documented by human experience, but the causes have not been pinpointed. The monkeys were sent up in straitjackets to stop them from pulling out electrodes, which were inserted into their brains and under their skin. Animal welfare groups in the US were outraged and protested that potential knowledge gain was only that already gathered from previous human experience in space. They deemed the loss and suffering of those animals as unnecessary and a waste of money. Whether such experiments are unacceptable is a moral question that lies at the heart of the debate in this area. What is one scientist's quest for knowledge is another person's unnecessary abuse of animal life. However, this particular experiment attracted scientific criticism because it was argued that restrained monkeys would hardly produce results comparable to active humans in space. The monkeys were finally launched into space in December 1997, and when brought back to Earth, one died and the other became ill. An independent panel investigated this form of animal experimentation and recommended that the United States should not involve itself in such experiments. This recommendation was accepted by the US government, and they have not been a part of such experiments since (New Scientist, 1997). The last country to send a primate into space was Iran in 2013, but the projects have largely been curtailed due to public concerns and scientific condemnation. It appears the court of public opinion draws lines in determining the rights and wrongs of animal experiments, but defining them in precise moral or legal terms remains elusive.

Aside from this high-profile case, many anti-vivisection groups have consistently argued that other, less spectacular or high-profile animal experiments are either morally wrong, harmful to humans as well as the animals, or, at best, of limited use: 'a large amount of the research which is done is trivial, and the knowledge has no medical importance' (Ryder, 1983, p. 11). Opponents of animal experimentation have often pointed to the notable failures of some drugs, certified for medical use after having been tested on animals, which turned out to have catastrophic effects. There are some notable and well-known examples: Thalidomide was given to women to prevent morning sickness and caused as many as 10,000 birth defects (Ryder, 1983, p. 32); Opren, an anti-arthritis drug, caused 70 deaths and some 3,500 cases of serious side effects in Britain before being withdrawn; Osmosin, an anti-inflammatory drug, caused 650 cases of serious side effects and 20 deaths (Singer, 1995, p. 57); and it is estimated that 88,000–139,00 United States citizens had heart attacks after taking Vioxx, which was withdrawn in 2004 (Alomar et al., 2019). The suffering of humans brought about by the mistaken belief in the safety of these drugs is one of the human costs that society has paid. Some people have been the unwilling victims of the utilitarian calculus of the potential benefits to be gained by animal experimentation against the potential risks to humans. The claims of the scientific lobby regarding advances in human health have also been disputed by many scientists, such as Dr Robert Sharpe, who doubts whether experiments involving animals have been the source of the advances in human health as claimed by the scientific community (Sharpe, 1988). Nobis (2011) also argued against much of the broad scientific acceptance of using animals, but the resolve of the majority of the scientific community seems to be in favour of its continuation. It is also somewhat ironic that science argues the need to use animals due to their being similar models to humans but neglects to see this as a reason to heighten their moral status.

Overall, the arguments for and against animal experimentation are difficult to resolve to come to one conclusion, and animal use continues even though there is evidence of experiments being unnecessary or medicine developed using animal models being dangerous to humans. The last part of this section will consider the alternatives to animal models.

Alternatives to animal experimentation and the Three Rs

Some immediate alternatives to using animals in research include: epidemiology, which involves the study of diseases; culturing cell tissue and organs from human sources; quantum pharmacology, which involves computer predictions of reactions based on existing knowledge; and clinical trials that study how people who have spontaneously contracted a disease respond to therapy or drug treatments. Advances in technology have increased the sophistication and reliability of some alternative models. For example, 3D bioprinting has been developed, which uses human cells to mimic organ functions to screen treatments and test drugs, and computer and mathematical models have been developed to predict how substances can impact organs such as the heart, lungs and kidneys (Kaylor, 2023). Computer models and software programs are used to develop new drugs before being used on animals, only in the final stages of testing (Doke & Dhawale, 2015). Cell and tissue cultures taken from animals and grown outside the body are used for preliminary drug screening, toxicity testing and assessing chemical reactions. Not only do these methods reduce and replace the number of live animals used in experiments, they can also provide more reliable outcomes when later used on humans. Other 'alternatives' now include other organisms, such as invertebrates or insects including fruit flies. Although these are still animals, some may be more comfortable with alternatives to mammals rather than alternatives to animals definitively.

The Three Rs principle was proposed in 1959 by Russell and Burch in their book *The Principles of Humane Experimental Technique*. These principles are:

1. Replacement: Avoiding or replacing the use of animals in experiments, wherever possible.
2. Reduction: Reducing the number of animals used by designing experiments that are both robust and reproducible.
3. Refinement: Minimising pain, suffering and distress in animals by improving their welfare and understanding how welfare impacts research outcomes.

As will be seen below, these three principles have been written into national and international legislation in the hope that they will reduce and eventually replace animals used in scientific experiments. This does not mean, however, that they have been extensively used, and it appears they have not had the huge impact anticipated. Reasons as to why this is the case will be explored later. It is difficult, however, to determine the success of the Three Rs in legislation, as the Home Office does not mention, never mind report, on their use and how many animals have not been used in experiments due to the development and operation of an alternative model. The National Centre for the 3Rs (NC3Rs) takes on the main responsibility of helping the research community develop technology to replace animal studies. The coalition government in 2014 attempted to provide further support to the NC3Rs through a delivery plan, but it did not go ahead and unfortunately has not been revisited since. In fact, successive governments in the UK have not paid much consideration to the welfare of animals used in research, as evidenced by the much-hailed Action Plan for Animal Welfare in 2021, which barely mentioned them. The Action Plan states only that the government will 'continue to commit to maintaining the high standards of protection where procedures are undertaken on live animals for scientific or educational purposes' and nothing about raising those 'high' standards. That said, the NC3Rs continue to help researchers adapt to alternative models, and by targeting early career academics, they will hopefully create a culture whereby live animal models are no longer the norm. Hubrecht and Carter (2019) highlight how seemingly small ways of advancing the Three Rs can have positive steps in the right direction, such as data and tissue sharing and better experimental designs to reduce the number of animals used. Additionally, they emphasise the importance of training protocols to reduce animal stress and increase welfare, which can help with refinement. Sparks and Brooman (2017, p. 9) argue that Brexit could be an 'opportunity for the UK to refocus funding and encourage the development of non-animal technologies.' This, however, will need greater commitment from the UK government to achieve the aims of the Three Rs.

International and European control

In 1985, the Council for International Organisations of Medical Sciences (CIOMS) published the International Guiding Principles for Biomedical Research Involving Animals, aimed at helping those countries lacking any legislative control regarding animal experimentation to introduce new controls. The principles encompass the need to 'recourse to experimentation on intact live animals of a wide variety of species.' They then go on to recommend several necessary, fundamental standards that have been embraced in many legal controls: the need to use alternatives where possible; proper housing and care of subjects; asking whether the experiments are necessary, and minimising pain and suffering. The principles also highlight the need for a suitably constituted review body where it is necessary to override any of the basic standards but do not give any substance as to what would amount to one that is 'suitably constituted' (Smith & Boyd, 1991, pp. 258–259). The principles are still relevant today, as the CIOMS has not published a more recent version. However, the methods employed to review and control procedures involving animals can be diverse across the globe, drawing some praise and, invariably, plenty of criticism.

At a European level, there have been three major international initiatives aimed at protecting animals used in experimentation. In 1985, the Council of Europe adopted a Convention for the Protection of Vertebrate Animals Used for Experimental and Other Scientific Purposes. Countries ratifying the convention are required to give legislative force to its provisions. It contains similar basic guidelines to the 1985 CIOMS Guidelines, encouraging humane care and killing of animals in pain as well as encouraging the search for alternatives. In 1986, the European Union (EU) introduced a Directive based on the 1985 Convention covering the 'approximation of laws, regulations and administrative provisions of the member states regarding the protection of animals used for experimental and scientific purposes' (Council Directive (86/609). This Directive set a deadline of November 1989 for member states to comply with its provisions. This required them to either strengthen existing laws or introduce a legal framework from scratch if necessary. The main provisions included the types of animals it covered, specifically, live non-human vertebrates (not embryos) used in product development and testing or research for the benefit of the health and welfare of humans/animals (Article 2). Additionally, it emphasised that alternatives to animal testing should be used where possible (Article 7).

Even though the 1986 Directive was the most stringent international attempt at regulation to date, there were concerns on both a moral and practical basis that there was still much to be done. Some EU Member States already complied with or went beyond the provisions of the Directive but Spain and Portugal, both of which had no specific laws concerning the use of animals in experimentation subjects, were required to introduce new legislation to comply. By 2001, the European Parliament was still reporting non-compliance with the Directive, such as Spain allowing the use of cats and dogs in experiments and Austria for failing to fully transpose the Directive into domestic law (European Parliament, 2002). The concerns of animal welfare groups appeared to be validated by the action against Luxembourg for failing to implement the Directive (*Commission of the European Communities* v. *Grand Duchy of Luxembourg*, 1996). However, the action was unsuccessful due to a technicality, and a full examination of the provisions of Luxembourg law relating to animal experimentation was never undertaken by the European court. Before detailing the most recent and stringent EU legislation, it is important to note that in 2009, following the UK's lead, the EU banned the testing of finished cosmetic products and their ingredients on animals. Additionally, the EU prohibited the sale of cosmetics, including ingredients and final products, that have been tested on animals anywhere in the world (EU Regulation 1223/2009).

Directive 2010/63

In 2010, the EU introduced a new Directive (2010/63/EU), which replaced and updated the 1986 Directive. The new Directive was similar to provisions the UK already provided in the ASPA, outlined below, but it created some strengthened changes for other member states in the EU. It is important to note that Article 2 of the Directive prohibits member states from increasing the protection provided under domestic legislation after it has been transposed, though member states who had greater protective measures before this could retain them if they were in force before November 2012. This means that member states are restricted from increasing the welfare of animals used in scientific procedures, which is an unusual provision in EU law.

The Directive has brought positive changes with it, including:

- The inclusion of breeding and supply within the law, rather than only regulating procedures. It also provided an extension to foetal mammals and cephalopods in the definition of animals (Article 1).
- The ban of the use of Great Apes (Article 8).
- The requirement of a harm-benefit assessment to be carried out, to determine whether the harm caused to the animals is justified by the expected outcomes (Article 38).
- The requirement of Member States to publish non-technical project summaries, project evaluations, and revised statistical data (Article 43).
- Data sharing between Member States and the prohibition of procedures where the data was already available in other Member States (Article 46).
- The promotion of the Three Rs (Article 47).

- The establishment of national committees for the protection of animals used in scientific purposes (Article 49).
- The introduction of severity limits for procedures which must be classified under Article 15, which are:
  - Non-recovery – 'procedures which are performed entirely under general anaesthesia from which the animal shall never recover consciousness'.
  - Mild – 'procedures on animals as a result of which the animals are likely to experience short-term mild pain, suffering or distress, as well as procedures with no significant impairment of the well-being or general condition of the animals'.
  - Moderate – 'procedures on animals as a result of which the animals are likely to experience short-term moderate pain, suffering or distress, or long-lasting mild pain, suffering or distress, as well as procedures likely to cause moderate impairment of the well-being or general condition of the animals'.
  - Severe – 'procedures on animals as a result of which the animals are likely to experience severe pain, suffering and distress, or long-lasting moderate pain, suffering and distress, as well as procedures that are likely to cause severe impairment of the well-being or general conditions of the animals…' (Annex VIII).

Though there have been many benefits brought by the Directive, there are some 'get out' clauses that can hinder its effectiveness. Article 15 prohibits procedures that cause severe pain, suffering or distress that is likely to be long-lasting and cannot be ameliorated. There is, however, a 'safeguard clause' in Article 55, providing an exception if there are exceptional and scientifically justifiable reasons, though the EU has reported that no member state has used this clause since the Directive took effect (European Commission, n.d.). This clause can also be used on the ban of the Great Apes. The publication of non-technical summaries are subject to 'safeguarding intellectual property and confidential information' – meaning there are exemptions to their publication. Further, Article 37 provides a waiver for projects classified as non-recoverable, mild or moderate, do not involve non-human primates and fall into specified categories of work providing non-technical summaries.

The UK had already included limits on severity in ASPA 1986, but the Directive has made improvements to how they operate. The new severity limits and retrospective assessments under the Directive are of beneficial, as they have replaced only documenting estimated harm before a project and allow for actual harm to be recorded after the project. It also allows for the individual assessment of animal suffering rather than taking an average, meaning that if the average animal would suffer moderate harm but one animal would experience severe suffering, it would be placed in the higher severity category. Lastly, it accounts for cumulative suffering, so that if a series of events taken together would be severe, it would be placed into the higher category, even if the interventions taken on their own would not be. An issue with the implementation of the severity limits is that there was little guidance or definition at the time of implementation, and there can be difficulties in calculating cumulative suffering (Beauchamp & Morton, 2015). This has resulted in procedures being placed in the moderate category when they should possibly have been classified as severe.

Regarding the Three Rs, though now a requirement for member states, there is a lack of training around alternative methods, non-availability in certain fields of alternatives, and not enough sharing of knowledge (European Commission, 2017a). The Directive has also failed to provide a strategy around the Three Rs and did not set targets for member states to reduce the number of animals used in procedures, and there is a lack of requirement to provide statistics on their use.

Member states are required to provide statistics to the EU on the number and classification of procedures carried out under the Directive. In 2017, the European Commission (2017b) carried out a review of the Directive across the member states, and whilst they stated 'the Directive's framework is generally considered to be a sound foundation for the regulation of animals used for scientific purposes', there were some key issues found. They related to the harmonisation of legislation within the EU, particularly for those member states that did not previously have formal structures for project evaluation, inconsistencies between project classifications, and slow uptake of the use of the 'Three Rs' (European Commission, 2017b).

The fact remains that the EU is committed to the use of animals in experiments because of their perceived role in improving the economic success of the community. Reliance on product innovation and consumer confidence has, in some circumstances, led EU and domestic legislation to require animal experimentation. If the EU is to fulfil its obligations under the Treaty of Rome, then animal testing is viewed as being an essential part of the jigsaw puzzle, not to be banned or further restricted unless there are suitable alternatives in place. Whether this is morally justifiable would be doubted by some considering the philosophical arguments of the animal welfare lobby, but it appears to represent underlying community economic philosophy. On the other hand, it may be that future developments in the use of alternative methods will produce more cost-effective methods of testing that are less reliant on the housing, care and feeding of animals. This would ensure that the economic arguments removed the European Union's reliance on animal testing before the moral arguments have been decided.

Domestic controls of animal experimentation in the UK

It is worth considering the UK in isolation because of its recognised influence on the development of worldwide legislation in the area (Dunn, 2021). Not only was it a forerunner in passing animal welfare legislation, but it continues to develop, or attempts to develop, and interacts with the development of notions of animal sentience. ASPA 1986 is still regarded by many as one of the most stringent pieces of legislation of its type in the world. The Act applies to the entire UK, and in England, Scotland and Wales, it is implemented by the Home Office. However, in Northern Ireland, responsibility is devolved to the Northern Irish Department for Health (2024), which releases its own reports and statistics. One of the major changes brought about by ASPA is the range of coverage it introduced. For example, the care and welfare of animals are not only covered when they are being used in procedures, but also in their care and housing before and after those procedures. Centres must be registered, as must the person responsible for the day-to-day care of the animals (known as a Named Animal Care and Welfare Officer [NACWO]) and a vet responsible for the animals' well-being. A code of practice for the Housing and Care of Animals Used in Scientific Procedures was issued in 1989. It is periodically updated to provide detailed guidance to those involved in the care and accommodation of the animals and is species-specific (UK Govt, 2014). The code does not set mandatory requirements for care and accommodation but is used to enable the Home Office to require programmes for improvement where establishments do not meet the code's standards. When Directive 2010/63 was implemented in 2013, ASPA was amended to make changes in line with the EU where it was needed. As the Directive was modelled on the UK system, minimal changes were required. The changes that were made are discussed below.

To conduct experiments legally, three licences are required under ASPA: an establishment licence (authorising the place where procedures can be carried out on any vertebrate), a personal licence (authorising specific individuals to carry out procedures), and a project licence (authorising the application of the regulated procedures). Under Schedule 2 of ASPA, an establishment licence is also needed when breeding an animal listed in the Schedule, if using them in regulated procedures or using their tissue or organs for scientific purposes. An establishment licence is also needed to keep animals that have been bred elsewhere and are to be supplied for the aforementioned reasons. The animals listed in Schedule 2 are now more extensive since the implementation of the 2010 Directive, which retains mice, rats, guinea pigs, hamsters, rabbits, dogs, cats and non-human primates, with any bird of the quail species, ferrets, gerbils, pigs and sheep if genetically modified, and certain species of frogs and zebrafish.

The main aim of the Act is to balance the research aims, that are considered essential and necessary, against the possible harm to animals. Section 5(3) outlines the permissible purposes of scientific procedures with this aim in mind:

- The prevention (whether by testing of any product or otherwise) or the diagnosis or treatment of disease, ill-health or abnormality, or their effects, in humans, animals or plants.
- The assessment, detection, regulation or modification of physiological conditions in humans, animals or plants.
- The protection of the natural environment in the interest of the health or welfare of humans or animals.
- The advancement of knowledge in biological or behavioural sciences.
- Education or training other than in primary or secondary schools.
- Forensic enquiries, and
- The breeding of animals for experimental or other scientific use.

The chief method of regulation used by ASPA is a two-tier licensing system of individuals (s.4) and projects (s.5). The personal licence allows experimenters to carry out individual programmes of work. As of 1 April 1994, all applicants seeking a personal licence must successfully complete an accredited training programme. The second tier is the project licence procedure, which now requires separate authorisation for each programme, in contrast to the 1876 Cruelty to Animals Act, which merely required the registration of a technique that could be repeated time and again with a new project and new animals. The greater use of licences specifically for each project aims to allow the Home Office to exert greater control of experimentation involving animals, including the conduct of the experiment itself. A critical tool to enable the Home Office to make its decision is the requirement created by s.5(4):

> In determining whether and on what terms to grant a project licence, the Secretary of State shall weigh the likely adverse effects concerned against the benefit likely to accrue as a result of the programme to be specified in the licence.

This has been advanced by the 2010 Directive, and s.5B(3)(d) now requires the Secretary of State to:

> Carry out a harm-benefit analysis of the programme of work to assess whether the harm that would be caused to protected animals in terms of suffering, pain and distress is justified by the expected outcome, taking into account ethical considerations and the expected benefit to human beings, animals or the environment.

Thus, the Act requires applicants to justify the severity of the procedures and the species of animals they propose to use, using a utilitarian approach. They must also sign a declaration to the effect that no alternatives will achieve the objectives of the project. Regarding the special relationship humans have developed with some species of animals, Schedule 2B provides that cats, dogs, non-human primates or equidae are not permitted to be used unless there is proof that no other species will be suitable. In 2022, only 0.97% of procedures were carried out on these specially protected species, which the Home Office stated was around 15,000 procedures (Home Office, 2023).

As stated above, the 2010 Directive introduced the publishing of non-technical summaries under Article 43 to increase the transparency of research conducted with live animals. This is important to avoid duplicate research studies and for the public to understand what studies they are financing (Hadley, 2011). The UK was doing this before the Directive, with approximately 400 abstracts a year published under a voluntary scheme (UK Gov. 2012). Though Article 43 requires publication of the summaries, there was a waiver in Article 37(2), which member states could include in their domestic law. Although there were many calls not to include this waiver in UK domestic law, the UK government transposed Article 37(2) as it stood (Home Office, 2012). Sometimes, however, these findings are not detailed enough or an exemption is used to avoid publishing the summary. David Thomas (2005) has outlined how research is usually published where it is found to be advantageous; there are no negative findings, and they often do not outline the animal suffering involved.

To determine if experiments have been carried out appropriately, it is possible to submit a Freedom of Information (FOI) request under the Freedom of Information Act (2000) (FOIA), which can be used to ascertain whether the Home Office has issued appropriate licences and that the procedures were carried out in line with the licence requirements. However, under s.44 of the FOIA, public authorities are prohibited from disclosing information if it is prohibited by another law. Animals used in scientific procedures are covered in s.24 of ASPA, which can be withheld by the Home Secretary, even when there is no objection from the provider for disclosure. The most commonly used exemptions of a FOI request are found in s.38 of FOIA, which exempts disclosure that would or would be likely to endanger the physical or mental health of an individual or the safety of an individual, and s.43 of FOIA exempts disclosure where the information constitutes a trade secret. These exemptions are used because, as outlined above, researchers have historically faced threats from animal activist groups, and research can contain commercial interests in need of protection.

These legal exemptions were argued in the case of *BUAV* v. *Newcastle University* (2010), where a FOI request was made for information on two project licences that allowed procedures in non-human primates. Newcastle University refused to release the requested information, citing s.38 and s.43 of FOIA and s.24 of ASPA, and BUAV complained to the Information Commissioner. The case was decided in the university's favour, and BUAV pursued this through the court. The First-Tier Tribunal agreed with Newcastle University, but it was held on appeal that s.24 did not apply and sent back to the First-Tier Tribunal for consideration. They maintained that the exemptions did not apply to all the information held and ordered the requested information to be disclosed with some redactions. The cost to Newcastle University was £250,000 in legal fees over three years, which they complained about in evidence to the Justice Committee during the post-legislative review of FOIA. BUAV responded that the cost was justifiably awarded against Newcastle University, as they had decided to dispute the FOIA (House of Commons, 2012). Cruelty Free International has continued these cases, one more recently with Imperial College London. Thomas (2017, p. 34) states that although the importance of s.38 is appreciated, 'it is all too easy for public bodies operating in controversial areas such as animal experiments to claim concern about safety and refuse to disclose information for that reason'.

There are clearly issues with the implementation of s.24 of ASPA. The National Anti-Vivisection Society (2013, p. 1) has previously outlined how s.24 has 'handicapped open public debate and wider scientific and ethical scrutiny of the use of animals in research, understandably contributing to public mistrust of government officials and those licensed to experiment on animals'. They further allege that s.24 did not comply with the 2010 Directive, which creates a requirement of transparency, and FOIA, which was introduced after ASPA, and means s.24 is now redundant. This has been reflected in the international Animal Protection Index rating for the UK, where it was awarded a 'C' (the highest standard being an A and the lowest a G) for protecting animals used in scientific research (API, 2024). This is compared to countries that have been awarded an 'A' for animals used in experimentation, such as Sweden and Denmark, which do not have a provision equal to s.24. The main reason cited by API is s.24 of ASPA, which they highlight makes the assessment of the effectiveness of ASPA difficult and recommend that it be repealed.

In 2014, the UK government undertook a consultation on whether to amend or repeal s.24, with the preferred option of the Home Office being to repeal the section but amend the legislation to include statutory prohibitions on the disclosure of information relating to specific people, places and intellectual property. This, they argued, would protect those involved and commercial rights (Home Office, 1986). Unfortunately, a response to the consultation was never released, and no further progress has been made despite continued calls to do so (Nature Watch Foundation, 2017).

The primary sanction under the Act is the removal of either the project or personal licence if the condition of the licence is breached, or if the Secretary of State deems it appropriate (s.11). The licence-holder is entitled to make representations if they are informed their licence is to be revoked (s.12). The Act also provides for the imprisonment and/or fining of up to two years if an offender is convicted on indictment.

The Animals in Science Committee (ASC), which replaced the APC, is tasked with 'providing impartial, balanced and objective advice' to the Home Office minister on matters relating to ASPA (Home Office, 2024). Under s.20, their functions include 'provid[ing] advice to the Secretary of State and Animal Welfare and Ethical Review Bodies on such matters relating to the acquisition, breeding, accommodation, care and use of protected animals as the Committee may determine or as may be referred to the Committee by the Secretary of State.' Therefore, the ASC has the power to report on any matter relating to the operation of the Act or as directed by the Home Secretary, which is unchanged from the APC. Examples of their functions and recommendations range quite widely, as illustrated in the following small number of instances from the APC/ASC:

- In chapter three of the 1992 report, the committee recommended the extension of the Act to cover cephalopods due to the evidence of pain and suffering noted in these animals (HMSO, 1993). This was implemented by an order that came into effect on 1 October 1993 extending the Act to cover *Octopus vulgaris* and was a remarkable change given that evidence was inconclusive and based on 'doubts'.
- They have regularly shown concern regarding the number of 'inadvertent infringements' due to a lack of understanding generally or the ignorance of new staff.
- Examples of continuing or specific areas of concern examined by the APC/ASC include the use of primates in research, the use of animals in toxicity testing and the reviewing the cumulative severity of suffering.

- Reviewing non-compliance with the Act and publishing 'lessons learnt' to help other establishments maintain standards set in law. They have published on infringements and to what extent information should be in the public domain.

How the new Animal Sentience Committee (detailed in Chapter 3) will work with other committees, such as the ASC, is yet to be seen. The Animal Sentience Committee's (2021) terms of reference state:

> In order to maximise its value-added, the Committee will likely be expected to take into account the extent to which some policy decisions are already subject to other scrutiny arrangements involving other bodies in respect to their impacts on animal welfare. For example, recognising existing advisory bodies and scrutiny mechanisms, such as the Trade and Agriculture Commission and the *Animals in Science Committee,* avoiding duplication of their functions [emphasis added].

It would seem, therefore, that the Animal Sentience Committee may also scrutinise policy alongside the ASC but will not where it will cause duplication. The recognition of animal sentience in law has been highlighted by Browning and Veit (2022) as the key component of animal welfare and should affect legislation by requiring 'scientists to develop ways of measuring subjective animal welfare as a consciously experienced state', which can impact their use and care in research. Therefore, it may be unlikely that the Animal Sentience Committee will publish reports on animals used in science. If it does, and if it is contradictory advice from the ASC, it is unclear which report or advice the government will follow.

Overall, the new legislation covering sentience is welcome, although the full effects will only emerge over time. The remaining sections of this chapter look more closely at whether the law has, overall, been effective and what further changes could be made to improve the protection of animals used in scientific research.

Has the law been effective?

It is difficult to say how effective ASPA has been due to the secrecy surrounding animal experimentation and the publication of types of research and outcomes of inspections. The only way, it seems, to determine whether the Act has been effective is by considering known outcomes such as the published numbers of animals used and the number of investigations and prosecutions for non-compliance with the Act. That does not, however, tell us much about the detail, as many technical reports and reports from bodies such as the Animals in Science Regulation Unit (ASRU) and Home Office provide only anonymised and amalgamated data, which makes it difficult to draw strong conclusions.

The number of animals used

One of the aims of the EU Directive and ASPA is to promote the Three Rs in order to use fewer animals in experiments. However, from looking at the statistics, this does not yet appear to have been achieved. Due to prior membership in the EU and reporting requirements under the 2010 Directive, accurate numbers are available of animals used in experiments across different member states. For example, in 2017, the UK used 2.57 million animals in research compared to Germany with 2.06 million, France with 1.91 million, the Netherlands with 477,550, and Portugal with 52,370 (European Commission, 2017a). In 2017, the UK used more animals in research than any other EU country and, along with Germany and France, made up 60% of animals used in the EU. Since the new Directive came into force, the number of animals used in experiments has stayed relatively stable, even with the inclusion of the Three Rs in the Directive, which attempted to reduce them. The UK, however, has reduced its numbers slightly since incorporating the Directive into ASPA, with 3.16 million animals used in 2015 compared to 2.57 million in 2017. This was the largest drop in the EU and has not been matched by other countries, such as Portugal, where numbers have increased.

Figures for 2022 in the UK (Home Office, 2023) show that 2.76 million procedures were carried out using live animals. There appears to be a steady decrease in the number of animals used in experiments since the introduction of the Directive, with a slight peak at the onset of the COVID-19 pandemic, presumably due to the search for a vaccine. It is difficult to know why numbers have been decreasing, as there is no reporting on how many experiments used alternative models rather than live animals, nor how many licences were rejected and why. Other information emerges from summaries published since the introduction of the legal requirement under the Directive, in an attempt to increase transparency of research (Home Office, 2023a), but there is also waiver of the summaries under Article 37(2). These summaries include details such as the number of animals to be used, justification for the species being used taking account of their sentience, a harm-benefit assessment, what will happen to the animals at the end of the experiment, and consideration of the Three Rs.

These are produced by the researchers, and it has been suggested that they may be prone to overestimate the benefits of the research and underestimate the severity limits animals would endure (CFI, 2015). However, it is difficult to draw any firm conclusions on whether the newly amended legislation is working.

One of the main concerns for lobby groups since the UK left the EU is the loss of intra-EU member data sharing. Regulation (EC) No. 1907/2006, which concerns the Regulation, Evaluation, Authorisation and Restriction of Chemicals (REACH), applies to all substances manufactured in or imported into the EU of one metric tonne or more. The main aim of REACH is to protect human health and the environment from the risks caused by chemicals. It also promotes the Three Rs through a central database and the sharing of results of all chemical substances and submits the results of any testing on animals.

The European Chemical Agency (ECHA), which oversees the operation of REACH, has made it clear that any studies on animals with reliable results must not be repeated and new tests may only be carried out where registrants 'have exhausted all other relevant and available data sources' (ECHA, 2024). ECHA also organises training sessions on alternative models to using animals, publishes advice and has made software available to companies to help identify relevant data.

Since Brexit, the UK has lost access to the REACH database, which can potentially cause an increase in animal testing by risking the unnecessary duplication of animal research (McCulloch, 2019a). It has been suggested that this could 'slow down progress' already made in the development and use of non-animal methods (Dunn, 2021). To combat this, the government created UK REACH, which 'grandfathered' the introduction of REACH into the EU, but only where UK registrants own the test data. The fallout is that the UK has lost access to a large database. The UK government also included a clause in an environmental bill that provided a commitment to reduce the number of animals used in research within the scope of REACH, with targets for reduction set by the Secretary of State until the situation is resolved. However, the proposed clause did not make it into the final version of the Environment Act 2021. Without these targets, there is no statutory target or firm duty placed on the Secretary of State, and annual statistics will need to be monitored closely to determine how much of an impact the loss of access to the EU REACH agreement has had. There have been some immediate issues resulting from the loss of EU REACH when the Home Office allowed for the testing of chemicals used in cosmetics on animals, where the data from EU REACH was lost. CFI sought a judicial review challenging the Home Office granting licences for such procedures, arguing several points, including that the policy had been unlawfully changed without communication or consultation and licences granted without a harm-benefit assessment carried out on a case-by-case basis. It was held that the Home Office should have maintained its policy and that it had to apply the harm-benefit assessment in each case. The judge also criticised the lack of transparency from the Home Office in the change of policy, stating the Home Office knew it would be politically unpopular and against the expectations of the public, though this was not a breach of their legal duties. Following this finding, the Home Office has now reinstated the ban relating to chemicals exclusively used in cosmetics (*The King on the application of Cruelty Free International* v. *Secretary of State for the Home Department* [2023]).

Investigations and prosecutions

Even since the passage of the 1986 Act, control of the use of animals in experiments has faced much scrutiny from anti-vivisection groups and has been reviewed on several occasions. Before its replacement, the APC referred many times in its annual reports to the inadequacy of their budget to fund research into alternatives, and, perhaps more seriously, they occasionally criticised the rejection of their recommendations by the Home Office.

At an institutional level, the operation of the 1876 and 1986 legislation has had little impact on the opening up of reporting and scrutiny, with only a handful of individual reports of infringement or bad practice alongside a general lack of recording of infringements under the newer Act. Some welfare groups saw this as one of the reasons that local ethics committees, introduced in the UK in 1999, would be an essential addition to the UK system. However, the requirement for a balanced membership of these committees and their effectiveness remains unproven.

The Home Office has stopped reporting infringements in their annual report since 2005, with this data now published by the ASRU Annual Report. The most recent report covering the period of 2019–2020 shows that in 2019 there were:

- 115 cases of non-compliance (involving a total of 21, 242 animals)
- 92 cases (involving a total of 2,692 animals) in 2020, and
- 112 cases (involving a total of 4,519 animals) in 2021.

Remedies against the institutions or individuals included inspector advice, letters of reprimand, retraining and suspension and compliance notices. During this time period, only five licenses were revoked (Home Office, 2022).

There have been no known prosecutions under the Act, despite annual reports detailing instances of many breaches of the legislation (Animal Protection Index, 2024). The ASRU is responsible for enforcing the Act and has published details of compliance investigations regarding animal testing since 2014 in the 'interests of transparency and openness' and to 'ensure that all stakeholders can learn from the outcomes'. There are five reports, all anonymised so that the establishments cannot be identified, with the latest at the time of writing. Of these, only one recommended a referral to the Crown Prosecution Service (CPS), which declined to act, and the reasons for this were not provided (Home Office, 2017a).

The ASRU annual report from the period of 2019–2021 identified a total of 329 cases of non-compliance, relating to the failure to adhere to licence authorities and failure to provide appropriate care, such as food, water and housing. The cases involved more than 28,453 animals, with some animal numbers or species not included in the report because of the perceived risk that it would compromise the establishment. In all cases, no prosecutions were brought, with the most common remedies being inspector advice and letters of reprimand or censure, followed by small numbers of retraining, suspension, compliance notices and revocation of licences (Home Office, 2022). In all the annual reports, dating back to 2011, there are only three noted referrals to the CPS. It remains very difficult to fully scrutinise the operation of the legislation in this area because the data regarding enforcement is at best non-specific and at worst less than transparent.

Governing bodies

For a law to be effective, it requires oversight by appropriate bodies. Whilst the Home Office is responsible for granting licences etc., it would appear to be important that there is a non-governmental, independent body to provide guidance and advice, and to scrutinise emerging evidence. When the 1986 Act was passed, the appropriate body was the APC. However, in the ten-year review of the Act in 1996, the RSPCA and BUAV were critical of the composition of APC members. At the time, membership included people who could certainly be described as supporting animal welfare stances: a member from the RSPCA, a member from the World Society for the Protection of Animals (now World Animal Protection), and the Director of Advocates for Animals. They numbered only three out of the 17 members in 1986, and the committee did not include members from groups that hold absolute prohibition views on the use of animals in experimentation. The group that the APC itself replaced in 1986, namely the Home Office Advisory Committee, was criticised because of its lack of effectiveness. In the House of Lords, Lord Platt said, 'I was on the Advisory Committee for eleven years, and we met only five times and advised on 19 cases' (Tatum, 1988).

The ASC, which replaced the APC in 2013, has a diverse membership ranging from veterinary science, law, philosophy to STEM research. In 2014, the Home Office conducted a triennial review of the ASC, a consultation that obtained views on the committee, its effectiveness in delivering on its terms of reference, and its membership. Overall, submissions tended to support the work of the ASC, which led the Home Office to conclude that the ASC was performing a necessary and expert function and that members should continue to be appointed to the committee based on their individual expertise and not representative of a group or organisation where their judgment could be influenced (Home Office, 2017b). In summary, the ASC appears to have brought some benefits, although World Animal Protection suggests that its membership should include a more diverse stakeholder group to provide a wider variety of views and perspectives, ensuring the perspectives of animal welfare organisations are not ignored.

What is the best way to control animal experimentation?

This section brings together some of the main challenges and themes from this chapter in order to identify areas for legal reform. Firstly, there is a lack of transparency surrounding experiments using live animals, which is necessary for accountability. Secondly, the level of investigations and lack of prosecutions needs further improvement. Thirdly, now that we have formal recognition of animal sentience in law, and in the Animal Sentience Committee, greater consideration needs to be given to animals used in research, particularly those with higher levels of sentience. Lastly, the Three Rs need to be better utilised and encouraged. So how can this be improved, and what is the best way to control animal experimentation? This section will highlight some of the main issues that could be improved immediately to improve control.

Greater transparency

Transparency is important for two reasons. Firstly, if researchers are open and honest about their findings and the impact on animals, it can help to prevent future unnecessary experiments, as results will be more reliable and translatable (Morosan et al., 2019). Secondly, there needs to be public accountability, to inform where research funding is directed and how it is used. The level of secrecy surrounding animal experimentation has caused public distrust in scientists and a lack of understanding of the research process (O'Sullivan, 2006). There has been an attempt to increase transparency through non-technical summaries. There are, however, many waivers to the publishing of these through s.24 in ASPA, and they are anonymised, so they cannot be linked to publications. Severity limit details are also not included, resulting in a lack of information about the harm suffered by the animals (Pound & Blaug, 2016). Further, Thomas (2005) noted that because publications often omit the suffering caused to animals or how this is alleviated, and negative results are often not published, this contributes to duplication.

The best way to drastically increase transparency in animal experimentation in the UK is to repeal s.24 of ASPA so that the public can know and better understand the licensing of animal experiments. It will also increase the scrutiny of licences granted, their purpose and compliance. There was a minor attempt to amend s.24 when a consultation was released in 2014 (Home Office). The consultation put forward the following options:

1. Retain s.24 as it is; or
2. Repeal s.24 and amend ASPA with a new legislative framework to:
   a. Introduce a criminal offence of maliciously disclosing information about the use of animals in scientific research; or
   b. Amend the legislative framework to include a statutory prohibition on the disclosure or information relating to people, places and intellectual property; or
3. Repeal s.24 – meaning all information could be publicly disclosed unless a FOIA exemption applied.

There was much support for repealing s.24, with or without a new legislative framework, with some groups noting that the FOIA now provides the necessary protection that came under Section 24 – meaning it is now unnecessary to have it in ASPA (National Anti-Vivisection Society, 2014). Unfortunately, nothing further came of this consultation, and the government has not revisited the issue.

It is important to note that the lack of transparency in animal research is not an issue particular to the UK. It has been highlighted that applications in Sweden need improvement, with research finding they were mainly not completed properly, with most applications reviewed not adequately covering the harm-benefit assessment and some not even mentioning the Three Rs (Jörgensen et al., 2021). The lack of transparency, or secrecy, surrounding animal experimentation in Sweden has potentially had a negative impact on public trust. However, there is a balance between transparency and exposing scientists to threats or violence against them (Holmberg & Ideland, 2012). Those working with animals may face some threats, and this can lead to 'selective openness' as Holmberg and Ideland call it, but it does not account for the lack of harm-benefit assessments or openness about the consideration of alternatives to live animals. Countries such as Sweden, however, is doing considerably better than some others, according to the Animal Protection Index. For example, both the UK and the US were awarded a 'C' for animals used in scientific research. For the UK, s.24 of the Act has played a large part in this lower score, and another recommendation is the creation of a multi-stakeholder group for the promotion of the Three Rs. Canada, surprisingly, has an 'E' for animals used in scientific research, due to there being no specific legislation relating to their welfare, and the country coming under the general criminal code relating to animal cruelty. Whilst there is room for improvement in the UK, with greater transparency contributing towards that, the fact that there is strong legislation in place is one less challenge to overcome.

To assist with increasing transparency, the APC in 2003 recommended releasing project licences to the public before Home Office approval (APC, 2003). They stated that 'we believe the pursuit of transparency is not about forcing disclosure of matters that have been kept secret but of revealing matters that have remained obscure' (APC, 2003, p. 75). Their recommendations, aimed at increasing confidence in the Act, included making the factors considered during an application review more explicit, providing more opportunities for consultation and comments on the cost-benefit assessment, and providing more 'meaningful information' about the outcomes of the animals used in experiments. They further advocated for the use of external/lay people participating in ethical review panels for licences, to help ensure the integrity of the review process. Pound and Baulg (2016, p. 169) highlight how this would have created a 'genuinely transparent process' and utilised 'the existence of a wealth of valuable, untapped knowledge held by expert members of the general public, animal welfare and protection organisations and animal replacement scientists.' This recommendation has not been adopted, and it remains to be seen whether we are employing the best possible control of animal experimentation with appropriate transparency and scrutiny.

Enforcement

The final question to raise here is whether animal experimentation has been subject to appropriate enforcement. The ASC reports details of non-compliance with ASPA and provides some evidence as to why it is, possibly, difficult to enforce. Their 'Lessons to be Learnt' report (ASC, 2015) was produced because a working group was established to provide advice following allegations of non-compliance and bad practice at a UK university. The report noted failings found by the Home Office inspector, namely: a lack of delivering improvement in the Three Rs, retrospective reviews of project licence holders not being undertaken, inadequate staffing, failure of culture and communication (relying too much on emails rather than face-to-face discussions), and a lack of clarity as to whether the NACWOs were appropriately responding to animal welfare concerns (pp. 1–2). Some of the issues that contributed to this were licence holders not being fully aware of their responsibilities under the Act or having a poor working knowledge of the conditions in the licence. The Home Office inspector, whilst noting some infringements, did not judge them as being involved in unacceptable animal welfare practices. It was found that the Home Office inspector acted properly in the inspection, and the report recognises that patterns of low-level concerns are difficult for the regulator to address. On their own, they did not amount to non-compliance, and no action was needed to be taken, but together, and over time, they may represent systemic failures. The ASC recommended a clear mandate for Home Office inspectors, with further guidance to ensure a consistent approach alongside a review of processes to ensure that risks of non-compliance are quickly identified.

In one of its final acts, the APC published a report in 2012 reviewing what information they believed should be in the public domain when infringements are reported. They acknowledged that the ASRU and Home Office publish some of the data they deem necessary in public reports but made some recommendations regarding the further details that could be released. This included information on the types of establishments, clarification on the classification/gravity of an infringement and how this was decided, why the infringement happened, why actions taken by the Home Office were deemed to be appropriate, and what actions were taken by the establishments. Some of these details are now included in ASRU reports, which are much more detailed as a result. This was a step towards providing adequate information for appropriate scrutiny and oversight to take place.

Encouraging the Three Rs

If researchers fully embraced the Three Rs and worked towards replacing all live animals used in experiments, there would be no need to control animal experimentation. Those using animals in experiments, however, need to take more steps to engage with alternative methods and better education and encouragement to engage with the Three Rs within research teams. The NC3Rs help to promote the Three Rs by providing training, grants for research into alternative methods and online resources for researchers. The centre encourages research that promotes the Three Rs and data sharing to identify further opportunities to replace, refine and reduce the numbers of animals used in experiments. In their latest vision report, they predict the demand for animals in experiments is likely to remain high, and therefore the need for their work to ensure that the Three Rs are properly considered in the planning of research is embedded (NC3Rs, 2015). Their vision for 2025 is that all scientists should understand the benefits of the Three Rs and commit to advancing them in their research. They also suggested that all universities have a framework for supporting the Three Rs, and better standardised objective measures of animal welfare to benefit the lifetime experience of animals and improve scientific quality. There is hope that with continued data sharing, better training and resources, and technological advances, animal experiments will be significantly reduced in the long term (Hubrecht & Carter, 2019).

Two countries that have been awarded a top score in the Animal Protection Index for animal use in experiments are Sweden and the Netherlands. One reason for this is their enshrining of the Three Rs into legislation, as well as the promotion and encouragement of them. For example, the Netherlands National Committee for the protection of animals used for scientific purposes (NCad) released a plan in 2016 to phase out animal experimentation, in some cases as soon as 2025. To reach this goal, they have transition strategies, which include investing in the acceptance of non-animal methods and better use of results from human subjects (NCad, 2016). The coalition government in the UK attempted something similar in 2014 and published a delivery plan outlining how to reduce the number of animals used in research. It included programmes on advancing and influencing the adoption of the Three Rs and promoting understanding about the use of animal models where there are no alternatives. This could be achieved by further supporting the NC3Rs and working with the Home Office to enhance the role of inspectors to help promote the Three Rs in their work. Unfortunately, these plans were not taken forward and have not resurfaced since. Any future government should revisit it as a priority.

In the UK, another positive step in the right direction was the creation of an all-party parliamentary group on Human-Relevant Science, which was formed in 2020. This group brought together Members of Parliament, Lords, third-sector groups and stakeholders. Supported by the Alliance for Human-Relevant Science, their aim was to advance human-relevant sciences in the UK by replacing poorly performing animal tests with human-relevant methodologies. To do this, their objectives included exploring current governmental financial support and funding opportunities to develop new methodologies and making proposals for change in the current regulatory framework. It was welcomed by several non-government organisations, such as CFI. The all-party parliamentary group held various meetings and heard evidence from experts on new research methodologies (APPG, 2020). Their recommendations were relevant, such as advocating for a more rigorous application of the harm-benefit assessment and an introduction into UK law of animal-free science aspirations. Their work may contribute to the advancement of the Three Rs a UK government is willing to consider and implement them..

Animal sentience

The growing recognition and appreciation of sentience has influenced our laws and how animals are treated to some extent. But how does recognising sentience impact animals in experiments? At the moment, it does not seem to have had much direct impact on animals used in experiments. The acknowledgement of sentience led to the addition of cephalopods, the one invertebrate species within the definition of animal, to ASPA in 2012. This was due to their capacity to suffer and feel pain, but they can still be used in experimentation. Recognising sentience goes beyond merely bringing them within the scope of the Act, and further consideration needs to be given to sentient animals. One of the strange aspects of the Act is the animals it gives greater protection to. The UK was the first country in the world to ban the use of the Great Apes in experiments, with the EU introducing the ban in the 2010 Directive. The UK and EU also have special requirements for the use of cats, dogs and horses. There seems to be little reason for this other than they are animals commonly kept as pets and believed at the time of the Cruelty to Animals Act 1876 as 'the most intelligent, and consequently most sensitive to pain' (Hansard, 1987, Col. 1151). We now know that these species are not exclusively intelligent and sensitive to pain, but public feelings towards them have given them a perceived higher sense of sentience and therefore greater protection within the law. For example, research has shown that the top two acceptable animals to use in research are rats and mice (most likely due to the common perception that they are pests), while cats and dogs (common domestic pets) are the least acceptable (Ipsos, 2018). Evidence of sentience, therefore, is not the only factor that affects which animals are used in experiments, but also includes our feelings towards them too (Cuthill, 2007).

The obvious way to realise sentience for animals used in experiments is to more widely adopt the Three Rs, with a specific focus on replacement. The idea of the Three Rs starts with our understanding of sentience (Hobson-West & Davies, 2018), in that we recognise animals can feel pain and suffer, and therefore we should aim to not use them in a way that causes negative welfare states. This, however, is likely to be a slow change, and only those animals deemed to be sentient will be awarded greater protection: the more sentient an animal is found to be, the greater their ethical status, and the more protection they are likely to be awarded (Brown, 2015). As highlighted in Chapter 2, the recognition of sentience comes with biases, both in terms of which animals are more relatable to humans being seen as sentient and those that have the benefit of research carried out to prove their sentience. For scientists, the issue with this is that some species, usually those that are more sentient (or deemed to be more sentient), are closer models to humans, such as non-human primates (Carvalho et al., 2018). There are clear ethical and moral issues with using non-human primates, and Carvalho et al. (2018) recommend adapting ethical guidelines used for human participants. For example, having legal guardians to provide informed consent on behalf of a non-human primate, as an adult parent would with a human child, and restrictions so that those who cannot provide their own consent can only participate if the research directly benefits them. We recognise that they are sentient and similar enough to humans for experimental purposes and reliability of data, yet we do not afford them the same level of protection. The moral dilemma posed by threats, such as a pandemic, is: how do you produce a safe vaccine quickly without the use of animals? This is the as-yet unanswered question that leads to the continuance of such experiments and divides many in the animal welfare lobby. It is an unresolved ultimate dilemma. Perhaps an alternative way to look at this is, where would we be with properly funded alternatives to animal use? Have humans done enough to freely advance the notion that 'there really is no other way'?

Conclusion

Using animals in scientific experiments is unlikely to cease anytime soon. Our current research cultures and processes simply do not allow for the sudden replacement of all animals in research. Although work is being done to encourage the making and use of alternatives, progress has been slow to drastically reduce the number of procedures carried out on live animals. The law has come a long way since the 1800s, when the first legislation regulating the use of animals in experiments was passed in the UK, but there are still challenges and issues that need to be addressed. The secrecy surrounding experiments, although better than it was with the introduction of technical summaries, is still omnipresent. This impacts public knowledge and understanding of the use of animals in research, and greater education in the area is needed. There is no strong enforcement, and prosecutions of infringements are practically non-existent. Compared to other areas of Animal Law, it can feel as though little meaningful progress can be made for animals used in experiments. With the work of non-government organisations, such as CFI, bringing judicial review cases to challenge their use, there is some accountability. The advancement of science and medicine to benefit both humans and animals is obviously highly desirable, but without appropriate development in non-animal models and technology, the large-scale use of animals in experiments will continue. This is why the Three Rs are so important and need more funding and support, as well as being enshrined in legislation. Current legislation in the UK is sector-leading but, as outlined throughout this chapter, could be stronger. It needs to be consistently reviewed in line with discoveries relating to care and sentience. As Sparks and Brooman (2017, p. 10) say, 'There is a pressing need to set in motion a mechanism for constant review, renewal and modification of regulation according to our expertise and evidence of animal suffering. This is what a nation genuinely committed to a moral view of the status of animals would do.'

CHAPTER FIVE

Companion animals

Introduction

Humans have kept animals as pets for thousands of years. It is a universal institution across all countries and almost all cultures. For pet ownership to have existed for so long and across all countries suggests it must provide significant advantages to humans. Are the advantages only for humans, or do the animals themselves benefit? Does society as a whole benefit from pet ownership? What are the disadvantages? This chapter will start by examining the origins of pet ownership and some of the obstacles it has survived. It will then examine the many advantages of pet ownership, especially for human physical and mental health. However, these need to be balanced against the disadvantages that can exist for the animals, for humans and the environment.

The risk of harm to animals kept as pets demonstrates the need for laws to protect them as vulnerable sentient beings, capable of experiencing pain and suffering. The sentience of animals is a key theme in Animal Law, and the animal welfare legislation in England is used to illustrate how laws can protect companion animals from harm. As in many countries, the law in England adopts a welfare approach. This means it is legitimate to use animals for human benefit, even where it may cause detriment to the animal, but animals are protected from unnecessary suffering. Protection from cruelty is a minimum baseline, and given the lifelong dependency of pets on humans, laws are needed to impose a positive duty on those responsible for the animal to meet their welfare needs. Once again, the legislation in England will be used to illustrate how this can be achieved.

A key theme arising from the law relating to companion animals is their legal status. Pets are deemed property in law, and as property, they can be bought, sold and gifted. It also means they can be humanely killed by their owners, even when healthy. As sentient beings that have feelings and can experience pain and pleasure, the legal status of domestic animals as property creates challenges, especially in the context of pets, because many people form close bonds with their companion animals. Some people perceive their companion animals as family members. Sharing an owner's home, even private and intimate spaces like their bedroom and bed (many cats and dogs sleep on their owner's bed), shows the unique nature of the human-companion animal relationship. This chapter will consider whether the law is out of sync with reality in treating companion animals as property. It will use three case studies: pet custody disputes, pets in rental housing and the abduction of pets, to examine some of the wider implications of the property status of pets. It will also consider if there are alternative ways to legally classify the human-companion animal relationship to better acknowledge its unique nature.

Defining companion animals

There is no definitive list of animals that can be kept as pets. There are particular species that are commonly kept as pets, such as dogs, cats, rabbits, guinea pigs, hamsters and mice, but there are also exotic animals, such as snakes, iguanas, spiders and turtles. Wild animals, such as primates, may also be kept as pets. Usually, pets live in our homes but some may live outside the home, such as a horse kept in a field or stable. There is no consensus on the terminology to use for this category of animals. Recent years have seen a shift from 'pet' to 'companion animal'. The more traditional terms 'pet' and 'owner', which reflect human ownership and dominance are being replaced with 'companion animal' and 'guardian' to better reflect the changing human-companion animal relationship (Huss, 2003). For example, in 2003, San Francisco in the United States amended its municipal codes to adopt the phrase 'pet guardian' instead of 'pet owner'. Campaigners for the change argued that the term guardian promotes greater responsibility and respect for the animals (AVMA, 2023).

DeMello (2012) uses the spatial distribution of animals as a vehicle for understanding how we incorporate animals into our society. In this way, companion animals are those that have been incorporated into the human domestic space, our homes. The link between homes and companion animals is vital, however, this definition is too wide, as not all animals living in the domestic space may be seen as companion animals. Working dogs may spend time in the home but are mainly kept for their ability to work and contribute economically. According to Serpell and Paul (1994, p. 129), 'The word pet is generally applied to animals that are kept primarily for social or emotional reasons rather than economic purposes'.

This chapter focuses on animals kept primarily for social or emotional reasons. The terms 'companion animal' and 'pet' are used interchangeably as appropriate but with a preference for the former.

The importance of the social category of an animal in law

The scholarly discipline of human-animal studies examines the interactions and relationships between human and non-human animals. It seeks to understand how animals are socially constructed. Once an animal is incorporated into the human social world, it is assigned a category, usually based on how it is used by humans. This social category is more important than the biology of the animal in determining the status and treatment of the animal both morally and legally. For example, a rabbit's biology classifies it as a member of the species *Oryctalygus cuniculus*, but the treatment of the rabbit under English law (as in many countries) depends upon its use: is it a pet rabbit? (protected by the Animal Welfare Act (AWA) 2006); or a rabbit bred for meat? (in which case, the Welfare of Farmed Animals (England) Regulations 2007 also apply); or is it a rabbit used in scientific procedures as an experimental test subject? (which would exclude the AWA 2006 and instead apply the Animals (Scientific Procedures) Act (ASPA) 1986); or is it a wild rabbit? (which is deemed a pest and generally excluded from the protection of the law unless under the permanent or temporary control of a human). Consequently, it is the social category bestowed upon the rabbit that determines its treatment under the law. As DeMello (2012, p. 10) observes, 'Animals' physical identity is less important to their status and treatment than their symbolic identification and their social meaning'. This use-based protection is a key theme in Animal Law. The extent of the legal protection a specific animal enjoys depends upon the social category given to that individual animal by humans.

In addition to how humans 'use' a particular animal, for example, as a companion, as meat, as entertainment, or as an experimentation subject, the 'relationship' the animal has with people can influence an animal's legal protection. The fact that humans have very close and personal relationships with their companion animals can give greater legal protection to specific species. For example, special consideration is given to cats and dogs under the legislation in England governing the use of animals in scientific procedures. It is more difficult to obtain a licence to experiment on dogs than rabbits, even though both are species commonly kept as pets in England. The nature of the bond between humans and their cats and dogs can be very strong, with these animals being perceived as family members or close friends. Recognition of this close bond has led to greater legal protection for all cats and dogs, even those not kept by humans as pets.

The history of pet ownership

Domestic animals, including companion animals, are deemed property in law. The origin of this legal status as property is thought to lie in the domestication of animals and the move from hunter-gatherers to pastoralists. The beginnings of livestock husbandry are dated approximately 9000 years ago, starting with sheep and goats, but our relationship with dogs is much older (Clutton-Brock, 1994). The conventional view is that humans first domesticated their hunting partner, wild wolves, 10–20,000 years ago; however, some suggest it was much earlier, approximately 100,000 years ago (Morrell, 1997). Using selective breeding to encourage the characteristics we desired – playfulness, subservience, dependence – dogs are the creation of humans. Beck and Katcher (1996, p. 176) suggest that 'Our affection for dogs may simply be a way of expressing the love that a creator has for his or her creation'. They hypothesise that 'the relationship between dogs and people is rooted in the evolution of both'. Given the long history we have with dogs, it is not surprising that they are a popular pet, with 13.5 million pet dogs in the UK in 2024 (UK Pet Food, 2024). The first evidence that a dog may have been a pet was found in Israel in 1978. A grave contained two skeletons buried together 12,000 years ago: an elderly human and a 5-month-old domestic dog. The person presiding over the burial 'carefully arranged the dead person's left hand so that it rested, in a timeless and eloquent gesture of attachment, on the puppy's shoulder' (Davis & Valla, 1978, p. 609).

Studies of pets in primitive societies hint at a significant paradigm shift as humans progressed from hunter-gatherers to agriculturists. Ingold (1994) adopted an 'indigenous perspective' to understand our domestication of wild animals. He sought to shed the dichotomies of 'wild versus domestic' and 'nature versus humanity' traditionally used in the West to tell the story of the history of our relationship with animals and instead sought to understand the nature of the relationship between hunter-gatherers and animals from the perspective of the indigenous people themselves. From their perspective, the natural world is not separate from and inferior to, the human world. It does not have to be conquered or controlled. Instead, animals are fellow inhabitants of the same world as humans.

Serpell (2000) observes much consistency across studies of hunter-gatherer societies who view animals as rational, sentient and intelligent beings with spirits or souls that can survive the body after death. For example, the Cree Indians of Northern Canada believed that animals intentionally presented themselves to the hunter to be killed, and on death, the soul of the animal was released to become flesh again. The hunter must be respectful and not wasteful, or the animal will remember the transgression and not present itself in the future. This view meant that the success of the hunter depended on establishing a continuing relationship with the hunted animals. According to Ingold, this relationship was based on trust. For him, 'The essence of trust is a peculiar combination of autonomy and dependency' (Ingold, 1994, p. 13). The hunter is dependent on the animal and takes a risk that the animal, as an autonomous being, will act in the interests of the hunter and present itself to be killed. In return, the hunter is respectful of the animal.

However, this egalitarian moral ideology was clearly incompatible with the shift to agriculture and the domestication of farm animals for meat. According to Ingold, the relationship the pastoralist has with animals is based on dominance not trust. Serpell (2000, p. 116) agrees that the 'ideological difference between hunters and herdsmen primarily involves a shift from human-animal relations based on trust to those based on domination'. The agricultural animals are selectively bred to be dependent on humans and therefore cannot exercise their own free will to present themselves to die. The animals have no control over their lives. This significant change created a moral dilemma for early farmers and necessitated seeing animals as objects as opposed to subjects worthy of respect. Ingold (1994, p. 6) argues that 'Domestication can be said to exist when living animals are integrated as objects into the socio-economic organisation of the human group'. Thus, the advent of animal domestication was dependent not just on biology but also on culture. Biology has enabled humans to adopt artificial selective breeding techniques to modify animals into what we want, and culture has enabled us to own animals as property through the development of law and government.

Arluke has explored the conflict in the treatment of animals in contemporary society – the fact that we shower our pets with love and treat them as one of the family but exploit and kill other domestic animals as utilitarian objects. He observes that, 'As with any cultural contradiction, these attitudes are built into the normative order, itself perpetuated by institutions that provide ways out of contradictions by supplying myths to bridge them and techniques to assuage troubled feelings' (Arluke, 1994, p. 145). In this way, our legal institutions that objectify domestic animals as property, serve to justify our use of animals, especially the animals we eat, and relieve any associated guilt. The property status of domestic animals may therefore be seen as a societal coping strategy to defuse the conflict we feel in exploiting sentient beings, especially farm animals. This conflict is less apparent with our companion animals because the majority of people treat their pets well.

Historically, our relationship with pets has been complex, with diverse influences coming into play over the years, such as religion, philosophy and culture. As an example and to show the diversity of influences on our relationship with pets, we can consider hunting and witchcraft in England. Firstly, the positive effect of hunting with dogs was that it strengthened the bond between people and dogs. In medieval times, the European church enjoyed a powerful position, and it had an open aversion to pet-keeping (Thomas, 1983). In fact, all monotheistic religions, not just Christianity, recognise humans as being superior to animals. Therefore, the move to domesticated farm animals and agriculture, together with Ancient Greek philosophy and major religious teachings, all promoted the concept of the supremacy of humans over animals. From this background, Menache (2000, p. 45) asks, 'When and how did medieval people abandon their comfortable status of absolute ruler over nature – which was accorded to them by divine will – and, exercising their free choice and acting in open defiance of theological tenets, place themselves close to dogs, to the point that they turned canines into their 'best friends'?' Menache argues that hunting in the late Middle Ages in Europe was an important step in the evolution of keeping dogs as pets. She identifies the 'ennoblement' of hunting that differentiated the nobility from the lower classes as a key influence. Laws were used to restrict hunting and the ownership of hunting dogs to the nobility; for example, in 1066, the council at Winchester made it a crime for commoners to keep greyhounds.

However, the concept of pet keeping suffered a significant setback in England during the 16th and 17th centuries, when witchcraft hunts made keeping pets dangerous. Legislation was passed in England creating the crime of 'necromancy' and the concept of a witch's familiar (in the form of animals, usually cats and dogs) was introduced. Serpell and Paul (1994, p. 134) observe, 'It was claimed that people were debased or dehumanized by the act of co-habiting on such egalitarian and intimate terms with animals'. A relationship with domestic animals based on domination and superiority was acceptable, for example, working horses or pigs kept for meat, but a relationship with a domestic animal such as a cat based on trust and equality was perceived as dangerous and consequently demonised.

Religious authorities discouraged people from keeping pets, and up until the 18th century, there were few pets except amongst the nobility. However, England underwent a transformation of its human-animal relationship in the 19th century. It went from being a nation that normalised visible cruelty to animals in popular forms of mass entertainment like bull-baiting, dogfighting and cockfighting, to being a nation of animal lovers, initiating the first major piece of animal welfare legislation in the world (The Cruel Treatment of Cattle Act 1822) and creating the Society for the Prevention of Cruelty to Animals in 1824 (later to become the RSPCA due to Royal patronage) to fund the enforcement of this new law. During this time, we see the beginnings of dog shows, with the first recorded in Newcastle Upon Tyne in 1859, with prizes awarded on appearance alone, regardless of the use of the dog (Garfield, 2020; Kean, 2000). The ownership of pedigree dogs became more popular, and the aspirational middle class started buying expensive pets to show their wealth.

The keeping of a companion animal was also seen as useful for the development of children, for them to learn responsibility and morality (Ferguson, 2019). Ritvo's (1994) analysis of attitudes towards animals in 19th-century England highlights the difficulty in understanding human-animal relations using a single narrative. Even today, there is much complexity and diversity in our attitudes towards animals, including companion animals. Blouin's typology of orientations towards pet dogs – humanistic, dominionistic and protectionistic – demonstrates the wide variations in people's attitudes towards dogs, from the humanistic owner who treats their dog like a human, usually a child, to the dominionistic owner who adopts a more hierarchical approach (Blouin, 2013). Such differences are evident in contemporary England, where some pet owners view their dogs as 'fur babies', fuelling the market for expensive lifestyle accessories and dog care services, while others inflict cruelty on their pets. Whatever the obstacles on the way, the institution of pet ownership has existed for thousands of years worldwide. For it to have persisted in this way suggests it must have many advantages for humans and society.

Pet ownership as a socially valuable asset for people and society

There are many disadvantages of pet ownership for an individual owner, including the financial costs of food; veterinary care and insurance; risks of bites, allergic reactions or other illnesses carried by the pet; concern arising from the destructive or anti-social behaviour of the pet; the need to clean up after the pet; time spent caring for the pet, and the significant emotional distress an owner faces when their pet is sick or dies. Pets usually provide no economic benefit to their owner, so given these disadvantages of pet-keeping, what motivates people to acquire a pet, and what does this tell us about the nature of the human-companion animal relationship and its protection under the law?

Developing social relationships

Research shows that pet ownership gives a person the opportunity to form a new social relationship with the companion animal and is a means of extending the person's network of relationships (Rook, 2018). Harker et al. (2000) applied Weiss' theory of relational provisions to understand the motivations for acquiring a pet. Weiss (1974) identified six categories of relational provision that ensure a person has an adequate social life and a sense of well-being (attachment, social integration, the opportunity to provide nurturance, reassurance of worth, a sense of reliable alliance and the obtaining of guidance). Weiss advocated that individuals need to maintain a number of different social relationships to ensure all the relational provisions are met. Harker et al. (2000) used a pet ownership questionnaire to examine Network of Relationship Inventory ratings from two groups of adults: those who were seeking to obtain a pet and those who were not. The study found that participants seeking to acquire a pet had expectations of positive relationship-like provisions – such as companionship, friendship and affection – which they believed would result from keeping a companion animal. This suggests that people acquire a pet to extend their network of relationships. However, what is the motivation to extend the network? Could pets be compensating for inadequacies in human-human relationships? Bonas et al. (2000) used a similar type of survey (based on the Network of Relationships Inventory and Weiss' theory of relational provisions) and found no evidence to support the idea that pets are used to 'plug the gap' where social provisions are lacking in human-human relationships. There is considerable support for the view that pets do not just substitute human relationships but complement and augment them (Serpell, 1996; Beck & Katcher, 1996).

The study by Bonas et al (2000, p. 219), to investigate whether pet ownership can be usefully conceptualised as a social relationship, gathered data on the participant's relationship with their immediate human family as well as their relationship with their pets, so that the data between the human-human relationship and human-companion animal relationship could be compared. They found striking similarities in the nature of the relationships, which adds 'empirical weight to the view that human-pet relationships are similar in nature to human-human relationships and, perhaps more specifically, that the supportive aspects of the two kinds of relationships are broadly similar'. Although the general socially supportive aspects are similar, the human-dog relationship gave higher scores for the attachment, nurturance and reliable alliance sub-scales of Weiss' social support index than human-human relationships, where the scores were higher for instrumental aid, affection and admiration, indicating a subtle distinction in the needs met by companion dogs compared to those met by fellow humans. Weiss advocated that individuals need a range of different social relationships for their well-being, and it appears that relationships with companion animals can play a valuable role in contributing to this variety.

Similar studies have focused on specific population groups. For example, a study that examined the bond between the elderly and their pets identified the most important social provision derived from the relationship as 'attachment, emotional closeness', followed by the 'opportunity for nurturance' and 'reassurance of worth' (Enders-Slegers, 2000). Another study that examined the human-pet relationship amongst people living with HIV in Australia demonstrated that pets benefit the emotional, physical and social lives of their HIV owners (Hutton, 2015). That pets fulfil one or more of Weiss' six relational provisions for psychological well-being is especially important for vulnerable groups such as the elderly, women suffering domestic abuse (Flynn, 2000) and homeless people (Irvine, 2013a). Irvine's (2013a) study of homeless pet owners in the United States identified four dominant narrative themes: the companion animal as 'friend and family'; a 'pack of two' (where the animal is described as meaning 'everything'); the animal as a 'protector'; and finally, the animal as a 'life changer' or 'lifesaver'. In these ways, the animals are viewed as respected significant others who bestow a sense of self-worth, provide a buffer against isolation, and in some instances, become redemptive figures who keep their owners alive or turn their lives around (Irvine, 2013a).

These studies suggest that it is the social relationship with the companion animal that motivates many people to acquire a pet and in anticipation of enjoying positive relationship-like benefits, such as companionship, they tolerate the expense, time and inconveniences of living with a companion animal. Having acquired a pet, research shows that many owners enjoy physical and mental health benefits from the social relationship.

The health benefits of the human-companion animal relationship

In 1980, groundbreaking research discovered that pet owners had better survival and recovery rates one year after discharge from a coronary unit than non-pet owners (Friedmann et al., 1980). Since then, many studies have examined the effects of pet ownership on human health (Friedmann et al., 2000; McNicholas et al., 2005; Friedmann et al., 2013). A recent example comes from a comprehensive study in Sweden, involving 3.4 million people over a 12-year period, which found that owning a dog lowered the risk of dying from cardiovascular disease, especially for single people (Mubanga et al., 2017). The study suggests that it is the relationship people have with their pets and the social support gained from this close bond that is significant to any physiological and psychological health benefits. This growing body of research is relevant to wider society and not just to the individuals affected. It is estimated that the health benefits of pet ownership in the UK may save the National Health Service up to £2.45 billion per year (Hall et al., 2017).

In contrast to this body of research, Herzog observes that those studies in which pet owners are more likely to have specified health 'problems', have been little publicised, thereby over-inflating the actual significance of what he calls 'the pet effect', which is at best inconclusive (Herzog, 2011). However, if it is the 'relationship' people have with their pet that is significant to any health benefits, mere pet ownership alone is not sufficient to test the validity of the claim that pets bring health benefits to their owners; the strength of the bond between the owner and the companion animal, as perceived by the owner, also needs to play into the equation. Hutton (2015, p. 211) argues that it is the owner's perception of support that matters; 'a person's belief in their animal's supportive presence may be sufficient to 'buffer' negative life challenges'. Someone who owns a pet but has a distant, functional relationship with the animal is unlikely to reap any health benefits that come from a close human-companion animal relationship.

Therefore, the evidence that pets provide physical, mental, emotional and social benefits to individuals is strong, but even where the strength of the medical evidence is lacking, it is the individual pet owner's perception of the benefits that is significant. It is not just individual pet owners that benefit; the ripple effects of pet ownership mean it has benefits beyond individual owners to wider society.

The benefits to wider society

Research shows that pet ownership can benefit society in a number of ways; for example, it can strengthen social capital in local communities and it can contribute to a healthy economy. Dogs can act as a social lubricant, facilitating the creation of social networks in local neighbourhoods and helping owners to make links within the community (Bulsara et al., 2007). Charles and Davies (2008, p. 8) observe that 'The social networks that animals help to create and in which they play an active part can be conceptualised in terms of bonding social capital.' Social capital refers to the connections between individuals in a community and the sense of reciprocity and trustworthiness that arise from these connections. A comprehensive study involving 2,600 people in Australia and the United States found that pet ownership increases social connectedness within local communities, creating higher levels of social capital and benefiting the community as a whole (Wood et al., 2017).

Figures published in the UK by the Office for National Statistics demonstrate how pet ownership contributes to a healthy economy through consumer spending on pet products and services such as pet food, toys and accessories, insurance, pet sitting, boarding and daycare, dog walking, animal trainers and behaviourists, and even pet photographers. Figures published in 2022 reveal that expenditure on pets and related products reached an annual value of £9.89 million, which represents an increase of 182% from 2005. Pet care is a thriving industry in the UK, with consistent growth every year, even during the cost-of-living crisis. There is a similar pattern in other countries, for example, the United States. Globally, the pet care market is worth $207.9 billion, with the figure estimated to reach $325.75 billion by 2028 (Martyn, 2023).

In conclusion, there are many benefits of pet ownership to humans and society. The longevity of the institution, lasting many thousands of years, is an acknowledgement of this. However, it is important to appreciate the detrimental effects. This is especially important from a legal perspective because the areas where there is a risk of harm to pets, people or the environment are the areas where the law can play a significant role.

Pet ownership as a philosophical problem

While recognising that living with a companion animal can be socially valuable for human health and well-being and consequently beneficial to society, there is growing evidence that pet ownership can be bad for the animals themselves, people and the environment. The advantages of pet ownership, discussed in the previous section, therefore need to be balanced against its detriments.

Is pet ownership good for the animals?

Pets are completely dependent on their owners in the home to provide nourishment, medical care and a suitable environment in which to live. This dependency, which lasts their whole life, makes them particularly vulnerable. Satz (2009, p. 80) observes, 'Domestic non-human animals are, for this reason, perhaps the most vulnerable of all sentient beings'. This vulnerability means pets are susceptible to abuse. Many people are responsible pet owners and spend considerable time and money ensuring their companion animals are well cared for and happy. However, some pets are subjected to cruelty and mistreatment, which can take many forms, some deliberate, some misguided and some unintentional. Examples include: deliberately injuring a pet, such as hitting or stabbing it; neglecting a pet by failing to feed it or provide appropriate shelter; failing to treat a pet's illness and disease; breeding pets with extreme traits that compromise the well-being of the offspring; training a status dog to intimidate other people or to take part in illegal dog fights; overfeeding a pet so that it becomes obese and suffers problems with joints or internal organs; keeping an animal that is unsuitable for living in a home, such as a primate. This is not an exhaustive list but seeks to illustrate the variety of ways in which animals can be harmed by being kept as pets.

Two examples are considered in more detail below with case studies to illustrate the way the institution of pet ownership can harm the animals themselves. Firstly, inappropriate dog breeding can lead to extreme conformations that can cause health problems for the offspring. Secondly, keeping primates as pets. In each case, the welfare concerns are identified, and potential law reforms to address these concerns are considered.

Dog breeding and extreme traits

Extreme conformation in dogs describes a physical appearance that has been significantly altered from the natural canine appearance by selective breeding practices that prioritise human aesthetic preferences over the health and welfare of the dog (Howe, 2023). An example of this is brachycephalic (flat-faced) dog breeds, such as pugs, bulldogs and French bulldogs. These breeds have become very popular in recent years, with a 3104% increase in French bulldog registrations with the Kennel Club in the ten years up to 2017 (British Veterinary Association, 2018). However, their exaggerated traits, caused by selective breeding, can cause them harm. For example, their skull shape can cause serious health problems such as breathing difficulties, sleep apnoea, eye disease and dental problems, and they can suffer from skin infections and may be unable to give birth naturally (Pratschke, 2017). The British Veterinary Association (BVA) (2018, p. 1) has highlighted this problem, observing that 'The rapid rise in the number of brachycephalic dogs in the UK is leading to a population-based increase of ill health and compromised welfare in these breed types'. Research indicates that owners of brachycephalic dog breeds show 'unrealistic perceptions of good health set against high levels of disease in relatively young dogs' (Packer et al., 2019).

To what extent can the law be used to address this problem? In England, the Animal Welfare (Licensing of Activities Involving Animals) Regulations 2018 concern the licensing of specified activities involving animals, including dog breeding. A breeding licence is required for anyone breeding three or more litters and selling at least one puppy in a 12-month period and for anyone advertising a business selling dogs. There are specific conditions in Schedule 6 for licence holders to satisfy to protect the welfare of the dogs, including 6(5): 'No dog may be kept for breeding if it can reasonably be expected, on the basis of its genotype, phenotype or state of health, that breeding from it could have a detrimental effect on its health or welfare, or the health or welfare of its offspring.' Could this provision be used to limit the breeding of brachycephalic dog breeds given that any breeding is likely to have a detrimental effect on the health of the offspring? Further guidance on the scope of this provision is needed.

Some countries have specifically legislated to ensure that breeders actively promote the well-being of their animals. The Norwegian Animal Welfare Act of 2009 states that breeding must encourage characteristics that promote the animal's good health (s.25). In 2023, the Norwegian Supreme Court ruled that breeding Cavalier King Charles Spaniel dogs was contrary to s.25 and was therefore unlawful *(Dyrebeskyttelsen Norge* v. *Norsk Kennelklubb, Norsk Bulldog Klubb, og Norsk Cavalierklubb [2023];* Eurogroup for Animals, 2023a). The Cavalier King Charles Spaniel breed suffers from numerous health problems, including syringomyelia caused by a small skull, brachycephalic obstructive airway syndrome, which impairs their ability to breathe, mitral valve disease and they are susceptible to ear and eye infections. The Supreme Court ruling only relates to breeding and does not prohibit owning or importing the breed. Nevertheless, the court's decision is a significant step in recognising the need to regulate extreme conformation in dogs and the harm that can be caused to offspring. The court ruled that breeding English bulldogs was permissible provided that the dogs had successfully undergone health screening prior to breeding.

The regulation of dog breeding is complex due to the large number of stakeholders involved (for example, breeders, dog owners, canine fertility clinics, vets, commercial enterprises such as dog shows or those that use dog imagery in advertising), and the financial incentives involved due to the consumer demand for brachycephalic dog breeds. This means robust legislation is needed to balance the various competing interests and to protect and promote the welfare of the dogs.

The recent legislation to regulate dog breeding (The Animal Welfare (Licensing of Activities Involving Animals) (England) (Amendment) Regulations 2019, also known as Lucy's law), put an end to puppy farms in 2020. The new law ensures that puppies and kittens (less than 6 months old) are sold in their place of birth, in the presence of their mother, and not sold or resold by a third party. However, it does not apply to imported dogs, meaning puppies can be imported from puppy farms abroad, and dogs with mutilations such as ear cropping or who are heavily pregnant can be legally imported. Therefore, further law reform is needed to prevent the UK Pet Travel Scheme from being used for pet smuggling purposes.

Keeping primates as pets

Concerns have been raised about the dramatic rise in exotic pet ownership in the UK since 2000. It is not illegal to keep wild animals as pets, but some species must be licensed. According to a 2022 survey of council licensing data in England, nearly 2,500 wild animals were found to be kept in private collections including 'capuchin monkeys, lemurs, mountain lions, alligators, hyenas, zebras, camels, grey wolves, honey badgers and ostriches' (Sample, 2023). The BVA has voiced concerns about the welfare of these non-traditional companion animals. Their survey of vets in the UK found that the majority of owners of non-traditional pets were not meeting the animal's welfare needs:

> Our 2022 Voice of the Veterinary Profession survey found that over eight in ten vets (81%) were concerned that the welfare needs of non-traditional companion animals (NTCAs) were not being met, with the most cited welfare issues being 'irresponsible animal ownership' (82%), 'irresponsible breeding or sourcing' (11%), and 'lack of specialist veterinary care' (10%). Vets who treat NTCAs report that over half (58%) of the NTCAs they see do not have their five welfare needs met . . . Of those vets, around nine in ten (92%) said that the 'need for a suitable environment' was often not being met, and over four in five (85%) felt that a suitable diet was often not provided. (BVA, BSAVA and BVZS, 2023)

Primates fall within the non-traditional companion animals category, and meeting their specialised welfare needs is particularly challenging. The RSPCA estimates that 4,000 to 5,000 primates are kept as pets in the UK (RSPCA, 2014). The Dangerous Wild Animals Act 1976 (DWAA 1976) was enacted to address the 1970s trend of keeping exotic pets, especially big cats. It requires local authorities to administer a licensing regime for some species of animals considered to pose a risk of injuring humans. The schedule of the Act lists the species that require a licence to be kept. While most primate species are listed in the Act, those that are most commonly kept as pets in the UK, such as marmosets, squirrel monkeys and tamarins, are not. In any event, DWAA 1976 is first and foremost public health and safety legislation and covers animal welfare only secondarily. Primates are highly intelligent, social animals that have evolved to live in the wild. A human home environment is unsuitable to meet their complex welfare needs, which include space to exhibit normal behaviours, being reared by their mother, primate companions and mental stimulation to prevent boredom. A House of Commons Environment, Food and Rural Affairs Committee report from 2014 on 'primates as pets' examined the arguments for and against a legislative ban in England on the keeping and trading of primates as pets. The arguments in favour of a ban include:

> Keeping primates in a domestic environment is incompatible with their complex social, behavioural, environmental and dietary needs, as well as their need for specialist veterinary care.
>
> Most people lack the expert knowledge required to care properly for primates, which is demonstrated by evidence of solitary primates being kept in small cages, being fed inappropriate diets, suffering physical and mental abnormalities and needing to be rescued.
>
> Primates have a high capacity to suffer if their needs are not adequately provided for, as they have complex brain physiology and advanced cognitive abilities.
>
> Keeping primates as pets creates public health risks, including the spread of zoonoses and the risk of physical attack. This reflects the fact that primates cannot be domesticated even if they are kept in a domestic environment and bred in captivity.
>
> The keeping and trading of pet primates can be detrimental to

> conservation efforts, encouraging the trapping and transportation of wild animals from their native habitats.

The committee report also summarises the arguments by those who oppose a ban, including:

> Primates should not normally be kept 'as pets' but this does not rule out the possibility of private keepers caring for these animals in a satisfactory manner.
>
> Keeping primates in a domestic setting in isolation and on inappropriate diets is already against the law, so there is little to gain from further legislation or a ban. Animal welfare is more likely to be protected by effective enforcement and application of existing legislation rather than new legislation or a ban.
>
> A wider ban on the trade in primates or on all private keeping of primates would mean that knowledgeable people who keep primates in appropriate conditions would be unable to continue to do so. This would penalise law-abiding, responsible owners because of the actions of irresponsible owners.
>
> A ban on the trade and keeping of primates as pets would force these activities underground and, in doing so, deny pet primates proper veterinary care because keepers could not take the animals openly to a vet to be looked at. (pp. 7–8 and 9–10).

The committee supported a ban in principle but felt a complete ban on keeping primates as pets was a draconian step that could only be based on strong evidence (which it felt was lacking at the time). It recommended that other options be pursued first but did not rule out a ban if these proved ineffective. It recommended the Government commission independent research on the number and type of primates being kept and traded as pets in the UK as the existing estimates were unreliable. It also proposed amendments to the Code of Practice for the welfare of privately kept non-human primates (2013) to address ambiguity and vagueness in its provisions and to include more species-specific details. The committee also recommended a public awareness campaign of the existing regulatory framework.

These recommendations did not elicit any changes in the law until the question of primates as pets was addressed in the Animal Welfare (Kept Animals) Bill 2021–2022, following a Defra consultation in 2020. The

Bill proposed implementing a prohibition on keeping primates without a licence. The licence holder would be required to meet high welfare standards, specified in regulations, to care for their pet primates. When the Animal Welfare (Kept Animals) Bill was withdrawn in 2023, the government announced that it would 'ensure that all primates in England are kept to zoo-level standards, which would in effect ban primates from being kept as pets.' (Defra, 2023). This approach avoids an outright ban but advocates that by raising welfare standards for keeping primates to the level of those required of zoos, it will in effect lead to a ban because private owners will be unable to meet these high welfare standards. In 2024, the Animal Welfare (Primate Licences) (England) Regulations 2024 created a specialist primate keeper licensing regime, which is operated and enforced through local authorities.

Whether this new licensing regime will be effective in improving the welfare of primates kept as pets in England remains to be seen, but whatever its effectiveness in practice, the new regulations ultimately perpetuate the concept of keeping primates as pets. This is unfortunate given the unsuitability of primates to be kept as pets in a home environment. Several European countries have already banned the keeping of all species of primates as pets, including Norway, Sweden, Belgium, Portugal, the Netherlands, Luxembourg and Romania.

This section has looked at two examples: extreme conformation in dogs and primates as pets, but there are many more examples of concerns for the welfare of animals kept as pets. In conclusion, it is evident that many animals are subjected to poor welfare or pain and suffering as a direct consequence of being owned as pets. While many people love and cherish their companion animals and ensure they are well cared for, not all animals benefit from their life as pets. For this reason, animal welfare legislation must exist to protect pets as vulnerable sentient beings. The law in England will be examined to illustrate how legislation can protect companion animals, but first, we explore societal problems that can arise from the institution of pet ownership.

What societal problems arise from keeping animals as pets?

The problem of pet dogs attacking people is one example of societal problems arising from pet ownership. In 2023, the tragic deaths of a number of people by dogs received considerable media attention in the UK (Goodier, 2023). Of the ten fatal dog attacks in the UK in 2022, six were attributed to the American XL Bully. The government response was swift, and in

2024 the American XL Bully was added to the list of banned breeds in the Dangerous Dogs Act 1991 (DDA 1991). It became a criminal offence to own an American XL Bully after 1 February 2024, without a certificate of exemption. The breed is relatively new (only recognised as a breed in 2004 by the American Bully Kennel Club) and it is difficult to define and identify because it is a crossbreed from a number of different breeds.

The problem with a breed-specific approach to a legislative ban is that it ignores the underlying cause of dog bite fatalities and fails to address unscrupulous dog breeders and irresponsible owners. Now that the American XL Bully has been added to the list of banned breed types under the DDA 1991, owners and breeders can simply switch to breeding and training other strong dogs and harness any disposition to aggressive traits. The UK Centre for Animal Law (2023) observes, 'The problem is not necessarily with certain dog breeds, but with the breeding, training and mutilation carried out deliberately to 'weaponise' dogs'.

The DDA 1991 is a controversial piece of legislation, having been hastily prepared following a number of dog attacks by pit bull-type dogs. The legislative process was completed in just four days. The Act is an example of breed-specific legislation that bans specified breeds or types of dogs in the UK (currently the Pit Bull Terrier, Japanese Tosa, Dogo Argentino, Fila Brasileiro and now the American XL Bully). None of these are recognised breeds in the UK, and no statutory definition of the dog breed types is provided in the Act. Identification of the breed type is based on a subjective assessment of what the dog looks like, and the burden of proof is reversed, so it is for the accused owner to prove that their dog is not of a type listed in s.1, DDA 1991. It is an offence to breed, sell, exchange, abandon such a dog or allow it to stray. The Act has been widely criticised as not tackling the underlying causes of dog aggression. The breed-specific ban has not been effective in reducing dog bites, and a study published in 2021 found that hospital admission rates for adults with dog bites tripled in England between 1998 and 2018 (Tulloch et al., 2021). This is because dog aggression is complex, and to take a single approach, focusing on the breed of the dog, is fundamentally flawed. The British Veterinary Association observes:

> All dogs, whatever their breed type or size, are capable of showing aggression. It is important to recognise that multiple factors can contribute to the development of canine aggression and dog biting incidents, including a dog's socialisation, rearing and training, environmental circumstances and human-associated risk factors. (BVA, 2021, p. 4)

It is therefore a complex problem that needs to be tackled on multiple fronts. Using breed to predict aggressive behaviour in dogs is unreliable and potentially dangerous. It unfairly punishes responsible owners and well-behaved dogs; even where a dog's behaviour poses no risk to public safety, the dog may be seized by the police and euthanised purely based on its appearance (Hansard, 2022). Under Section 3(1), DDA 1991, an owner of 'any' dog, or the person in charge of the dog at the time, can be guilty of an offence if the dog is dangerously out of control in any place (whether it is a public place or not). This is a general provision and is not specific to a particular breed. A dog is considered dangerously out of control if it injures someone or there are grounds for reasonable apprehension of injury to a person, whether or not injury actually occurs. Dog attack fatalities is a very emotive subject; however, it is important that legislation to address this social problem is not an emotive response but rather adopts an evidence-based approach that tackles the underlying causes.

There is one detrimental effect of pet ownership on society that has only recently attracted attention, and consequently, there is little academic research in this area to date. It is the detrimental impact of pet ownership on the environment. For many years the concept of 'One Welfare' has recognised the interconnections between human, animal and environmental well-being (Garcia et al., 2016), but there has been little consideration of the negative impact of pet ownership on the environment, in particular how pets harm wildlife and contribute to the climate crisis. Cats provide an example of the detrimental effect on wildlife, as cats kill wild birds and mice. Vettese (2023) notes that 'Cats have extinguished 63 species worldwide.'

One area of negative impact on climate change is pet food consumption. Research suggests that the food emissions for an average dog of 22 kg is 530 kg of CO2 each year (Alexander, 2023). As global pet ownership rises, especially of cats and dogs, so too do the environmental impacts of pet food, with estimated greenhouse gas emissions 'equivalent to the total emissions from countries such as Mozambique or the Philippines' (Alexander et al., 2020, p. 1). In addition to pet food consumption, the environmental impact of plastic pet toys and accessories together with pet transport also need to be considered. A more extreme example of pet transport is a UK-based charter firm that, in 2023, launched a private jet service enabling people to fly with their pets (Gayle, 2023). Given the current climate crisis, the environmental impact of pet ownership will become increasingly important.

Cruelty and domestic abuse

Domestic abuse adversely affects humans, animals and society, so it is examined separately. Research has discovered a link between domestic abuse and companion animal abuse (Flynn, 2009). Pet ownership can exacerbate the negative impacts of domestic violence in the home in a number of ways: Firstly, the institution of pet ownership creates a situation in which the pet is vulnerable to suffering abuse in the home. The abuse of companion animals is a coercive tactic used by perpetrators to control the human victims, motivated by anger, revenge and punishment. Secondly, the victim of domestic abuse may delay leaving the home for fear of leaving the pet behind with the perpetrator, as many domestic abuse shelters will not accept pets (Ramsey et al., 2010). Pet ownership therefore can prolong the suffering of the victim; Thirdly, children may witness violence to the pet, which is distressing for the child and can also create a cycle of violence to animals, making the child more likely to abuse animals in the future. The child learns to react to their own frustration and anger with violence, and this is directed towards the companion animal, being the only one in the home more vulnerable than they are (McDonald et al., 2015; Levitt et al., 2016).

It is a complex situation, and more research is needed to better understand the role of the animal in the dynamics of domestic abuse. However, it is clear that the human-companion animal relationship can be a vital source of support for the victims (Flynn, 2000). Many victims see their companion animals as family members that give them strength and 'a reason to live' (Fitzgerald, 2007). Sadly, this strong emotional bond makes the victims (both human and animal) vulnerable to exploitation by the perpetrator.

What this research shows is that legislation to protect human victims from domestic abuse needs to be extended to include the protection of animal victims. For example, in 2016, the State of Alaska in the United States amended its legislation on domestic abuse to permit the inclusion of pets in protective orders. This allows courts to include companion animals in restraining orders against the perpetrators of domestic abuse, which thereby provides direct protection for the animal itself. More recently, in 2023, the State of Delaware included pet abuse in the definition of domestic violence. It added pets to Domestic Violence Protection-from-Abuse Orders and allows courts to award custody of the pet, for example, from the perpetrator to the victim. The United States is making progress in protecting animal victims of domestic abuse. The National Link Coalition observes that 'The measure makes Delaware the 39th state [in the US] with Pet Protection orders and the 13th state where coercive-control animal abuse is also defined as domestic violence' (The Link, July 2023). Since then, Nebraska has become the 40th state to include pets in Domestic Violence Protection Orders.

In 2021, the UK enacted the Domestic Abuse Act 2021 (DAA 2021). It provides a statutory definition of domestic abuse that emphasises that abuse is not limited to physical violence but can also be emotional, controlling or coercive abuse. The statutory guidance to the DAA 2021 gives examples of controlling or coercive behaviour, which includes 'using animals to control or coerce a victim, e.g., harming or threatening to harm, or give away, pets or assistance dogs' (Domestic Abuse: statutory guidance, Chapter 2, Understanding Domestic Abuse, 2022, para.50). Recognising how companion animals can be used and abused in situations of domestic abuse is a significant improvement in the law. However, the law also needs to provide a means for protecting the companion animal and removing them from the abusive environment, especially if the perpetrator is their owner. The DAA 2021 provides for a new Domestic Abuse Protection Order as well as placing a duty on local authorities in England to provide safe accommodation for victims of domestic abuse, but unfortunately, neither of these measures includes companion animals. Fortunately, some charities provide support; for example, the Dogs Trust runs the Freedom Project, which provides free, temporary fostering of dogs for owners fleeing domestic abuse at home.

In 2023, the United Nations Committee on the Rights of the Child, which has responsibility for the interpretation of the Convention on the Rights of the Child, published General Comment 26 on children's rights and the environment, with a special focus on climate change. The General Comment is legally binding on countries that are signatories to the convention. The committee recognises the negative impact witnessing abuse to animals can have on children. The General Comment states: 'Children must be protected from all forms of physical and psychological violence and from exposure to violence, such as domestic violence or violence inflicted on animals' (United Nations, 2023, Section G, para.35).

Having practical ways to remove pets from the home where they are being abused as part of domestic abuse is an effective way for signatory countries to meet their legal obligations under General Comment 26. Including companion animals in domestic abuse protection orders and giving courts the power to decide on the custody of the pet (regardless of which party has the better claim to the legal title of the animal) helps reduce the risk of children witnessing cruelty to companion animals in the home.

Having identified how animals can suffer from being pets, the next section will consider how legislation can be used to protect them.

The legal status of companion animals as property is a key theme in Animal Law and raises a number of challenges. Property status is at odds with reality given that pets are increasingly perceived as family members. Their property status in law promotes the idea of pets as disposable items and trivialises the importance of the human-companion animal relationship for many people. A forced separation from a companion animal, whether caused by a family split, a covenant in a lease, or theft, can be devastating for the owner and animal, and relegating this to the realms of property loss fails to appreciate the magnitude of the harm caused. An alternative legal framework is needed for companion animals. A relational approach that addresses the legal treatment of animals based on their relationship to humans, for example, as family members, is an attractive option and promises to better protect companion animals given our unique relationship with them – a relationship that leaves them dependent and vulnerable but also elicits very strong emotional bonds between pets and their humans.

Legislating to protect companion animals

Two of the key themes in Animal Law are the sentience of animals and the legal status of domestic animals as property. Given that companion animals are classed as property in law, legislation must exist to restrict the way people can deal with their property. There is nothing to stop someone from breaking the legs of their chair, but laws are needed to prevent someone from deliberating breaking the legs of their dog. It is because the dog is a sentient being with welfare needs that their position is very different to the chair, and this raises questions as to the appropriateness of animals being classed as property in law in the same category as inanimate objects like chairs. Given the sentience of animals, legislation exists around the world to protect companion animals from harm and suffering, and in some countries, to promote their welfare. This chapter examines the law in England and Wales as a case study to demonstrate how legislation can protect companion animals and the challenges that can arise with the drafting, interpretation and enforcement of such legislation.

The Animal Welfare Act 2006 – a case study from England and Wales

The principal legislation in England and Wales relating to companion animals is the AWA 2006. It prohibits certain types of harm, such as unnecessary suffering, to most domestic and captive animals and imposes a positive duty on people to meet the welfare needs of animals for which they are responsible. Many Western countries have legislation that prohibits unnecessary suffering to domestic and captive animals, for example, Sweden (Animal Welfare Act 2018), Germany (Animal Protection Act), US state law (such as Florida Statutes, Chapter 828) and Australian state law (such as Western Australia's Animal Welfare Act 2002). The European Convention for the Protection of Pet Animals is a Treaty of the Council of Europe and has been ratified by 26 countries (Council of Europe, 2023). Article 1 prohibits causing unnecessary pain and suffering to companion animals.

This type of legislation is welfarist, meaning that it seeks to protect the welfare of these animals but does not challenge the human use of animals, even if that use compromises the welfare of the animal. It is only unnecessary suffering that is prohibited; necessary suffering of animals is permitted under the law. Consequently, assessing the necessity of an animal's suffering is a vital component of animal welfare law. Some argue legislation such as the AWA 2006 is really about protecting our continued use of animals rather than protecting the animals themselves. Satz (2009) adopts the 'interest-convergence' principle from critical race theory and applies it to Animal Law, arguing that far from protecting animals, animal welfare law actually asserts our right to use animals and thereby authorises the many ways we harm them. For Satz, animal welfare laws exist only as far as protecting animal interests converge with human interests. Therefore, to say that the purpose of these laws is the protection of animals is fundamentally misleading, as the real purpose is to assert our right to use the animals.

Defining animals within the scope of the legislation

Any legislation to protect companion animals needs to define the animals that come within the scope of the Act. In England and Wales, to come within the protection of the AWA 2006, an animal must be a vertebrate (other than human) (s.1(1), AWA 2006). The explanatory notes to the AWA 2006 (commentary on s.1) explain the rationale for restricting the scope of the Act to vertebrates as being based on the fact that 'these are currently the only demonstrably sentient animals'. Therefore, the rationale for legally protecting animals from pain and suffering is their sentience. This makes sense, but difficulties can arise in identifying which animals are sentient.

There is scope for the definition of animals to be extended to include any invertebrates if scientific evidence shows them to be sentient. Some countries include decapod crustaceans (such as lobsters, crabs, crayfish, prawns and shrimp) and cephalopods (such as octopus, squid, cuttlefish and nautilus) in their animal welfare legislation; for example, New Zealand (Animal Welfare Act 1999), Switzerland (Swiss Animal Welfare Act 2008) and Norway (Norwegian Animal Welfare Act 2009). In the UK, scientific research supporting the view that decapod crustaceans and cephalopods are sentient (Birch et al., 2021) led to their inclusion in the Animal Welfare (Sentience) Act 2022, as outlined in Chapter 2, meaning they are officially recognised as sentient animals for the purposes of this legislation. Section 5(2) of that Act gives power to the Secretary of State to make regulations 'to bring invertebrates of any description' within its remit, and therefore more species of invertebrates may be included in the future. Given the available scientific research, the definition of animal under the AWA 2006 needs to be extended to include sentient invertebrates.

Although the definition of animal under the AWA 2006 currently includes all vertebrates other than humans, Section 2 restricts the reach of the Act to domestic and captive animals. It does not apply to wildlife living in the wild:

> Section 2: An animal is a 'protected animal' for the purposes of this Act if –
>
> (a) It is of a kind that is commonly domesticated in the British Islands, or
>
> (b) It is under the control of humans, whether on a permanent or temporary basis, or
>
> (c) It is not living in a wild state.

Most species of animals kept as companion animals fall within (a); for example, dogs, cats, rabbits and hamsters are commonly domesticated in the British Isles. More exotic species of pets, such as snakes, iguanas, chinchillas and primates, come within (b); They are not commonly domesticated in Britain but are under the control of those humans who are keeping them as pets. Since the three tests are independent and only one needs to be satisfied for an animal to fall within Section 2, a stray cat is a protected animal because it is commonly domesticated in the British Isles even though it is living on the streets and is not under the control of a human owner. An example of a situation that falls within category (c) is where an animal is not commonly domesticated in Britain, for example, a monkey and has escaped from where it is being kept, whether from the home of a private individual or a wildlife park/zoo, and is therefore not under the control of a human owner, but it is not living in a wild state.

Defining which animals fall within the protection of legislation can be problematic, but evidence of sentience is surely the minimum threshold. Therefore, wherever science demonstrates the sentience of an animal, it should benefit from legal protection from unnecessary suffering. However, defining unnecessary suffering is the next challenge.

The offence of unnecessary suffering

There are two main themes to the AWA 2006: the prevention of harm to animals protected by the Act and the promotion of their welfare. There are a number of offences to prevent specific forms of harm: mutilation such as the ear cropping of dogs (s.5), tail docking of dogs (s.6), poisoning (s.7) and animal fighting (s.8). However, within the preventing harm theme the most common offence is causing unnecessary suffering to a protected animal (s.4). This is one of the key offences under the Act and has a long history; the concept of prohibiting unnecessary suffering to animals has existed in England since the first piece of animal protection legislation in 1822 (The Cruel Treatment of Cattle Act 1822) made it an offence to wantonly and cruelly beat, abuse or ill-treat specified animals, including horses, sheep and cattle. The offence under the AWA 2006 has a number of components:

> Section 4: Unnecessary suffering
>
> (1) A person commits an offence if –
> (a) an act of his, or a failure of his to act, causes an animal to suffer,
> (b) he knew, or ought reasonably to have known, that the act, or failure to act, would have that effect or be likely to do so,
> (c) the animal is a protected animal, and
> (d) the suffering is unnecessary.

The concept of unnecessary suffering is a pivotal concept in animal welfare law globally, with many countries adopting it or something very similar. For example, Florida in the United States defines animal cruelty to include 'every act, omission or neglect whereby unnecessary or unjustifiable pain or suffering is caused' (subject to exceptions such as the interests of medical science) (Florida Statute 828.12).

The use of the word 'unnecessary' in the AWA 2006 has a significant impact on the protection given to companion animals. Whether there has been unnecessary suffering is a question of fact. In practice, the judiciary is involved in a balancing exercise, weighing competing factors such as the suffering of the animal, the purpose to be achieved by the actions that cause the suffering, and whether the suffering is proportionate to that purpose. This is a subjective exercise. Recognising this subjectivity in determining the necessity of animal suffering, Radford (2001, p. 242) states, 'That courts may come to different conclusions upon similar facts is therefore an inherent characteristic of the process'. Similar concerns have been expressed in the US, where Schaffner (2011, p. 26) observes that the use of 'unnecessary suffering' means that 'the definition of what constitutes cruelty is highly discretionary'. In practice, the test of necessity is crucial to determine whether an offence has been committed. In England, there are statutory considerations to assist a court in deciding whether the suffering is necessary or unnecessary. These are set out in Section 4(3) of the AWA 2006:

> Section 4(3): The considerations to which it is relevant to have regard when determining for the purposes of this section whether suffering is unnecessary include –
>
> (a) whether the suffering could reasonably have been avoided or reduced;
> (b) whether the conduct that caused the suffering was in compliance with any relevant enactment or any relevant provisions of a licence or code of practice issued under an enactment;
> (c) whether the conduct that caused the suffering was for a legitimate purpose, such as –
> (i) the purpose of benefiting the animal, or
> (ii) the purpose of protecting a person, property or another animal;
> (d) whether the suffering was proportionate to the purpose of the conduct concerned;
> (e) whether the conduct concerned was in all the circumstances that of a reasonably competent and humane person.

Assessing the necessity of the animal's suffering therefore involves a balancing exercise. The court will take all the relevant considerations into account and weigh them against each other to reach its decision. No offence is committed if the suffering is for a legitimate purpose and is proportionate to achieving that purpose. For example, if a pet dog is attacking a child, it would be justifiable to cause some harm to the dog as a means of stopping the attack.

The Section 4(3) statutory considerations created a loophole in the law in cases of attacks on service animals like police dogs. The defendants, who attacked the police dogs, could rely on Section 4(3)(c) AWA 2006 to claim self-defence. This demonstrates the challenges legislators can face when drafting animal welfare legislation, which is to apply in different situations. Wording that may be effective for companion animals may not work so well for domestic animals used in different ways, such as farm or service animals. The loophole led to the enactment of the Animal Welfare (Service Animals) Act 2019 to rectify the problem. The campaign to change the law followed an attack on police dog (PD) Finn in 2016. PD Finn was stabbed in the head and chest with a large hunting knife while trying to detain a robbery suspect. The defendant could not be found guilty of causing unnecessary suffering to PD Finn because of the defence in Section 4(3)(c) AWA 2006, which permits inflicting suffering on an animal to protect a person. The Animal Welfare (Service Animals) Act 2019 (known as Finn's law) ensures that where a person injures a service dog that is being reasonably used by an officer in the course of their duties, they cannot use Section 4(3)(c) AWA 2006 to claim that the injury to the dog was justified. In 2019, the Act was used for the first time against a defendant who, in trying to evade arrest by the police, stabbed PD Audi in the head. The defendant was convicted of causing unnecessary suffering to a service animal under the AWA 2006 as amended.

The offence of unnecessary suffering is a vital part of animal protection law for pets, given their vulnerability to abuse due to their lifelong dependence on humans. However, preventing unnecessary suffering is the minimum baseline of protection. Companion animals are dependent on their owners to provide for their welfare, for example, appropriate food, a suitable environment, social interaction and medical care. Therefore, legislation to protect companion animals also needs to provide a duty to meet the animal's welfare needs. The law in England and Wales took this step in 2006 and created a new welfare offence.

The welfare offence

The AWA 2006 introduced a new positive duty to ensure the welfare of any animal for which a person is responsible. This has the advantage of allowing preventative action to be taken before an animal has suffered. Responsibility for an animal is a wider category than ownership and ensures someone who is temporarily in charge of an animal falls within the scope of the welfare offence. An owner is always regarded as being responsible for their pet even when someone else is temporarily in charge of the pet, for example, boarding kennels while the owner is on holiday. The welfare offence means anyone responsible for an animal is legally obliged to take reasonable steps to meet their needs and provide a minimum level of care. Under the repealed Protection of Animals Act 1911, which preceded the AWA 2006, if an owner was not meeting the welfare needs of their pet, there could be no intervention until the animal was suffering. This was clearly an unsatisfactory situation given the complete dependency of the animal on humans, so the welfare offence constitutes a significant improvement in the law.

In the first 10 months of 2006 (before the AWA 2006 came into force), the RSPCA discovered many animals living in poor welfare conditions: 31,199 animals without access to water; 73,008 animals kept in a dirty or unsuitable environment; and 29,185 animals unable to express normal behaviour patterns (RSPCA). In all these cases, if the animal was not actually suffering, the RSPCA could do nothing to force an unwilling owner to improve conditions. Section 9 AWA 2006 addresses this problem and imposes a positive legal duty to meet the welfare needs of an animal on those responsible for the animal. The welfare offence is defined as:

> Section 9(1): A person commits an offence if he does not take such steps as are reasonable in all the circumstances to ensure that the needs of an animal for which he is responsible are met to the extent required by good practice.

Therefore, a person responsible for an animal is required to take such steps as are reasonable in all the circumstances to meet the welfare needs of the animal. The word 'reasonable' creates an objective standard of care – what steps would a reasonable person take in these circumstances? Section 9 refers to meeting the welfare needs of the animal to 'the extent required by good practice'. For some animal species, Codes of Practice exist that provide guidance on how to meet their welfare needs; for example, the Department for Environment, Food and Rural Affairs (Defra) has a Code of Practice for the welfare of dogs. Failure to comply with a Code of Practice is not a criminal offence, but it can be used in evidence to support a prosecution for a welfare offence.

Section 9(2) sets out the welfare needs of an animal based on the five freedoms that originated in the Brambell Report in 1965:

> Section 9(2): For the purposes of this Act, an animal's needs shall be taken to include –
>
> (a) its need for a suitable environment,
> (b) its need for a suitable diet,
> (c) its need to be able to exhibit normal behaviour patterns,
> (d) any need it has to be housed with, or apart from, other animals, and
> (e) its need to be protected from pain, suffering, injury and disease.

In deciding what is reasonable in all the circumstances, the court can have regard to any lawful purpose for which the animal is kept.

> Section 9(3): The circumstances to which it is relevant to have regard when applying subsection (1) include, in particular –
>
> (a) any lawful purpose for which the animal is kept, and
> (b) any lawful activity undertaken in relation to the animal.

This means that where, for example, a person keeps an Alsatian dog primarily as a guard dog and keeps it tethered outside for long periods, the owner's purpose in using the dog as a guard dog can be taken into account by the court. However, Section 9(3) does not provide an absolute defence. It is one factor to be taken into account and weighed in the balance. An owner cannot justify failing to meet the welfare needs of a dog simply because it is used as a guard dog. An example of this can be found in the case of *Gray and others* v. *RSPCA* [2010] EW Misc 8 (EWCC), which concerned the severe neglect of over a hundred horses. In challenging a charge of failing to meet the welfare needs of the horses, the defendants raised the lawful purpose of the horses as a relevant consideration. The horses were farmed animals, being bred for their meat. The expert witness for the defence, who was a vet (and also a magistrate), argued that the systems for feeding, bedding and cleaning that were used at the farm were reasonable, bearing in mind the use of the horses as food. He argued that the lawful purpose of being bred and slaughtered for meat justified the 'hunger stimulus' feeding regime used by Mr Gray because there is an economic balance to be struck by a farmer. The judge was not persuaded by this argument on the facts, saying that the feeding regime amounted to 'deprivation' and the system of bedding and cleaning was 'deplorable'.

The welfare offence is a vital component of the legal protection of companion animals. Given their lifelong dependence on humans, legislation is needed to ensure owners meet their welfare needs. The European Convention for the Protection of Pet Animals, a Treaty currently ratified by 26 countries, recognised the importance of this back in 1987 with Article 2 creating a duty of care on pet owners to meet the health and welfare needs of their animals. English law provides an example of such legislation, but it is important that the purpose for which the animal is kept is not used to justify a poor standard of welfare. It is not enough that protection for companion animals is written into the statute book; the legislation must also be adequately interpreted and enforced. For example, the European Convention for the Protection of Pet Animals contains no enforcement mechanisms, which significantly impacts the overall effectiveness of the Treaty to protect companion animals.

Interpretation and enforcement

For animal welfare legislation to be effective, it must be appropriately interpreted by the courts and properly enforced by the relevant authorities. Interpretation and enforcement are therefore key themes in Animal Law. Two examples are given below to illustrate challenges arising from restrictive interpretation of statutory provisions by the courts. One example concerns animal fighting, and the other relates to the penalty of disqualification under the AWA 2006.

Challenges arising from statutory interpretation

The AWA 2006 includes an offence of animal fighting. Under s.8, a person commits an offence if they take part in an animal fight in one of many ways; for example, organising or attending a fight, training animals, publicising a fight, taking bets or supplying a video recording of an animal fight. Animal fights, such as dog fighting, can cause animals extreme suffering and exist purely for human entertainment. The RSPCA states that dog fighting is sadly still prevalent in England and numbers are rising (Evans, 2023). Although a ban on animal fighting existed under Section 1, Protection of Animals Act 1911 (now repealed), its scope was severely restricted by the court's decision in *DPP* v. *Barry* [1989] Crim LR 645. This case demonstrates how restrictive interpretation of statutory provisions can leave animals unprotected and at risk of harm. The case concerned badger baiting, and after the defendant's dog was sent down a badger set and injured by a badger, the court held that no offence of animal fighting had been committed. Under the Act, it was an offence to 'cause, procure, or assist at the fighting or baiting of any animal', but the court interpreted the wording restrictively, stating that all the animals involved in the fight had to be domestic or captive for an offence to have been committed. The badger that fought the defendant's dog was wildlife and was not protected under the Act. This restriction was thankfully removed under the AWA 2006, with Section 8 making it clear that the offence of animal fighting includes a protected animal being set up to fight wildlife, such as setting a dog on a badger.

In Section 8(7) AWA 2006: 'animal fight' means an occasion on which a protected animal is placed with an animal, or with a human, for the purpose of fighting, wrestling or baiting.' It is fortunate that the legislature was able to rectify the court's restrictive interpretation of animal fighting, but there is not always parliamentary time for this.

The next example concerns the court's interpretation of sentencing powers under the AWA 2006. Where a person is convicted of an offence under the AWA (a prevention of harm offence or a welfare offence), the court has the power to make a disqualification order. Section 34 explains what a disqualification order does:

> Section 34: Disqualification
>
> (1) If a person is convicted of an offence to which this section applies, the court … may … make an order disqualifying him … for such period as it thinks fit.
> (2) Disqualification under this subsection disqualifies a person –
> (a) from owning animals,
> (b) from keeping animals,
> (c) from participating in the keeping of animals, and
> (d) from being party to an arrangement under which he is entitled to control or influence the way in which animals are kept.

Disqualification can be in relation to all animals or in relation to a specified kind, for example, dogs or horses. The disqualification can be for life or for a specified time, for example, ten years. If a pet owner receives a disqualification order in relation to dogs, it affects all the dogs owned by that person. A person who breaches a disqualification order commits an offence. On paper, this looks like comprehensive wording to protect animals from having to continue living with someone who has been convicted of harming animals.

However, the decision in *Patterson* v. *Royal Society for the Prevention of Cruelty to Animals (RSPCA)* [2013] EWHC 4531 (Admin) severely limits the effectiveness of disqualification orders to protect animals. Mr Patterson was convicted of an offence of animal fighting contrary to Section 8 AWA 2006. A disqualification order was made in relation to all animals. Later that year, an RSPCA inspector visited the home where Mr Patterson lived with his wife and children and found many animals, including ducks, chickens, rabbits and eight dogs. Mr Patterson told the RSPCA inspector he had passed the title to all the animals to his wife, who was now solely responsible for them. The RSPCA inspector believed that Mr Patterson was in breach of his disqualification order because he was able to influence the manner in which these 55 animals and birds were kept, exercised some control over them, and participated in their keeping, especially when Mrs Patterson was out at work and he was alone at home. The magistrates took a similar view, and Mr Patterson was convicted of breaching his disqualification order and his wife was convicted of aiding and abetting him. In addition, they were both convicted of several animal cruelty offences due to the neglect of some of the animals. On appeal, the Divisional Court quashed his convictions for breach of his disqualification order and for animal cruelty. The court focused on the word 'entitled' used in Section 34(2)(d) AWA 2006, which states the defendant is disqualified from 'being party to an arrangement under which he is entitled to control or influence the way in which animals are kept'. Whilst the court accepted that Mr Patterson may be able to control or influence how the 55 animals and birds were kept, there was no evidence that he was entitled to do so.

Patterson v. *RSPCA* [2013] EWHC 4531 (Admin) Mr Justice Blake:

> 21. ... It is not sufficient that you are able to control or influence the way in which animals are kept, you must be entitled to control or influence the way in which they are kept under an arrangement to which you are a party.
>
> 22. The court is conscious of the practical difficulties for inspectors of the RSPCA understandably seeking to police disqualification orders when they will not usually have 24-hour coverage of what is going on in particular premises. Of course, this is an area in which a successful prosecution may be founded on inferences drawn from primary facts whether undisputed or found by the justices to be the case. But this being a criminal prosecution the rule is that before a case can proceed to a finding of guilt by way of

inferences to the criminal standard, the inference must not only be one that can be drawn from the evidence but the only sensible inference, the evidence is inconsistent with any other inference save guilt.

23. It is accepted that there is no direct evidence that Mr Patterson has cared for or was responsible for or was party to an arrangement by which he was entitled to care for any of the animals that he said he had transferred both ownership and responsibility for to Mrs Patterson. Of course, whilst Mrs Patterson is out of the house Mr Patterson would have the opportunity to have cared for the animals, but it does not necessarily follow that he has used the opportunity to do so and if he has not done so, it is difficult to see what evidence there was that he was entitled to do so. There may be cases where the length of absence of any other responsible custodian is such that the justices are able to conclude by process of elimination that the disqualified person must have been the person who cared for the animals: fed them, watered them, exercised them and such like. But the case stated that the justices did not direct their minds to the question of whether there was an entitlement to care for or control the animals, and secondly, do not set out with any particularity why the facts in this case were so strong as to exclude any other inference but that Mr Patterson had at some point during the 6 months before December 2011 done things that he knew he was prohibited from doing. The account given consistently by the couple on initial inquiry, investigation and during the trial was that all responsibility had been transferred to Mrs Patterson and there had been no breaching or crossing of that division by the couple in the months following the disqualification and the visit to the inspectors.

As acknowledged by the court in the above extract, the decision in *Patterson* v. *RSPCA* creates very practical difficulties for RSPCA inspectors in trying to ensure a defendant does not breach a disqualification order.

In *Barker and Williamson* v. *RSPCA* [2018] EWHC 880 (Admin), the court confirmed that the purpose of a disqualification order is to protect the animal and not punish the defendant. However, the effect of Patterson appears to be that someone convicted of cruelty to animals and subject to a disqualification order can simply transfer ownership and responsibility for their pets to another person living in the same house. The court's restrictive interpretation of the wording in Section 34 AWA 2006 is unfortunate as it leaves vulnerable animals living in close proximity to the very person they are supposed to be protected from and makes policing disqualification orders extremely difficult in practice.

Problems with the enforcement

Enforcement of animal welfare legislation can be difficult for a variety of reasons. In the UK, animal welfare issues are a devolved issue, meaning each nation will have their own enforcement strategies. In England and Wales, the enforcement of the AWA 2006 is delegated to local authorities. There are a variety of difficulties associated with this. Firstly, local authorities receive no central funding from the government to enforce the legislation, and with limited resources, many do not prioritise animal welfare. It is unclear how many inspectors are appointed under the AWA 2006 currently, but during the Wooler Review, it was highlighted that just over 60% of local authorities in England had appointed one, with little of this resourcing on companion animals. Of these local authorities, 40% said they would always refer matters concerning companion animals to the RSPCA, which at the moment does not have statutory powers of enforcement (Wooler, 2014). The second issue is when local authorities outsource work, they do not always have inspectors trained in animal welfare and health. For example, in inspections for animal licensing activities, it is common for a trading standards inspector to be sent, who will have knowledge and experience in licensing generally but potentially not animal welfare. This can result in them failing to identify animal welfare concerns.

The RSPCA is currently the main body investigating animal welfare issues and bringing any private prosecutions, particularly those concerning companion animals. This has, however, caused criticism in the past, with organisations like the Countryside Alliance claiming the RSPCA is pushing an animal rights agenda (Countryside Alliance 2017). This criticism led to a House of Commons debate in 2013, which led to the Wooler Review, published in 2014. The review focused on RSPCA prosecutions and provided recommendations for improving their operations. The RSPCA responded positively to the report, but its new strategy to implement its recommendations (RSPCA Strategy 2030) has caused some concern in the animal welfare sphere. The RSPCA has decided to relinquish its prosecution role and hand over prosecutions to the Crown Prosecution Service (CPS) and to focus more on investigations, hoping to gain statutory powers under the AWA 2006.

There have been several concerns raised regarding this decision. Firstly, the CPS may not prioritise animal welfare cases, meaning fewer prosecutions against those harming animals. There is evidence that crimes involving companion animals are not prioritised by enforcement agencies; for example, in the area of puppy smuggling, a report by the Environment,

Food and Rural Affairs Select Committee observes, 'There is evidence that the current rules are not being enforced at the border, making it easy for pets to be illegally brought into the country … Increasing prosecution rates must also be a priority, as prosecution rates are proportionately low given the estimated size of the trade' (Moving Animals Across Borders, 2021). Secondly, even where prosecutions are brought, prosecuting lawyers may not have specialist knowledge of Animal Law, resulting in fewer successful prosecutions. These concerns are not without evidence as the RSPCA statistics show a high success rate; for example, their 2019 Prosecutions Report outlined a 93.7% success rate. In a House of Commons debate in 2013, Caroline Lucas MP highlighted that, at that time, the RSPCA had a 98% success rate in its prosecutions, while the CPS had only a 50% success rate (House of Commons, 2013).

The role of the RSPCA in ensuring the enforcement of the AWA 2006 for companion animals has been vital. The role of having responsibility for both investigations and prosecutions for animal welfare offences has been successful in other parts of the world. For example, the RSPCA in New South Wales, Australia, has statutory powers under the state's animal welfare legislation and also brings any subsequent prosecutions. Unfortunately, the RSPCA in England has not managed to continue this harmony, which could have a huge impact on the future of enforcing animal welfare laws.

Summary of the challenges in legislating to protect companion animals

There are a number of challenges in legislating to protect companion animals. The law in England has been used to demonstrate these challenges, but similar issues can arise in other countries. Firstly, the challenge of drafting legislation so that it provides adequate protection for animals; for example, in deciding the scope of the protection, are sentient invertebrates included? England does not currently include any invertebrates in the scope of the AWA 2006 but given their inclusion in the Animal Welfare (Sentience) Act 2022, there are calls for the definition of animals under the AWA 2006 to be extended (Rook et al., 2023). Secondly, the challenge of interpreting the legislation in a way that provides animals with the best protection possible within the confines of the wording used. If courts interpret the legislation in a restrictive way that fails to give animals the best protection under the Act, it can leave them vulnerable to the risk of harm. Thirdly, the challenge of enforcement means that crimes involving companion animals may not be identified, prioritised or dealt with by those with the appropriate specialist knowledge. Inadequate enforcement is a significant problem across all areas of Animal Law, as was seen with animals used in scientific procedures in Chapter 4 and will be seen when looking at farmed animals in Chapter 6 and wildlife in Chapter 7.

A key theme in Animal Law is the property status of domestic animals, and this is an underlying factor in the three challenges identified above – drafting, interpretation and the enforcement of laws. Property status perpetuates the perception of crimes against animals as being of low importance. Until recently, in England, harsher sentencing for criminal damage to property existed than for animal cruelty. This led to the bizarre situation in 2020 of a defendant, known in the media as the 'Brighton cat killer', being charged with 16 counts of criminal damage to property for horrendous knife attacks on pet cats. Nine cats died and seven were seriously injured (Slawson, 2021). The CPS chose not to charge the defendant with an offence under the AWA 2006 because, at that time, it attracted a much lower sentence compared to an offence of criminal damage to property. Since then, the Animal Welfare (Sentencing) Act 2021 has been enacted, which provides for higher custodial sentences for the prevention of harm offences under the AWA 2006. On summary conviction, the term of imprisonment can be up to 12 months, but the more serious cases can now be tried on indictment in the Crown Court with the availability of a term of imprisonment on conviction of up to five years.

The reform of the sentencing laws was in response to a public campaign to increase penalties for animal cruelty offences and shows how public opinion is often a key factor in improving legislation to protect animals. The public campaign arose following two animal cruelty cases reported widely in the media (for example, Lewis, 2016). In 2016, the Frankish brothers, aged 22 and 19, were convicted of causing their pet dog, Baby, unnecessary suffering. A distressing video of them abusing the pet bulldog circulated on the internet. It shows them repeatedly throwing Baby down the stairs, stamping and jumping on her while laughing and joking. Baby was later euthanised after losing the use of her back legs. The brothers pleaded guilty to causing unnecessary suffering but were not given a custodial sentence. A public petition of almost 800,000 people called for the brothers to be jailed, and in April 2016, an aeroplane towing a banner 'Jail the Frankish brothers' flew over Middlesbrough football stadium while a game was in play (Johnson, 2016). The following year, two men were each sentenced to four months imprisonment after a failed attempt to kill a 16-year-old blind terrier pet dog that belonged to one of the men. The dog was hit over the head with a hammer and had a long nail driven into his skull before being buried alive in a local wood, where he was later found still alive. The sentencing in these cases was woefully inadequate given the seriousness of the animal suffering and caused a public outcry, instigating a change in the law.

This section has examined how legislation can be used to protect companion animals from harm and to promote their welfare. It has identified some of the themes and challenges that can underlie animal welfare legislation. The next section will examine some of the wider implications of the property status of companion animals and the challenges this gives rise to.

The implications of the legal status of companion animals as property

In most countries, companion animals are deemed property in law. This sits uncomfortably with extensive research from across the world that people often perceive their companion animals as family members, for example, in Australia (Power, 2008), Israel (Shir-Vertesh, 2012), the UK (Charles & Davies, 2008) and the USA (Irvine & Cilia, 2017). Defining family membership is complex. There is a set of relationships based on blood ties where there is consensus, such as mother and child, and recognised legal ties such as husband and wife, but there is uncertainty beyond these formal categories. In recent decades, there has been a move away from defining family as a heterosexual conjugal unit based on marriage and co-residence engaged in raising children (the traditional nuclear family) towards embracing the diversity of families, for example, single-parent families, same-sex families and families living across households. This diversity is not a decline or disintegration of family but simply a change to reflect evolving patterns in society, such as shifting gender relations and sexual orientations. Sociologists Silva and Smart (1999, p.1) observe that 'the family is not expected to remain unchanged and unchanging. It is seen as transforming itself in relation to wider social trends, and sometimes it is seen as a source of change itself, which prompts changes to occur in public policy'. If the diversity of families has crossed the species boundary and pet owners are treating their companion animals as family members, could this be the source of change Silva and Smart refer to that prompts changes in public policy and law?

This section uses a case study approach to demonstrate how the law, in treating companion animals as property, is increasingly out of sync with reality. This has led to calls for changes in the law to better recognise and protect the human-companion animal relationship. The three case studies examined here are pet custody disputes, the use of 'no pet' covenants in rental housing, and pet abduction. In each of these areas of law, the property status of companion animals is at odds with the perception of many pet owners who see their pet as a member of their family. Property status fails to acknowledge the strength of the human-companion animal bond and the significance of the relationship to the parties.

In 2023, the United Nations Committee on the Rights of the Child, which has responsibility for the interpretation of the Convention on the Rights of the Child, published General Comment 26 on children's rights and the environment. The General Comment is legally binding on countries that are signatories to the convention. The committee acknowledges the potential positive impact of interactions between children and animals. The General Comment states: 'The development of children is intertwined with the environment in which they live. The developmental benefits of a healthy environment include those linked to opportunities to experience outdoor activities and to interact with and play in natural environments, including the animal world' (United Nations, 2023, Section C, para. 23). This transparent recognition by the committee that the welfare of children and animals is connected has been described as 'groundbreaking' and may represent 'the entry of animal protection into international human rights law' (Pressat, 2023). It may pave the way to use human rights arguments in the future to prevent children being separated from their cherished companion animals in instances of pet custody disputes and/or the use of 'no pet' covenants in rental housing.

Pet custody disputes

In February 2015, the Law Society in England issued a press release highlighting a largely neglected area of family law – disputes over pets. Family law solicitors are being asked for legal advice as to the residency of a pet following a family break up. On the basis of research by the animal charity the Blue Cross, which found that over one in four divorces in England include a dispute over pets, the Law Society recommends the use of 'pet-nups' (pre-nuptial agreements in respect of pets). There is a lack of reported case law in England on pet custody disputes (technically the dispute is over ownership of the pet, but 'custody' is regularly used in the literature), but cases in other jurisdictions demonstrate the difficulty courts face when deciding disputes over pets. The difficulty arises from the fact that pets are a unique type of personal property that is both living and sentient.

Two divergent approaches have developed to resolve pet custody cases in the United States. Firstly, the application of pure property law principles arising from the status of the pets as property. Under this test, custody of the pet is awarded to whichever person is able to prove the better title to the property. Secondly, the application of an 'animal welfare' or 'best interests of the animal' test where the welfare of the pet may lead to custody being given to the person with the weaker property title. In the United States, the law governing divorce is a state matter dependent upon the applicable jurisdiction, and therefore it is not surprising that there are conflicting decisions across states. While in most cases the court attempts to apply a property law test, some decisions show an underlying inconsistency between the court's insistence that animals are personal property and its reluctance to rely on a pure property law test to resolve the dispute. For example, several cases have awarded visitation rights to one of the parties in recognition of the close bond that exists between a person and their pet. For example, in *Arrington* v. *Arrington* [1981], a Texas trial court emphasised that pets are property and refused to apply a 'best interest of the pet' test but nevertheless awarded custody to the wife and visitation rights to the husband. Visitation orders are not normally given in respect of personal property, so the court is acknowledging the special relationship a person can develop with a companion animal.

The case of *Raymond* v. *Lachman* [1999] concerned two flatmates rather than a couple. The New York appellate court overturned the trial court's decision, which had awarded custody of a pet cat to its legal owner – the person with the stronger claim to the property title. Instead, the appeals court considered the age and life expectancy of the ten-year-old cat and allowed it to 'remain where he has lived, prospered, loved and been loved for the past four years'. Therefore, the welfare of the cat trumped the property rights of the owner, demonstrating the willingness of some judges to look beyond a pure property law test to resolve the dispute.

In contrast, in Israel, the courts are willing to apply the 'good of the animal' test to decide pet custody disputes. The case of *Ploni* v. *Plonit* [2004] concerned an unmarried couple who had rescued a street cat and a sick dog. When the couple separated, the woman moved out, taking the animals with her. Subsequently, the man petitioned the court for custody. The court adopted a 'good of the animal' test, and after hearing evidence from an expert on animal behaviour, it decided that both animals remain with the woman. In this case, the judge openly acknowledged the inadequacy of the law to resolve pet custody disputes, observing that 'The concept of companion animals as property does not provide the legal system with tools to adjudicate and resolve the petitions and bring them to a suitable solution'.

What these cases demonstrate is that a pure property law test is not always appropriate to resolve a pet custody dispute because companion animals constitute a unique type of property – property that is both living and sentient (Favre, 2010). Two consequences flow from this recognition of pets as living and sentient property (Rook, 2014): Firstly, as sentient beings, animals have 'interests' such as avoiding pain and suffering. This may lead to custody being given to the party with the weaker property title. For example, in *Juelfs v. Gough* [2002], the Alaskan Supreme Court upheld the award of sole custody of the family dog to the husband even though the wife had the better property title. The wife had moved into a property with her new partner, who had dogs. The family dog was at risk of serious physical injury from her new partner's dogs, and therefore, the interest of the family dog in avoiding physical injury prevailed over the wife's property rights. Secondly, strong emotional bonds can develop between the owner and their living, sentient property, creating a special relationship that can be perceived as akin to family. The irreplaceability of this special relationship means that the dispute cannot be resolved by simply buying another pet of the same breed and type.

Given the difficulty facing the courts in deciding pet custody disputes, some countries and states have passed legislation. In 2003, Switzerland amended its Civil Code to provide a test that considers the interests of the animal, enabling the animal's interests to trump the property rights of the owner. In 2017, Alaska became the first state in the United States to require courts in divorce cases to take 'the well-being of the animal' into consideration when resolving a pet custody dispute. The politician who sponsored the bill cited the recognition of pets as family members as a justification for this change in the law: 'Pets are truly members of our families. We care for them as more than just property. As such, the courts should grant them more consideration.' (Pallotta, 2017). Other states that now allow the courts to consider an animal's best interests include California, Delaware, Illinois, Maine, New Hampshire and New York. In 2023, British Columbia became the latest jurisdiction to enact such legislation.

No pet covenants in rental housing

A second case study that demonstrates how the legal status of companion animals as property is out of sync with reality is the use of 'no pet' covenants in residential rental housing. A 'no pet' covenant is a leasehold covenant (or policy incorporated into the tenancy agreement) that prohibits or restricts the tenant from keeping companion animals in their rental housing accommodation. Research has shown that the problem of restricting pets in housing is a global phenomenon affecting pet-owning tenants worldwide (Jegatheesan et al., 2024; Rook & Jegatheesan, 2024).

There is no reliable data on the scale of the use of 'no pet' covenants in rental housing but their use is prevalent across the sector, for example, in England a government press release in 2020 stated that in the private rental sector 'around 7% of landlords advertise homes as suitable for pets' (Ministry of Housing Communities and Local Government, MHCLG, 2020). Studies conducted in the UK, United States and Australia investigating the reasons for relinquishing dogs to a shelter found that the restrictions imposed by landlords played a key role (Shore et al., 2003; Coe et al., 2014). There are expenses involved when animal shelters and charities need to rehome companion animals so the fact that these animals have families who want to keep them is a waste of societal resources (Stavisky et al., 2012). For the animals themselves, a forced separation raises serious welfare concerns. They face the stress of being separated from their owners, living in kennels, adapting to a new home or, in some cases, the animals will be euthanised (Fox & Ray, 2019).

The character of the human-companion animal relationship as a close, dynamic, supportive social bond that extends kinship ties means that pet-owning tenants suffer serious harm when they are forced to rehome their pets due to 'no pet' covenants. The legal status of domestic animals as property disguises the seriousness of the loss for the pet-owning tenant. Relegating the loss to mere property loss downplays the magnitude of the harm suffered by tenants and encourages the idea of pets as disposable items, permitting landlords to feel it is acceptable to request a tenant to surrender their companion animal to secure housing.

An alternative outcome for a pet-owning tenant is to relinquish their home rather than their companion animal, which can also have detrimental effects on their health and well-being. For example, in 2017, Bob Harvey, an 87-year-old man from Scotland, left his residential care home after being threatened with eviction by the new manager unless he gave up his 10-year-old Schnauzer dog, Darcie, for rehoming (Rook, 2018). Bob and his wife got Darcie as a puppy, and when Bob's wife died, Darcie became his sole companion in the home. The strength of Bob's sentiment towards Darcie is displayed in his words, 'He means everything to me. Everything. He's my life now' (BBC, 2017). For the love of his dog, Darcie, Bob was forced to give up his home, where he had enjoyed the benefits of security, home support, meals and a sense of community with the other residents, and moved to a property in an unfamiliar town where he felt isolated and struggled to find adequate home support.

Vulnerable people are especially susceptible to being disadvantaged by the use of 'no pet' covenants because they often lack choice over where they live. The elderly, mentally ill and homeless are more likely than the average population to need to move into care or sheltered accommodation due to their health and care needs or their personal circumstances. If the accommodation prohibits pets, the vulnerable person is faced with the difficult choice of giving up their companion animal or their housing place.

Research by the National Landlords Association in England shows that the use of 'no pet' covenants by landlords and letting agents is driven by a desire to avoid damage to property or annoyance to neighbours (NLA, 2017). It is reasonable for landlords to want to protect the value of their property, but the probability of harm must be considered. For example, research in the UK by Cats Protection found that 89% of the private landlords surveyed who permit tenants to keep cats had not experienced any damage to their furniture or fittings (Cats Protection, 2019). If the probability of damage to property is small and the majority of pet-owning tenants are responsible pet owners with well-behaved pets, then the degree of risk to the landlord's interests is small. In these circumstances, does the extensive use of 'no pet' covenants constitute disproportionate harm to tenants given the magnitude of the harm caused when forced to rehome a companion animal?

A number of countries and states have legislation regulating the use of 'no pet' covenants in residential leases, including France, which passed legislation in the 1970s (Article 10 of the Law of 9 July 1970), Ontario in Canada under its Residential Tenancies Act 2006, and in 2020 the state of Victoria in Australia gave tenants the right to keep pets (through an amendment to its Residential Tenancies Act). In England, the Renters' Rights Bill 2024-25 proposes to change the law to allow tenants to keep pets with the landlord's consent, which cannot be unreasonably refused. In each case, the legislation includes exceptions and exemptions to balance the competing interests of the respective parties (landlords, pet-owning tenants, neighbouring tenants, companion animals and wider society). It permits responsible pet owners to live with well-behaved pets while addressing the needs of landlords and other tenants to protect their property or their enjoyment of their home environment.

The growth of pet-positive housing laws and policies in the rental sector is to be welcomed, but the likely increase in the size of pet populations in each country or state needs to be considered. An increase in pet ownership inevitably raises animal welfare concerns; for example, should there be limits on the number of pets permitted in one property or limits on the size of the animal? Is a small apartment in a high-rise block of flats suitable for a large, energetic dog breed such as an Alsatian? These questions highlight the complexity of balancing the rights and interests of all parties involved.

Pet abduction

The Pet Abduction Act 2024 came into force in England and Northern Ireland in August 2024. Under the Act, a person convicted of stealing a pet dog or cat in England or Northern Ireland can receive a maximum penalty of up to five years imprisonment, a fine, or both, and significantly, the welfare of the animal is a consideration in sentencing. In 2020, there were approximately 2,000 thefts of pet dogs reported to the police in England and Wales, although reliable data is limited as there was no separate identifiable offence of pet theft at that time (Pet Theft Taskforce report, 2021). Prior to the 2024 Act, the theft of a pet dog came under the Theft Act 1968 and was not distinguished from the theft of inanimate property such as jewellery. In relation to the total population of dogs in the country at that time (approximately 9 million in the UK in 2020), 2,000 cases of dog theft may seem like a relatively small figure. However, this crime has a serious impact on the victims (Allen et al., 2022) due to the close human-companion dog relationship causing the owner significant emotional trauma and seriously compromising the welfare of the dog.

In 2021, in response to an increase in pet thefts driven by the COVID-19 lockdowns the government in England established the Pet Theft Taskforce that was commissioned to gather evidence and make recommendations. The Taskforce noted the Animal Welfare (Sentience) Act 2022 and the legal recognition of animal sentience. Based on this, the Taskforce examined ways 'to better reflect the view that stolen pets are not mere property but sentient beings' (Pet Theft Taskforce report, 2021, p. 9). The Taskforce recommended a new 'pet abduction' offence, and the use of the word 'abduction' as opposed to 'theft' is significant. Rather than create a new offence of pet theft that perpetuates the idea of pets as property and focuses on the owner's loss, the Pet Theft Taskforce proposed a new 'pet abduction' offence that makes the welfare of the animal a primary consideration when sentencing defendants.

The key theme underlying this law reform is the legal status of companion animals as property and the challenges this has posed for police and criminal courts when dealing with pet theft cases. Property status does not reflect the seriousness of the offence and its impacts on the victims and has led to low prosecution rates and lenient sentences. Anna Firth, who introduced the Pet Abduction Bill into Parliament as a Private Members Bill in 2023, said, 'The golden thread running through this bill is that dogs and cats are sentient beings. They are not mere property; animals and humans can and do form emotional bonds, and there is a devastating impact when animal abduction takes place, both on people and on pets' (HC Deb c1168, 19 January 2024). In backing the Bill, the Environment Secretary recognised 'what treasured members of the family dogs and cats are. It is a deeply traumatic experience for both the owners and the pet when they are stolen' (Defra, 2024). The Pet Abduction Act 2024 gives the theft of companion cats and dogs the recognition it deserves so that the offence is taken seriously and the impact on the victims, including the animals as sentient beings, informs the sentencing of the defendants.

These three case studies demonstrate the need for changes in policy and law to better protect the human-companion animal relationship. In each case, the property status of pets creates problems and raises the question of whether an alternative legal framework is needed for companion animals. One such alternative is a relational approach to categorising companion animals in law. A relational approach addresses the legal treatment of animals based on their relationship to humans. Kymlicka (2017, p. 125) advocates a social recognition strategy that includes domesticated animals into 'everyday legal categories of social membership'. This approach could be used to categorise companion animals as family members, for example, within housing law. Although this approach reinforces the objectification of animals by differentiating them on the basis of their use to humans, it is nevertheless a more politically feasible strategy for protecting the interests of companion animals at law than being trapped 'in a paralyzing debate about whether categorising animals as 'persons' instead of 'property' will improve their legal protections' (Satz, 2009, p. 66). Categorising pets as family members may help resolve pet custody disputes and housing disputes by allowing the interests of the companion animal to be considered, but could be problematic in other areas, for example, negligence claims against veterinarians or those who provide pet services such as boarding, grooming or walking, leading to higher costs for these services for all pet owners.

Conclusion

The overarching theme in this chapter is the unique relationship humans have with companion animals. The fact that pets live in our homes and can be agents in the social construction of family life means our relationship with these animals is very different from all other animals on the planet. This relationship can be beneficial for human owners, the animals and wider society. The fact that the institution of pet ownership has persisted across the globe over thousands of years points to significant benefits for humans. However, there is a darker side to pet ownership that can expose animals to the risk of abuse and mistreatment. Examples include inappropriate breeding practices leading to extreme traits in dogs, puppy farms and puppy smuggling, including importing dogs with mutilations such as ear cropping, exotic pets that are unsuitable for living in human homes, pets as victims of domestic violence, pet theft, neglect, abandonment and cruelty.

Pet ownership can also pose problems for wider society, such as dog attacks on members of the public as well as its contribution to environmental concerns, such as the climate crisis. This raises a serious philosophical question as to whether the institution of pet ownership is flawed. More research is needed on the positive and negative effects of pet ownership on society, the environment and the animals themselves to enable an informed public debate on the future of pet ownership. What would be the consequences of a ban on pets? The health benefits derived from keeping pets are well researched, so there would be a clear loss here, but what are the wider effects? For example, does the close bond we share with companion animals increase the empathy humans feel for all animals? If we lost the institution of pet ownership and human interaction with animals significantly decreased, humans may become less empathetic towards other animals, such as wildlife (Gómez-Leal et al., 2021).

If it is felt that the benefits of pets are so significant that the institution should be retained, there needs to be robust laws to regulate pet ownership to protect humans, companion animals and the environment. Many countries have laws to prohibit unnecessary suffering to companion animals, but this is only a minimum baseline, and given their vulnerability and lifelong dependency on humans, more is needed to ensure the welfare needs of the animals are met. Legislation needs to be drafted, interpreted and enforced in ways that ensure good protection for the animals.

CHAPTER SIX

Farmed animals

Introduction

For people who feel inspired to improve the protection of animals in society, there is no better place to start than with farmed animals. This is due to the staggering number of animals within this category. The number of farmed animals slaughtered each year across the globe is in the billions, so large it is difficult to fully appreciate the scale of it. Attempts have been made to try to make the scale comprehendible. For example, in 2010, approximately 900 million farmed animals were killed in the UK, and the chair of the then Farm Animal Welfare Council (FAWC) said, 'This number of individual animals is almost impossible to imagine: if they all marched past at two per second, it would take over 14 years from the first to the last' (Wathes, 2010). According to Wolfson and Sullivan (2004), 98% of all animals people in the United States interact with are farmed animals. Considering all the different non-human animals people engage with, including companion animals, wildlife, animals used in entertainment, and scientific procedures, this is an incredible statistic. It emphasises the importance of getting the law that governs farmed animals right; if it is right, billions of animals will benefit.

This chapter will focus on the law and ethics relating to farmed animals. Law and ethics are inextricably intertwined here, as the assessment of whether the law protecting farmed animals is adequate depends on the ethics of using animals for food. The law in England, as in many countries, prohibits causing unnecessary suffering to farmed animals, but necessary suffering is permitted. Therefore, the reach of the law to protect farmed animals from suffering is governed by the concept of necessity. As explained in Chapter 5, necessity is a subjective concept, and someone who is vegan is likely to have a very different opinion from someone who eats meat on the necessity of any suffering caused to animals through intensive farming practices. If we accept that pigs suffer in intensive farms, the question of whether that suffering is necessary or unnecessary will vary depending upon whether eating pork is accepted as a legitimate purpose. Cultural norms influence what type of meat is deemed acceptable. Until recently, South Korea's ancient custom of eating dog meat meant it was acceptable to farm dogs for meat, but in 2023, the government announced its intention to enact a law to ban the dog meat trade by 2027 (Sarkar, 2023). Therefore, understanding the law (and assessing its adequacy to protect farmed animals) is dependent on cultural norms and societal perceptions around animal meat and requires the application of ethical theories. This chapter will consider meat-eating as an ethical decision and consider some of the wider factors that come into play, especially the environmental concerns arising from the meat industry's significant contribution to the climate crisis.

A key underlying theme in animal law is the welfare versus rights debate discussed in Chapter 3. The current legal framework governing farmed animals is a welfarist approach. It allows the use of farmed animals as products, for example, for meat, fur and leather, but seeks to reduce animal harm and even promotes their welfare in some circumstances. This raises an important question: Does welfare-based law adequately protect farmed animals? The reality is that any success in applying a rights-based approach to animals in the foreseeable future is unlikely to extend to farmed animals, especially given the vested interest humans have in continuing to use these animals as meat and by-products of the meat industry. Therefore, it is important that welfare-based law adequately protects farmed animals in three ways: firstly, the law must be sufficiently comprehensive in content; secondly, it must not be restrictively interpreted by the courts; and thirdly, it must be appropriately enforced by the relevant authorities. This is needed to ensure the best protection for farmed animals at all stages of their lives – on the farm, during transport and at the slaughterhouse.

This chapter starts by examining the legal definition of farmed animals. It then considers the concept of sentience given its importance as the characteristic of farmed animals that necessitates their need for legal protection. The need for the law to keep pace with science is considered as new evidence emerges of the sentience of some invertebrates used as food. The chapter sets the historical context of intensive farming practices in England and asks whether modern practices lead to animal suffering. However, evidence of suffering on its own is not unlawful, and therefore the legal concept of unnecessary suffering is applied to farmed animals. Legislation to protect farmed animals raises challenges that are specific to our use of the animals as products for food, cooking, clothing and fashion. Humans have a vested interest in continuing to use farmed animals in this way on a massive commercial scale and by the most cost-effective means. This vested interest can affect the interpretation, implementation and enforcement of animal welfare legislation thereby limiting its effectiveness to improve the welfare of farmed animals. It can also make legal reform challenging. The chapter ends by considering some of the anthropocentric arguments against intensive farming practices focusing on some of the adverse effects on human health, the environment and food security. This is relevant to the ethics of meat eating and the recognition that what we choose to eat is a moral decision worthy of thoughtful consideration.

Defining farmed animals

'Farmed animal' is a socially constructed category. Animals are not born farmed animals. Instead, they become farmed animals by virtue of the way humans use them. For example, a rabbit may be a farmed animal if it is bred or kept for food or for its fur. However, the same rabbit could be a companion animal if it is kept as a pet, or it could be a wild animal living in a field. Not all animals that are kept for food are protected as farmed animals under the law. Some animals are excluded. For example, in England, The Welfare of Farmed Animals (England) Regulations 2007 define farmed animals as:

> an animal bred or kept for the production of food, wool, skin or other farming purposes.

The regulations exclude the following animals:

> (a) a fish, reptile or amphibian;
> (b) an animal whilst at, or solely intended for use in, a competition, show or cultural or sporting event or activity;
> (c) an experimental or laboratory animal; or
> (d) an animal living in the wild.

Although excluded under the regulations, these animals may come within other animal welfare legislation such as the Animal Welfare Act (AWA) 2006. If a horse is kept on a farm in England for the purpose of food production, the horse will come within The Welfare of Farmed Animals (England) Regulations 2007 but if the horse is kept on a farm for the purpose of sport, such as horse racing, the regulations will not apply. Either way, the horse will fall within the scope of the AWA 2006 as a 'protected animal' being a non-human vertebrate, domesticated in the British Isles and under the control of humans.

There is a growing market for edible insects such as crickets and locusts. The insects as food and feed (IAFF) industry farms over 1 trillion insects a year and is continuing to grow. It is estimated that by 2030, over 8 trillion insects will be farmed for food (Barrett & Fischer, 2023). Based on our existing knowledge of insect sentience, it is arguable that eating insects does not raise the same ethical concerns as eating mammals; however, more research is needed as there are very few studies examining whether insects are sentient (Gibbons et al., 2022). Sentience is the quality of being able to experience pain and pleasure. It is the fact that farmed animals like pigs, chickens and sheep are sentient that makes eating them a moral decision. As sentient beings, farmed animals can suffer in intensive farming and slaughter practices. The current state of knowledge of insects is inconclusive on whether they are sentient (Van Huis, 2021). If we accept that insects do not experience pain and pleasure as a subjective experience like mammals do, then there is little risk of harm to the insects if they are bred and killed for food. Edible insects could become a more ethical alternative to eating mammals. However, if scientific research emerges on the sentience of edible insects, then ethical concerns arise. It is the presence of sentience that matters, and therefore, sentience is a vital characteristic when considering the legal protection of farmed animals.

The sentience of animals

According to Broom (2019), 'sentience means having the capacity to have feelings' such as pain and pleasure. Acknowledging the sentience of animals was key in the implementation of animal welfare laws. Descartes (1596–1650) is well known for advocating that animals were incapable of suffering pain, and his views justified invasive scientific procedures being performed on animals without the use of any pain relief. Over time, views changed as people recognised animals as capable of feeling pain. Bentham identified the capacity to suffer as the key characteristic for moral consideration and famously said, 'The question is not, Can they reason? nor, Can they talk? but, Can they suffer?' (Burns & Hart, 1970, p. 283). It was this recognition of the capacity to suffer that ultimately led to the enactment in 19th century England of the first major piece of animal welfare legislation in the world, The Cruel Treatment of Cattle Act 1822. Kean emphasises the importance of seeing everyday cruelty to farmed animals on the streets of London as a significant factor in bringing about change. She highlights 'the importance of the role of sight in developing the relationship between seeing ill-treatment and creating change' (Kean, 2000, p. 30). To what extent does the invisibility of farmed animal suffering inhibit changes in current times? In Western countries, intensive farming practices and slaughter practices in abattoirs are almost exclusively behind closed doors and out of sight.

A significant step in legally recognising the sentience of farmed animals occurred in Europe in 2009. Article 13 of the Treaty on the Functioning of the European Union was amended (by the Lisbon Treaty) to recognise animal sentience. It requires Member States to pay 'full regard' to animal welfare when implementing specified policies, including agricultural policies. Following Brexit, the English Parliament enacted the Animal Welfare (Sentience) Act 2022. The Act enshrines animals as sentient beings in domestic law and creates a new Animal Sentience Committee with the authority to scrutinise government policy and report on any detrimental effects on the welfare of animals as sentient beings. This means the committee can make recommendations as to how agricultural policy is formulated or implemented in such a way as to ensure that 'all due regard' is given to the adverse effect of the policy on farmed animals as sentient beings.

We accept that farmed animals that are mammals, such as pigs, cattle, chickens and sheep are sentient, but what about lobsters, prawns, crabs and other marine life that are regularly caught and kept for food? The legal protection of decapod crustaceans (such as lobsters, crabs, crayfish, prawns and shrimp) and cephalopods (such as octopus, squid, cuttlefish and chambered nautilus) has developed in recent years in line with emerging scientific research that suggests they may be sentient. In the field of animal experimentation, European Directive 2010/63/EU extended the protection of animals used in scientific procedures to 'any living cephalopod', and this was implemented into domestic law in England in 2012 when cephalopods were added to the definition of 'protected animals' in s.1, Animals (Scientific Procedures) Act 1986 (ASPA 1986) (SI 2012/3039), which up until that time was restricted to 'any living vertebrate other than man'. The decision to include cephalopods was based on the emergence of increased scientific evidence of their likelihood to feel pain. Decapod crustaceans are protected in animal welfare legislation in New Zealand (Animal Welfare Act 1999), Switzerland (Swiss Animal Welfare Act 2008), and Norway (Norwegian Animal Welfare Act 2009) but were not included in the EU Directive (2010/63/EU) nor the consequent amendment of ASPA 1986 in England.

The legal protection of cephalopods and decapod crustaceans is confused by conflicting approaches in the legislation. In England, cephalopods and decapod crustaceans are not protected from unnecessary suffering under the Animal Welfare Act 2006. Animals to which the Act applies are defined in s.1 as 'a vertebrate other than man'. However, s.1(3) permits for the extension of this definition of animal to include invertebrates if 'the appropriate national authority is satisfied, on the basis of scientific evidence, that animals of the kind concerned are capable of experiencing pain or suffering'. The Animal Welfare (Sentience) Act 2022 defines animals as including 'any cephalopod molluscs' and 'any decapod crustaceans' (s.5). In 2021, when the Bill was going through parliament, it was amended to include these invertebrates following the publication of a government-commissioned report on their potential sentience (Birch et al., 2021). This means there are conflicting messages in the legislation in England, with their sentience being acknowledged in the Animal Welfare (Sentience) Act 2022 but disregarded in the Animal Welfare Act 2006.

Interestingly, some of the secondary legislation governing farmed animal welfare in England does include invertebrates. For example, the Welfare of Animals (Transport) (England) Order 2006 includes cold-blooded invertebrates in the definition of animals and provides it is an offence to transport any animal in a way that causes or is likely to cause unnecessary suffering. The Welfare of Animals at the Time of Killing (England) Regulations 2015 (WATOK) include invertebrates in Schedule 4 and require the humane killing of these animals. The fact that English law now recognises some invertebrates used in food production as sentient means that their killing must be carried out without causing unnecessary suffering to the animal. It appears that the existing practice of boiling crabs and lobsters alive in restaurants and homes in England has therefore become unlawful because the law now recognises these animals as sentient (Rook et al., 2023).

Plans for the world's first commercial octopus farm in Spain demonstrates the problem of excluding invertebrates from legislation protecting farmed animals. The farm intends to raise a million octopuses a year for food, but expert scientists oppose it, arguing that the conditions the octopuses will live in will lead to stress, conflict and high mortality (Kassam, 2023). The prospect of a large-scale commercial octopus farm highlights the need for welfare laws protecting farmed animals to keep pace with the science on animal sentience.

The growth of intensive farming practices

Although animals have been closely associated with human development for thousands of years, the causes of modern welfare problems for farmed animals are the result of much more recent events in human history. With the end of the Second World War in 1945 came the beginning of a new era of increased demand for the production of meat and other animal products. This demand led the farming community to search for methods to produce high yields of food at the cheapest possible price for the consumer.

Farming techniques were introduced that were designed to maximise productivity and drive down the chief production costs of manpower and land required for traditional expansive husbandry systems. The increased use of antibiotics and other health products enabled farmers to place more animals into conditions of close confinement, which, as Bernard Rollin notes, might have been a recipe for disaster in preceding times:

> If a 19th century agriculturalist, let alone an ancient one, had dreamed of keeping thousands of chickens in one building, such a scheme would have been corrected by nature, for it would be a rapid path to ruin, bringing quick spread of animal disease, death, and financial disaster. Producers did well if and only if animals did well, and – this is critical – 'did well' for the animal meant playing out its biological nature in an environment for which those powers had been selected by both natural and artificial selection. Society, therefore, did not need laws mandating good husbandry for animals – that was dictated by self-interest and reinforced by the ancient ethic of care. (1995, p. 7)

Traditional expansive farming practices generally involved small-scale farms with fewer animals and more space per animal, but the emergence of intensive farms (sometimes called factory farms) led to large-scale operations with large numbers of animals confined in ever smaller spaces. In 1964, a public outcry and intense media coverage followed the publication of the book *Animal Machines* by Ruth Harrison, which was serialised in *The Observer*. She brought these new intensive farming practices into the limelight and described in detail the adverse effects on the farmed animals. Within two months of her book, the Brambell Committee, under the chairmanship of Professor Roger Brambell, was set up to investigate the conditions under which farmed animals were kept and to recommend legislative change. Its report ran to 85 pages and detailed numerous principal findings and recommendations. The committee noted the difficulty in defining intensive farming and acknowledged increasing public concern for the welfare of farmed animals:

> Principal findings
>
> 6. It is difficult to define precisely the term 'intensive livestock husbandry'. We have considered the keeping of poultry of all sorts, whether hens, turkeys or other birds, entirely within doors on deep litter, slats or wire in battery cages; the keeping of rabbits under comparable conditions; beef, veal calf, sheep and pig production under cover, as falling clearly within our terms of reference. All these methods result in the rapid production

> of animal products by standardised methods involving economy of land and labour. All are capable of exploitation on a large scale, and units of varying sizes, some very large and some quite small, are in operation. A high degree of mechanisation and automation is a feature of the larger establishments.
>
> …
>
> 9. Historically the evolution of our society has been marked by increasing concern for the welfare of animals. Many cruel practices, such as badger baiting and cockfighting, have been proscribed by law. Others, including castration or dehorning of adult cattle, can now be carried out only under anaesthesia. The movement and slaughter of animals for food are controlled in the interest of the animals. Indeed, this committee was established in response to widespread concern for the welfare of animals under systems of intensive husbandry. It appears to us reasonable to anticipate continuing development of concern for animal welfare and that conditions which appear to us tolerable today may come to be considered intolerable in the future ...

Within its principal findings, the committee made controversial (for the time) observations about the confinement of farmed animals:

> 37. ... In principle we disapprove of a degree of confinement of an animal which necessarily frustrates most of the major activities which make up its natural behaviour and we do not consider such confinement or restraint permissible over a long period unless the other advantages thereby conferred upon the animal are likely to be very substantial. An animal should at least have sufficient freedom of movement to be able without difficulty, to turn round, groom itself, get up, lie down and stretch its limbs …

Ultimately the committee recommended the need for new animal welfare legislation to safeguard farmed animals (which led to the enactment of the Agriculture (Miscellaneous Provisions) Act 1968):

> Principal recommendations
>
> 1. ... we have concluded that the use of such [intensive husbandry] methods should not in itself be regarded as objectionable and may often benefit the animals; but certain practices are contrary to animal welfare and need to be controlled ...

> 4. The existing animal welfare legislation does not adequately safeguard farm animals and a new act is needed incorporating a fuller definition of suffering and enabling Ministers to make regulations requiring conditions for particular animals ...

Some of the recommendations of the Brambell Committee were implemented in the Agriculture (Miscellaneous Provisions) Act 1968. (This Act was subsequently repealed and replaced by the Animal Welfare Act 2006). Radford advocates that the Brambell Committee report was a 'game-changer' (Radford, 2023). It recognised the mental well-being of farmed animals as a relevant component of their welfare. It appreciated the need for scientific evidence of animal behaviour in assessing their welfare and thereby laid the foundation for the development of animal welfare science, which has played a vital role in animal welfare law reform. The report led to the setting up of the Farm Animal Welfare Council (now the Animal Welfare Committee) and the creation of the highly influential 'Five Freedoms' paradigm. The Five Freedoms have played a pivotal role in assessing the welfare of farmed animals and will be examined in the next section.

Do farmed animals suffer in intensive farming practices?

Legislation generally seeks to prevent farmed animals from experiencing pain and suffering and to provide for their welfare. But what is meant by these terms, and can animal suffering be proved? To what extent should we legislate, and against which farming practices in particular? Defining prohibited farming techniques that cause 'pain and suffering' or providing for practices that promote 'welfare' requires precise definitions of those words. Webster and Margerison (2022, p. 9) define welfare as 'the state of body and mind of a sentient animal as it attempts to cope with its environment'. The word 'welfare' is used to cover different types of treatment of animals – direct or indirect ill-treatment of farmed animals involving abuse or neglect, alongside the comparatively recently recognised form of welfare concern, 'quality of life'.

As a basic illustrative guide to terms that are extremely difficult to pin down to specific practices, abuse might be said to involve direct and deliberate actions resulting in actual injury/pain, fear or distress in an animal. Neglect is an indirect form of welfare violation involving either overworking animals or simply being negligent in, for example, their dietary requirements. Alongside the forms of physical abuse that have been prohibited in legislation since 1911 (in the now repealed Protection of Animals Act), has come legislation aimed more at the quality of life given to farmed animals to provide for their physiological and other needs, such as s.9 of the Animal Welfare Act 2006, which requires those responsible for farmed animals to provide a suitable environment and an opportunity to display normal behaviour patterns.

The 'Five Freedoms and Provisions', which were initially drafted by the FAWC in 1993, identify the elements for the well-being of farmed animals and the husbandry resources needed to promote those freedoms:

1. Freedom from hunger and thirst, by ready access to water and a diet to maintain health and vigour.
2. Freedom from discomfort, by providing an appropriate environment.
3. Freedom from pain, injury and disease, by prevention or rapid diagnosis and treatment.
4. Freedom to express normal behaviour, by providing sufficient space, proper facilities and appropriate company of the animal's own kind.
5. Freedom from fear and distress, by ensuring conditions and treatment that avoid mental suffering (Farm Animal Welfare Council, 2009).

Over the years, the Five Freedoms have played a pivotal role in UK law and policy governing farmed animals. However, more recently, there has been criticism that the freedoms set a low threshold for animal welfare by focusing on preventing negative experiences; for example, freedom from discomfort, rather than promoting positive experiences, such as the need for an environment that promotes the well-being of the animal. In 2009, the FAWC acknowledged this low threshold, and in light of the positive obligation in AWA 2006 to meet the welfare needs of domestic animals, the council advocated that 'At a minimum, each farm animal should have a life that is worth living to the animal itself and not just to its human keeper' (Farm Animal Welfare Council, 2009, p.1).

Mellor and Reid (1994) formulated the 'Five Domains' model for assessing animal welfare, which has its origin in the Five Freedoms paradigm. The Five Domains are nutrition, environment, health, behavioural interactions and mental state/experiences. While there is similarity with the Five Freedoms, the Five Domains model explores the mental state of an animal in more detail and reinforces the importance of an animal's emotional needs. The domains model demonstrates how minimising negative physical and mental states is not on its own enough to provide a farmed animal with a 'life worth living'. Farmed animals need the opportunity for positive experiences, for example, by providing an environment that encourages the animals to express rewarding behaviours. The domains model was initially devised for assessing the welfare of animals used in scientific procedures but has since been used for a diverse range of animals (Mellor, 2017). For example, the model was cited in a defamation case in 2023 brought by Chris Packham, a naturalist and television presenter, against an online magazine that accused him of lying to raise funds for a wildlife sanctuary caring for tigers rescued from a Spanish travelling circus. Packham won the case and was awarded damages and in reaching its decision the High Court judge, Mr Justice Saini, referred to the domains model:

> The expert evidence left me with the firm overall impression that the modern peer-reviewed literature supports the proposition that it is indeed inherently harmful to tigers for them to be kept in travelling circuses. That conclusion is based on applying what the literature calls the 'domains' model for assessing animal welfare which considers nutrition, physical environment, health, behavioural interactions and mental state. (*Packham* v. *Wrightman* [2023] EWHC 1256, para.48)

Although this case did not involve farmed animals, it nevertheless illustrates the courts willingness to use the domains model for assessing animal welfare.

It should be noted that not everyone agrees that animals experience 'pain' or 'suffering' that can be equated with the pain and suffering of humans. Peter Carruthers, for example, distinguishes between 'conscious' and 'non-conscious' mental processes in relation to pain, as well as the levels of suffering endured by different species, claiming that the capacity for pain and suffering is much greater in humans because of their greater intelligence. Carruthers proposes that animals think in a 'non-conscious' way, somewhat akin to the way humans can perform a task, such as driving a car, without really thinking about the specifics of the task in hand and whilst 'consciously' thinking about what they are going to do that evening. This leads him to conclude that, as there are no reasons to protect non-conscious thoughts, animals are not worthy of our moral concern. Applied to intensive farming, he regards the apparent suffering or pain of animals, evidenced by the observation of measurable physiological changes, as amounting to no more than non-conscious reactions that carry no moral weight (Carruthers, 1992). Peter Singer (1995, p. 11), however, is of the opposite view:

> Nearly all the external signs that lead us to infer pain in other humans can be seen in other species, especially the species most closely related to us – the species of mammals and birds. The behavioural signs include writhing, facial contortions, moaning, yelping or other forms of calling,

> attempts to avoid the source of pain, the appearance of fear at the prospect of its repetition, and so on. In addition, we know that these animals have nervous systems very like ours, which respond physiologically as ours do when the animal is in circumstances in which we would feel pain: an initial rise in blood pressure, dilated pupils, perspiration, an increased pulse rate, and, if the stimulus continues, a fall in blood pressure. Although human beings have a more developed cerebral cortex than other animals, this part of the brain is concerned with thinking functions rather than with basic impulses, emotions, and feelings. These impulses, emotions, and feelings are located in the diencephalon, which is well developed in many other species of animals, especially mammals and birds.

Since the work in the 1980s of Marion Stamp-Dawkins of the Animal Behaviour Research Group at the Department of Zoology in Oxford, there has been a growing body of research demonstrating that farmed animals are capable of suffering pain. Stamp-Dawkins conducted 'preference testing' with farmed hens to establish which kind of environment they preferred and found that, despite an initial reluctance to move away from the close confinement of the battery cages, the birds' curiosity eventually led them to investigate and then move into a more free-range environment (Stamp-Dawkins, 1980). She asserted that no single scientific test can determine the subjective experiences of animals and that it is possible to examine a variety of evidence to determine whether animals are 'suffering' such as their physical health, behaviour, productivity, their preferences (as identified from preference testing), and comparisons to any wild counterparts.

Pigs can be used to illustrate this approach by examining their psychology and natural behaviours to help assess if they suffer in intensive farming practices. Domestic pigs are descended from wild boars, a highly gregarious species, with the first phase of domestication occurring approximately 9000 years ago (Giuffra et al., 2000). The selective breeding of pigs has focused on traits for food production, such as growth, meaning that modern domesticated pigs are cognitively and behaviourally not dissimilar to their ancestors, the wild boars (Held et al., 2009). Strong parallels are evident between domestic pigs and wild boars in their social behaviour, especially their reproductive and parenting behaviours (Marino & Colvin, 2015). Pigs are highly social animals and a typical social unit comprises of several females and their offspring. Pigs rely on tactile information, which plays an important role in their behaviour. They use their snouts for interacting with their environment, such as rooting, foraging and carrying, and for social interactions. Marino and Colvin's review of the literature on the psychology of domestic pigs concluded that, on the evidence available, pigs appear to be cognitively complex and share a number of traits with intelligent animals such as chimpanzees and dolphins. For example, they demonstrate complex object discrimination requiring a long-term memory; they have very good spatial cognition enabling them to acquire, remember, organise and use information about their spatial environment; they are playful, display inquisitiveness and seek novelty; they can take the perspective of other pigs and use this information to manipulate each other:

> In one study, pigs foraged for food in pairs. Only one pig was shown the location of the food. The uninformed pig followed the pig-in-the-know to the food source and then took the food first. In response to this behavior, the informed pigs altered their behavior in later trials to reduce the chances that they would be followed and increased their forging speed to stay ahead of their exploiters [Held et al., 2000]. These types of strategies and counter strategies are a complex form of perspective-taking called tactical deception, a capacity also observed in great apes and ravens (Marino & Colvin, 2015)

Pigs display emotional contagion (the ability to feel the emotional state of another from the other's perspective), which is thought to be a simple form of empathy:

> In one study, naïve test pigs were exposed to pen mates who had been trained to anticipate upcoming rewarding events (receiving straw and chocolate raisins) or aversive events (social isolation). When the naïve pigs were placed in the company of the trained pigs, they adopted the same emotional anticipatory behaviors (e.g., ear and tail postures, increased cortisol release) as the trained pigs with the direct experience. These findings show that not only can pigs connect with the emotions of other pigs, but they can also do so with pigs who are responding emotionally in anticipation of future events (Reimert, Bolhuis, Kemp, & Rodenburg, 2013). (Marino & Colvin, 2015)

Although Marino and Colvin concluded that pigs are cognitively complex based on the evidence available, their review of the literature found a significant gap in our knowledge of domestic pigs and identified the need for further non-invasive research. Having considered some aspects of the psychology and natural behaviours of pigs, we can better appreciate how pigs cope with intensive farming practices and whether this causes them to suffer.

One of the prominent international groups leading the campaign for improved conditions for farmed animals is Compassion in World Farming

(CIWF). It is campaigning to end the use of cages for farmed animals, and for pigs, cages are used for breeding sows. The UK has banned the use of sow stalls but permits the use of farrowing crates. A sow stall is a narrow metal cage where a pregnant sow is kept for the entire 16-week pregnancy. She can only stand up and lie down; the sow stall is too narrow for her to turn around. The floor is usually bare concrete or a metal slatted floor. Sow stalls are illegal in the UK and Sweden, and there is a partial ban in the EU, but they are still used in many parts of the world. A farrowing crate is a metal cage used to house a pregnant sow from just before giving birth until the piglets are weaned and taken away from her. The farrowing crate is similar to a sow stall except it also has space to the side for the piglets. Metal bars prevent the sow from accessing the lying area for the piglets. These crates severely restrict the sow's movement and frustrate her natural behaviours of foraging, rooting and exploring her environment. In particular, the crates frustrate the sow's strong instinct to build a nest before giving birth. The routine use of farrowing crates is banned in Sweden, Norway and Switzerland, with Germany and Austria committed to implementing partial bans. The crates are extensively used in the rest of the world, including the UK.

It has been argued that farrowing crates do not comply with the obligations under English law to meet the welfare needs of the sows (McCulloch, 2022). Farrowing crates are justified based on reduced piglet mortality rates because the crate reduces the risk of the sow crushing her piglets. However, alternative systems exist where sows are kept outdoors with access to a hut for shelter. Access to straw allows the sows to build a nest (hence reducing any risk of crushing her piglets) and to enjoy natural behaviours such as foraging, rooting and wallowing in mud (to keep cool). Evidence that free farrowing systems (without the use of crates) achieve comparable, or lower, piglet mortality rates challenges the rationale for the use of farrowing crates and questions its continued legality in England. In a judicial review case in 2020, New Zealand's High Court held that new regulations and minimum standards relating to the use of farrowing crates were unlawful because they circumvented earlier laws to phase out the use of the crates. It was accepted that the severe confinement of the sows was not compliant with the country's Animal Welfare Act, which has welfare obligations based on the five freedoms, including the ability to display normal behaviour patterns. The High Court said the agriculture minister must now consider new regulations to phase out the use of farrowing crates (Anthony, 2020).

Pigs that are bred for meat are usually housed in pens with concrete or metal slatted floors. In these crowded and barren conditions, pigs can readily become bored and frustrated. To reduce injury caused by fighting and biting, piglets may have their teeth clipped and their tails docked, sometimes without any pain relief. The pigs are slaughtered at approximately 6 months old. Transport to the slaughterhouse is especially problematic for pigs because they do not have sweat glands and can overheat during transport. Their ability for emotional contagion exacerbates their susceptibility to suffering stress during transport and pre-slaughter handling. CIWF (n.d.) observes that 'Internationally, significant numbers of pigs die each year in transport or in lairage at slaughterhouses as a result of stress'. Alternative systems exist, such as higher welfare indoor systems where pigs are housed in smaller groups with solid floors and access to straw for rooting and bedding, or systems that allow for the outdoor and/or free-range rearing of pigs. CIWF estimates that worldwide approximately 1.4 billion pigs are slaughtered every year. They estimate that at least half of these 1.4 billion pigs are raised in intensive farming systems. These statistics illustrate the importance of assessing whether pigs suffer in intensive farming practices. If suffering is caused by cages for breeding sows, crowded and barren indoor living accommodations for young pigs, and the stresses of transport and slaughter methods, it raises an important question as to what laws and policies are needed to address these welfare concerns.

CIWF advocates that farmed animals do suffer in intensive farming practices. It provides numerous examples, two of which will be considered here: broiler chickens and dairy cows. The first example concerns broiler chickens, which are farmed for their meat. They are reared in large, barren, windowless sheds. They have been selectively bred to grow very fast, which puts a strain on their hearts and lungs and causes painful leg disorders. High concentrations of ammonia from droppings cause burns on their legs, chest and feet. As they grow, the sheds become overcrowded, and the chickens have little space to move, making it difficult to reach the food and water, especially if they are lame. Catching, crating and transporting the chickens to the slaughterhouse is stressful for the birds and can result in bruising and broken bones. At the slaughterhouse, the chickens are usually hung by their feet on shackles while conscious. They are stunned by being dipped, headfirst, into an electrified water bath before their throats are cut. However, stunning may be ineffective if the birds raise their heads. All this provides evidence of the suffering of the birds, according to CIWF. The second example of animal suffering concerns dairy cows. They have been selectively bred over many years to produce very large quantities of milk; an average yield in the UK is 22 litres a day. This puts tremendous strain on the cow's body, and they are usually slaughtered after three or four lactations because their milk production falls. Prolonged standing on concrete floors can lead to lameness. Mastitis (the inflammation of the udder) is a painful bacterial infection caused by contamination of milking equipment or bedding. In the UK, most dairy cows are put out to graze in fields in the summer, but worldwide 'zero-grazing' systems are increasingly used for large-scale operations, which means the cows are kept indoors all year round and denied access to natural grazing. In these ways, dairy cows suffer, according to CIWF.

In each case, assessing whether an animal suffers from such practices requires evidence from various sources, including physical health, comparison to natural behaviour and wild counterparts, and any evidence from research on the animals' preferences. However, from a legal perspective, evidence of suffering is not enough on its own. The law in England, and in many other countries, prohibits unnecessary suffering to domestic and captive animals but allows necessary suffering. Therefore, in the context of farmed animals, the concept of unnecessary suffering is vital in determining which intensive farming practices are legal.

The law: the concept of unnecessary suffering as applied to farmed animals

Francione talks of 'moral schizophrenia' to describe how humans acknowledge animals as sentient beings and want to protect them from suffering but feel justified to use animals for their own benefit even if it causes the animals harm (2004). According to Francione, this moral schizophrenia results in 'the institutionalised exploitation' of millions of animals in 'factory farms'. The concept of unnecessary suffering in law goes some way to address the inherent inconsistencies apparent in this moral schizophrenia. It prohibits animal suffering that is unnecessary while permitting that which is necessary. It is a welfarist concept that seeks to justify the continued use of sentient beings as products while allaying any uncomfortable feeling of guilt on the part of humans. According to Satz (2009), the real purpose of animal welfare legislation is to assert our right to use animals for our own benefit.

The Animal Welfare Act 2006 (AWA 2006) governs the offence of unnecessary suffering in England. Under s.4, AWA 2006, a person is guilty of a criminal offence if their act (or failure to act) causes a protected animal to suffer unnecessarily and they knew or ought reasonably to have known that it would have that effect. Farmed animals, such as pigs, chickens and sheep, come within the definition of a protected animal being vertebrates, domesticated in the British Isles and under the control of humans. However, invertebrates that are kept for food, such as lobsters caught in the wild and kept alive in water-filled containers prior to slaughter, are excluded. This anomaly in the law, whereby some invertebrate food is recognised under the Animal Welfare (Sentience) Act 2022 as sentient but denied protection from pain and suffering under the AWA 2006 needs to be addressed with the appropriate extension of the definition of animals to include sentient invertebrates.

Suffering is a pre-requisite to a s.4 offence of unnecessary suffering, but once suffering is established, the court must then consider the question of necessity. There are several statutory considerations set out in s.4, which were developed through case law under the previous legislation (the Protection of Animals Act 1911, which included a similar offence of cruelty). Two of the key statutory considerations are legitimate purpose and proportionality. There must be a legitimate purpose for the act that caused the animal to suffer, and there must be proportionality between that legitimate purpose and the means of achieving it. Proportionality is a legal concept used in human rights law that involves a balancing exercise – the need to weigh various factors in the balance, sometimes conflicting interests, to ensure that no one suffers disproportionate harm. Relevant factors must be identified and allocated an appropriate weighting for the balancing exercise to take place.

Israel has a similar concept of unnecessary suffering in its animal welfare legislation, and the Israeli Supreme Court decision in *Noah* v. *The Attorney General* (HCJ 9232/01, 215) is an excellent example of the subjectivity involved in assessing necessity. The case demonstrates proportionality in practice and shows how a slight shift in the factors identified as relevant or the weighting allocated to those factors in the balancing exercise can lead to different outcomes. The case concerned the intensive farming practice for foie gras production by inserting a tube into the oesophagus of geese and force-feeding them until their livers become abnormally large and fatty. At the time of the case, more than 500 tonnes of foie gras was produced in Israel each year, and hundreds of farmers were dependent on the industry. The court had to consider whether this farming practice caused the geese unnecessary suffering contrary to Israeli law. In assessing proportionality, the majority of the judges identified the key relevant factors to be the suffering of the geese against the production of a food delicacy enjoyed by humans. On this basis, the court held that the suffering of the geese was not justifiable for an unnecessary luxury food item. In contrast, a minority of the judges identified food production in general and the livelihoods of farmers in the foie gras industry as relevant factors. The minority view was that the suffering of the geese was necessary, as the harm to humans would be greater if a ban on foie gras production in Israel was implemented. This case is unusual because, in the balancing exercise to decide the necessity of the animal suffering, the interests of the animals ultimately outweighed those of humans; in practice, this is rare. Cases from England demonstrate a more restrictive interpretation of how unnecessary suffering can apply to farmed animals.

In *Roberts* v. *Ruggerio* (1985), the organisation CIWF sought to challenge the veal crate system, which was then in use in England. Male calves from dairy cows are used to produce veal, which is an expensive, pale-coloured meat. To produce the right colour and texture for the meat, the calf was individually confined in a narrow stall, unable to turn around and with no access to roughage in the diet. Did this method of rearing the calves cause them unnecessary suffering? The court accepted that the calves did suffer but held that the suffering was necessary. The court accepted that all animal husbandry involves some suffering and that 'the suffering of the calves was not beyond that which was general in animal husbandry'. Significantly, the court would not consider alternative methods of raising calves for veal that caused less suffering. Since alternative (less harmful) farming practices were deemed irrelevant, the actual test that the court applied was that the suffering of the calves was not beyond that expected in this 'particular type' of animal husbandry, i.e., the veal crate. This suggests that in avoiding unnecessary suffering, farmers do not have to use farming practices that cause the least suffering. No offence is committed even if there are alternative methods that cause less suffering to the animals and achieve the same end. The court took the view that it would only consider suffering beyond that which is to be expected from the use of the veal crate. Soon after this case was decided, the British Government passed legislation to prohibit the use of the veal crate system because of the suffering of the calves. The law came into force in 1990, and the EU eventually followed suit and banned the use of veal crates from 2006.

The older case of *Ford* v. *Wiley* (1889) offers a different approach to the narrow approach adopted by the court in *Roberts* v. *Ruggiero.* In this case, young cattle at a farm in Norfolk had their horns sawn off very close to their heads using a common saw. It was accepted that the cows suffered extreme and prolonged pain. The farmer sought to justify this procedure on a number of grounds, including profit and convenience. The court held that the practice of dishorning caused unnecessary suffering. Significantly, the court was prepared to consider alternative, comparatively painless, methods to achieving the objective sought, and this was a relevant factor in considering the necessity of the suffering.

In *Roberts* v. *Ruggiero*, Stephen Brown LJ said that alternative systems of raising veal were irrelevant, and he sought to distinguish the case from *Ford* v. *Wiley* on the basis that the veal calves had not suffered beyond that which was general in animal husbandry. Presumably, he felt that the dehorned cattle had. However, there was expert evidence that the practice of dehorning was gaining support in the county, having been discontinued many years beforehand. On this basis, if the practice of dehorning had still been widespread at the time of the trial, the court could have excluded the suffering of the cattle as being no more than that which would be expected from that particular type of animal husbandry. On Stephen Brown LJ's reasoning, the 'hideous torments' of dehorning, which were found to be totally disproportionate to the object to be achieved, would not have been illegal if the practice was still widespread. These two cases indicate two different approaches. The *Roberts* v. *Ruggerio* case suggests that any suffering directly caused by the use of intensive farming methods is excluded as 'general husbandry' and alternative, less painful, methods are not relevant to the question of necessity, whereas the *Ford* v. *Wiley* approach takes alternative methods, which cause less suffering, into account in assessing necessity.

The approach of the court in *Roberts* v. *Ruggerio* raises an interesting comparison to the criminal law in the United States, which prohibits cruelty to animals. Numerous states apply what is known as the 'customary farming practice' as an exemption to the criminal offence of causing unnecessary suffering. A 'customary farming practice' means that a majority (or even a significant minority) of farmers use it (Wolfson & Sullivan, 2004). This means that if a farming practice causes suffering to animals, it is not illegal if the practice is used by a large number of farmers. What is significant here is that it is the agribusinesses themselves who are defining what is meant by a customary farming practice. Wolfson and Sullivan conclude that 'in effect, state legislators have granted agribusiness a license to treat animals as it wishes' (Wolfson & Sullivan, 2004, p. 215). The idea of not being able to challenge suffering caused by a customary farming practice raises serious concerns for animal welfare. It is hoped that English courts will always be willing to consider suitable alternative methods of husbandry that cause less suffering when assessing the necessity of any suffering to farmed animals.

It is interesting to note the response of an English judge to an attempt to use the concept of 'customary farming practice' in a defamation case in the English courts. The case (known in the media at the time as the McLibel trial) arose in the 1990s when the fast food company McDonald's sued two people for defamation when they distributed a leaflet criticising McDonald's for, among other things, the cruel treatment of farmed animals. McDonald's legal team raised the customary farming practice exemption, but the judge rejected it, noting that to use it 'would be to hand the decision as to what is cruel to the food industry completely, moved as it must be by economic as well as animal welfare considerations' (Wolfson, 1999, p. 39). Although the McLibel trial concerned the tort of defamation and not the criminal offence of unnecessary suffering, the judge's observation highlights the risks inherent in the use of the customary farming practice exemption.

The effectiveness of legislation specific to farmed animals

It is not enough to have legislation that purports to protect farmed animals from suffering and improve their welfare; the legislation also needs to be interpreted and implemented in effective ways. In relation to farmed animals, the interests of the animal to have a life worth living can diverge from the interests of society to obtain large quantities of meat or other animal products quickly and cheaply. This divergence of interests can adversely affect how animal welfare legislation is interpreted and implemented, thereby limiting its effectiveness in improving the welfare of farmed animals.

In England, there is secondary legislation in the form of regulations (authorised under s.12 AWA 2006) specifying how farmed animals are to be kept and slaughtered. Much of the content of these regulations comes from EU law. For example, the Welfare of Farmed Animals (England) Regulations 2007 give detailed instructions on how to keep farmed animals, much of which was transposed from EU Directive 98/58/EC. Regulations purport to ensure minimum animal welfare standards exist in farming, but limitations arise from their interpretation and implementation. Two examples are considered below to illustrate these limitations.

The Welfare of Farmed Animals (England) Regulations 2007 and 'Frankenchickens'

The 2007 regulations implement EU law (as was required at that time) and provide minimum animal welfare standards. Schedule 1 outlines general conditions that apply to all farmed animals on matters such as staffing, inspections, building and accommodation, the use of mechanical equipment, diet and breeding procedures. For example, there is a provision regulating freedom of movement that provides:

> The freedom of movement of animals, having regard to their species and in accordance with good practice and scientific knowledge, must not be restricted in such a way as to cause them unnecessary suffering or injury. (para. 9)

Schedules 2 to 9 provide additional conditions that apply to specific animals; for example, Schedule 8 applies to the keeping of pigs. In addition to the regulations, the Department of Environment, Food and Rural Affairs (Defra), which is the central authority with responsibility for farmed animal welfare, provides recommendations and codes of practice for specific species; for example, there is a code of practice for the welfare of meat chickens and meat breeding chickens (Defra, 2018). These codes of practice are not legally binding in themselves, but a failure to comply with one may be used as evidence of a welfare offence under the AWA 2006.

In 2023, the Humane League bought a judicial review case against the Secretary of State for Environment, Food and Rural Affairs, the central issue being the construction of paragraph 29 of Schedule 1 to the Welfare of Farmed Animals (England) Regulations 2007, which states:

> Animals may only be kept for farming purposes if it can reasonably be expected, on the basis of their genotype or phenotype, that they can be kept without any detrimental effect on their health or welfare.

The case concerned the use of fast-growing broiler chickens that have been selectively bred since the 1950s to grow large and fast to produce large quantities of meat in a very short time. The media referred to them as 'Frankenchickens' (Halpin, 2023).

Over one billion meat chickens are slaughtered in the UK each year, and 95% are reared in large, closed buildings with high stocking densities (para. 13–15). They reach a slaughter weight of approximately 2.2kg in five to six weeks. Their legs cannot always support their heavy muscle weight, and this leads to lameness and chronic leg disorders, and, in some cases, an inability to stand or walk, leading to hock burns to their skin caused by the ammonia in the faeces on the floor. They can experience organ failure and fatal heart attacks. The Humane League argued that the Secretary of State for Environment, Food and Rural Affairs had adopted and maintained policies and practices in relation to the rearing of fast-growing broiler chickens that were founded on a legal error. They argued that the use of these fast-growing birds was illegal under paragraph 29 because their genetics could cause serious health and welfare problems and that the Secretary of State had misdirected herself as to the meaning of paragraph 29. The Secretary of State said there is no consensus in the current science that fast-growing meat chickens cannot be kept without detriment to their welfare.

Her defence demonstrates the importance of continued research in animal welfare science to provide robust evidence of animal suffering where it exists. This case illustrates the multidisciplinary nature of Animal Law as a subject that calls for collaboration between lawyers, scientists and ethicists. The High Court ruled that the Secretary of State had acted lawfully. It is important to appreciate that judicial review challenges the way a decision has been reached, and therefore the court was reviewing the lawfulness of her decision rather than the rights and wrongs of using fast-growing chickens. The judge accepted the Secretary of State's view that, although there may be a higher risk of health problems with fast-growing chickens, they 'can be kept without detriment to their welfare since environmental conditions can have an influence on the health and welfare of birds with both fast- and slow-growing breeds' (para.102). Therefore, the Secretary of State had not acted contrary to her legal duties.

In 2024, the Court of Appeal dismissed Humane League's appeal, stating it was not an appropriate case to make a declaration in the abstract. However, the court gave valuable direction on the scope and effect of para.29. It said the High Court judge had erred in not differentiating between those detrimental characteristics which can be mitigated and those that cannot. If the fast-growing chickens do suffer from heart problems and leg disorders then no improvement in environmental conditions, such as lower stocking densities, can mitigate this. The Court of Appeal recognised that 'those consequences would be inherent in the particular breed of chicken and the keeping of such a breed would be prohibited by Paragraph 29' (para. 52). It went on to say that any prohibition on keeping a breed of animal that suffers inherent health problems because of its genetics 'applies regardless of any commercial advantages which it may have' (para.60).

In 2022, 82 million chickens in the UK died before reaching slaughter weight, which is a mortality rate of almost 7% and led to calls for the industry to switch to slow-growing breeds (Ungoed-Thomas, 2023). The British Poultry Council argued that the unusually high mortality rate was due to avian flu, which led to all flocks being kept indoors at a time when the UK was experiencing extreme summer temperatures resulting in heat stress on flocks. They argue that ultimately there is not consumer demand for slow-growing breeds as it would increase the price of chicken meat and consumers are unwilling to pay the higher price.

This example illustrates the limitations of the law. The law specifically states that it is only permissible to use breeds where, based on their genetic type, it is reasonable to expect no detrimental effect on the health of the animal. However, in practice, there is extensive use of fast-growing broiler chickens, and millions die in the UK every year before reaching slaughter weight due to significant health problems caused by their genetic make-up (Ungoed-Thomas, 2023). It is not enough for a law to be effective on paper; it also must be interpreted and implemented in a way that protects farmed animals in practice. Another example of the limitations of the law is considered below.

The Welfare of Animals at the Time of Killing (England) Regulations 2015 and the stunning of pigs with carbon dioxide

The WATOK 2015 require that farmed animals be stunned prior to slaughter (subject to some religious exemptions). The purpose of stunning is to make the animal unconscious before they are bled so they do not experience pain or suffering at the point of death. In England, as in many other countries, the most common stunning method used for the commercial slaughter of pigs is exposure to high concentrations of carbon dioxide gas (CO_2). As the pigs inhale the gas and their blood oxygen levels decrease, they experience respiratory distress. Their behaviour in the chamber, gasping, jumping, lateral head movements, retreat and escape attempts, and high-pitched vocalisations, indicate distress and suffering. In 2003, the Farm Animal Welfare Council (a government advisory body) stated that 'the use of high concentrations of CO_2 to stun and kill pigs is not acceptable, and we wish to see it phased out in five years' (FAWC, 2003). Instead, its use has increased from 50% in 2013 to 86% in 2018 (government review of WATOK, 2021). In 2020, a report by the European Food Safety Authority stated: 'Exposure to CO_2 at high concentrations … is considered a serious welfare concern by the panel because it is highly aversive and causes pain, fear and respiratory distress' (EFSA, 2020, p.100). Even the National Pig Association accepts that this method of stunning pigs raises welfare concerns: 'While we acknowledge gas stunning isn't perfect, it is the best, most humane and efficacious commercially available option, and often the most reliable slaughter method for ensuring consistency' (Colley & Wasley, 2023). A review of the literature between 2004 and 2021 found very little empirical research had been conducted to find an alternative method of stunning pigs (Sindhøj et al., 2021) and without research, there is unlikely to be a change in the method used soon. WATOK 2015 defines stunning in the same way as the EU Slaughter Regulation as 'any intentionally induced process which causes loss of consciousness and sensibility without pain' (No.1099/2009, Article 2). It is argued that exposing pigs to high concentrations of CO_2 cannot come within the legal definition of stunning because it causes the pigs pain due to the respiratory distress it induces (ALaw, 2023). The definition of stunning under WATOK specifies it is 'without pain'.

The stunning of pigs by exposure to high concentrations of CO_2 gas demonstrates Satz's 'interest-convergence' principle (Satz, 2009). The law purports to protect pigs from unnecessary suffering, but even though there is undisputed evidence that exposing pigs to high concentrations of CO_2 causes them distress and pain (Colley & Wasley, 2023), the practice is retained and deemed lawful. This is because declaring the use of CO_2 unlawful conflicts with human interests for cheap meat produced on a commercial scale. Does WATOK assert our right to use pigs as food and authorise how we harm them by exposure to carbon dioxide?

These two examples illustrate the limitations of the regulations governing farmed animal welfare due to how they are interpreted and implemented. It is not enough for laws to exist on paper; to be effective, the law needs to be adequately interpreted, implemented, and enforced in a way that benefits the animals it is seeking to protect. The next section will examine the crucial issue of enforcement.

The enforcement of legislation

A significant challenge in ensuring adequate legal protection for farmed animals is enforcement. How do we ensure that welfare laws are effectively enforced? In England, the AWA 2006 and regulations relating to farmed animals are centrally overseen by Defra. At ground level, the responsibility for enforcing this law is mainly delegated to local authorities. It does make sense for this to be overseen by local authorities, with control over their specific areas and the need for local enforcement. They have not, however, received any funding from the government to enforce this legislation, and many have failed to do so due to tight resources. Enforcement is implemented through a system of farm inspections. However, there is an insufficient number of inspectors, and there are no set procedures or rules on when and how often farm inspections should be conducted, meaning some may never be inspected. In practice, many farm inspections result from a complaint, but with most farming happening in remote areas and behind closed doors, complaints may be rare, making this an unsatisfactory basis for an inspection. With approximately 300,000 farms in operation in the UK and a lack of investment by the government for inspection and enforcement of welfare legislation, it is not hard to appreciate the issues local authorities face in their role of enforcer. Morton et al. (2020) have highlighted how in jurisdictions where government agencies are responsible for animal law enforcement, few, if any, details on enforcement activities are made publicly available.

A lack of enforcement can also be an issue where there is a spread of responsibility between various government departments, which have limited resources. A 2022 report titled 'The Enforcement Problem' by the Animal Law Foundation and Animal Equality showed that only 2.95% of UK farms were inspected over a three-year period from 2018 to 2021, and of those, one-third identified non-compliance with welfare legislation.

Of these, only 0.33% of farms were prosecuted. Contributing to this poor enforcement is the fact that not all local authorities have appointed inspectors under AWA 2006. The Wooler Review (2014) found that just over 60% of local authorities had appointed inspectors, and nearly 40% stated that they would always refer such matters to the RSPCA.

The lack of inspections by local authorities means that enforcement falls to non-governmental organisations, which may have little to no statutory authority. In England and Wales, this is mainly the RSPCA, which has historically taken on a central role in investigating and prosecuting animal welfare crimes. Looking at the statistics of investigations and prosecutions, we can see that they have played a vital role in the effectiveness of AWA. There are claims that the RSPCA have been responsible for 90% of prosecutions (Morton et al., 2020) and, though the Crown Prosecution Service (CPS) do bring some prosecutions, it has been acknowledged that they only have a 50% success rate, compared to up to 98% success rate for the RSPCA (Lucas, 2013). Due to a highly politicised landscape over animal welfare, which led to the Wooler Review, the RSPCA has now decided to hand over their private prosecutorial role to the CPS and focus more on investigations, hoping to gain statutory powers under AWA 2006 (RSPCA, n.d.). It is too early to know the impact this will have on the enforcement of animal welfare legislation, but it could have a drastic impact. The RSPCA gaining statutory powers could strengthen investigations, but stopping prosecutions may result in even fewer cases making it to trial.

The enforcement of legislation designed to monitor activities on farms behind closed doors, for example, the requirement for CCTV in slaughterhouses also raises challenges. The Mandatory Use of Closed-Circuit Television in Slaughterhouses (England) Regulations 2018 require operators of slaughterhouses to install CCTV that provides a complete and clear image of killing and related operations in all areas of the slaughterhouse where live animals are present (s.3). These regulations were a response to a public outcry about the poor treatment of animals in abattoirs following a number of reports in the media of cruelty to farmed animals awaiting slaughter. For example, in 2011, Animal Aid filmed pigs in an abattoir who were punched in the face by workers, who also stubbed their cigarettes out on them, seemingly for fun. One lame pig was dragged into the slaughter pen by their ears, and an electric goad was used on the face of one pig, with many not stunned properly and not rendered unconscious prior to slaughter (Backler, 2012). The workers involved were successfully prosecuted, but without undercover footage, these acts of cruelty would have gone unknown, sparking public petitions and lobbying for CCTV in slaughterhouses. Under the regulations, arrangements must also be made for the storage of any images and information captured by the CCTV for 90 days from the date it is obtained (s.4). An inspector who has entered premises to enforce WATOK 2015 can, under s.5, inspect a CCTV system, seize or copy images/information captured by the CCTV system, and require any person to provide assistance or information as is reasonable, without delay, amongst other enforcement powers. They can issue enforcement notices, and prosecutions may be brought for non-compliance.

There is little to no research on whether the CCTV regulations have been effective in protecting farmed animals and reducing non-compliance with the welfare legislation. Before the CCTV regulations came into force, FAWC asserted that the use of CCTV in slaughterhouses could be effective but should not be used as a substitute for direct managerial oversight or inspections, and that good training for operators is a necessity (FAWC, 2015). In the 2023 post-implementation review, it was highlighted that the effectiveness of the regulations was difficult to measure as numerous slaughterhouses already had CCTV in place, though the requirement that all slaughterhouses now use CCTV offered consistency across the jurisdiction (Defra, 2023a). Whether or not the CCTV acted as a deterrent was unclear, but it allowed for more instances of non-compliance to be recorded, and it is estimated it resulted in a 30% reduction of welfare non-compliance in 2020/21 compared to 2019/20 (Food Standards Agency, 2021). Further, the use of CCTV proved useful to support enforcement action when non-compliance was identified and was used to support enforcement activity like issuing welfare enforcement notices and prosecutions. Overall, there is some evidence that CCTV helps to strengthen and aid the enforcement of slaughterhouse regulation compliance.

The 'enforcement gap' is a key challenge in the success of animal welfare laws. Wolfensohn has highlighted how the ideal animal welfare law '… has a clear enforcement responsibility, involves an enforcement body with sufficient power and funds, and includes education of the public and industry' (Wolfensohn, 2020, p. 5). The difficulties in investigating animal welfare concerns and enforcing welfare legislation, especially with insufficient funding, means the law may have little practical impact. Local authorities who do carry out animal health and welfare inspections on farms do not usually prosecute cases, given the time and costs involved in doing so.

In 2023, the organisation Animal Equality released a report named 'The Enforcement Solution' that outlines several recommendations to strengthen the enforcement of laws relating to farmed animals. One recommendation is for a licensing system. Farms would pay a licence fee that would fund increased local authority inspections every one to three years depending on the size of the farm and number of animals. Further, it suggests penalties must be robust, including fines, suspension or non-renewal of licences, or prosecution (Animal Equality, 2023). There are also recommendations for the storage and sharing of CCTV footage in slaughterhouses being transferred to the Food Standards Agency (FSA) and being stored for three years, with reviews on a regular basis and compliance issues published in public reports. The post-implementation review of the CCTV regulations by the government supported some of these recommendations, and changes may be made in the future (Defra, 2023a).

Overall, improvements can be made to the enforcement of legislation relating to farmed animal welfare. Changes include more investment by the government into the hiring and training of local authority inspectors, rather than relying on non-governmental organisations to fill this gap in enforcement.

Having examined the challenges with existing legislation in terms of scope, interpretation by the courts, and enforcement, the next section will consider some of the challenges in reforming the law governing farmed animals. It highlights the significant difficulty in implementing the changes that benefit farmed animals where they clash with human interests and the importance of public support with campaigns for law reform.

The challenges for legal reform

The legal protection of farmed animals can be challenging because of the vested interests many people have in continuing to use farmed animals as products; for example, for meat, fur and leather. It makes legal reforms, to better protect farmed animals and improve their welfare, difficult and reform can be very slow. One example of this is the campaign in England to ban exports of live farmed animals.

For decades, the export of live animals for slaughter and fattening has been a controversial subject, inciting passionate protest. Howkins and Merricks (1995, p. 88) researched the history of live animal exports in the UK and noted that:

> Opposition to the transport of live animals has a long history. The Humanitarian League ran campaigns between 1897 and 1903 (if not later still) against the transport of cattle across the Irish Sea. More emotional in appeal, and securing wider support, were campaigns between the 1900s and the 1960s to stop the shipping of live horses to continental Europe for slaughter. In the 1950s, as a result of the demands of the US forces, who argued that British abattoirs failed to come up to American standards, an export trade in live animals developed.

Despite numerous campaigns to stop the practice in the 1960s and 1970s, there was a large increase in the export of live animals, especially sheep and cattle, in the 1980s. In 1993, with the creation of a Single European Market, regulations governing the transport of live animals were relaxed. Howkins and Merricks describe the protests against the export of live animals that took place in 1993 and 1994 at a number of ports, for example:

> On 2 January, the first attempt was made to load animals at Shoreham. About 200 demonstrators confronted a handful of police. As lorries carrying the animals tried to turn into the narrow dock road, the protesters sat down. After a few minutes the lorries turned around and left. The next night similar scenes occurred, although now both the numbers of police and protesters had increased … The following night 1,300 police were brought in, lorries were taken through another entrance, and what the local press called 'the siege of Shoreham' began. For the next three weeks, at the cost of some £2m, the port was kept more or less open, although the demonstrations continued. Locally the demonstrators were widely supported. (1995, p. 93)

Howkins and Merricks observe that the most effective change was achieved through consumer pressure on the airlines and ferry companies involved in transporting live animals, with British Airways and the ferry company P&O both announcing bans on carrying live animals in 1994. However, the export of live animals continues into the 2020s in the UK and across the world. There are laws that offer some protection to animals during transport, such as Council Regulation (EC) No.1/2005, which regulates transport between EU member states, but questions have been raised about the poor enforcement of the law (CIWF, 2016). Globally, millions of animals endure long journeys only to be slaughtered on their arrival at their destination. Numerous welfare concerns are associated with live exports, including overcrowding causing stress and injury, exhaustion due to insufficient rest, hunger and dehydration from insufficient food and water, heat stress caused by overheating in the summer months, and fear and stress due to increased handling, unfamiliar surroundings and poor conditions during transit.

There are also many examples of tragic events; for example, in June 2023, the livestock carrier Al Badir capsized when leaving Sudan for Saudi Arabia with 15,000 sheep onboard, all of whom drowned. In March 2021, 2,700 cattle were stranded in the Mediterranean Sea for three months after being refused entry to several countries because of suspected outbreaks of the bovine disease bluetongue. The surviving animals were eventually taken back to Spain for immediate slaughter. A report by Spanish veterinary officials described 'dire welfare conditions' on the ship, and almost 200 cattle died in transit (Kevany, 2021). In 2017, over 2,400 sheep died from heat stress during a journey on the carrier Awassi Express from Australia to the Middle East. In relation to the number of carriers capsizing and sinking, Miller observes that, 'According to Lloyd's list there have been seven losses of livestock carriers in the past decade, leading to the deaths of 50,000 animals and 170 seafarers' (Miller, 2022).

It is not just the journey that can be perilous for animals; once they arrive at their destination, they will be slaughtered or fattened first before slaughter. The country that exported the animal no longer has any control over the conditions under which the animals are kept or slaughtered. Britain purports not to export animals to the non-European countries where welfare standards are lower, but in 2020, the BBC news reported that British cattle were being slaughtered, without stunning, in a Lebanese abattoir after being transported from the UK to Spain. Once in Spain, the cattle were transported to the Middle East to be slaughtered (Ironmonger, 2020).

The alternative to the export of live animals is for animals to be raised and slaughtered as close as possible to their place of birth and any trade to be in meat carcasses and not live animals.

A number of countries have passed legislation to prohibit all, or some, live animal exports including Great Britain which passed such legislation in 2024 with its Animal Welfare (Livestock Exports) Act 2024. Germany and Luxembourg had already prohibited live animal exports beyond the EU, and together with the Netherlands, Sweden, Belgium and Denmark, are calling for an EU-level ban. Israel has implemented restrictions and plans to phase out the practice altogether. In 2023 legislation came into force in New Zealand banning the export of live animals by sea (NZ government, 2023). The momentum for the ban was fuelled by the sinking of a cargo ship, Gulf Livestock 1, which sank in 2020 in a typhoon on route to China with the deaths of 43 crew members and almost 6,000 dairy cows. New Zealand is the second largest exporter of lamb meat in the world, yet all its lamb has been exported by way of refrigerated carcass meat for many years. It is notable that 'the first ever refrigerated shipment of meat sent to the United Kingdom in 1882' was lamb exported from New Zealand (USDA, 2023, p. 3). New Zealand demonstrates that the trade in meat carcasses is clearly viable as an alternative to live animal exports, and this raises questions about the necessity of animal suffering caused by live export.

Brazil is currently a major exporter of live cattle, with 150,000 animals exported in 2022. Nevertheless, in April 2023, a Brazilian trial court made a historic ruling to ban live animal exports from all the country's ports. The ruling came after the National Forum for the Protection and Defense of Animals, a Brazilian non-governmental organisation, filed a lawsuit in 2017 requesting that all live cattle exports be banned based on animal welfare concerns. The ruling must be reviewed and analysed by the Federal Regional Court, after which the government can appeal the decision, a process that could take many years. In the meantime, the judgment is a significant recognition of the harm live export causes to animals and the need for a ban. The court acknowledged that the long journey by ship and the method of slaughter in the destination country can cause animal suffering that would be unlawful if it occurred in Brazil. There is an anomaly in requiring animals to be stunned when slaughtered in Brazil but permitting the animals to be exported for slaughter in countries where stunning is not required. The federal judge, Djalma Gomes, stated that:

> Animals are not things. They are sentient living beings, that is, individuals who feel hunger, thirst, pain, cold, anguish, fear. (Eurogroup for Animals, 2023)

The judge went on to say,

> To our eternal shame, Brazil was the last country to abolish the slave regime … May we not become the last country to effectively respect the right of non-human animals, but may we be at the forefront in abolishing inappropriate handling and in eradicating all types of cruelty against animals. (Animals Australia, 2023)

In Britain, the Animal Welfare (Livestock Exports) Act 2024 prohibits the export of 'relevant livestock' for slaughter and fattening overseas. A person who commits the offence of exporting relevant livestock will be liable on summary conviction to imprisonment and/or a fine. The definition of 'relevant livestock' includes cattle (and other bovines), horses (and other equines), sheep, goats, pigs and wild boar (s.1(4)). However, other farmed animals, such as rabbits and chickens, are not included in the ban. This is concerning given the large numbers of animals it could affect. In 2018 (before Brexit), the UK exported tens of millions of chicks every year in an industry worth £139m (Kevany, 2021). Post-Brexit, live animal exports to mainland EU stopped due to a lack of border control posts in EU mainland ports. Even though there have been no live exports since 2020, the Animal Welfare (Livestock Exports) Act 2024 is important because it prevents live exports from recommencing in Great Britain. Together with countries like New Zealand and Brazil, it supports the international campaign to ban live exports. Given the availability of a suitable alternative in the form of trade in meat carcasses, it is difficult to justify the necessity of the export of live animals for fattening and slaughter. There is a strong case for arguing that the suffering animals endure during live export, such as injury, disease and dehydration, constitutes unnecessary suffering.

The next section will examine two areas of farming that are ripe for law reform: fish farming and fur farming. Fish are often excluded from laws to protect farmed animals mainly because, until relatively recently, fish were not thought to be sentient. Now there is growing evidence that fish are sentient, greater legal protection is needed (Lambert et al., 2022). The fur trade (and fur farming as an integral part of that trade) is an area where a serious interest (i.e., the animal avoiding suffering and death) is balanced against a trivial interest (a human wearing fur as a fashion item). Therefore, there is a lot of public support for banning the fur trade (Born Free, 2022) and this support makes the chances of successful law reform more likely.

Fish farming

Fish farming raises its own challenges for Animal Law, especially as legal protection is weaker than that for farmed mammals due to the fact that the recognition of fish as sentient is relatively recent in comparison. However, the numbers of fish involved in farming are massive; for example, in the UK, up to 77 million fish are farmed and killed each year for food, leading to calls for better legal protection for farmed fish (Canham, 2022). In England, fish are specifically excluded from the Welfare of Farmed Animals (England) Regulations 2007; however, they are protected by the AWA 2006, which means that unnecessary suffering in fish farming is prohibited. For the purposes of slaughter, fish come under WATOK 2015 regulations, but there are no fish-specific regulations to take account of the needs of different species. In summary, there are no laws relating specifically to the handling, stunning and slaughter of fish. The sentience of fish is now well documented, but fish are seldom afforded the same consideration or legal protection as warm-blooded farmed animals (Lambert et al., 2022; Brown, 2015), even though there is public support for this (The Humane League, 2021a). Given fish sentience and intelligence, farming practices need to be assessed to determine whether fish suffer in fish farms and, if there is evidence of suffering, whether that suffering is necessary.

The RSPCA raises a number of welfare concerns for farmed fish in the UK, including water quality, handling, stocking densities, transport and slaughter methods (RSPCA, n.d.). Some of the issues that arise during slaughter include fasting, which is common with farmed salmon, to reduce their metabolic rate and physical activity before handling and reduce water fouling by emptying their stomachs to aid hygienic processing (CIWF, 2018). There are four ways that fish welfare can be impacted during farming according to Saraiva et al. (2022): ethological, physiological, human-induced and environmental. Ethological relates to the impairment of behavioural functions and the ability to cope with the environment, such as restricting free movements. Physiological relates to the health of the fish, such as infections and parasites. Human-induced challenges include handling and slaughter. Environmental challenges are usually found in the water, such as water quality, light conditions and temperature, as well as transfer between salt water and fresh water. They recommend that welfare is assessed by reference to the species of fish being farmed to inform the farm design and practices used.

Enforcement on fish farms has been shown to be particularly poor. In 2021, The Humane League found that no official public institution, such as Defra or the Animal and Plant Health Agency (APHA), carries out welfare inspections of fish at slaughter, each not wanting to take responsibility (The Humane League, 2021b). Since then, the Scottish Government has appointed APHA Scotland to carry out mandatory welfare inspections. There are, however, multiple bodies involved in the oversight of fish farming. For example, in England and Wales, the Fish Health Inspectorate carries out inspections, on behalf of APHA and Defra, to prevent the introduction and spread of diseases. The Centre for Environment Fisheries and Aquaculture Science (Cefas) is an executive agency sponsored by Defra, that provides evidence and advice to the UK on different matters, such as safeguarding human and animal health and food security and carries out inspections on fish and shellfish farms to investigate serious outbreaks of disease (Cefas, n.d.). They do not, however, have any official enforcement powers like the Fish Health Inspectorate. There needs to be more consistency and cohesion between the different bodies, with robust legislation and enforcement mechanisms.

Further, the CCTV regulations at slaughter do not extend to farmed fish, even though poor practices have been recorded, such as fish having their gills cut while still conscious or being thrown aggressively by workers to the floor and left to asphyxiate (Conservative Animal Welfare Foundation and Animal Equality UK, 2018). There are calls for the CCTV regulations to be extended to fish slaughter premises (Animal Equality, 2022), and this is yet to be implemented in England.

It is important to note that the recommendations by animal welfare groups such as The Humane League and Animal Equality through campaigns and research are not new. In 2014, the FAWC recommended the extension of the Welfare of Farmed Animals (England) Regulations 2007 to include fish, with suitable modifications and reviews of compliance and enforcement of relevant legislation by responsible bodies (FAWC, 2014). These recommendations have not been implemented to date. Only by reconsidering our laws relating to fish can we provide greater protection to the most farmed animal in the country.

Fur farming

The Humane Society International reports that one hundred million animals are bred and killed each year for their pelt to supply the fashion industry, though there has been a decline in the industry in recent years (Humane Society International, n.d.). Over 95% of fur sold globally originates from fur farms, with the rest from trapped live animals in the wild (Fur Free Alliance, n.d.(a)). The most common animals killed for their fur are mink, racoons, arctic foxes and red foxes. The main difference between fur farming and farming for food is that animals bred and killed for their pelts are wild animals that have not been domesticated and therefore struggle in their contained environment. For example, mink are solitary quasi-aquatic creatures that will build up to 24 dens around the lake or riverbank where they live to store food and rest. On fur farms, they cannot carry out natural behaviours, as they are confined to small cages with many other mink, which causes them to suffer considerable stress and can result in behaviours such as fur chewing and biting. Mink also suffer from sores from the wire cages and may be overfed to create a larger pelt, which can cause obesity. The slaughter method used on fur farms is species dependent, with carbon dioxide gas commonly used for mink and electrocution commonly used for foxes.

Fur farming has been banned in England and Wales since 2003, when the Fur Farming (Prohibition) Act 2000 came into force, making it the first country to do so. This Act made it illegal under s.1(1) to keep animals 'solely or primarily for slaughter for the value of their fur.' Bans were then implemented in Scotland with the Fur Farming (Prohibition) (Scotland) Act 2002, and Northern Ireland followed with the Fur Farming (Prohibition) (Northern Ireland) Order 2002. At the time of the ban, mink was the only animal used for fur farming in the UK and operated on a license system. Many countries are following this ban, with Lithuania the most recent. China is one of the biggest producers of fur; Europe is not far behind, though this has been declining steadily since 2014 with some key producers introducing bans, such as Norway, which, in 2019, introduced a ban to phase out fur farms entirely by 2025. Though reluctant to entirely ban fur farming (Grove, 2023), the EU introduced legislation to provide for the welfare of animals on fur farms. For example, Directive 98/58/EC provides that keepers in Member States must ensure animals are not caused any unnecessary pain, suffering or injury. There are also welfare provisions, for example, ensuring the conditions in which the animals are kept have regard to their species and there are specific provisions relating to accommodation, food and water, as well as breeding provisions. Animals on fur farms also come under Council Regulation (EC) 1099/2009 for the time of killing, which states the animals should be spared any avoidable pain or suffering at the time of killing (Article 3) and sets out requirements for the various methods used, such as carbon dioxide gassing and electrocution.

Although fur farming is prohibited in England and Wales, it is still lawful to trade in fur by importing it from overseas (subject to exceptions). Therefore, to protect animals, it is not enough to simply ban fur farming, the international trade in fur also needs to be addressed. The EU has introduced some species-specific bans to the market, such as Regulation EC No 1523/2007, which bans dog and cat fur from being placed on the market or imported or exported within the EU. A similar ban on seal products was introduced in the 1007/2009 Regulation, though there is an exception for seal fur that has been obtained by traditional hunts conducted by Inuit or other indigenous communities. As the UK was a member of the EU at the time, it implemented these bans and following Brexit the ban has been implemented into domestic law under the European Union (Withdrawal Agreement) Act 2020 (The Cat and Dog Fur (Control of Movement etc) (EU Exit) Regulations 2022).

In the last decade, there have been issues with real fur being used on fashion items that are then marketed and sold as faux fur. This means that consumers are buying a product that may not align with their ethics due to dishonesty or a lack of care on the part of the seller. For example, in 2019, an online clothes retailer sold a pom-pom jumper that contained real animal fur, most likely rabbit, but advertised it as faux fur (BBC, 2019). Other popular fashion websites were found to be doing the same. This is becoming a long-standing issue, with Fur Free Alliance reporting in 2016 that 17 large, high-end retailers were found to be selling real fur advertised as faux fur (Fur Free Alliance, 2016). This misleading of consumers is clearly unacceptable, whether intentional or not, particularly as a YouGov poll from 2020 found a 75% support for the ban of fur product imports, with the majority believing fashion brands selling fur products to be unethical or cruel, and only 3% currently wearing real fur.

A result of the mis-selling of faux fur products led to a Defra inquiry in 2018, finding retailers mis-selling some products as faux fur, which actually contained fur from rabbits, racoons and mink. Defra noted that in most cases the retailers were not intentionally selling real fur products, and confusion can be caused by the 1007/2011 Textile Labelling Regulation from the EU (Efra, 2018). This regulation stipulates that any textiles containing fur (and other animal products like leather and bone) include a label with the wording 'contains non-textile parts of animal origin' (Article 12) so that the consumer is aware of the animal content. This means that a coat that includes a real fur trim on the hood must include that wording (although it doesn't have to specify what part of an animal is present, just the fact that it is fur). However, for a garment to fall within the scope of the Textile Labelling Regulation, 80% of its weight must be comprised of textiles, and fur is not a textile. This leads to the anomalous situation of a coat including a real fur trim on the hood falling within the regulation and requiring a label to indicate the presence of animal parts, whereas a coat made almost entirely of fur would not come within the regulation and no label is required. Therefore, the labelling of fur products can be confusing for consumers and can ultimately result in people unknowingly buying products that contain real fur.

Following these various investigations, the UK government explored a ban on the import and export of all fur products and a prohibition on their sale but potential challenges to Freedom of Goods whilst still a Member State of the EU needed to be explored. In 2021, Israel became the first country to prohibit the sale of fur (Fur Free Alliance, n.d.). Following Britain's departure from the EU, the issue has been considered further, and in 2024 the Fur (Import and Sale) Bill 2024-25 was introduced into the English Parliament as a Private Members Bill. If passed into law it will extend the existing ban on the import and trade in cat, dog and seal fur to include other animal fur. In 2022, the UK imported £42 million worth of fur and exported £14.5 million in fur and fur products, primarily in clothing and apparel products (Parliament: House of Commons, 2023).

Since leaving the EU, the debate has focused on the World Trade Organisation (WTO) rules rather than EU trading laws and whether a ban on the fur trade would breach GATT Article XI. This Article stipulates that no prohibition or restrictions on imports or exports of any product, other than duties, taxes or other charges, can be instituted by a contracting party, though there are exemptions to this. There is precedent from the WTO for animal welfare concerns allowing for bans on imports that carry animal welfare and ethical concerns, such as the case brought by Norway and Canada against the EU. This case concerned Regulation (EC) 1009/2009, which prohibited the import and sale of processed and unprocessed seal products, except for products derived from Inuit or indigenous community hunts or those for marine resource management purposes.

Norway and Canada argued that this ban breached various trade laws and challenged the legislation (WTO, 2014). The EU successfully argued an exemption under Article XX(a) of GATT that there are public morals concerning animal welfare (Offor & Walter, 2017). It can therefore be concluded that a UK ban on the import and sale of fur would be allowed under the WTO, particularly considering the public support for the ban and public concern over animal welfare (Dunn, 2019).

Why farmed animal health and welfare is important – the anthropocentric factors

This section moves away from animal welfare and the concept of farmed animals having a 'life worth living' and considers the impact of intensive farming on the human population to assess the anthropocentric arguments against current intensive farming practices. After all, the dominant theory as to the cause of SARS-CoV-2 and the subsequent COVID-19 pandemic, is that it emerged from our treatment and relationship with animals used for food. This has had severe consequences for human health as well significant effects on businesses and economies worldwide (Schuck-Paim et al., 2023).

Food security and the environment

The impact of intensive farming, including food and fur farming, on the environment is becoming more apparent. There is insufficient space here to provide details on all the environmental impacts, but this section will provide a brief overview of some of the main issues. According to a 2017 report produced by the Pew Commission on intensive farming in the United States, intensive farming results in three main causes of environmental degradation: firstly, the production of large volumes of animal waste; secondly, a lack of appropriate management and disposal of waste; and thirdly, unsustainable water usage and soil degradation from associated feed production. Food production uses double the volume of water than all other human activities combined (Richardson et al., 2016). The intensive methods of farming are having a drastic impact on the environment, with it being responsible for approximately 20% of the greenhouse gases produced by human-generated emissions (Horrigan et al., 2002).

The pollution caused by intensive farming can cause risks to human health. For example, some intensive farms release large amounts of toxic air emissions, like ammonia (Michener, 2015). Odours from these farms can also interrupt the enjoyment of the natural environment by attracting flies and rats (Gerber et al., 2008). Studies have found that living near an intensive animal farm can contribute to illness, causing asthma-like symptoms due to poor air quality (Sigsgaard & Balmes, 2017). The intensive farming of chickens provides a good example of the concerns for human health. Chickens have become the most farmed land animal in the world, with CIWF (n.d.) stating more than 50 billion chickens are reared annually for food. The intensive farming of chickens causes multiple environmental impacts, including excess waste materials that can contaminate water and soil, gases that can diminish human health, and the use of microorganisms and pharmaceuticals that can lead to antimicrobial and multidrug resistance in both human and non-human animals (Gržinić et al., 2023). Chicken waste pollution in the River Wye, which has starved the river of oxygen and caused algae, has led to a multi-million-pound court case against one of the UK's biggest food producers, seeking to compensate those living near the river (BBC, 2024).

Another common result of intensive and unsustainable agricultural practices is land degradation, defined as the 'temporary or permanent decline in the productive capacity of the land' (Scherr & Yadav, 1996, p. 3). This damage to the land has impacts on the environment, but also on humans generally, as a decrease in the productivity of the land can adversely affect a country's food supply and trade. When land degradation occurs, other land is sought to replace the degraded land and this pushes farmland into natural habitats, causing further land destruction, depletion of water sources, loss of biodiversity and contributes to climate change (Steinfeld et al., 2006). The causes of land degradation can be connected and complex (Gupta, 2019). Deforestation carried out to create more space for agriculture can lead to flooding and soil erosion by water and wind. The impact of agricultural expansion is causing nearly 90% of global deforestation, and 38.46% of this is used for livestock grazing (FAO UN, 2020).

Intensive meat production raises food security concerns. To sustain the large numbers of livestock reared for a high-demand meat market, much of the crops grown contribute to livestock feed. Research estimates that 36% of calories produced by the world's crops are used for animal feed, and only 12% of these calories are returned to the human diet (Cassidy et al., 2013). This results in an inefficient system, whereby we spend more calorie energy feeding the livestock and eating meat rather than directly eating the grain. If we were to instead grow the plant crops exclusively for human consumption, it could potentially feed an additional 4 billion people globally (Cassidy et al., 2013). This grain, if used instead for direct human consumption, could contribute to solving global hunger as the feed from plant protein can go directly to humans, rather than through meat protein, which returns fewer calories (CIWF, 2009). Another predicted challenge of food security is caused by the effects of climate change creating difficult growing conditions, such as heat stress, to produce enough food to meet the demands of a growing population (CIWF, 2009). This also means there will not be enough crops to feed the livestock, which is heavily contributing to the climate crisis. To help slow climate change and to ensure food security, eating less meat and using the grains fed to livestock to feed humans is a more sustainable system. There is a need to produce more food to meet population demands, but sustainably achieving this is challenging (Xiong et al., 2022).

A way to combat this is to adopt a plant-based diet. It is difficult to know how many vegans there are in the world, and there are varying figures, but there are estimates from 79 million to 230 million people (Ipsos, 2018). There are various reasons why people adopt a vegan diet, including animal welfare, the environment and for health reasons (McKeown & Dunn, 2021). In the UK, the driving factor is animal welfare, followed by the environment (Jones, 2020). Research shows that adopting a meat-free and dairy-free diet is the most effective way to reduce environmental footprints (Scarborough et al., 2023) and advocates for plant-based and flexitarian diets (Springmann, 2018). Another way to help improve the negative impacts of intensive farming is regenerative agriculture, which is seen as a stepping stone from industrial farming to organic farming practices, which are better for the environment (Hargreaves-Méndez & Hötzel, 2023).

Spread of diseases and pandemics

The UK is considered one of the nations where the distribution risk of zoonotic emerging infectious diseases is high, and poor farmed animal welfare and health is a factor in this (Allen et al., 2017; Enticott et al., 2011). The outbreak of H5N8 (Bird Flu) in 2020 was widely reported, leading to millions of birds, mainly chickens, turkeys and ducks, being culled at farms (Kevany, 2022). It also spread to domestic pets and wildlife (WHO, 2023), with cases reported in wild birds and mammals. Other outbreaks the UK has faced, such as E. coli and Salmonella, have shown the link between animal and human health and demonstrate how the mismanagement of animal health can have social and economic consequences. For example, the outbreak of foot and mouth disease in 2001 cost the taxpayer an estimated £8 billion (Enticott et al., 2011). The need for better farming practices to protect all species is becoming more apparent, not just for animal welfare but for the general welfare of the world. In response, the World Health Organization advocates for One Health, an integrated approach 'that aims to sustainably balance and optimize the health of people, animals and ecosystems' (WHO, 2023b), recognising that they are all linked and interdependent.

Though many countries have laws aimed at protecting the welfare of all domestic animals, it has been noted that farmed animals are often implicitly or explicitly exempt from this protection (Wadiwel, 2002). For example, in many US states, there is a 'customary farming practice' exemption from animal cruelty legislation (Wolfson & Sullivan, 2004). Eisen (2019) argues that this exemption from welfare laws, however, is not just contained on a national level but also in areas such as international trade law, where there needs to be a free flow of goods between borders. This softening of welfare legislation for farmed animals, mostly for economic reasons, has drastic impacts on animal welfare and, ultimately, human health. The increase in intensive farming has meant a decrease in animal welfare due to the huge numbers needing to be farmed. These intensive farming practices have been associated with more than 50% of zoonotic diseases that have emerged in humans since 1940 (Rohr et al., 2019). Research shows that fur farming is a risk to human health and represents a significant transmission hub for viral zoonoses (Zhao et al, 2024). The UN Environment Programme highlighted in their 2020 report that to prevent further pandemics we need to de-risk our food system by enhancing the monitoring and regulation of food systems and strengthening animal health. The report stresses the need to move from short-term political responses to long-term political commitments, which must include the entire food chain (UN, 2020).

In England and Wales, the legislation in place to safeguard the welfare of farmed animals, including areas such as husbandry and slaughter, largely derives from European Union Directives that have been transposed into domestic legislation. Whilst it should be celebrated that we have this welfare legislation, the law needs to keep pace with advances in scientific research, particularly in preventing disease transmission, and there is the need to revisit the legislation in terms of both protection and enforcement. A report in 2006, commissioned by Defra, highlighted the complexity of current farmed animal welfare regimes resulting in inconsistency of results, and stated the risk to animal health/welfare and human health were 'simply too great' (Eves, 2006). The UK government has had opportunities to improve farmed animals' health and welfare in recent legislation, for example, during the implementation of the Agriculture Act 2020, but has failed to do so (McCulloch, 2019b). Though the Agriculture Act 2020 allows farmers to be rewarded financially when increasing animal welfare, it has not prevented the government from forming detrimental trade deals, including importing meat from countries where the welfare standards are much lower than our own (ResPublica, 2022). This may result in driving down welfare standards in the UK, as domestic farmers struggle to compete with cheaper imports (UK Centre for Animal Law and Wildlife and Countryside Link, 2023). This in turn may have a drastic impact on animal and human health. Considering that current and new zoonotic diseases emerge from animals consumed for food at various stages of the animal food supply chain (Morse et al., 2012), legislation must be effective at all stages, from farm to slaughter. Defra and APHA published the Animal Health and Welfare Framework, a strategy for local authorities to work with communities to safeguard the farming industry and help prevent animal disease, which in turn promotes animal welfare and protects human health. This includes the enforcement of international and national animal health and welfare legislation, sharing data and intelligence, and ensuring the training and qualification of officers who are responsible for the delivery of animal health and welfare controls (APHA and Defra, 2018).

Human welfare in food production

Research is starting to focus on the impact of farmed animals on human welfare, namely workers in food production, though it still needs to be developed. People often forget that the food on their plate has had multiple human contacts along the way: on the farm, during transport, and at abattoirs for slaughter. The people who work in these various industries may suffer too, and from a wider social justice perspective, the negative impact of intensive farming across the globe is huge. This is an important but often invisible issue that should be confronted. Not to do so 'is to ignore a key cornerstone of the intersectional labyrinth that is the pursuit of social justice' (Muller, 2018, p. 82).

Working conditions in slaughterhouses vary worldwide. Research in Kenya found that slaughterhouses often do not provide workers with protective equipment and cleaning facilities, which has resulted in a high level of illnesses being reported in workers (Cook et al., 2017). Injuries have also been reported in Western societies, including severe injuries caused by knives used to cut through bone or caused by animals kicking or falling from apparatus as they struggle (Dillard, 2008; Eisnitz, 2006). In the United States, in extreme cases, deaths have been reported caused by poisonous fumes inhaled when cleaning tanks for blood collection (Muller, 2018).

More recently, consideration has been given to the mental well-being of staff in slaughterhouses with reports of alcohol abuse and suicide causing concern (BBC, 2020). Research in Denmark found that some workers, at the start of their employment, suffered from feelings of shame and guilt. To deal with the negative impacts of their work, some slaughterhouse workers adopt psychological defences, becoming emotionally detached from their work (Baran et al., 2016), leading to expressions of anger that had an impact on their home life in the form of domestic or sexual abuse (Victor & Barnard, 2016; Fitzgerald et al., 2009). Despite the gruelling nature of the job, the wages of slaughterhouse workers have fallen below that of average manufacturing wages (Dillard, 2008). The workers must maintain high production speeds, especially with increases in meat production due to greater consumer demand for meat. Some reported conditions in the United States, particularly those in post-slaughter production, include workers being prohibited from taking toilet breaks, causing health issues (Oxfam, 2015). Thus, the eating of meat is very much a human social justice issue, as well as an animal welfare and ethical issue.

The ethics of meat eating

If farmed animals suffer as a result of farming practices, does eating meat become a moral decision? If we know that our actions will cause harm to another sentient being, should we take reasonable steps to prevent or alleviate that risk of harm? Singer thinks that people have a moral duty to be vegetarians. He is a utilitarian and argues that being a utilitarian requires a person to be a vegetarian: 'I am a vegetarian because I am a utilitarian. I believe that applying the principle of utility to our present situation – especially the methods now used to rear animals for food and the variety of food available to us – leads to the conclusion that we ought to be vegetarians' (Singer, 1980, p. 325).

Utilitarians will find out as much as possible about the consequences of their actions and carry out a cost-benefit assessment to ascertain what action (in this case, whether to eat meat) will bring about the best outcome for minimising pain and maximising pleasure. However, identifying the factors to go into the cost-benefit assessment and deciding on the relative weighting to attach to these factors can be difficult. For example, when assessing the costs involved in eating meat, the following factors may be relevant: animal suffering, environmental costs and risks to human health. Allocating what weight, if any, to give to these factors is subjective and will depend on the cultural, religious and geographic context as well as the beliefs and values of the individuals concerned. There is evidence that animals suffer in intensive farming practices (for example, McCulloch, 2022; RSPCA, 2020a), but different people will have different views on the importance of this in the cost-benefit assessment. Vegans are likely to find any animal suffering unacceptable, whereas meat-eaters are likely to feel some suffering is inevitable in intensive farming practices and justifiable to provide food for humans. Transparency is important to ensure people have full and accurate understanding of the suffering farmed animals endure. In his book *Animal Liberation*, Singer gives detailed information about the living conditions of farmed animals because knowledge is an important component of the cost-benefit assessment. This is also true for the environmental costs of meat production; accurate knowledge of the costs is vital. Two influential United Nations (UN) reports by the Food Agriculture Organisation in 2006 and 2013 provided valuable information on the contribution of livestock to climate change. The UN report in 2013 identified three key concerns:

> First, the production of animal protein, particularly when fed on dedicated crops, is typically less efficient than the production of equivalent amounts of plant protein. Second, extensive livestock are often kept in remote environments where deforestation and land degradation reflect weaknesses in institutions and policies. Lastly, intensive livestock production tends to cluster in locations with cost advantages (often close to cities or ports) where insufficient land is available for the recycling of waste from livestock, leading to nutrient overloads and pollution.

Globally, the livestock sector is one of the largest contributors to greenhouse gases and one of the leading causal factors in the loss of biodiversity, as well as being the main source of water pollution (United Nations, 2006). In addition to the costs to farmed animals and the environment, there is growing evidence of risks to human health from the consumption of red and processed meat (Papier, 2021; Bouvard, 2015). Against these costs, the benefits of eating meat must be identified and weighed in the balance. Meat is a valuable source of protein, especially in countries where it is difficult to access alternative sources. Many people enjoy the taste of meat and eating it is a source of pleasure for them. Another consideration is the livelihoods of the many people who work in the meat industry. Regan is critical of Singer's utilitarian approach as applied to the moral dilemma of eating meat. He argues that utilitarianism does not require a person to be vegetarian; only a rights approach will do this. In constructing his argument against the utilitarian theory, he emphasised the significance of people's livelihoods. He lists farmers, feed producers and retailers, cage manufacturers, slaughterers and those who package and ship meat as all being invested in the continuation of eating meat. Since their interests need to be weighed in the cost-benefit assessment and considerable weight is likely to be allocated to these human interests, it may, according to Regan, result in a utilitarian deciding to eat meat. Regan has the same goal as Singer. He wants people to stop eating meat, but he advocates that only an animal rights theory requires people to be vegetarians because they must respect the inherent value of animals as subjects-of-a-life. There are numerous ethical theories that can be applied to the question of eating meat. This section applies the utilitarian theory as one example with the aim of illustrating the point that eating meat is a moral decision because animals are sentient. It should not be done without thought to the lives of the animals that are being eaten and consideration of whether they are suffering in farms, transport vehicles, markets and slaughterhouses.

Conclusion

The number of farmed animals raised and slaughtered each year worldwide for their meat, fur and other parts is so enormous it is difficult to comprehend. Since farmed animals are sentient (with the possible exception of insects, although research is underway to determine the question of sentience in insects), laws are needed to protect them from pain and suffering. There are challenges in drafting such laws, not least because of the vested interest humans have in continuing to use farmed animals as our resources and in ways that satisfy the huge demand for their meat and as cheaply as possible. This means that even when we know animals are suffering, for example, the CO_2 gassing of pigs, we continue to use this method of slaughter because it is efficient and cheap for meeting human demand.

In drafting legislation to protect farmed animals, we need to ensure it protects all those that are sentient (with the capacity to include new species as scientific research advances) and that there are not wide exclusions (such as the 'customary farming practice exemption' in the US) that radically narrow the scope of the legislation.

Where we have existing legislation that seeks to protect farmed animals from suffering or meet their welfare needs, there are challenges in ensuring these laws are adequately interpreted by the courts and enforced by relevant enforcement bodies. Since farmed animals are seen as human resources, it is difficult for their interests to be given the moral weighting they deserve as sentient beings. It is easy for enforcement agencies with limited funds to put the welfare of individual farmed animals low down in their list of priorities.

This chapter has explored some of the key themes in Animal Law relating to farmed animals: their sentience; their legal status as property; the legal concept of unnecessary suffering, and the vital link between law, science and ethics, especially in law reform. In the context of these themes, the chapter has identified some of the challenges in Animal Law: the need for legislation to keep pace with advances in science – for example, to bring sentient invertebrates under its protection; the need for legislation to be interpreted by the courts in a way that is true to the aim and purpose of the legislation, and the need for legislation to be adequately enforced to better protect farmed animals from suffering and to better meet their welfare needs.

CHAPTER SEVEN

Protecting wildlife from cruelty

Introduction

This is the first of two chapters looking at the challenges seen in the law relating to wildlife. The chapter considers how wildlife is protected from cruelty, which in law is seen as unnecessary suffering. The next chapter will consider Animal Law in the context of wildlife extinctions and biodiversity loss. These chapters, although split for ease of understanding, are really parts of the same issue and need to be read together as the information overlaps (Johannsen, 2020, 2022). However, there is also a dichotomy in terms of how the law deals with wildlife issues, as '…[i]nternational wildlife law addresses conservation and sustainable use issues requiring international cooperation, while animal law pursues humane treatment of the individual animal and moral considerations of wildlife well-being. Generally, conservation lawyers want to ensure that the species does not go extinct, while animal lawyers aim for the well-being of individuals of the species' (Adam & Schaffner, 2017, p. 1). This chapter concentrates on the Animal Law issue of cruelty, so the well-being of the individual animal and the next chapter on conservation, but it is important to remember that whilst the law protecting individual animals and to protect habitats are distinct in terms of their aims they often work together in terms of their effects.

In terms of the adequacy of the law to protect wildlife from cruelty, the risk of harm to wild animals demonstrates the need for laws to protect them as vulnerable sentient beings capable of feeling pain and suffering. As in many countries, UK law adopts a welfare approach; however, this only applies in limited situations to wild animals, so the legal protection they have is from the limited baseline of protection from cruelty. So, whilst all animals can be used for human benefit, even where it may cause detriment to the animal, the law provides more protection to domestic and farmed animals.

The chapter will begin by considering how the law has viewed wildlife historically, then examine wildlife protection against cruelty before moving on to explore some of the wider issues, particularly relating to the culling of badgers, hunting, shooting, fishing, keeping wildlife in captivity and animals used in entertainment. The chapter will consider the balance between human and animal interests and discuss how the law can improve the lives of animals. Additionally, it will highlight the challenges in enforcing the law to protect wild animals from acts of cruelty. As in previous chapters, the UK will continue to serve as a primary case study due to our familiarity with its legal system and historically it has been at the forefront of legal protections. However, we will also briefly consider the EU's approach and international law, where they influence domestic legislation.

Definitions are important in law, and there are semantic and ontological discussions that can be had about all the terms referred to. For example, the terms we use for environmental issues can affect our perception of them, so using the term climate crisis rather than climate change, global heating rather than warming may better reflect the reality of the situation we are facing more. But do these terms reflect the whole range of impacts on the planet? We use wildlife to include 'animals and plants that grow independently of people, usually in natural conditions' (Cambridge Dictionary, n.d.). Wild animals are animals in their natural state that have not been domesticated. This includes non-domesticated animals living freely in the natural environment as well as those living in captivity, whether kept as pets or for other reasons such as entertainment. We use the term 'wildlife' to include all the wild things on the planet, but in this chapter the law often relates to just wild animals, and so both terms will be used as appropriate.

History of the protection of wildlife and land use

It is only recently that the law has sought to protect wild animals in their own right, rather than because they are of some economic value. In the past, law viewed wildlife through an anthropocentric lens, as pests, food or quarry (Reid, 1994). Wildlife was captured and kept for entertainment, as illustrated by Blunt (1976, pp. 15–17):

> Julius Caesar mentions in his *Commentaries* that even in those days, rich English landowners had parks in which they kept hares, geese, and chickens, not for eating but almost as 'pets'. The Norman lords who came over with the Conqueror appropriated parks such as these and stocked them with deer for the chase and sometimes with less common animals also. There is a record of a nobleman receiving a bear from William

> Rufus, and William of Malmesbury tells us that Henry I had at Woodstock lions, leopards, lynxes, camels, and other animals, including a remarkable owl which had been sent to him by William of Montpellier. Henry III, who in 1252 transferred the Woodstock collection to London, had a polar bear for whose maintenance at the Tower of London the City's sheriffs were made responsible; they were also obliged to furnish it with a muzzle and an iron chain, and a stout rope to hold it when, to save expense, it was taken down to the Thames to fish for its supper. In 1254 Henry was sent by his son-in-law, King Louis IX of France, a sensational present: the first elephant ever to be seen in England. Again, the unfortunate sheriffs had to bear the substantial cost of feeding it and of constructing a cage, 40 feet by 20, to house it ... The animals at the Tower were miserably housed in Stuart times, and Evelyn, when in Florence in 1644, commented that the city's wolves, cats, bears, tigers, and lions, kept in a deep-walled court, were "therefore to be seen with much more pleasure that those at the Tower of London, in their grates".

The view of wildlife was also tied into the view of the land and the wildlife on it being a form of property, particularly in the case of wildlife being seen as game (Kirby, 1933). So, to understand how the law has developed in terms of protecting wildlife from cruelty, it is necessary to consider the historical context of land use in England and Wales, particularly its use as land for 'field sports'.

Much of the English landscape has been changed over the centuries. Deforestation occurred as wood was required for building and other purposes. During the Middle Ages, land ownership was seen as a reward for loyalty and as a way of acquiring wealth. Many of the restrictions on the commoners' use of land, as well as the types of activities permitted, were fixed after the Norman Conquest and are still evident today. William the Conqueror put England under the heel of a landowning class of knights and claimed all the land for the Crown. After this, land would be owned by permission of the King. William the Conqueror therefore created the legacy that this group of landowners would enjoy a privileged status and an associated passion for hunting. Forests had some legal protection from this time until the 14th century, as the Crown saw them as a way of raising revenue through deforestation, the killing of game, and enclosure. Originally, the Royal Forests had covered a quarter of England. By 1330, the area of Royal Forest had shrunk to two-thirds of what it had been in 1250. This led to restrictions being placed on the use of this land by commoners who had previously enjoyed many rights over it (Shoard, 1997, p. 28). This set the foundation for much of the view of land use we see, particularly in England today.

The difference in terms of class that flowed from property rights led to differences in the law as to who was undertaking the activities. The law makes a distinction between the use of animals to fight as sport and the hunting of wildlife as sport. Hunting, like the fighting of animals, has a long history. But unlike the latter, which is largely a working-class preoccupation, hunting has long been tied into the ownership and rights over the land. Thus, fighting using animals has long been prohibited under the law. In 1835, animal fighting, such as dogfighting, cockfighting, bear-baiting and badger baiting became illegal (under the Cruelty to Animals Act 1835). This can be contrasted with the use of land for the hunting and shooting or fishing of wildlife either for 'sport' or for food, where hunting with dogs was not legislated against in England until the Hunting Act 2004.

In the past, cruelty laws were not applied to wildlife, and wildlife was seen as 'other', not part of the protections given to other animals instead being seen by the law as objects for human gain and entertainment (Kean, 1998). So, whilst hunting has a long history as a means of obtaining food for our ancestors, hunting as a pastime or 'sport' in the UK began in the Anglo-Saxon and Norman periods and was a driver of land use and was seen as an elite sport (Richards, 2014; Griffin, 2007):

> The evidence suggests that the origins of hunting lie in the Anglo-Saxon and Norman period. It was the conception of the Norman Court that hunting was an exclusive and entertaining sport which required both ritual and etiquette in its practice...The historical evidence shows that hunting very quickly became established as the exclusive occupation of the elite who preserved that exclusivity by harsh penalties for other classes indulging in the same activity. During the period between the Conquest and the Industrial Revolution the traditions and rituals of hunting were most assiduously observed by those who aspired to elite status, most particularly by the squirearchy which rose to prominence during the late Middle Ages. (Thomas, 1983, pp. 11–12)

In law, wild animals were not protected unless they were property. Under the common law in the UK, the term wild animals *ferae naturae* was applied to animals that were not domesticated or in captivity. In consequence, there was no absolute property in wild animals while living unless they were goods or chattels (*Case of Swans* 1592 7 CO Rep). Qualified property could be acquired over wild animals *per industrium*. This arises by lawfully taking, taming, or reclaiming them, or until they regain their natural liberty (*Blades* v. *Higgs* 1865 11 HL Cas 621). Qualified rights could be claimed under *ratione soli and rationae priavalegii*, where the owner of the land could take, kill and hunt wild animals unless they granted a licence, shooting or sporting rights to another when the grantee obtained qualified privilege above the rights of the landowner (*Blades* v. *Higgs* 1865 11 HL Cas 621). The common law controls over animals are now superseded by statutory controls; for example, the Wild Creatures and Forest Laws Act 1971 abolished prerogative rights (historical powers of the Crown) over animals and birds, and these rights are now limited to fish and swans (the King owns unmarked mute swans swimming in open waters).

So, we can see that in terms of specific protection from cruelty, wildlife has been treated differently to domestic animals. Whilst domestic animals in England and Wales received a degree of protection from cruelty since 1822 under Martin's Act, wildlife had a much longer wait. For centuries, wildlife has been open to direct and indirect destruction unless they happen to be rare or protected as game. Captive wildlife was protected under the Wild Animals in Captivity Protection Act 1900, which was replaced by later legislation and now comes under the Animal Welfare Act 2006. Whilst other pieces of legislation did give some protection, wildlife not in captivity had to wait a lot longer to be protected from specific acts of cruelty under the Wild Mammals Protection Act 1996.

The law on cruelty to wild animals

Unlike domesticated animals such as farm animals, wildlife was not protected from cruelty under the Martins Act 1822. Wild animals could only get protection under the Protection of Animals Act 1911 (which was the legislation protecting domestic and captive animals at the time) if they were captive. However, cases such as *Rowley* v. *Murphy* and *Hudnott* v. *Campbell* highlighted the problems underlying the Protection of Animals Act 1911 in terms of when a wild animal was captive and so came under the protection of the Act. In *Rowley* v. *Murphy*, a wild stag, which was being hunted, jumped over the hedge of a field on to a main road, slipped on the tarmac surface, and went under a stationary furniture van between its front and rear wheels. The stag was dragged from beneath the van by two or three men, partly dragged and partly carried some few yards through a nearby gate into an enclosure, where it was killed with a knife. The carrying of the animal to the enclosure took some five to ten minutes; the killing of it took, so it was said, a matter of seconds. The master of the hunt was charged with cruelly terrifying an animal by cutting its throat with a knife, contrary to s.1(1)(a) of the Protection of Animals Act 1911. It was held that a mere temporary inability to get away was not a state of captivity, and as the words 'captive animal' mean an animal in captivity or confinement, the stag was not a captive animal within s.15(a) of the Protection of Animals

Act 1911 and was not within the protection of that Act. In the second case, *Hudnott* v. *Campbell*, a hedgehog was beaten, and it was held that beating a wild animal so as to maim it and bring it under the domination of the person beating it does not make it a captive animal.

After much lobbying of the government, the Wild Mammals Protection Act 1996 was passed, providing some protection from intentional cruelty to wild mammals in certain situations. Under s.1, if any person mutilates, kicks, beats, nails, or otherwise impales, stabs, burns, stones, crushes, drowns, drags or asphyxiates any wild mammal with intent to inflict unnecessary suffering, they shall be guilty of an offence unless one of the exceptions set out in s.2 applies. The exceptions set out in s.2 include acts of mercy in certain situations and where the wild mammal has been injured; for example, during a lawful shoot or pest control, including the use of poisons, and if the act was done using any snare, trap, dog or bird lawfully used for the purpose. Section 3 states 'wild mammal' means any mammal that is not a 'protected animal' within the meaning of the Animal Welfare Act (AWA) 2006.

In terms of being protected from unnecessary suffering under the Animal Welfare Act 2006, any reasonably known act or failure to act that causes unnecessary suffering to a protected animal is an offence. A protected animal is defined in S.2 as (a) it is of a kind that is commonly domesticated in the British Isles; (b) it is under the control of any person, whether on a permanent or temporary basis; or (c) it is not living in a wild state. This means that wildlife is not included in the definition of a protected animal under the AWA 2006, s.2(c), except in very limited circumstances, such as if it is a feral animal originally from domestic stock, if it is permanently or temporarily held captive, or if it has escaped from captivity; for example, from a zoo (Natural England, 2019). This means that wildlife rarely falls within the protection against unnecessary suffering under AWA 2006 s.4.

As we set out below whilst there is a plethora of legislation covering wildlife, around conservation, the issue of what is seen as cruel and what causes unnecessary suffering under the law can depend upon the type of wildlife, the situation it finds itself in, and the view of it by humans. This then impacts on the level of protection it has from unnecessary suffering and from practices that many consider cruel.

The law on conservation

In Victorian times, concerns arose regarding the conservation of birds due to a decrease in seabirds and other birds, and as a result, many statutes were passed to protect them. The Sea Birds Preservation Act of 1869 protected various types of sea birds, and this was followed by the Wild Birds

Protection Act of 1872 and the 1876 Wild Fowl Preservation Act. The legislation was finally consolidated with the introduction of the Wild Birds Protection Act in 1880. After that Act, many similar statutes were passed dealing with the protection of birds, including the Wild Birds Protection Acts of 1881, 1894, 1896, 1902, 1904 and 1908, the Sand Grouse Protection Act 1888, the Wild Birds (St Kilda) Act 1904, the Captive Birds Shooting (Prohibition) Act 1921, the Protection of Birds Acts 1925, 1933, 1954 and 1967, the Protection of Lapwings Act 1928, the Quail Protection Act 1937, and the Wild Birds (Ducks and Geese) Protection Act 1939. Other animals did not receive the same degree of protection until the Wild Creatures and Wild Plants Act 1975, which was replaced by the Wildlife and Countryside Act in 1981. Some animals have their own protection. Seals were covered by the Grey Seals (Protection) Act 1914, which was then replaced by the Conservation of Seals Act in 1970 and The Conservation of Seals (England) Order in 1996 (Reid, 1994).

In terms of conservation, the main piece of legislation currently protecting wildlife in the UK is the Wildlife and Countryside Act 1981 (as amended), which provides some protection for wildlife, plants and habitats; however, there are separate provisions for game birds (except for in some limited parts of the Act). In terms of birds, it protects them, their nests, and eggs (with some exceptions). There are other wildlife offences 'such as bat persecution and bird of prey persecution through poisoning, trapping, shooting, disturbance of nest and/or theft of chicks, egg theft/collection' (CPS, 2022). The case of *Kirkland* v. *Robinson* (1987) established that the possession of birds is a strict liability offence (which means that no blameworthiness is needed for a crime, just the criminal act) under s1(2) of the Wildlife and Countryside Act 1981 and that criminal culpability occurs when a person chooses to take possession of such items (Wandesforde-Smith & Hart, 2015). This legislation is there to provide conservation-led protection rather than to protect the birds from cruelty or unnecessary suffering, although of course some of the provisions do this by keeping them alive and safe.

Wild animals are now considered sentient beings if they fall under Animal Welfare (Sentience) Act 2022 s.5 which defines an animal as a) a vertebrate other than *homo sapiens*, b) any cephalopod mollusc and c) any decapod crustacean) and whilst this term is problematic in terms of its definition as set out in chapter 2, at a basic level it means animals have feelings such as suffering and feeling pain as well as having a level of consciousness. However, as much of the law around protecting wild animals from cruelty is not based on sentience but instead the legal protection against cruelty often depends on the context of the activity involving the wild animal. Specifically, it often hinges on the reasons for carrying out the activity.

Therefore, wildlife protection and concurrent issues around cruelty often come up against other pressures such as agriculture and the influence of the hunting, shooting and fishing lobby. There are often tensions between the need to conserve wildlife, the control of wild animals considered pests to farmers and other landowners, and issues of cruelty. This can be seen most specifically in relation to badgers.

Case study – badgers

Badger baiting was first made illegal in the Cruelty to Animals Act 1835 (for a full history, see Cassidy, 2019). However, loopholes in the Act meant that badger setts could be interfered with when hunting with dogs. Badgers were protected under the Badgers Act 1973, which made it a criminal offence to 'cruelly ill-treat' a badger or use badger tongs while killing, taking, or digging for a badger. However, due to pressure from hunters, the Act emerged from parliament with a serious flaw – landowners and their agents were exempted from the prohibitions on badger persecution on their own land. This meant that 'badger setts were still being dug, bulldozed, blocked or the animals were cruelly killed' (RSPCA, n.d.). In 1981, the law was tightened up in the Wildlife and Countryside Act – parliament removed the 'landowner's loophole' and made it an offence to be in possession of a badger or any part of a badger. Further attempts to tighten the law by protecting badger setts as well as the badger failed due to objections from the hunting fraternity. The loophole allowing the interference with badger setts when hunting with dogs meant that hunters could claim they were looking for foxes when digging, leading to difficulties in proving their intentions. When the Wildlife and Countryside (Amendment) Act was passed in 1985, the government reversed the onus of proof in cases brought against those suspected of digging for badgers. In 1991, two Badger Bills were passed to create a new criminal offence of interfering with a badger sett without a government licence. The 1973 and 1991 Badgers Acts have now been consolidated into the Badgers Act 1992. It is illegal to wilfully capture, injure or kill a wild badger, be in possession of a live or dead badger, or destroy or obstruct access to an active badger sett. The 2004 Hunting Act made the stopping up of badger setts completely illegal (Bengston, 2012) and legislation to protect badgers was aimed at preventing a violent form of abuse against badgers (Legge & Brooman, 2020, p. 206).

Other offences include badger baiting and lamping, which involves using high-powered spotlights to transfix the animal so that shooting or dogs can be used to kill them at night (Badgers Trust, n.d.). Whilst badger baiting is illegal, there is a concern that the law is not acting as a deterrent due to the inadequate penalties available under the Badgers Act 1992 and the Wildlife and Countryside Act (Badgers Trust, n.d.). The reason why this is an issue is because whilst prosecutions for the offence of animal fighting do take place under the Animal Welfare Act 2006, these are aimed at the protection of the dogs that are sent down the badger setts rather than the badgers themselves (Darnell, 2022). The Badgers Trust considers the law inadequate and seeks harsher penalties to protect badgers.

As we can see, a mixture of specific cruelty legislation and conservation legislation has been passed to both protect badgers as a species and also to protect individual badgers from specific acts of cruelty. However, in relation to badgers in the UK, it has been suggested that the inclusion of a licensing get-out clause in the 1992 Act has actually resulted in a government-sanctioned badger slaughter (Legge & Brooman, 2020). Licences have been granted to cull badgers to stop the spread of bovine TB in cattle (Animal and Plant Agency, 2022). The cull takes place in licensed areas, mainly in the West of England, outside the badger breeding season under licences issued by Natural England (s.10(2)(a)). Since 2013, half of Britain's badger population has been killed through this method. Some suggest it is an inherently cruel and inhumane policy, and yet the killing continues (Badgers Trust, n.d.).

There are some arguments in favour of the cull that need to be addressed, particularly the recognition that there is an emotional and economic cost to farmers of losing their cattle as well as the direct detriment to cattle. However, the cull has been extremely controversial (Wood et al., 2022), and it is unclear whether it has been effective (Langton et al., 2022) and figures for the cull have been condemned as 'appalling' (Veterinary Record, 2020), with over 230,000 badgers culled from 2013 to 2023 (Badgers Trust, n.d.). Despite these numbers, it is unclear whether it has in fact had a long-term reduction in TB (Jenkins et al., 2010) and there is a concern that it is counterproductive as it 'perturbates' badgers, driving them away, which further spreads the disease (O' Hare, 2019). These and other concerns have led to a campaign to vaccinate badgers and cattle rather than culling badgers (Dorset Wildlife Trust, n.d.).

While badger baiting is rightly considered to be cruel, the culling of badgers is allowed, due to the interests of landowners and farmers, based on science that is not conclusive (Bishop, 2012). In Northern Ireland, a consultation to allow farmers to shoot badgers to prevent TB was found to be flawed (Northern Ireland Badger Group and Wild Justice Application, 2023). In Wales and Scotland, where devolved powers apply, badgers have not been culled; instead, there has been a focus on cattle-based solutions such as restricting when they can be moved and other biosecurity measures.

A complaint has been lodged under the Berne Convention against the UK government because of its approach (UK 19/4), with the response being that badger vaccinations, enhanced surveillance and monitoring of badgers are being developed. New measures for a bovine tuberculosis eradication strategy: 'include a survey of the badger population for the first time in a decade, a wildlife surveillance programme, the launch of a Badger Vaccinator Field Force and a badger vaccination study to end the cull by the end of this parliament. The Government has also stated that it aims to bring the badger cull to an end within this Parliament and the strategy will be an important part of the effort to eliminate bovine TB by 2038' (Defra, 2024c). Whilst this is to be welcomed it was hoped that the end to badger culling would happen sooner as the cull appears to be based on doubtful science, and action is urgently needed to prevent badger populations from disappearing. The culling of badgers brings into stark focus the contradictions and failings of the law in relation to wild animals.

Hunting, shooting, and fishing ('field sports')

The contradictions and failings of the law relating to badgers are also witnessed in relation to hunting, shooting and fishing. Whilst the badger cull takes place for economic reasons, most of the activities in this section such as hare-coursing and fox-hunting are done for 'entertainment', although there may be limited activity for economic reasons. Fishing, for example, is both an entertainment and a form of income. In this respect, UK wildlife is subject to demand in the same way as the trophy hunting of large species, such as lions and elephants, and it is fair to say that both are unnecessary to humankind, other than for entertainment.

Some forms of wildlife are often seen as 'pests', and it is argued that they need to be culled in the interests of maintaining game shooting or protecting livestock. This issue was raised in the mid-20th century by one of the first inquiries into this area, where the Scott Henderson Committee (1951) noted that:

> [S]entimental concern about animals is directed mainly towards particular animals such as foxes, deer and rabbits, which are beautiful or attractive creatures and are viewed as such by those who are not concerned with the damage they may cause. Few people seem to be in the least concerned about what happens to rats, which are generally regarded as vermin and arouse considerable feelings of revulsion. Yet the rat is an intelligent and highly sensitive creature ... Any field sport which has a reasonable measure of support and is a traditional activity of the countryside, and which has

> some utilitarian value, should not be interfered with except for some very good reason. Interference on the grounds of cruelty would be justified only if it was shown that the amount of suffering involved was excessive or unreasonable. (British Field Sports Society, n.d., p. 1)

The committee recommended that fox-hunting be allowed to continue, which it did, controversially and with much direct protest and sometimes violence, until the election of Tony Blair's Labour Government in 1997. A manifesto promise led to the Burns Inquiry (Burns et al., 2000) on fox-hunting and a seven-year 'battle' to determine a legislative formula that would work.

The Hunting Act 2004 marked a significant moment for the hunting of wild animals in the UK. Whilst its basis was clearly the welfare of the animals being pursued, the outcome was more of a compromise than might have been anticipated by the anti-hunting lobby – hunting was permitted to continue with restrictions on how foxes can be killed (Legge & Brooman, 2020). The Act bans chasing wild mammals with dogs (ss.1 and 3) and the use of land in England and Wales to do this (s.3). However, despite this, the focus of attention is very much concerned with species of animals, including foxes, deer, hares, badgers, otters, and mink that, paradoxically, are still persecuted through illegal hunting and other associated crimes. Hunting of these species can continue under the exemptions allowed under Schedule 1 of the Act, including using a specified number of dogs to stalk and flush out wild mammals, including for the purpose of falconry, to protect birds used for shooting, hunting of rabbits or rats, or retrieving hares that have been shot, and the rescue, capture or observation of wild mammals. In Scotland, the situation has changed as legislation has been enacted to protect wildlife further than in England and Wales, revealing how different levels of control are emerging in each UK region.

Since the 2004 Act, hunts most often participate in 'trail-hunting', where hounds follow a pre-laid trail of scent, either a fox-based or artificial scent. This, in turn, becomes one of the defences that can be used with those engaging in hunt-like activities that commence with no intention to hunt. Other defences include wrong identification, a temporary lapse or, under s.4, that the defendant reasonably believed the hunting was exempt (CPS, 2019).

The police are empowered to search and seize evidence under s.7 and can arrest under the Serious and Organised Crime and Police Act 2005 (SOCPA). However, the courts have held that the meaning of 'hunts' does not include the mere searching for an as yet unidentified wild mammal (*DPP (Crown Prosecution Service CCU Southwest)* v. *Anthony Wright*; *The Queen on the Application of Maurice Scott, Peter Heard & Donald Summersgill* v. *Taunton*

Deane Magistrates Court). Hence, once an illegal hunt begins, only a person who engages or participates in the pursuit of an 'identified' wild mammal is guilty of an offence (CPS, 2019).

Perhaps inevitably, the defences above have resulted in criticism that the Act has not stopped hunts from participating in illegal hunting. In 2021, in England and Wales the number of actions for breaches of the Hunting Act increased to 80 (Wildlife and Countryside Link, 2021, p. 22). In addition, the policing of hunts remains as long-standing a contentious issue as it ever was, with a UNODC Report (2021, pp. 11–12) stating that the Act's exceptions make policing it very difficult. The report recommends that a review be conducted, particularly focused on delivering clarity for law enforcement on when and how to enforce the Hunting Act 2004.

Other issues around hunting include the fact that hunts often trespass onto private land even though the hunt itself has a legal responsibility to respect the rights of other property owners, as established in *League Against Cruel Sports Ltd* v. *Scott and Others*, which also raised animal welfare concerns for the keeping of the hounds. Other associated crimes are dealt with under other legislation such as the Protection of Badgers Act 1992, the Deer Act 1991, the Wildlife and Countryside Act 1981, and the Conservation of Habitats and Species Regulations 2017 (Wildlife and Countryside Link, 2021, p. 25). The overall effect of the Hunting Act is far from clear in terms of improving the welfare of animals both those hunted and used for hunting, leading to calls for the abolition or re-design of the legislation (Legge & Brooman, 2020, p. 205). It is to be hoped that all hunting will be ended by the Labour Government by closing the loopholes in the existing legislation.

The killing of hares

Hare-coursing was also banned by the Hunting Act 2004. Hare-coursing is the pursuit of hares with sight hounds, which chase the hare by sight and not by scent. This type of offending can also be known as hare poaching and can take the form of organised events where betting takes place on the skill of the dogs in hunting the hares and often involves "substantial sums of money"' (CPS, 2022). Whilst the Hunting Act has reduced hare-coursing, many rural communities have seen the activity continue, with a consequential impact on the local hare population. Section 30 of the Game Act 1831 is the legislation most used to prosecute offenders when hare-coursing takes place during the day (S. 1, of the Night Poaching Act 1828 covers when it takes place at night). This is because there is no requirement under this Act for anything to be actually chased or caught for the offence to be committed – trespassing on land to look for something to chase is sufficient (CPS, n.d.).

Section 5 of the Hunting Act does not encompass what might be described as hare-coursing that is recreational. The offence requires proof of a competition, meaning that, whilst it may cover large, well-organised hare-coursing events, such as the old Waterloo Cup, it is much more difficult to prove in other circumstances unless there is strong supporting evidence of competitive elements such as betting on the outcome (CPS, 2022). Tougher sentences for coursing have been introduced through the Police Crime Sentencing and Courts Act 2022, which sees offenders liable for an unlimited fine and up to six months imprisonment. However, brown hares are defined as game under the Game Act 1831 and so can be shot. There is no closed season, just a limit on shooting them on Sundays and Christmas Day. The Hares Preservation Act 1892 makes it an offence to sell, or expose for sale, any hare or leveret between the months of March and July. Despite a government statement that a closed season would be introduced (Defra, 2021), this has not yet happened. Farmers are also able to shoot hares in order to protect their crops.

Hare-coursing, often seen as a working-class activity, has deservedly been made illegal. However, it occupies a contradictory position when compared with another form of organised persecution of hares that is generally considered to be carried out by wealthier classes – the shooting of hares as game. The shooting of animals and birds as game often takes place to supplement income on landowners' estates. Historically, the law dealt harshly with those who sought to abuse or disrupt game thereby underlining the predominance of protecting property rights, even at the expense of animals. Those wishing to afford themselves similar rights of access to wildlife may be prosecuted for poaching or selling game under the Game Act 1831. Trespassing on land with dogs to hunt game would be rendered unlawful under the Hunting Act 2004, so the property protection element is held firmly in place.

The killing of birds

Landowners can shoot game birds, but a licence is needed. The law sets closed and open seasons for shooting game birds as well as other controls (BASC, 2024). These require consultation with, for example, Natural England (the government's adviser for the natural environment in England) when game birds are to be released near specially protected areas. These are sites of high nature conservation of species, but it seems that Natural England's advice is not always being followed (*Wild Justice* v.

Natural Resources Wales [2021]). This is problematic as there can be a conflict of interest between protecting wildlife and raising game for shooting (Lees et al., 2013).

The conflict between game and wildlife can be seen in relation to buzzards and pen-reared pheasants. These conflicts often represent social and cultural issues as much as the perceived impact of the wildlife on game (Redpath et al., 2013). This has led to the illegal killing of birds of prey, and some initiatives to protect raptors and work with game managers have broken down (Horton, 2023). There are also concerns for the welfare of the grouse themselves, and there are calls for changes to driven grouse shooting, where grouse are flushed out by beaters over a line of people with guns. This involves particularly intensive game rearing, which has a deleterious effect on the environment due to peat burning of the moors to encourage the growth of younger shoots that the grouse eat and the establishment of a monoculture in terms of the habitat (RSPB, n.d.).

The killing of deer

The Animal Welfare Act 2006 covers captured deer, tame deer, or injured deer under treatment. The Act does not apply to the stalking of wild deer. Wild deer are protected under the Deer Act 1991 and the Regulatory Reform (Deer) (England and Wales) Order 2007, which set out offences in relation to poaching (s.1), taking or killing deer intentionally at night (s.2) or during the closed season (s.3) and to the sale or purchase of any such venison covered by the offences set out in the Act (s.10). There are some exceptions, including having a licence (s.8) and shooting deer where the shooter had reasonable grounds for believing the deer (or one of the same species) were causing damage to crops, or other property on the land, and further serious damage was likely unless the deer was shot (s.7).

Therefore, deer are often shot both as a food source and because they are seen as a 'pest' as they have no natural predator in the UK. Wild animals kill each other for food in a way that is sustainable if they are operating in healthy ecosystems, but over the centuries we have driven some predator species to extinction, which has allowed certain species to flourish in the absence of such predation, which, in turn, causes knock-on issues. As we encroach more on wild animals' ecosystems and give them less space to live, our perception of them as 'pests' increases. The outcome for deer is that numbers may have doubled since 1999, according to the Deer Initiative (which promotes the sustainable management of wild deer). This impacts on farmers and conservationists who fear the impact that deer have on crops and wildlife, leading to some scientists calling for deer-culling to take place. Each year, as many as 350,000 deer are culled (Defra, 2009).

Deer are stalked and shot for food (Lewis & Parr, 2023), and due to climate change, it has been suggested that deer might be a better source of food to mitigate the detrimental climate effects of, for example, raising cows for beef (Suzuki et al., 2022). In terms of conservation, whilst some argue that there should be selective culling, others argue that this should not be the first option and that fencing deer in may help, as might restricting food for deer or controlling their numbers through fertility control. Another suggestion is to re-wild areas to restore the natural balance by introducing predators such as wolves.

The killing of fish

Fishing is exempt from controls in the Animal Welfare Act 2006. Section 59 states that 'Nothing in this Act applies in relation to anything which occurs in the normal course of fishing.' The explanatory note explains that the term 'fishing' should be understood as applying to the ordinary activities of fishermen and anglers and the ordinary activities of those who own and run stocked ponds and allow fishing activities to take place using their ponds.

There are some legal controls to the extent that fishing with a rod for freshwater fish (salmon, trout, course fish and eels) requires a rod licence and compliance with national and local bye-laws (UK Government, 2024). For sea-fishing, controls are set out by local Inshore Fisheries and Conservation Authorities. The setting of minimum landing sizes and conservation reference sizes is used all over the world to manage fish stocks (Angling Trust, n.d.). In terms of cruelty and unnecessary suffering, fish are vertebrates and are included in the definition of animal in the Animal Welfare (Sentience) Act 2022. This raises the question of what constitutes unnecessary suffering for a fish. It is argued that:

> When caught, these fish are not killed instantly upon leaving the water, but exposed to an environment they are not designed to cope with. Primarily, they can't breathe. Other factors include stress imposed due to the sudden change in temperature, noise, vibration, oxygen concentration, light intensity, and damage to a protective mucous layer. If fish survive this ordeal, they are often put into a keep-net. These nets are designed to keep fish underwater, before being released at the end of the fishing session. However, many fish will receive injuries from the net mesh or from being

> squashed together with other fish and many will die due to depletion of oxygen over a period in these devices. Keep-nets are most popular at fishing matches, enabling each angler to weigh his complete catch at the end of the match. (Hunt Saboteurs Association, 1992)

It is argued that even catching and releasing fish is cruel because:

> Studies show that fish who are caught and then returned to the water suffer such severe physiological stress that they often die of shock. Fish often swallow hooks, and anglers may try to retrieve a hook by shoving their fingers or pliers down the fish's throat, ripping out not just the hook but some of the fish's throat and guts as well ... When fish are handled, the protective coating on their bodies is disturbed ... These and other injuries make fish easy targets for predators once they are returned to the water … Along with suffocation fishing tackle can also cause injury to other wildlife through injuries caused when entangled in fishing line or if they swallow fishhooks. (PETA, 2024)

Angling is justified on the grounds of its role in conservation. Anglers, it is argued, are wildlife guardians, being in a good position to report pollution offences, including over abstraction, and putting pressure on water companies to clean up or maintain river quality for angling. Angling, it is also claimed, is good for mental health (Angling Trust, 2022), and it can provide a cheap source of protein in times of economic hardship. However, the conflict between human uses and wildlife can be seen in the Angler's Trust campaign on otter predation and its calls to add cormorants and goosanders to the general shooting licence along with pigeons, crows and magpies, subject to an annual review to ensure the conservation status of the birds is not threatened. At present, in 2024, attempts are being made to persuade Natural England and the Environment Agency to carry out pilot projects in three river catchments to measure the impact this might have (Angling Trust, n.d.).

Whilst angling has grown into 'a significant cultural activity and tourism industry in its own right' (Mordue, 2009), there are concerns that it is inherently cruel and leads to conservation clashes. Whilst there are a few pressure groups who want fishing to become illegal, others see it as having a vital place in the conservation of fish and in protecting rivers, as well as leading to human benefits in terms of its social and mental health benefits. As is the case in much of this chapter the issues around angling reflect the anthropocentricism evident in the limits of legal control of this sport and recreation.

Arguments for and against the killing of wildlife

The arguments for hunting (see the Report of the Committee of Inquiry into Hunting with Dogs in England & Wales, 9 June 2000) include that it is a traditional rural activity (Harrop, 2005; Harrop, 2006). Supporters of shooting and hunting claim the activities help with the management of wildlife populations and the protection of farm animals from predation. It is often claimed, for example, by the Gamekeepers Association and Rural Sports, that wildlife does not suffer, and that it is hypocritical to be concerned about this when other animals are killed as pests or for food. The field sports lobby argue that the ethical basis of all field sports is the same and that the motivation of the pursuer is irrelevant, even if done for sport – a pest is a pest, they argue. In addition, the anthropocentric benefit is again stressed – it protects agriculture and provides employment.

Arguments against killing wildlife raise a number of objections to these arguments. The casual referral to wildlife as pests certainly lowers their potential status, as pests can be viewed as deserving of their fate. Questions are also raised about how effective hunting is for population control and that there are better ways to do this, as mentioned in relation to badger and deer culling. Research conducted before the ban on hunting was implemented suggests fox hunts had little effect on fox populations (The League Against Cruel Sports, n.d.; Hunt Saboteurs, n.d.):

It was argued by Dr Harris in 1987 that left alone by humans, fox populations will be higher in areas with an abundance of food and lower where food is scarce. This can be seen in towns and cities, where large numbers of foxes survive on refuse and rodents. A three-year study at the University of Aberdeen found that, in the absence of any form of fox control, there was neither an increase in fox numbers nor in the number of lambs lost. Foxes form stable family groups that defend their own territory against intruding foxes and generally reproduce at a similar rate to their fatalities. The fox population would, therefore, not explode if all methods of fox killing were suspended (The League Against Cruel Sports, n.d.).

The need to control animals that encounter human populations will be considered in relation to biodiversity in the next chapter, as will the trade in animals hunted and shot but the arguments around the economics, conservation value and welfare implication of sport hunting should lead to alternatives to this activity (Feber et al., 2020). There is a clear moral dichotomy between how the control of wild animals is formulated compared to those that are domesticated or captive and the levels of cruelty considered acceptable in each case. In Chapters 2 and 3, the rising importance of knowledge about animal sentience was discussed as a major

21st-century driver for improving the welfare of animals, but this does not always seem to apply in the case of wild animals.

There are ethical discussions (Humphreys, 2014; Cahoone, 2009), to be had about whether these activities should be allowed in law (which go hand in hand with definitions of animal cruelty) as there is clearly a good deal of inconsistency between species of equivalent sentience. In some instances, lawmakers do act – there are specific controls around practices that are seen as exceptionally cruel, so for example, the EU has directives banning methods of trapping such as leg holds used for trapping animals for fur (Council Regulation (EEC) No 3254/91) and lead shot. However, lead shot can still routinely be found in game sold in UK supermarkets (Wild Justice, 2023) and the Health and Safety Executive (HSE) is looking into this issue (HSE, October 2023).

It cannot be denied that many of the activities set out above would be defined as cruelty if done to domestic animals, and some of the methods of killing wild animals, such as hunting, shooting and trapping, would be seen as unacceptable practices for captive animals. In addition, the control of wildlife as 'pests' does not only include controlling their numbers through hunting or shooting, as foxes and other wild animals can be caught in snares, which are promoted as being an effective way to control fox and badger populations to protect lambs and ground-nesting birds such as snipe.

In Wales, the government banned the use of snares (Harris, 2022). It is to be hoped that the Labour Government will ban the use of snare traps in England. The decision to ban this cruel practice along with other wild animal proposals around hunting and shooting has traditionally seen 'push-back' from farming and hunting lobbies who argue that there is a culture war between town and country. Additionally, populist politicians have used these issues to claim votes.

We suggest that the use of such methods of capture, sometimes killing or maiming, is an unacceptable method of control in modern society, especially as alternative methods are available.

The use of glue traps to kill rodents has been made illegal in the UK, but other traps can be used, such as spring traps or humane traps. It might be argued that as wild animals are killed on the roads or by pollution, then such killing aligns with the unfortunate eventualities of life. However, hunting, shooting, and fishing are different in a unique way – they happen out of a desire to make sport of their killing, and these activities seem to carry a discriminatory deference to property ownership in the case of 'game' – even the term 'game' evokes an unfortunate levity to a very serious issue. It seems particularly cruel to kill wild animals for trivial reasons, even if done in the name of tradition. A cruel method remains a cruel method even if it has been done for centuries, and this raises considerable questions regarding necessary and unnecessary suffering (Spark, 2014).

Wildlife kept in captivity

Wildlife is protected under the Animal Welfare Act (AWA) 2006, where it comes within the definition of a 'protected animal' under S. 2. This occurs where wildlife is permanently or temporarily held captive or where animals have escaped from captivity, such as in a zoo, and are not living in a wild state. Wild animals can be found in a number of captive situations, including zoos, wildlife parks, and sanctuaries, as pets and in more temporary situations for use in entertainment. (Bostock (1993, p. 55) suggests that animals in zoos may not be 'wild' in the sense they have been tamed or domesticated and may even have been born in captivity.) Keeping a wild animal in captivity can be seen as problematic as it limits the natural behaviour of an animal and places both their mental and physical well-being at risk as they often lack adequate shelter, food, room to roam, and environment control to keep their body at the temperature it needs to be. Human beings, when keeping animals in captivity, are not equipped to provide wild animals with the care necessary to fulfil all their intrinsic needs (World Animal Protection, 2020).

Zoos and wildlife sanctuaries

The rationale in favour of zoos is usually based on their role in conservation or their care for individual wild animals in the zoo (Braverman, 2012). The welfare of zoo animals is covered by the AWA 2006 and the Zoo Licensing Act 1981. The AWA allows action to be taken where there is evidence of cruelty to an animal or a failure to provide for its welfare. It also sets out five needs, and there is a legal duty to provide for these needs that include a suitable environment and diet, a chance to exhibit normal behaviour patterns, the need to be housed with, or apart from, other animals and the need to be protected from pain, suffering, injury and disease. Further to these general provisions, the welfare of animals in zoos is specifically covered by the Zoo Licensing Act 1981. Under this Act, zoos must comply with comprehensive animal health, welfare and husbandry standards, and are subject to an annual local authority inspection. Zoos must be inspected at least every year by a local authority, with an inspection every two to three years using inspectors drawn from a list of qualified zoo inspectors kept by Defra (Department for the Environment, Food and

Rural Affairs). The Zoo Licensing Act 1981 (Amendment) (England and Wales) Regulations 2002 increased the enforcement powers for zoos in terms of closing them, modifying licence conditions, and give effect to conservation measures to complywith the Zoos Directive (Council Directive 1999/22/EC). However, despite the Directive, concern over welfare standards in zoos across Europe has been highlighted in a report by the Aspinall Foundation. There is a concern that the European Association of Zoos and Aquaria (EAZA) cannot maintain and enforce animal welfare requirements within its accredited member zoos (Born Free Foundation, 2024).

Defra also maintains the Secretary of State's Standards of Modern Zoo Practice. These are detailed standards for zoo management with which zoos are expected to comply. These standards are kept under review by Defra's Zoos Expert Committee (ZEC), which includes leading animal welfare experts. The ZEC's role is to provide independent, technical advice to the UK Government on zoo matters. These standards will become more important from 2026 as a licence will be needed to own animals such as orang-utans, chimpanzees, lemurs, and monkeys under the Animal Welfare (Primate Licences) (England) Regulations 2024, which ensure that only private keepers who can provide zoo-level welfare standards will be able to keep primates.

Wildlife can often be found in sanctuaries run by individuals or charities. These animals are covered by AWA and regulations made under that Act, and as they are in captivity, they may be covered under the Dangerous Wild Animals Act 1976. Such sanctuaries do not require a licence to operate, and they are not inspected by local councils or other official bodies. Many are set up in the interests of wildlife, either for their welfare or conservation.

The arguments against zoos, and sometimes wildlife sanctuaries, often centre around the issues of animal welfare. However, zoos provide the counter-argument that captive wild animals enjoy many benefits over their wild counterparts:

> No wild animal is free in the sense understood by the average citizen. Each living creature is confined by a maze of restrictions. These may be environmental or may involve the presence of other animals or members of its own species, or the availability of food. If these factors are taken into consideration and the animal's normal biological needs are catered for, what does it suffer by being captive? As our scientific knowledge improves, so does the lot of the zoo animal. It is infinitely better off than its wild counterpart (and also the average pet hamster), for it has a regular, well-balanced diet, constant shelter, no territorial disputes, plus the benefits

> of the most up-to-date advances in surgery and medicine. Is it to be wondered at that the zoo specimen can expect a longer life than it would in the wild? (Jordan & Ormrod, 1978, pp. 13–14)

However, Jordan and Ormrod questioned whether, at that time, this was actually the case in the UK. Brando and Chapman (2023) also argue that cruelty issues arise in keeping wild animals in captivity and that the longer life spans of captive animals and the corresponding issue of how to care for aging animals raises welfare issues.

Wild animals used as entertainment

Wild animals can also be kept in captivity for entertainment, such as in marine parks and circuses. Cetaceans in parks can suffer from shorter lives, attacks, repetitive behaviours, and dorsal fin collapse and may be given drugs to calm them (Whale and Dolphin Conservation, n.d.). The cruelty involved in using animals for entertainment and economic gain in this way has been recognised in UK law. Whilst there is no ban, the effect of strict welfare requirements has led to the effective cessation on the keeping of cetaceans in parks.

In recognition of concerns over using wild animals for tourist entertainment, the Animals (Low-Welfare Activities Abroad) Act 2023 prohibits the sale and advertising of activities abroad that involve low standards of welfare for animals. This Act is unusual as it regulates activities beyond the boundaries of a national state and is a proactive form of legislation. It allows the government to bring forward a ban on the advertising and sale of specific unethical activities abroad where animals are kept in captivity or confinement, subjected to cruel and brutal training methods, forced to take 'selfies', or are ridden, drugged or declawed. However, at the time of writing the Act had not been implemented "as ministers must create a statutory instrument listing the banned activities to make the law enforceable" (Tapper, 2024). The recognition of the cruelty inherent in using wildlife in circuses has meant that the use of wildlife in circuses across the world has decreased in recent years. In the EU, 24 of the 27 members restrict the use of animals in one form or another (Eurogroup for Animal Welfare, n.d.). In the UK, the Wild Animals in Circuses Act 2019 makes it illegal to use wild animals in a travelling circus.

Temporary captivity can occur when wild animals are used in films, TV or as part of social media. In terms of protecting animals from cruelty, S. 1 of the Cinematograph Films (Animals) Act 1937 states that:

> 1. No person shall exhibit to the public or supply to any person for public exhibition (whether by him or another person) any cinematograph film (whether produced in the UK or elsewhere) if, in connection with the publication of the film, any scene required in the film was organised or directed in such a way as to involve the cruel infliction of pain or terror on any animal or the cruel goading of any animal to fury.
>
> 2. In any proceedings brought under this Act in respect of any film, the court may (without prejudice to any other mode of proof) infer from the film as exhibited to the public or supplied for public exhibition, as the case may be, that a scene represented in the film as so exhibited or supplied was organised or directed in such a way as to involve the cruel infliction of pain or terror on an animal or the cruel goading of an animal to fury, but (whether the court draws such an inference or not) it shall be a defence for the defendant to prove that he believed, and had reasonable cause to believe, that no scene so represented was so organised or directed.

The Performing Animal (Regulation) Act 1925 and the Animal Welfare (Licensing of Activities Involving Animals) (England) Regulations 2018 require any person who exhibits or trains any performing (vertebrate) animal to have a licence.

In the UK, the Online Safety Act 2023 provides that animal cruelty must be removed from social media platforms. Schedule 7(38) sets out priority offences, including where social media shows actions that are an offence under S. 4(1) of AWA (unnecessary suffering of an animal). Section 62(7) sets out the content that may be considered harmful to children, which (a) depicts real or realistic serious violence against an animal and (b) depicts the real or realistic serious injury of an animal in graphic detail.

It remains to be seen how effective the Act will be in protecting animals from cruelty, as the legislation in question has an anthropocentric aim that may only incidentally carry benefits for animals alongside it.

Enforcement of cruelty legislation for wild animals

There is always the need for effective enforcement if the law is to protect animals, and this is also the case in relation to wildlife crime. In the UK:

> …the CPS works closely with the police, the National Wildlife Crime Unit (NWCU), Defra, and other interested organisations to tackle all types of wildlife crime. The CPS sits on several working groups to tackle wildlife crime, including the National Wildlife Crime Unit's (NWCU) UK Tasking

> and Coordinating Group (UKTCG), which sets wildlife crime priorities and the Partnership for Action Against Wildlife Crime (PAW UK) ... The resultant priority areas are the ones which have been assessed as posing the greatest current threat to either the conservation status of a species or which show the highest volume of crime. (Crown Prosecution Service (CPS), n.d.)

In 2023 the CPS set out its priorities as:

1. Badger persecution.
2. Bat persecution.
3. Convention on International Trade in Endangered Species (CITES) issues (Current priorities of European eel; illegal trade in raptors; ivory; medicinal & health products; reptiles; rhino horn and timber).
4. Freshwater pear mussel (FWPM).
5. Poaching (deer poaching/coursing, fish poaching and hare-coursing).
6. Raptor persecution (including poisoning, egg theft, chick theft, taking from the wild and nest disturbance/destruction and to concentrate on golden eagle, goshawk, hen harrier, peregrine, red kite, and white-tailed eagle).
7. Cyber-enabled wildlife crime (CPS, n.d.).

This is an instructive list as it covers issues across these two wildlife chapters and shows some of the contradictions inherent in the law. As observed above, badgers are subject to cruelty and persecution in the current wave of government-sponsored culling, but stopping badger persecution remains a priority for the CPS when enforcing the law to prevent badger persecution. In addition, poaching, which, as stated above, can be seen as an economic crime against property, is viewed by the CPS as another priority area. However, hare-coursing, the working-class pursuit, is prioritised but not the illegal hunting of foxes. For the law to be adequately enforced it needs to be more consistent in terms of what is considered cruel.

Adding to the issues around cruelty to wildlife that are covered by the law, Darnell (2022) argues that there are differences between the various penalties (ranging from fines to imprisonment) for cruelty to wild animals and domestic and captive animals. The Animal Welfare (Sentencing) Act 2021 increased maximum penalties for offences under AWA that cause harm to animals. But AWA only protects wildlife where it is either captive or under the temporary control of a person. The difference in penalties has been recognised by Defra (2022), which has suggested that 'minimum penalties for wildlife and poaching offences should be harmonised across all wildlife provisions to ensure the protection of all species and … should be comparable to those recently introduced for animal welfare offences'.

In terms of wildlife crime, it is often NGOs that fill the gaps of underperforming statutory agencies (Nurse, 2013, p. 306). So, for example, the pressure group Wildlife and Countryside Link (WCL) has published reports highlighting the changing nature of wildlife crime, and they provide useful recommendations for reform. For example, much wildlife crime is not recorded centrally. However, WCL provides updates: 'In the absence of official police figures (due to a lack of notifiable status for most wildlife crimes, meaning that police forces are not obliged to officially report them back to the Home Office), this report provides the reader with an overview of the type and extent of wildlife crime' (WCL, 2021, p.2).

The need for a national plan is set out by the Wildlife and Countryside Link:

> The United Nations Office on Drugs and Crime (UNODC) 'Wildlife and Forest Crime Analytic Toolkit Report: United Kingdom of Great Britain and Northern Ireland' report provided a comprehensive blueprint for tackling wildlife crime in the UK. Over 200 pages and through 72 separate recommendations, covering legislation, enforcement, prosecution, sentencing and monitoring, the report set out how more wildlife can be protected from the suffering and species losses, extending from mammals to invertebrates, inflicted by wildlife criminals. (Wildlife and Countryside Link, 2021, p. 3)

It sets out three recommendations for reform:

1. Making wildlife crimes notifiable (UNODC recommendation number 23)
2. Increasing resources for wildlife crime teams (UNODC recommendation numbers 6 and 8)
3. Reforming wildlife crime legislation (UNODC recommendation numbers 1 and 19). (Wildlife and Countryside Link, 2021, p. 3)

The need for the reforms is set out in the report:

> There are domestic challenges across the UK regarding its wildlife crime legislation, not least that the legislation is scattered, with disparities between the approach taken towards priority concerns in Northern Ireland, England and Wales, as compared with Scotland. There is strong interest within the Department for Environment, Food and Rural Affairs (Defra) to harmonise England's existing wildlife crime legislation, which officials acknowledged as having inconsistencies. It was estimated that there are between 30 and 40 statutes on wildlife and wildlife management that need to be harmonised. (UNODC, 2021, p. 11)

Wildlife and Countryside Link states that, in terms of enforcement, it welcomes the increase in sanctions for hare-coursing offences through the Police, Crime Sentencing and Courts Act 2022. However, it argues that the 191 year delay since the last penalty increase in the Game Act 1831 demonstrates how slowly necessary changes are implemented. It argues that antiquated legislation used in most wildlife crime prosecutions needs to be updated much faster (Wildlife and Countryside Link, 2021, p. 50). However, the United Nations Office on Drugs and Crime (UNODC) report (2021, p. 11) states that increasing penalties is inadequate without using specialised investigative techniques and along with these changes is a need to change the view of such crimes.

Rayburn et al. (2020) examined public perceptions of wildlife crime to understand how consumers view these offences and how marketing might influence their reduction. They argue that working with policymakers and marketers can create strategies that benefit businesses, society, consumers, and wildlife alike:

> Analogous to animal welfare promoted in food marketing and packaging contexts (e.g., certified humane, grass-fed certified, cage-free, animal welfare approved), marketers can help create thriving ecosystems of wildlife protection, where constituents benefit from policy and strategy that protect wildlife, curb animal cruelty, and reduce wildlife crime. For example, wildlife protection models like national land trusts provide a framework for marketers in their attempt to save and secure wildlife now and for future generations. (Rayburn et al., 2020, p. 1653)

Perhaps this is the way forward through education, changing public perceptions and purchasing decisions.

The enforcement of laws to protect animals in zoos is the responsibility of zoo inspectors, and there are concerns about how adequately this is being done through a licensing regime (Tyson, 2021). Similar issues are observed with marine parks (Van der Meer et al., 2018). The Euro Group for Animal Welfare argues that there is a lack of consistency in the regulation of standards in licensed zoos under the Zoos Directive and raises concerns about those that remain unlicensed. In the United States, this has led to multiple court cases by the Nonhuman Rights Project to free wild animals from captivity, as discussed in Chapter 2.

In relation to circuses, enforcement is problematic because circuses move frequently and there are different laws in place to govern them across Europe (Eurogroup for Animals, March 2021).

The growth in the number of internet and YouTube videos showing instances of animal cruelty involving wild animals is a growing problem;

for example, in 2024, a British woman pleaded guilty to being part of a global monkey torture network (BBC News, 2024b). She was part of a private online group that funded the torture and killing of baby monkeys in Indonesia to watch online. There are clear difficulties with enforcing animal protection laws across international borders and in enforcing guidelines against such online content (Carvalho et al., 2023). It will be interesting to see how effective the Online Safety Act 2023 will be in this regard. For all forms of wildlife crime, effective enforcement using the best possible evidence is central:

> Veterinary forensics is becoming increasingly important in civil and criminal court cases, mainly for the acquisition of evidence of abuse, intoxication or force trauma associated with animal cruelty (including neglect and abuse), unlawful killing, violation of wildlife law, and medical malpractice, all of which are punishable offences in many countries. (Takenaka et al., 2023, p. 1; see also Rolo et al., 2013)

The enforcement of wildlife crimes to ensure effective regulatory compliance depends on political will and the corresponding funding of the agencies tasked with performing these duties. With economic pressures affecting many countries and the corresponding tightening of public finances, effective mechanisms to hold policymakers and enforcement agencies to account are under considerable strain.

Conclusion

How should the law be reformed to protect wild animals from cruelty?

Cruelty to wild animals is a problematic issue whilst specific instances of cruelty have been made illegal the lack of protection from unnecessary suffering is an anomaly even if the context of what is necessary is often contested. Spark (2014, p. 494) suggests that 'extending S. 4(1) of AWA to protect wild animals from unreasonably caused unnecessary suffering, thereby affording them the same level of protection as non-wild animals, would not cause any problems in practice and can be justified in principle'. Defining cruelty is based upon anthropomorphic views, often placing low-level human interests such as 'fun' or recreation above those of animals. However, the increase in knowledge regarding animal sentience casts doubt on many human activities that cause harm and suffering to wild animals. It is hard to see how some of the activities discussed in this chapter can be justified when examined through the lens of consistency between the species. As Garlick et al. (2011, pp. 161–175) argue:

> Fostered by institutional failure, greed and selfishness, and the worst aspects of human disregard, the objectification of animals has its roots in longstanding Western anthropocentric philosophical perspectives, post colonialism, and a global uptake of neoliberal capitalism. Conservation, animal rights and welfare movements have been unable to stem the ever-growing abuse of wildlife, while 'greenwash' language such as 'resource use', 'management', 'pests', 'over-abundance', 'conservation hunting' and 'ecology' coat this violence with a respectable public veneer.

Castelló (2022, p. 112–21) argues that 'wild animals should have a right to immunity from being mere objects of property rights'. This would form part of a wider reform of the law to encompass higher legal rights, including political representation and internal self-determination (autonomy without a right to secession), which, he argues, should be based on legal animalhood rather than claims for personhood, which are discussed in Chapter 3.

Singer's (1977) argument that animals have intrinsic value due to the ability to feel pain and Regan's (1983) mental capacity as mirrored in consciousness have impacted the development of law and legal strategies. Much of the law is focused on animal welfare and has been centred around the treatment of farm and domestic animals in law to the exclusion of wild animals.

As we have seen in this chapter whilst the law has recognised sentience in the UK and Europe, this has not as yet led to significantly more protection for wild animals from cruelty.

There are difficult discussions to be had as to how the law can adequately protect wildlife whether from its use as entertainment, as a sport or through their control as 'pests' or whether it perpetuates activities that are cruel and cause suffering, unnecessary or not. It would seem ethically clear that using wildlife as entertainment is not acceptable. Wildlife as food is a harder ethical discussion. There is an ethical discussion to be had about using terminology such as 'pests' being applied to wild animals. When wild animals such as foxes and badgers kill chickens kept as pets or for laying eggs, the owners feel upset, and wild animals are branded as pests in need of controlling – be that culling or hunting. The view of nature as red in tooth and claw (Murray, 2008) and so by analogy, inherently cruel, seems to mean that we do not think more closely about what we are doing to animals who inhabit the natural world or the impact our activities have on them. The ethical 'leap' will be to accord as much concern for wildlife as there is for species kept closer to home.

This chapter has examined a range of controls and protections for wild animals, some of which specifically protect them from cruelty. Returning to Adam and Schaffner's (2017) argument that animal lawyers aim for the well-being of individuals of the species, we can see that the law is often found to cover the low baseline of direct cruelty. Higher-level welfare requirements, which impose positive duties to meet an animal's welfare needs, are only applied in limited situations, such as when wild animals are kept in captivity.

The conflict between wildlife conservation and human activities such as agriculture, hunting, shooting and fishing means that legal protection from cruelty to wild animals is often seen as problematic and directly at odds with human interests. Cruelty legislation has not kept up with the advances in the scientific recognition of sentience in animals or the growing recognition of their consciousness and individual lives. How to remedy this and define what is unnecessary in relation to suffering for wild animals is highly contested. Clearly, the very term 'unnecessary suffering' carries with it different ethical, moral, and political viewpoints, which may have failed to catch up with scientific discovery and philosophical thinking. In accordance with Adam and Schaffner's (2017) argument that Animal Law concerns itself with the humane treatment of individual animals and Wildlife Law with conservation, we may be left with contradictory practices that see animals kept in zoos to conserve a species at the expense of their own welfare. Whilst this chapter has concentrated on the first issue, the issue of conservation and how wild animals and humans interact and find a place on Earth will now be considered in the next chapter.

CHAPTER EIGHT

Wildlife protection: extinction and the loss of biodiversity

Introduction

This chapter examines the adequacy of wildlife law and the challenges it faces to halt extinctions and protect biodiversity. There is some debate about how to define biodiversity (Wilson, 1992; Toepfer, 2019), but the Convention on Biological Diversity (CBD) Article 2 defines biodiversity as 'the variability among living organisms from all sources, including inter alia, terrestrial, marine and other aquatic ecosystems and the ecological complexes of which they are part; this includes diversity within species, between species and of ecosystems'.

International wildlife law is considered by some to have different aims than Animal Law:

> International wildlife law addresses conservation and sustainable use issues requiring international cooperation, while animal law pursues humane treatment of the individual animal and moral considerations of wildlife well-being. Generally, conservation lawyers want to ensure that the species does not go extinct, while animal lawyers aim for the well-being of individuals of the species. (Adam & Schaffner, 2017, p. 1)

This chapter builds on the previous discussion around cruelty to wildlife but concentrates on the issues of conservation, particularly around extinction and the loss of biodiversity (Visseren-Hamakers, 2022: Schapper et al., 2022). In particular, this chapter addresses the legal challenges to the recognition of sentience and how law should be reformed to ensure the effective protection wild animals.

The development of the law in relation to wild animals has been based on the view of wild animals as 'other' and not given the protection afforded to domestic and captive animals.. Whilst the last chapter considered cruelty to individual animals this chapter will consider nature in the whole. The claim that humans need to view nature more holistically is not new. James Lovelock explained the interdependence of life on Earth in his books on Gaia (Lovelock, 2007, 2015a, 2015b). Our understanding of the impact of our actions on the world was set out in stark form in Rachel Carson's series of books, the most famous being *Silent Spring*, which detailed the human and environmental harms caused by pesticides (Carson, 1968). We need to understand how we have reached this point of mass extinctions (McGubbin, 2023; Carew, 2023) and a rapid rise in biodiversity loss, and why we have not heeded earlier voices. Habitat loss and fragmentation are also having a considerable impact on efforts to conserve and save endangered species. However, we contend that habitat destruction does not have to be an inevitable consequence of our existence on Earth. Conservation of endangered species, the reverse of biodiversity loss and the protection of habitat must be achieved through enforceable and workable legal solutions if we are to conserve the world around us and the wildlife in it.

The causes of species and habitat loss are many, but occur particularly through slaughter, war (Milburn and Van Goozen, 2021, Peters et al., 2023; Lercier et al., 2024), and the damage humans have caused to the climate. As urban areas increase, the pressure on the countryside increases, and so too on wildlife. The land is under pressure from, for example, agriculture and general urban development such as housing. Rivers come under pressure from pollution, over-abstraction and dams, whilst the seas are also under pressure from pollution and overfishing (Appleby & Harrison, 2019).

To understand the present, we also need to consider how the law has developed, its effectiveness in terms of raising consciousness (Dunn et al., 2023) and how well it is enforced. We begin by considering the history of extinction and biodiversity loss and then consider how international law (Peters, 2021) has developed in relation to wildlife (Offor, 2020 and 2023) in particular with regard to the protection of migrating species, the control of invasive species and the impact of trade on endangered species. The chapter will not, however, consider the wider trade issues in relation to animals (Sykes, 2021). The chapter will look at conservation efforts, including the role of zoos and habitat protection and explore the marine environment, including a case study on whales. The impact of the climate emergency is a theme that runs throughout this chapter, the effects of which are becoming more apparent and serious with every report (Ripple et al., 2023; EEA, Report No. 1/2024). The chapter also considers how people and wildlife can coexist and the way in which the law can take this into account and deal with conflicts.

International law is central to protecting the 'global commons', those parts of the planet that fall outside national jurisdictions and to which all nations have access (UN, 2013b). Specific regional approaches, such as those taken in the EU or by individual countries, are also important, but it is impossible to consider all of these. Whilst recognising that environmental pressures have a fundamental impact on biodiversity, the great range of legal measures to protect the environment from air, water and waste pollution cannot be covered in detail here, however, there are other sources available that cover environmental law (Bell et al., 2024).

A brief history of extinction and biodiversity loss

The history of life on Earth has been one of extinction and biodiversity loss (Humboldt, 1845–1862; Wulf, 2015). It is difficult to know the true numbers of species that have become or are in danger of becoming extinct (Greenspoon et al., 2023) and the effect this will have on biodiversity (WWF, 2022). The UN suggests that '... around 40,000 species are documented to be at risk of extinction over the coming decades, 10 million hectares of forest (an area the size of Iceland) are being destroyed each year, and more than half of key biodiversity areas remain unprotected' (United Nations Department of Economic and Social Affairs, 2022).

Extinctions have occurred over time due to natural events (Kolbert, 2014) but also, and increasingly, due to human activities:

> Over the past two million years there have been seven so-called Ice Ages or glacial periods, which have been interrupted by warmer interglacial periods. These fluctuations have resulted in numerous extinctions. However, when our ancestors entered the scene between one and four million years ago the loss of species accelerated dramatically. Primitive Stone Age hunters caused extinctions of large mammals. Humans continually developed more sophisticated hunting techniques, ensuring ever greater levels of extinction. But now, in the 20th century, the wave of extinction is reaching levels quite unprecedented in the history of our planet. (Stuart & Stuart, 1996, pp. 3–4)

It is becoming harder for species to adapt to rapidly changing circumstances, with the increasing extinction rate showing how some wildlife is finding it impossible to survive.

The International Union for the Conservation of Nature (IUCN) has a '"red list" of those species at high risk of global extinction and divides them into nine categories: Not evaluated, data deficient, least concern, near-threatened, vulnerable, endangered, critically endangered, extinct in the wild and extinct"' (IUCN, 2024). Birdlife International explains that the list highlights that 49% of bird species worldwide (5,412) have declining populations, while 38% (4,234) are stable, with just 6% (659) increasing, and 6% (693) having unknown trends. It is further concluded that:

> Declines are not restricted to rare and threatened species – even common and widespread species are declining rapidly in some cases. Although decline rates in these common species may not be great enough to classify them as globally threatened, the substantial reduction in the number of individuals is likely to impact ecosystem function and the provision of ecosystem services. (Birdlife International, 2023, p. 14)

Evidence of the worldwide loss of biodiversity and the 'state of nature' is found across the globe, as illustrated by the House of Commons Environmental Audit Committee (2021), Burns (2023), the European Commission (COM/2020/635), WWF (2024) and the IUCN. However, whilst these provide a useful snapshot of the current situation, there may be '[t]ime-delayed biodiversity responses to environmental changes (ecological lags) [that] are often absent from models of biodiversity change, despite their well-documented existence … so, these need to be part of any models of biodiversity change' (Cornford et al., 2023, p. 1). This is important as reductions in the number or diversity of wildlife may be difficult for us to recognise.

The picture is complicated by the unfortunate fact that the imperative to deal with biodiversity loss may be impacted by how succeeding generations perceive the losses in their world:

> Among scientists, it is now recognised that we all suffer from 'shifting baseline syndrome', a phenomenon whereby we accept the world we grow up in as normal, although it might be quite different from the world our parents grew up in. Evidence is emerging that we humans are also poor at detecting gradual change that takes place 'within' our lifetime … In the last 50 years, we have reduced the abundance of wildlife on Earth dramatically. Many species that were once common are now scarce. (Goulson, 2021, pp. 88–71)

Barnes (2018) highlights the importance of being aware of nature in our surroundings in order to be able to fully appreciate it. Being aware and accurately recognising the loss we face of biodiversity and from extinction is a significant challenge for the development of Animal Law.

The stresses on nature

The stresses on wildlife are not easing (Rigal et al., 2023, Hannah et al., 2019; Shaw et al., 2024; Wilson, 2019c)) and include, along with the issues outlined above, the impacts of domesticated animals such as cats (Trouwborst & Somsen, 2020), (; Lawrence et al., 2015), the clearing of land (Luther, 2013), which can lead to zoonotic diseases (Greger, 2007;; Richardson et al., 2016; Wierucka et al., 2023; Minias, 2023), human population growth (Reaka-Kudla et al., 1997, pp. 10–13), introduced species, habitat destruction and the breaking up of habitat, as well as water scarcity or flooding.

There are also effects from intensively farmed land on water pollution from nitrates, soil structure and the loss of hedgerows and other habitats for wildlife, waste and climate change (Zahar, 2023). Other effects include hidden stressors such as light and noise pollution (Cravens & Boyles, 2019; Goodyer, 2022) road building, dams, infrastructure projects and housebuilding. These have been exacerbated by the climate emergency (Gaget et al., 2020; Ripple et al., 2023) and the concern that Earth is now moving towards a tipping point leading to irreversible changes (Russill, 2015; Willcock et al., 2023).

A tipping point is defined as, 'In the context of climate science, a tipping point refers to a critical threshold in the Earth's system or related processes which, if passed, can cause sudden, dramatic or even irreversible changes to some of the Earth's largest systems, such as the Antarctic ice sheet or the Amazon rainforest' (Met Office, 2023) and this may also be the case for wildlife. There also needs to be a recognition of 'ecological overshoot' which is defined as, 'the human consumption of natural resources at rates faster than they can be replenished and entropic waste production in excess of the Earth's assimilative and processing capacity' (Mertz et al., 2023).

As can be seen above, the variety and breadth of human impacts on wildlife and biodiversity is diverse and challenging, with much of it hidden from view. This chapter considers how the law deals with these issues at an international, regional and national level, and whether the law is effective to prevent more extinctions and biodiversity loss and so improve the situation for all wildlife on the planet.

The role of international law

International public law is a subject in its own right (Klabbers, 2023), with a specific branch dedicated to the environment (Harrison, 2023). Whilst most environmental law does not necessarily concern itself with animals in particular (Boyle & Redgwell, 2021; Dunoff et al., 2023), it is useful to see how and why international environmental law developed alongside conservation and biodiversity protections in terms of international wildlife law to consider nature as a whole. Whilst most of the law developed after the Second World War there was earlier international protection in terms of trade and conservation:

> Regulation of international wildlife trade began with a focus on African species and the signing in 1900 of the 'Convention Designed to Ensure the Conservation of various species of wild animals in Africa, which are useful to Man or inoffensive' (British Parliamentary Papers, 1900). While hailed as the first international treaty on nature conservation, it never came into force. Thirty-three years later, the 'Convention Relative to the Preservation of Fauna and Flora in their Natural State' was adopted and came into force in 1936. Known as the 'London Convention,' its primary aim was to protect African species by prohibiting hunting, killing, and capture, and by regulating internal and international trade in their trophies (Cioc, 2009). The London Convention eventually paved the way to a discussion on institutionalizing (sic) conservation, which led to the creation of The International Union for the Conservation of Nature (IUCN) in 1948. (Kelleher & Kenchington, 1991, pp. 3–5)

Since it was set up in 1948, the IUCN members:

> … include national and subnational governments and government agencies as well as non-governmental and indigenous peoples' organisations from over 160 countries … The IUCN Members convene every two to four years to debate and agree major policy issues and approve the organisation's programme. A major outcome of these meetings are the Resolutions and Recommendations. These efforts guide global conservation efforts by, for example supporting the preparation of the World Conservation Strategy and contributing to the development of environmental treaties. Members have issued over 1400 Resolutions since the organisation's founding in 1948. These have been the Union's most effective means of influencing conservation policy, at species, site, national and global levels. (IUCN, n.d.)

The most significant development in international law was the establishment in 1945 of the United Nations, which was given the task of working on global issues and developing mechanisms to uphold international law. The United Nations Environment Programme was set up in 1972. The programme works on a range of issues that include sustainable development and the climate emergency and works with other stakeholders through the United Nations Environment Assembly that sets 'priorities for global environmental policies and develops international environmental law' (United Nations Environment Programme [UNEP], n.d.):

> During the 1970s, there was increasing recognition and mounting concern regarding many environmental problems. In 1971, the Convention on Wetlands of International Importance especially as Waterfowl Habitat (known as the Ramsar Convention) was developed. In 1972, the Convention for the Protection of the World Cultural and Natural Heritage (known as the World Heritage Convention) was developed. Also, in 1972 at the Stockholm Conference, the Governing Council of the United Nations Environment Programme (UNEP) was given the task of reviewing the international situation to ensure that emerging environmental problems of wide international significance receive appropriate and adequate consideration by governments. (Kelleher & Kenchington, 1991, pp. 3–5)

As the impact of what was then called global warming, which then became known as climate change (Coplan et al., 2021), became apparent, so did the development of international law. The Intergovernmental Panel on Climate Change (IPCC) is the UN body that assesses the science relating to climate change. It was established by the United Nations Environment Programme (UNEP) and the World Meteorological Organization (WMO) in 1988 to provide political leaders with periodic scientific assessments concerning the risks and implications of climate change, as well as to put forward adaptation and mitigation strategies (UNEP produces many reports; see UNEP, 2024a). In the same year, the UN General Assembly endorsed the action by the WMO and UNEP in jointly establishing the IPCC. It has 195 member states (IPBES secretariat). The UN Framework Convention on Climate Change (UNFCCC) came into force on 21 March 1994. The law is developed at the Conferences of the Parties (COP) – the decision-making body of the UNFCCC. All states that are parties to the convention are represented at the COP, during which they review the implementation of the convention and any other legal instruments that the COP adopts, and then decisions are taken to promote the effective implementation of the convention, including institutional and administrative arrangements.

The COP aims to limit global warming through the setting of targets (Mayer, 2022; Reins & Verschuuren, 2022; LSE, 2024). There have been a number of important milestones, including the Rio Conference in 1992, the Kyoto Protocol (adopted on 11 December 1997 and came into force on 16 February 2005), the Paris Agreement in 2015, and the Warsaw Mechanism for International Loss and Damage was agreed in 2013 and a loss and damage fund was finally established and made operational in 2023. This is then implemented (or not) on a regional level (Holwerda et al., 2021), such as the European Climate Law (Regulation (EU) 2021/1119), and at national levels, such as in the UK, the Climate Change Act 2008 (and the work of the Climate Change Committee).

The international protection from extinction

One of the first recorded indicators for extinctions and the pressures that lead to them was the creation of the IUCN red list:

> Established in 1964, the International Union for Conservation of Nature's red list of Threatened Species has evolved to become the world's most comprehensive information source on the global extinction risk status of animal, fungus and plant species. (IUCN, n.d.)
>
> In much the same way as a barometer measures atmospheric pressure to help us prepare for adverse weather conditions, The IUCN red list measures the pressures acting on species, which guides and informs conservation actions to help prevent extinctions ... This is why The IUCN red list is often referred to as a 'barometer of life'. (Dubois et al., 2017; IUCN, n.d.)

The IUCN Red List Categories and Criteria are intended to be an easily and widely understood system for classifying species at high risk of global extinction. It divides species into nine categories: Not Evaluated; Data Deficient; Least Concern; Near Threatened; Vulnerable; Endangered; Critically Endangered; Extinct in the Wild; and Extinct (IUCN, 2024).

This list is important as it does not just consider some of the iconic species, such as pandas, but focuses on other wildlife. For example, in the UK, the hedgehog is on the red list following its assessment as being of 'Near Threatened' in 2024 moving from its previous listing of 'Least Concern', as illustrated by falling population numbers in rural areas due to agricultural intensification, roadkill, and modern garden design, although the numbers of urban hedgehogs are beginning to recover (Barrow et al., 2022).

The importance of the red list is seen in relation to controls on trade in endangered species, so in the case of eel smuggling to China, the fact they are endangered and on the red list means they have become subject to fishing and distribution quotas, and it is illegal to trade them outside of Europe (Jones, 2023). However, a problem with the red list is that it focuses on vertebrates in the list species (Hutchinson et al., 2022, p. 193) and only a small number of species have been assessed, so that some, deemed as 'data-deficient', may be at risk, although this is not yet officially recognised through their inclusion on the list (Borgelt et al., 2022, p. 2). The red list and the state of nature reports are useful as together they shine a spotlight on the wildlife at risk of extinction.

The international protection of biodiversity

The focus on biological diversity in international law was developed by the Convention on Biological Diversity, which was signed by 150 countries in June 1992 at the United Nations Conference on Environment and Development. The convention aimed to conserve biological diversity, provide for the sustainable use of the components of biological diversity, and ensure the fair and equitable sharing of the benefits arising out of the utilisation of genetic resources. Article 6a of the Convention on Biological Diversity states that each contracting party should 'develop national strategies, plans or programmes for the conservation and sustainable use of biodiversity' (The Convention on Biological Diversity, n.d.). The implementation of these is monitored at the COP, which is the governing body of the convention and implements the convention at its meetings.

There are two protocols to the convention: First, the *Cartagena Protocol on Biosafety to the Convention on Biological Diversity*. This is an international agreement that aims to ensure the safe handling, transport, and use of living modified organisms (LMOs), which can include genetically modified animals and plants resulting from modern biotechnology that may have adverse effects on biological diversity, taking also into account risks to human health. The Protocol was adopted on 29 January 2000 and came into force on 11 September 2003. Second is the *Nagoya Protocol on Access to Genetic Resources and the Fair and Equitable Sharing of Benefits Arising from their Utilization to the Convention on Biological Diversity*. This aims to facilitate the sharing of benefits arising from the utilisation of genetic resources in a fair and equitable way. It came into force on 12 October 2014 and includes protection for indigenous and local community knowledge around genetic resources.

At COP 15, a global target was included to protect 30% of nature on the planet by 2030 (known as '30 x 30'). This was part of the Kunming-Montreal Global Biodiversity Framework and as part of 23 targets that nation-states were given the responsibility to report on from time to time. At COP 28, a global stock take took place and a recognition that biodiversity issues also need to be considered by governments when developing their climate action plans along with a goal to halt and reverse global deforestation by 2030. However, whilst COP 28 included an acknowledgement that indigenous communities can play a positive role there are still concerns about how the 30 x 30 approach can impact local communities because it 'revolves around fortress conservation, which means that biodiversity should be protected by creating protected areas, which can be seen as being very old school' (Goodyer, 2022, p. 22). This is because there is a concern about how the development of protected areas impacts local communities, particularly those that are relocated (Büscher et al., 2016; Mahalwal & Kabra, 2023). Goodyer (2022) explains:

> So, depending on how you implement it, it can involve quite negative practices in terms of relationships with local communities. The second major criticism of the 30 x 30 approach concerns the question of quantity over quality. So, 30 per cent by 2030 is a sort of arbitrary target. We know that many areas, effectively, only exist on paper and that biodiversity has declined even as protected areas have increased. If we only think about designating more areas for protected status, we're going to be missing a big part of the problem. (Goodyer, 2022, p. 22)

It will need funding and focusing on the areas that are in most need, and '(w)e should be looking at how we are integrating communities into the management of those areas and how we can ensure that community lands are adequately supported to protect nature' (Goodyer, 2022, pp. 22–23).

There have also been some concerns about the speed and comprehensiveness of the implementation of the treaty (Dias, 2020 and Carbon Brief 2024). This can be seen in Europe where, although the EU has set out the EU Biodiversity Strategy, the move towards a Nature Restoration Law (COM/2022/304) proposed by the European Commission and agreed by the European Parliament was adopted by the European Council with a narrow majority after some resistance from some EU states. In terms of developing the law, the analysis of biodiversity targets in the UK (Defra, 2023) and the EU suggests that it is difficult to compare headline targets 'as they are all set out in broad and mostly ill-defined differing terms' and they are often not quantified or are difficult to interpret (Tucker, 2022, p. 29). Tucker also suggests that, in terms of the specific biodiversity outcome objectives, the EU's targets are more comprehensive and focused, whereas those in the UK are too broad, less focused on priorities, and seem to have lower ambitions and urgency, which could lead to the loss of important species (Tucker, 2022, p. 30).

Protection of biodiversity in Europe

The development of a European approach to protecting biodiversity was set out in 1979 by the Council of Europe. The Bern Convention (1979) aimed to promote European cooperation on the conservation of wild flora and fauna and their natural habitats (Rodriguez Goyes, 2021). The convention now extends to some African states. Parties to the convention agree to consider 'the impact that other policies may have on natural heritage and recognise the intrinsic value of wild flora and fauna, which needs to be preserved and passed to future generations' (Council of Europe, 2024a). The Bern Convention has led to several EU initiatives, including Natura 2000, a network of core breeding and resting sites for rare and threatened species. It also led to the designation of some rare natural habitat types, which are listed under both the Birds Directive and the Habitats Directive (Council of Europe, 2024b). There has also been development at a national level arising from the convention. The UK has committed to work alongside existing organisations to set about biodiversity 'net gain' (Natural England, n.d.), including for the marine environment (Natural England, n.d.). This aims to measure overall net losses and benefits and to mitigate environmental damage through planning or environmental improvements. For example, a habitat might be created in the UK to offset the environmental impact of a new housing development.

The effectiveness of the Bern Convention depends upon how it is implemented by different countries. The discretion within the convention leads to different approaches depending on the interpretation given in national law (Sollund, 2020). For example, Sollund suggests that some large predators, which were under threat due to a variety of human actions have experienced a resurgence in many European countries as a result of the convention (Sollund, 2020, pp. 357–358). But Sollund (2020, p. 364) goes on to argue that whilst the Bern Convention has shaped the legislation and wildlife conservation policies of parties to the convention, due to the discretion given to each country it still means that large predators can be killed by licence for example, provided the entire species are not wiped out.

The regional nature of enforcement and the discretion given to individual countries means that wildlife can lack sufficient protection and this can be particularly the case for migrating species as they cross borders, moving from one jurisdiction to the next which means that there is even more need for well-organised cooperation and consistency in cross-border enforcement.

The issue of migrating species

The need for cross-border cooperation in the conservation of species that migrate across national boundaries or between areas of national jurisdictions and the high seas was first recognised in the 1979 Convention on the Conservation of Migratory Species of Wild Animals (the Bonn Convention), which arose from a recommendation of the 1972 United Nations Conference on the Human Environment.

There are two appendices to the convention: Appendix I lists species in danger of extinction and states that habitats should be conserved and restored where feasible:

> …to prevent, remove, compensate for, or minimize, as appropriate, the adverse effects of activities or obstacles that seriously impede or prevent the migration of the species; and control or eliminate exotic species where feasible and appropriate. Animals should only be taken for scientific purposes, enhancing the propagation or survival of the affected species, to accommodate the needs of traditional subsistence users of such species or extraordinary circumstances so require so long as such exceptions are precise as to content and limited in space and time. Such taking should not operate to the disadvantage of the species.

Appendix II lists those species that are migratory and have an 'unfavourable conservation status'. These are those that require international agreements for their conservation and management, as well as those with a conservation status that would significantly benefit from the international cooperation that could be achieved by an international agreement. The UN published its first report on the state of migratory species in 2024.

There are concerns about how effective the Bonn Convention has been for animals. Sellheim and Schumacher (2022, p. 369) argue that by focusing the protection of migratory species in terms of habitat protection means that it applies too much of an ecosystem-based approach rather than one based on the species concerned, and that it has 'struggled to gain full global approval'. At the time of writing, 133 states have ratified the convention, although it is notable that the United States, the Russian Federation, China, Japan and Canada—all of which are extremely important states for global conservation—are not parties to the convention. Consequently, the Bonn Convention plays a small role in the international discourse about conservation, as its effectiveness is hampered by its structure and composition.

Sellheim and Schumacher (2022, pp. 379–380) also suggest ways to mitigate the weaknesses in the Bonn Convention in that contracting parties could tighten their enforcement to ensure compliance and thereby protect endangered species. They argue that if they are not willing to do this, then no international panel exists that could hold these states accountable. Instead, parties would have to resort to 'soft' compliance mechanisms such as non-binding resolutions and declarations. However, as Fasoli and

McGlone (2018, p. 28) explain other, more traditional means of enforcement in international treaty obligations, such as countermeasures, exceptio non adimpleti and the rules on state responsibility, might be more effective. Although commencing more formal proceedings before a judicial body, such as an international court or tribunal, might be regarded as 'confrontational and adversarial'.

Whilst the Bonn and Berne Conventions work together with the Birds Directive and the Convention on International Trade in Endangered Species there can still be a lack of protection for migrating birds. The need for effective enforcement mechanisms is illustrated by the large number of birds killed around the Mediterranean basin as they migrate between Europe and Africa. An estimated 25 million birds are killed every year, negatively impacting populations of migrating wild bird species in the EU and beyond. The European Commission has set out an updated roadmap to eliminate the illegal killing, trapping and trade of birds and the EU has a sustainable hunting initiative (European Commission, 2023). The effect of the killing is that these migratory species have little chance to recover during their migration, and this is a major barrier to their recovery (Birdlife International, n.d.). Much of this loss is down to hunting, which can be for food (Safety of Wild Game Regulation (EC) 852/2004 and Regulation (EC) 853/2004, the EU Food Hygiene Regulations) or as a 'sport', both of which have impacts on conservation efforts. In 1990, for example, the straits of Messina were shown to be a particular hot spot for shooting, and many of the hunters were from Italy (Birds International, 1990, p. 7). Since stricter enforcement of the regulations in previous hunting areas, such as Italy and Malta, much of the activity has moved to the Balkan countries where there is less regulation, highlighting the need for stricter regulation throughout Europe (Birdlife International, n.d.).

Invasive non-native or alien species

The movement of animal species can create issues, whether this has occurred naturally or through deliberate or accidental introduction, this movement can lead to a species becoming problematic as an 'invasive species'. However, defining any species as 'invasive' is controversial, and decisions by countries to do so are often seen as being value-laden, with variations according to which country is doing the labelling (Kapitza et al., 2019). In general terms, the designation as an invasive non-native species applies to species introduced by humans to environments outside their natural range, which then go on to have adverse effects on native species and ecosystems through resource competition, disease transmission, hybridisation, predation and habitat modification (Simberloff, 2013). Examples from the animal kingdom include species that became invasive after being imported often as part of colonisation or brought as exotic pets, escaped from captivity, or were brought in to tackle other wildlife seen as pests (Coates, 2023). Invasive non-native species are one of the major threats to global biodiversity, as they can lead to a decline in biodiversity and to extinction (Bhagwat, 2018; IPBES, 2023).

The International Union for the Conservation of Nature (IUCN) listed:

> 100 of the world's worst invasive species in order to boost awareness of some of the most damaging, distinct, and representative invasive species globally. Inclusion on the list is both on the basis of the severity of impacts on biodiversity and human activities and the species' potential to represent important issues in relation to biological invasions (Lowe et al., 2000, p.3). As such, species on this list are known to impact upon the structuring and functioning of ecosystems and the biodiversity they support, as well as on key human endeavours. Importantly, absence from the list does not imply lesser impact or lower risk to ecosystems or economies, and the list aims at communicating on biological invasions in general rather than a subset of species. (Cuthbert et al., 2022, p. 1896)

An example is the introduction of the non-native grey squirrel into the UK, which then forced the native red squirrels into a few small, protected areas. In other areas of the world, the crazy ant has caused a collapse in the number of grey land crabs as well as reducing the reproduction of a variety of arthropods, reptiles, birds and mammals on the forest floor and canopy (Lowe et al., 2000, p. 4). However, the 'true' cost of these invasive species is yet to be seen (Cuthbert et al., 2022, p. 1895).

Internationally, invasive alien species are formally addressed in the Global Strategy on Plant Conservation. In the EU (Regulation (EU) No 1143/2014) and in the UK, there are strategies for tackling the existing and growing threat posed by non-native species under the Invasive Alien Species (Enforcement and Permitting) Order 2019 (Defra, 2023). There are specific legal controls in place; for example, in the UK, it is illegal to release a grey squirrel into the wild or allow one to escape. Instead, they must be humanely killed, or it is considered an offence under Schedule 9 of the Wildlife and Countryside Act 1981. Whether they can be eradicated is problematic for practical reasons – they are a highly robust and widely established species (Crowley et al., 2017; García-Díaz et al., 2021; Frank, 2021). The need for a workable international legal framework to stop the spread of invasive species is further complicated by climate change, which means that non-native species can flourish in new areas (Broughton et al., 2022, p. 1291–1292; IUCN, 2021), along with the fact that whilst some species move on their own accord, some are introduced by the trade in wildlife.

The trade in wildlife

There are two forms of trade in wildlife, legal and illegal. The legal trade often masks the illegal trade worth millions of pounds to organised crime so hindering enforcement. The history of both types of trade is linked to colonialism, the effects of which still overshadows the law today.

History and background of the trade in wild animals

The trade in wild animals for various purposes, such as for use in circuses, has a long history as does the link between colonialism and extinction (Gandy, 2022). The taking of wildlife for circuses evidenced by:

> The circus as we know it today owes its origins to Philip Astley, a one-time Sergeant Major in the 15th Light Dragoons, who gave his exhibitions of equestrian expertise, and later performing animals, in London in the 1770s. But these can be traced by the historically minded to similar shows and performances of wild beasts seen in the Circus Maximus and the Amphitheatres of Ancient Rome. These in turn were derived from the wondrous exhibitions of exotic animal species and perhaps from chariot racing in Egypt and Greece. (Croft-Cooke & Cotes, 1976, pp. 7–8)

Croft-Cooke and Cotes (1976, pp. 7–8) suggest that both earlier and 18th-century circuses, and their use of animals were influenced by imperial colonists and explorers who procured animals from their colonies. 'Rome, like Greece before it, had established links with India and Persia, which facilitated the supply of animals from these countries, just as the establishment of British rule in India made it easy for the followers of Astley to obtain elephants to enrich their shows'. The arrival of these animals from a new country highlighted its invasion or colonisation and reflected the view of animals and people as property in the new capitalist mercantile system of trade.

The ongoing economic incentive for trade can be seen in the various reasons that animals are taken from the wild: 'Demand for products such as elephant ivory, tiger skins and pangolin scales create a powerful financial incentive for poaching and smuggling, which drastically undermines ongoing conservation efforts. That demand is driven by the desire for medicinal products or investment in luxury trinkets' (Environmental Investigation Agency, 2024). Wildlife can also be taken for trophies, as pets (and to appear on social media (Spee et al., 2019).

The trade in wild animals also leads to several negative issues, including ecological problems (Hughes et al., 2023), the transmission of infectious diseases, injuries and concerns relating to animal welfare (Shotton, 2023). Animals are often transported under poor conditions. These problems are exacerbated by the perception of animals as property rather than as individuals with rights, which limits the effectiveness of the controls that might otherwise be provided under international law (Sollund, 2011, p. 448).

International law on the trade in endangered species

Trade in all animals is governed by trade law (Peters, 2021), but trade in endangered species is regulated by the Convention on International Trade in Endangered Species (CITES – also known as the Washington Convention), which was signed in 1973 and came into force on 1 July 1975. CITES is a voluntary international agreement between states, and it aims to prevent the hunting of endangered species by prohibiting the trade in animals or artefacts taken from them, such as horns or tusks made into ornaments. Once a state agrees to be bound by the agreement, it is subject to a legally binding framework that must be implemented by the state concerned; however, it does not replace national law. It aims to ensure that scientific evidence is used to regulate international trade in specimens of wild animals and plants and that the trade does not threaten species' survival (Smith et al., 2011). It allows, for example, some controlled trade in species that are not yet endangered but may become so. There are four types of trade covered, these being import, export, re-export and introduction from the sea.

CITES sets out three appendices to prohibit trade in those species threatened with over-exploitation. Species are grouped in appendices according to how threatened they are by international trade. Some whole groups are included, such as primates, cetaceans (whales, dolphins and porpoises), sea turtles, parrots, corals, cacti and orchids. In some cases, only a subspecies or geographically separate population of a species (for example the population of just one country) is listed (CITES, n.d.).

Appendix I includes species threatened with extinction. Trade in specimens of these species is permitted only when the trade is not commercial, for example for scientific research. Appendix II includes species not necessarily threatened with extinction, but where trade must be controlled using export permits or re-export certificates. Animals can be moved from one appendix to another at the biannual Conference of the Parties (COP). The COP has agreed in Resolution Conf. 9.24 (Rev. COP17) on a set of biological and trade criteria to help determine whether a species should be included in Appendices I or II.

Appendix III contains species that are protected in at least one country, which has asked other parties to CITES for assistance in controlling the trade. Changes to Appendix III can be made unilaterally by any party at any time. Countries can make reservations that they will not be bound by the convention. This, it has been suggested, occurs where countries wish to continue with an illegal trade, often for commercial reasons. These:

> reservations act as a tool for countries to dispute a CITES listing while continuing to trade the species legally. The seven species with the most current reservations are mammals used in the fur industry … Five further species, including the whale shark, minke whale, basking shark, and two seahorses – all have five reservations each. These are all either consumed or made into medicine. Twenty-six species have been deleted from CITES, although they remain on the IUCN red list. (Hutchinson et al., 2022, p. 203; see also Challender et al., 2023)

The convention has a documentation system for importing, exporting or re-exporting a specimen of a CITES-listed species. The appropriate documentation needs to be obtained and presented for clearance at the port of entry or exit, depending on each country's laws. CITES requires that the system is overseen at a domestic level by a management and scientific authority and there is an international body to oversee the workings of the permit system. CITES aims that by 2030, all trade in listed species should be legal, traceable and sustainable (CITES Secretariat, 2022). There are also requirements to report legal and illegal trade annually. The top exporting and importing regions are Europe (for example in relation to shark fins see Shea et al., 2022) and Asia. In 2022, CITES reported that approximately half of the estimated annual average value of global CITES-listed animal exports originated from Asia, while almost two-thirds of the estimated annual average value of global CITES-listed plant exports was attributed to exports from Africa.

One significant concern is the export of ivory from Africa (Caton, 2023). In the UK, the Ivory Act 2018 came into force in 2022 and means there can be no dealing of items containing, or made of, elephant ivory unless they are registered or certified as exempt. The illegal sale of ivory and other items was highlighted in a case in Derby, where a man was prosecuted for trading ivory on eBay without a licence (Naylor & Astley, 2023). The seizure of seven tonnes of smuggled ivory in a container in Vietnam highlighted the transnational nature of illegal trade (Swann, 2023). The shipment was re-routed from Africa to disguise its original port of embarkation and to deter suspicion. Smugglers often disguise the shipment's origin in the hopes it will allow them to avoid detection (UNODC, n.d.). The other issue in relation to ivory is the storage and management of the existing stock so it does not re-enter the illegal market, and there are protocols and guidelines on how this should be done (CITES, n.d.).

In the EU, CITES has been implemented through Council Regulation 338/97/EC, 865/06, 338/97 and 792/2012 (as amended). The regulations provide control of the sale and possession of wild animals, birds and plants normally found in the EU, as well as CITES-listed species. The EU Wildlife Trade Regulations go beyond CITES in a number of respects, including the designation of species, import controls, transport and housing, as well as internal EU trade (Eurogroup for Animals, n.d.). The EU has a wildlife trafficking action plan (COM/2022/581), which contains four main priorities:

- To prevent wildlife trafficking and address its root causes by reducing consumer demand for illegally traded wildlife, supporting sustainable livelihoods in source countries, and tackling corruption at all levels.
- To strengthen the legal and policy framework against wildlife trafficking by aligning EU and national policies with international commitments and the latest evidence and engaging with civil society and business sectors involved in the wildlife trade.
- To enforce regulations and policies to fight wildlife trafficking effectively by improving the rate of detection of illegal activities within the EU, focusing on capacity-building along the entire enforcement chain. Encouraging coordination and cooperation within and between member states and increasing efforts in tackling the online aspects of wildlife trafficking.
- Strengthening the global partnership of source, consumer and transit countries against wildlife trafficking.

In the UK, enforcement provisions are primarily contained in The Control of Trade in Endangered Species (COTES) Regulations 2018 and the Customs and Excise Management Act 1979 (CEMA), as well as retained EU law in this area.

How effective has CITES been?

The Environmental Investigations Agency highlights the historical importance of CITES:

> Prior to 1989, between 70,000 and 100,000 elephants were being poached every year to supply the international ivory trade. Africa's elephant population was halved from 1.3 million elephants in 1979 to just 624,000 in 1988. Highly organised poaching gangs swept down from the north to east, west, central and southern Africa throughout the 1970s and 1980s. High-level corruption, wars, murder and escalating prices for ivory caused poaching to intensify. The CITES ban caused ivory prices and elephant poaching to drop dramatically virtually overnight.
>
> As leading consumers of these products of now illegal trade, Europe, Japan and America closed their markets to ivory imports and the impact was considerable. In another turn, which turned out to have its own associated animal welfare problems, countries are now more aware of their elephants as tourist attractions (Head, 2023) and are 'therefore a previously untapped source of revenue which should be protected'. (Environmental Investigations Agency, 1994, p. 5)

However, there are issues raised in terms of the enforcement of CITES requirements due to a lack of documentation, and lack of awareness by exporters and importers of CITES requirements, particularly tourists. The relatively high cost of obtaining CITES compliance permits can lead to breaches of the regulations, and low fines and lack of legal trade options can incentivise illegal activity (CITES Secretariat, 2022). Often, these violations are part of a wider system of organised crime (Harrison et al., 2016; Stringham et al., 2023). The campaign group End Wildlife Crime has called for the creation of additional protocols to tackle wildlife crime under the UN Convention on Transnational Organised Crime. However, as the International Union for Conservation of Nature (IUCN) (n.d.) suggests, there appears to be a lack of political will to do this, which can lead to a weak criminal justice response, often exacerbated by corruption and a lack of resources in combatting such crime.

The legal trade in endangered species

There are a number of concerns about the legal trade in endangered species. The first relates to the growing trade of animals bred specifically for this purpose, particularly as most trade is now from the captive market). Green et al. (2023, p. 8) estimated that at least 487 wildlife species are farmed across the world. This comprises of at least 27 amphibians, 133 reptiles, 249 birds and 79 mammals. Of these documented species, 34% are considered either 'near threatened', 'vulnerable', 'endangered' or 'critically endangered' on the IUCN red list of threatened species, and 62% are listed on the Convention on International Trade in Endangered Species of Wild Fauna and Flora (CITES) appendices.

The commercial breeding of a species from Appendix I sees them moved into Appendix II if they have been bred in captivity, meaning they can be traded (Natali, 2023, p. 210). Breeding may be useful in driving illegal trading down by providing another source of products and protecting the species through breeding programmes (Natali, 2023, p. 210). However, there are problems related to this as the farming of Appendix I species can see pressure continue on wild populations, distorting the authenticity of trade flows and generating further demand for those species that farmed supplies fail to meet (Natali, 2023, p. 211).

This is compounded by the fact that it can lead to further animal welfare concerns for those captive animals, for example:

> Conditions often associated with wildlife farms – including high concentrations of animals, poor hygiene, and close contact with caretakers – can increase the risk of disease emergence and create opportunities for pathogen transmission between wild animals and humans, and from captive wild animals to free-ranging populations ... Similarly, a range of animal welfare concerns have been documented for the commercial farming of wild animal species, including disease, malnourishment, stress-induced behaviours, injuries, infected wounds, cannibalism and premature death. (Green et al., 2023, p. 10)

Green et al. (2023) further suggest that strong governance is needed if the trade in farmed or captive animals is to help in the conservation of species. However, they argue that a transition away from commercial breeding is needed because there are plenty of alternatives that can aid population recovery and conservation, which do not result in such negative impacts. Bans, social marketing for demand reduction strategies, and reducing the social acceptability of wildlife products have all previously been shown to play a role in mitigating wildlife exploitation.

In terms of enforcement, a key problem is that legal trading often covers up illegal trading, as it may be difficult to establish the origins of a wild bird or animal; for example, breeding Appendix I animals can make it hard to differentiate them from the illegal trade when the same species has been taken from the wild (Natali, 2023). This is compounded by the increasing trade in 'second generation wildlife' – the offspring of illegally traded wildlife that is difficult to identify as originating from wild parents other than by DNA sampling, as was the situation in *ET* v. *Ministerstvo* životního *prostředí* (2022).

The reform of CITES

Despite the apparent success of CITES, concerns remain that the legal and illegal trade in endangered species is still causing problems for wildlife and their welfare. The operation of CITES has been criticised, for example, by Hutchinson et al. (2022, p. 206), who argue that species' market value, charisma and survival status together form a complex set of characteristics that leads to in-demand species continuing to be traded despite the threat of extinction.

Protecting those species not yet placed on the CITES remains a problem (Watters et al., 2022). CITES has adopted the precautionary principle, meaning it acts prudently to place animals under protection even if the need to do so is unclear. Even so, it is argued that for animals protected under Appendix I, there needs to be a change in emphasis from listing those that cannot be traded to listing those animals that 'can' be traded. It is suggested that this would make implementation easier for enforcement officers and reflect the precautionary principle rather than being reactive (Hughes et al., 2023). While there is a lack of consensus on what exactly the precautionary principle is (Sandin, 1999; Chapman, 1999), it is felt that being 'better safe than sorry' is an effective approach to regulatory decision-making (Marchant, 2003, p. 1799).

In the EU, some states have adopted legislation including 'positive lists' of those animals that are allowed to be kept and traded as pets (Warwick et al., 2018). Other EU States have continued with negative lists of banned species, but these often lack clarity because of the emergence of new species that importers seek to exploit (Eurogroup for Animals, no date). However, the use of lists does not solve the underlying fundamental issue that, from an 'anthropocentric and a welfarist perspective, it seems that 'unnecessary' animal suffering is an unavoidable part of the trade', whether legal or illegal (Wyatt et al., 2022, p. 70).

Added to the concern about the welfare impact and the issue of unnecessary suffering inherent in both the illegal and illegal trade, is the effect of the law on indigenous communities and traditional practices. This is recognised in Article 116 of the Treaty for the Establishment of the East African Community which undertakes to develop a collective and coordinated policy for the conservation and sustainable utilisation of wildlife and other tourist sites in the Community. It is argued that there needs to be more recognition of why hunting takes place and that trophy hunting, debated in the UK during the passage of the Hunting Trophies (Import Prohibition) Bill 2023–24, is different from subsistence or cultural hunting (Hare et al., 2023). Trophy hunting does not add to the conservation or sustainability value and ignores the sentience and moral considerations of wildlife (Prisner-Levyne, 2020), but subsistence or cultural hunting is often viewed differently (Hare et al., 2023). It is to be hoped that the Bill will be reintroduced by the Labour Government.

It is important to reduce both the legal and illegal trade in wild animals so that illegal activities are prevented, and practical solutions can be found that support local conservation efforts. This includes implementing educational programmes and developing alternative income-generating opportunities (World Animal Protection, n.d.). Ensuring that conservation actions are respectful and rooted in local communities is essential. For example, the Ewaso Lions community initiative (Ewaso Lions 2024 is a fully African wildlife conservation organisation that engages with key demographic groups, such as warriors, women, elders and children, to develop strategies to reduce human-carnivore conflict.

Other reforms are also needed, such as the creation of artificial trophies (Dhar, 2023). There is a need to ensure that alternatives to markets and trade in illegal wildlife products are supported by countries such as the UK. An example is the Illegal Wildlife Challenge Fund, which tackles illegal wildlife trade by supporting projects worldwide that develop sustainable livelihoods for local communities. The fund also helps strengthen law enforcement, supports legal systems and reduces demand for illegal wildlife products (Illegal Wildlife Challenge Fund, 2024).

Sollund argues that a problem with CITES is that it regards wildlife as 'resources' whose trade needs regulation so that species can be conserved primarily for human benefit. Therefore, reforming the convention's rationale could see CITES move to being a promoter of conservation and a protector of individual species' rights. Sollund highlights that this is 'essential in the preservation of non-human animal species and ecosystems, and of course for all sentient beings' (Sollund, 2022, p. 1048). However, changing international law can be a lengthy process, and it needs to be based on collaboration.

Morton et al. (2022, p. 1007) argue that such change would offer space for constructive collaboration to change the status quo and help CITES deliver on its core mission to protect endangered species. This would also be in accordance with the fundamental principle of changing regulation based on openness, participation and consultation (Graham & Prosser, 1988).

Zoos – exploitation or conservation?

The protection and preservation of species is seen as the key rationale for maintaining zoos. Some of the legal trade in wildlife discussed above takes place in order to provide wildlife for breeding programmes in zoos. This, it is argued, is a way of reducing extinctions and the loss of biodiversity. But does the reality of zoos support these aims?

The history of zoos

The Zoological Society of London was founded in 1826 by Davy and Raffles, and the zoo at Regents Park was opened a year later (Blunt, 1976, pp. 15–17). Zoos opened in Paris, Vienna and Dublin shortly after (WSPA/Born Free Foundation, 1994). However, conditions were grim, deaths were frequent, particularly in the case of chimpanzees, and capture and delivery was 'barbaric and incredibly wasteful' (Leahy, 1991, pp. 237–238). Synthetic captive breeding in something approaching a natural setting was not put into practical effect until the opening of the UK's Whipsnade Zoo in 1931.

> In the 19th and early 20th centuries, 'not much thought was given to the purpose of zoos. Davy and Raffles, in London, had the provision of specimens for scientific research in mind but no sense of the need for conservation as the term is now used. (Synthetic captive breeding in something approaching a natural setting was not put into practical effect until the opening of the UK's Whipsnade Zoo in 1931.) There were 19th-century critics who were outspoken not only about the conditions in which the animals were kept but also the indignities and baiting they were subjected to in order to please an unruly public. This campaign led to the Cruelty to Wild Animals in Captivity Act of 1900.' Since then, the number of zoos has grown, but never more so than in the 1950s and 1960s, when municipalities in search of status and businessmen in search of profit put money into zoos.

> What had previously been the preserve of nations, cities, and the occasional wealthy individual became *de rigeur* throughout the developed and many parts of the developing world. During these boom years, zoos were no more than recreational facilities that displayed animals to satisfy the curiosity of the general public. Even the long-established scientifically based zoos paid only marginal attention to a more serious agenda. For instance, such research as was conducted centred on efforts to breed and maintain wild animals more successfully in captivity. Hardly any zoos looked beyond their immediate circle towards their responsibilities in the wild. During the 1970s and 1980s, three factors arose which were bound to confront and challenge such an introspective attitude:
>
> - The development of sophisticated televised natural history documentaries which conveyed a more accurate interpretation of the natural world.
> - Expanded opportunities for global travel, which made it possible for more people than ever before to see and appreciate wildlife in its natural habitat.
> - Increased recognition of the welfare implications of captivity as information became available about the causes of stereotyped behaviour in zoo animals.
>
> These developments linked to the issues of animal welfare, conservation, and education, led people to increasingly question the acceptability of zoos (World Society for the Protection of Animals/Born Free Foundation, 1994, p. 10). (Leahy, 1991, pp. 237–238)

The law relating to zoos

A zoo is defined as any establishment where animals of wild species are exhibited to the public, meaning that regulation applies to sanctuaries and rescue centres with similar core activity (Draper, 2011, p.20). Zoos and other facilities tend to base the rationale for their existence on conservation, science and education, which is reflected in the law at a domestic level in the UK and at EU level in the Zoos Directive (Council Directive 1999/22/EC). The directive states in Article 1: 'The objectives of this directive are to protect wild fauna and to conserve biodiversity by providing for the adoption of measures by member states for the licensing and inspection of zoos in the community, thereby strengthening the role of zoos in the conservation of biodiversity'. This is supported by Article 3, which requires states to ensure that zoos adhere to Articles 4, 5, 6 and 7 and implement the following conservation measures:

- Participating in research from which conservation benefits accrue to the species, and/or training in relevant conservation skills, and/or the exchange of information relating to species conservation and/or, where appropriate, captive breeding, repopulation or reintroduction of species into the wild.
- Promoting public education and awareness in relation to the conservation of biodiversity, particularly by providing information about the species exhibited and their natural habitats.
- Accommodating their animals under conditions that aim to satisfy the biological and conservation requirements of the individual species, inter alia, by providing species-specific enrichment of the enclosures and maintaining a high standard of animal husbandry with a developed programme of preventive and curative veterinary care and nutrition.
- Preventing the escape of animals to avoid possible ecological threats to indigenous species and preventing intrusion of outside pests and vermin.
- Keeping up-to-date records of the zoo's collection appropriate to the species recorded.

Are zoos centres for conservation?

Zoos often justify their existence by emphasising their roles in conserving endangered species (Cohn, 1991; Colodner & Bechert, (eds), 2023), advancing science and providing education (Jensen, 2014). It is argued that zoos are necessary to keep some endangered species alive as, too often, it is not realised that a species is under threat 'until their numbers have crashed to dangerously low levels and this is a trend that is only likely to continue' (Hone, 2017).

Whether zoos are effective in conservation is questioned by some, as zoos often focus on iconic species rather than those that are most beneficial to the planet (Gill, 2023). It would certainly seem to be the case that a zoo of insects may not be as effective in terms of attracting visitors as one full of elephants, chimps, giraffes, meercats, lions, etc., as these are iconic species that provide 'entertainment' rather than those being 'most vital for nature' (Hancocks, 1995, p. 11).

The conservation focus of zoos has also been questioned regarding how effective they are in reintroducing species back into the wild. There are two broad issues underlining these doubts. Firstly, there are concerns about where wildlife is released, as it is important that the habitat they are released back into is protected and that the animals themselves are protected from stressors such as hunting. The importance of this can be seen in the fact that, panda numbers are rising in the wild, and they are now on the improved status of 'vulnerable' on the red list, due to a reduction in poaching and expansion of their protected habitat (Howard, 2017). However whilst wild panda conservation is financed in part from the rent of captive pandas in zoos only six pandas have been released into the wild in the last 50 years. Zoos have had some successes in introducing wild animals back into the wild, such as the partula snail, northern bald ibis, and fen raft spider, among others, with some breeding endangered species such as the critically endangered West Lowland gorilla (London Zoo, 2024).

Secondly, there are questions about the effectiveness of breeding programmes; for example, in relation to northern white rhinos where there are just two infertile females left but where embryo transfers have been tried but so far have failed (Morelle & Francis, 2024; Janssens & Trouwborst, 2018). Breeding programmes are also taking place in relation to elephants, monkeys, tigers and pandas (Pilcher, 2023, pp. 59–60). There are also debates about whether species should be re-engineered for survival or whether animals should be brought back from extinction (Allen et al., 2020; Sandler, 2012, 2020; Wienhues et al., 2023) although this is not yet a reality (McMahon & Doyle, 2020; Friese & Marris, 2014; Stanton et al., 2019). The key question appears to be whether we need to accept that some species will become extinct (Nijhuis, 2021).

In terms of direct animal welfare, questions are raised as to whether wild animals can be kept in a natural state in zoos (Learmonth, 2019). This raises the ethical question of whether, in efforts to conserve a species, we are in fact causing unnecessary suffering to individuals of that species held in captivity. Gill (2023) states that 'suffering is inevitable in a life of captivity'. However, Bostock (1993) argues that the valuable conservation work performed by zoos justifies efforts to improve them rather than shutting them down. These arguments become more complex when considering the state of the environment animals might be released back into. Protecting individual animals or groups is insufficient if their natural habitats are no longer viable.

Habitat protection and the survival of wild animals

The stresses and impact of human activities on wildlife go hand in hand with the need to protect the habitat that wildlife need to survive (Mancini et al., 2023). This section explores the laws relating to habitat protection in more detail.

International laws protecting habitats

In terms of international habitat protection, the Ramsar Convention on Wetlands is one of the oldest conventions. Established in Ramsar, Iran, in 1971, it focuses on wetlands of international importance, especially waterfowl habitats. The convention recognises the need to cooperate internationally to promote wetland conservation and has since widened its aims:

> The convention covers all aspects of wetland conservation and 'wise use'. The convention defines wise use of wetlands as "the maintenance of their ecological character, achieved through the implementation of ecosystem approaches, within the context of sustainable development". Wise use can thus be seen as "the conservation and sustainable use of wetlands and all the services they provide, for the benefit of people and nature" (Ramsar, n.d.). It has three main 'pillars' of activity:
>
> - the designation of wetlands of international importance as Ramsar sites.
> - the promotion of the wise use of all wetlands in the territory of each country; and
> - international cooperation with other countries to further the wise use of wetlands and their resources. (JNCC, n.d.)

Whilst the initial emphasis was on selecting sites of importance to waterbirds, other features are increasingly taken into account that have a much more anthropocentric leaning. This is reflected in the following guidance: 'Under the Convention Strategic Plan 2016–2024, a series of actions are directly related to sustainable development, including water, livelihoods, biodiversity, disaster risk reduction, resilience and carbon sinks. Also, parties have adopted a specific framework on water, including river basin management, water allocation and ground water' (JNCC, n.d.).

There are concerns about the effectiveness of the Ramsar Convention and that it lacks teeth in the absence of any substantial enforcement mechanisms as it 'cannot punish member states for violations' (Cawardine, 2016). However, Cawardine (2016) argues that despite this the convention is often instrumental in protecting sites under threat and has raised awareness of the importance of wetlands generally. Gaget et al. (2020, p. 6) emphasise its importance as it has had indirect effects, such as leading to international and national conservation policies in wetland legislation and improved waterbird conservation measures, not just in Ramsar designated sites but as a basis for other initiatives its success should be enlarged to include 'international and national waterbird conservation'. However, whilst it may have raised the profile of wetlands (Finlayson et al., 2022), it is also noted that it has not been signed by several nations, and implementation by those that have signed it is inconsistent. Gaget et al. (2020, p. 2) observe that 'the Ramsar Convention is not necessarily supported by legal regulations nor accompanied by binding measures, meaning that conservation effectiveness may depend on the country's governance'.

European protection of habitats

In the EU, habitats are specifically protected through the Habitats Directive, but they are also protected through other environmental legislation covering water and air pollution along with controlling waste emissions (Burns et al., 2023; Kramer & Badger, 2024). Adopted in 1992, the Council Directive 92/43/EEC of 21 May 1992 on the conservation of natural habitats and of wild fauna and flora aims to promote the maintenance of biodiversity, taking account of economic, social, cultural and regional requirements. Under the directive, each member state must compile a list of Special Areas of Conservation (SACs), which are areas containing the habitat types and species listed in the directive, and it sets out the scientific criteria for doing this. These specified flora and fauna are given strict protection to prohibit their deliberate capture, killing, destruction, disturbance, or sale. Other, less threatened species may be managed or taken from the wild provided this can be done sustainably, that is, without threat to the conservation of the species.

This directive forms the cornerstone of Europe's nature conservation policy with the Birds Directive (Directive 2009/147/EC). Under the Birds Directive (Article 4), the network must include Special Protection Areas (SPAs) designated for 194 particularly threatened species and all migratory bird species (European Commission, n.d.). The importance of EU protection can be seen in relation to the case of *R* v. *Secretary of State for the Environment, ex p Royal Society for the Protection of Birds (Port of Sheerness Ltd intervening)* (1996), which considered whether a port could be extended into a Special Protection Area. The European Court of Justice (ECJ) held that the government could not let economic requirements override the ecological objectives or public interest as set out in the directive. The EU-wide Natura 2000 ecological network of protected areas safeguarded against potentially damaging developments is designated under the Habitats and Birds Directives:

> [Natura 2000 protects] over 1000 animal and plant species, as well as 200 habitat types, listed in the directive's annexes are protected in various ways. The European Commission has published guidance on species protection to help member states implement correctly the directive's provisions. EU Species Action Plans are developed to restore the populations of certain species across their range within the EU. The European Commission also promotes the conservation of Europe's five species of large carnivores, the brown bear, the wolf, the wolverine and two species of lynx and supports the European Red Lists of Threatened Species, developed by the IUCN to provide an overview of the conservation status of 11,000 European species, so that appropriate action can be taken to protect those threatened with extinction. (European Commission, n.d.)

The EU has developed a biodiversity strategy up to 2030 and a forest strategy under the aegis of the European Green Deal (European Council of the European Union, n.d.).

The effectiveness of the EU Habitats Directive is generally seen in positive terms when taken with its commitment to expand protected areas to 30% of the overall EU area. Moreno-Saiz et al. (2021, p. 6) argue that this creates an 'umbrella effect' protecting and conserving both plant and animal species and maintaining biodiversity. However, there is concern that the directive takes an elitist and anthropocentric view of wildlife and 'entails preliminary fundamental animal rights as a by-product of a human interest in biodiversity' (Platvoet, 2023, p. 103). Platvoet (2023, pp. 81–82) argues that 'certain animals are deemed higher on the list of priorities for humanity and receive an elite treatment in comparison to other animals'. He argues for moving to protecting the individual rights of animals rather than indirect protection through habitat. To avoid the elitist approach 'wild animal rights need to be grounded in the protection of the moral rights of individual animals, not in the human interest in biodiversity. To establish a legal instrument on conservation that would entail fundamental rights in a moral sense, a shift in conservation law is required' (Platvoet, 2023, p. 82).

The protection of habitats at national level in the UK

In the UK, the Habitats Directive was implemented by the Conservation (Natural Habitats &c.) Regulations 1994 (as updated in 2017). Changes have been made to the Conservation of Habitats and Species Regulations 2017 (as amended) by the Conservation of Habitats and Species (Amendment) (EU Exit) Regulations 2019. The importance of these regulations in protecting habitats can be seen in planning decisions relating to housing developments; for example, in the case of *Wyatt R. (on the application of)* v. *Fareham Borough Council* (2022) and in relation to housing and nutrient neutrality, as seen in *C. G. Fry & Son Ltd* v. *Secretary of State for Levelling Up Housing and Communities* (2023). However, there is a plethora of legislation in the UK covering wildlife and the environment (Bell et al., 2024).

The founding legislation on which many of the site protection measures are based is the National Parks and Access to the Countryside Act 1947. This allowed the introduction of specific management measures for nature and landscape conservation at designated sites and has since been updated and superseded by the Wildlife and Countryside Act 1981 (as amended), including the Countryside and Rights of Way Act 2010 and other conservation-related legislation. It was hoped that the designations would provide an integrated approach to protecting wildlife, 'taking into account both local needs and national priorities' (Cooke, 1996, p. 21), but this has arguably not been the case. It has instead led to a fragmented approach to protecting various forms of habitat and led to unlinked areas of conservation (The Wildlife Trust n.d.; Natural England's annual action plans) and the loss of important habitats such as rainforest and the degradation of the chalk streams of Southern England by pollution. The UK is now one of the most nature-depleted countries in the world (Mancini et al., 2023).

The need for more joined-up thinking has been recognised through the development of 'super nature reserves', such as that in Purbeck, Dorset. There have been several national initiatives, such as the 25-year Environment Plan, the National Planning Policy Framework (Mills, 2023), the Environment Act 2021, an Environmental Improvement Plan, and a new framework for National Parks and National Landscapes. However, there still appears to be a need for more connected and wider thinking on this issue (Scott, 2021). This is not helped by the withdrawal of the UK from the EU (Lowther et al., 2018; and Agyepong-Parsons, 2020;), because the UK will no longer have to comply with habitat protection legislation in the EU, with only wider international law remaining (Reid, 2021). This has led to a concern that having to rely on the 'toothless' Bern Convention and other international biodiversity treaties means that the UK will lack the protection afforded by the enforcement mechanism of the EU court (Agyepong-Parsons, 2020). There are other methods of accountability such as that provided by the Office of Environmental Protection (OEP), whose powers are set out in the Environment Act 2021. For exmaple, the OEP is, as we write in 2024, investigating possible failures to comply with environmental law in relation to Special Protection Areas (SPAs) for wild birds (OEP, 2024).

The need for law reform on habitat protection

Several fundamental issues need to be considered when reforming the law regarding habitat protection, including the importance of setting clear objectives and the need to expand the areas of protection (Nature Conservancy Committee, 1984, p. 41). Added to these are issues such as the social impact of protecting habitats, the need for local engagement in decision-making, and how to deal with biodiversity outside of these spaces (Büscher et al., 2017, pp. 408–409). It may not be enough to have some habitat areas protected if other areas are not (Stuart & Stuart, 1996, pp. 3–4). This has led to calls for 'wildlife corridors' to facilitate animal movement whichi also recognises the fact that habitat protection is an issue for both urban and rural areas and not just a countryside problem.

Conflict between humans and wildlife

To combat the effect that humans have on wildlife, initiatives have been suggested, such as 'rewilding'(Carver et al., 2021), the creation of wildlife reserves, or using areas of land to offset the loss of biodiversity. These suggestions are subject to economic pressures that could be alleviated by ecotourism, but each of these solutions has encountered concerns about how wildlife and humans coexist.

Conflict in rewilding

Rewilding to improve biodiversity, which involves, for example, the reintroduction of apex predators such as the Lynx to the UK, has been suggested for some time (Heatherington et al., 2008). There have been programmes to reintroduce wolves back into some European countries

(Ledger et al., 2022), but this may be under threat as the EU Commission is considering reducing the protection given to these species (Barkham, 2024). Such programmes are also threatened, as the wolves may be at risk from wolf-dog hybridisation (Salvatori et al., 2020).

As Timperley explains (2021, p. 87) Foreman (2004) first set out a definition of rewilding in the 1990s and since then it has developed to cover the 3 Cs – conservation of Cores, Corridors, and Carnivores. The introduction of core areas protected and connected along with the introduction of apex predators keeps down the number of other animals, such as deer, which may then benefit other wildlife. It has also been suggested that rewilding might help sequester carbon, as indicated by a study in Brazil (Strassburg et al., 2020). The study suggested that if 15% of ecosystems, were restored including former forests, degraded grasslands and wetlands such action might capture as much as 30% of all CO2 released since the industrial revolution and avoid 60% of expected extinctions (Timperley, 2021, p. 87). This is needed more than ever as some of these natural carbon sinks are now declining or vanishing. Timperley also suggests that 'to its advocates rewilding goes further than traditional conservation to recognise the vast scale of the ecological disaster the world is now facing. It aims to bring back nature as much and as fast as possible' (Timperley, 2021, p. 89). However, the conservation benefits are important, as Lewis and Parr (2023) explain, a natural balance between herbivores and carnivores would bring wide-ranging benefits for habitats, species and entire ecosystems. and re wilding has now grown to be more than introducing wild animals to ecosystems to putting 'nature back in the driving seat, allowing habitats to evolve, shift to find their own way' (Tree & Burrell, 2023, p. 7).

The reintroduction of beavers into Scotland has led to some of them being culled as they are viewed as pests by farmers and anglers. However, the reintroduction programme is expanding in England and has led to beavers from Scotland being reintroduced into England rather than being culled. In other parts of the world, there is evidence of conflict between wolves and farmers, although in certain regions in Europe, such as Spain, this conflict has been mitigated by better protection measures for livestock.

Overall, there is much work to do in defining the scope of such rewilding and what and where is wild in terms of which species should be reintroduced and their potential location (Lorimer & Driessen, 2016). Interestingly, Tree and Burrell (2023) have called their new book '*Wilding*'. This may reflect a more future-facing way of considering the issues, rather than it being seen as a move towards the past; instead, it can be seen as a reimagining of the practical steps needed to move to the future. There are other debates, such as the role of cattle and other farm animals, such as sheep, being used as part of wilding and their role in climate change (Monbiot, 2023), and for the alternative view, see Tree & Burrell, 2023).

Sollund (2020, p. 366) argues that trying to manage wildlife is reflective of humans' anthropocentric notion that we need to 'control' wildlife and this tends to do more harm than good as it attacks ecosystems, impacts environmental security, and exposes endangered carnivores to attack by angry farmers. Rewilding/wilding could be viewed as an impetus for change at all levels of land use, such as gardens and urban spaces, providing us with a framework to rethink our relationship with wildlife. This is already apparent in the move in the UK to 'No Mow May' (Plantlife, n.d.), which is an attempt to rectify the loss of nearly 97% of flower-rich meadows since the 1930s. The idea behind No Mow May is that by not mowing grass in the month of May, 'a healthy lawn with some long grass and wildflowers benefits wildlife, tackles pollution and can even lock away carbon below ground' (Plantlife, n.d.). Similar moves to involve people with their local wildlife, such as counting birds and butterflies in various surveys, may help bring public attention to the damage done, in terms of both species diversity and biodiversity loss.

Human wildlife conflict – fortress conservation

Concerns have been raised about creating wildlife reserves or taking land for biodiversity offsetting because these activities can be seen as problematic (zu Ermgassen et al., 2020) but they can also lead to 'fortress conservation' (Baldauf, 2020;and Kopnina & Washington, 2020). The term 'fortress conservation' was first defined by Nash (1990), who argued that conservation often led to the removal of people from nature and was based upon a Western epistemology of the mid-19th century that, like much of the normative rhetoric of the Anthropocene, focused on the ways in which humans harmed nature. The idea was that taking land for conservation purposes could protect wildlife like a fortress. The other issue with this approach is that whilst it acknowledges the positive impacts on certain species, it has been used at the expense of indigenous peoples and local communities, whose lives continue to be 'threatened, criminalised and lost where this model is applied' (Weber & Barron, 2023, p. 132). The need for humans and animals to be able to coexist is important, and it is important that measures to protect conservation and biodiversity include social and ecological justice (O'Riordan & Stoll-Kleemann, 2002; Kopnina & Washington, 2020; Armitage et al., 2020; Baldauf, 2020; Washington et al., 2024).

Many stories have revealed the pressure species are facing across the globe, with wildlife often coming into sometimes fatal contact with humans. These stories include, for example, lions in Ethiopia, leopard attacks in Uttar Pradesh, conflicts involving elephants in Africa and Asia (Ethirajan, 2023) and cheetahs in India. This is compounded by other environmental changes, such as drought in Kenya, which has caused more predation on livestock.

Economic pressures and human-wildlife conflict

Economic pressures can often lead to human-wildlife conflict, as seen in the example of Borneo, where the economic impetus for food production and the corresponding environmental and wildlife harm have long been in evidence. Borneo saw consecutive decades of rising unemployment and ethnic conflict from the 1990s to the early years of this century. The rise in popularity of palm oil, a product of Borneo, led to a dash by local officials and residents to cash in (Gaveau et al., 2016). However, this led to the environmental destruction of irreplaceable forests, which are invaluable as they act as 'carbon sinks'. This is still the case and the World Wildlife Fund (WWF, n.d.) has raised concerns that deforestation is having a serious effect on several species that depend on this habitat, for example, orangutans, Borneo elephants and Sumatran tigers, all of which are being pushed closer to extinction. Smallholders and indigenous people who once inhabited and protected the forest for generations are often driven from their land, sometimes violently. WWF also documents other impacts from this, such as the growth of the illegal wildlife trade as cleared forests provide easy access to more remote areas and a rise in uncertified palm oil being sold in other market areas, such as animal feed. Whilst there have been moves to make the production of palm oil more sustainable, there is a need for it to be accurately certified as such. To emphasise the global nature of this problem, this destruction is often driven by the demand for palm oil products by consumers in wealthier parts of the globe, such as in the UK (Luskin et al., 2017). In Europe, the EU Parliament has approved an import ban on commodities linked to deforestation; however, Malaysia has stated that it will give orangutans as gifts to countries that buy its palm oil. This has aroused considerable concern from conservationists who suggest that money would be better spent on conserving the animals in situ along with their habitat (Ratcliffe, 2024).

In the case of deforestation in places such as Borneo, the effects on wildlife could be alleviated and reformed by some of the examples discussed previously, such as providing wildlife corridors for wildlife to move freely between different areas of forest (Hance, 2023), although the term 'wildlife corridor' is itself problematic (Fletcher et al., 2021; Maulana, 2023). There is also a need to engage the community in changes (Oram et al., 2022; Wildlife Trust of India, 2021), ecotourism is a way of providing human benefits in terms of income (Purwoko et al., 2022; Bagniewska & Macdonald, 2010).

Human wildlife conflict – ecotourism

The 'ecotourism' concept was introduced in the 1960s by Hetzer (Jurkus et al., 2022) and was developed by Ceballos-Lascurain (1996) to promote responsible and sustainable travel. However, replacing traditional livelihoods with tourism comes with its own problems, including the direct impact this can have on wildlife (Moorhouse et al., 2015, 2017). Some activities are clearly not responsible or sustainable, such as hunting, shooting and fishing, but even if the activities are generally responsible and sustainable, tourist activities, such as safaris, buying wildlife souvenirs and using animals as entertainment, can disturb wildlife.

Other indirect impacts include sewage and other forms of pollution, including noise and light pollution, and the impact of climate change caused by flying (One Planet Sustainable Tourism Programme, 2021), as well as over-visitation. The impact on wildlife can also come from structural development, such as the building of roads and railways. In the UK, very few wildlife highways have been created, even though they have long been advocated in other countries (Natural England, 2015; Brooman & Legge, 1997, pp. 372–373; Sugiarto, 2023; Paemelaere et al., 2023). Other less visible impacts include the creation of waste, the spread of disease through reverse zoonosis (Köndgen et al., 2008) and the effects of litter. This may also lead to more scavenger animals visiting an area and the animals' natural routines being disturbed (RSPCA, 1995; Ceballos-Lascurain, 1996, pp. 67–71). Therefore, although people may benefit from experiencing the natural world, it should be balanced against the problems created by ecotourism. It is suggested that when developing new ecotourism ideas, the right provisions are in place to benefit animals and local communities (Rushby, 2023; Thompson, 2022; Jurkus et al., 2022; Luyt & Van Der Merwe, 2022).

The role of law in regulating human-wildlife conflict

At a fundamental level, there is a need for humans to learn to share the Earth's limited space with wildlife (Erin, 2013) by developing our ability to coexist (König et al., 2020). Dubois et al. (2017) suggest that this involves moving away from viewing animals as pests when they happen to enter the human zone of activity. They suggest there are certain criteria that could be employed to achieve a greater ability to share space with wildlife, including:

- Can the problem be mitigated by changing human behavior?
- Are the harms serious enough to warrant wildlife control?
- Is the desired wildlife control outcome clear and achievable, and will it be monitored?
- Does the proposed method carry the least animal welfare cost and to the fewest animals?
- Have community values been considered alongside scientific, technical and practical information?
- Is the control action part of a systematic, long-term management program? Are the decisions warranted by the specifics of the situation rather than negative labels applied to the animals?. (Dubois et al., 2017, p. 758)

The function of law is to detail how these balances are measured and put into practice and by whom, through creating a framework of regulation and enforcement built on the right moral and ethical foundations.

Case study on habitat protection – the marine environment and the protection of whales

The largest habitat in need of protecting is that of the marine environment, and one of its iconic inhabitants is the whale. Water makes up around 71% of the Earth's surface, and 96.5% of that water is in the oceans. Given its importance to all life on Earth, it provides us with a useful and key case study of the role and limits of the law.

The history and the law on protecting the marine environment

Whilst the marine environment is protected by all the international agreements set out above, there is also some more specific protection:

> The need to devise methods to manage and protect marine environments and resources became apparent during the 1950s and early 1960s. Thus, the First World Conference on National Parks (1962) considered the need for

> protection of coastal and marine areas ... In 1958, four conventions known as the Geneva Conventions on the Law of the Sea were adopted. These were the Convention on the Continental Shelf, the Convention on the High Seas, the Convention on Fishing, and the Convention on Conservation of the Living Resources of the High Seas. The High Seas Conventions formed the basis for the establishment of the Intergovernmental Maritime Consultative Organisation (IMCO) in 1959 – later to become the International Maritime Organisation (IMO). (Kelleher & Kenchington, 1991, pp. 3–5)

The IMO is responsible for the safety and security of international shipping as well as acting to prevent pollution being discharged from ships (IMO, n.d.). In 1982, the United Nations Convention on the Law of the Sea (UNCLOS, 1982) came into effect, providing some regulation of oceans and ocean resources. There have been other international agreements on various aspects of the marine environment, such as the United Nations (UN) declaration on the 'ocean decade' (UN Decade of Ocean Science for Sustainable Development 2021–2030). The UN expressed its desire to promote ocean science and develop scientific knowledge and partnerships to improve the state of the ocean system and facilitate the sustainable development of this vast marine ecosystem (UN, n.d.). In an advisory opinion requested by the Commission of Small Island States (COSIS) on climate change and international law, the International Tribunal for the Law of the Sea stated that greenhouse gases are a form of pollution and that states should take all necessary measures to prevent it (International Tribunal for the Law of the Sea, 2024).

In 2023, the UN adopted a resolution for the Conservation and Sustainable Use of Marine Biological Diversity of Areas Beyond National Jurisdiction known as the 'High Seas Treaty':

> 1Once ratified, the High Seas Treaty will allow the establishment of marine protected areas in the high seas at global level, safeguarding the ocean from human pressures in a major contribution to reducing climate change, to protecting biodiversity and achieving the objective to protect at least 30% of the planet by 2030' (European Commission Directorate-General for Maritime Affairs and Fisheries, 2023). This is important as 'only about 1% of the high seas is currently protected'.
>
> The Treaty will also ensure a framework for a number of issues, including the fair and equitable sharing of the benefits from marine genetic resources, the transfer of marine technologies to developing countries, as well as a voluntary fund to support developing countries to achieve UN Sustainable Development Goal 14 on *Life Below Water* (European

> Commission Directorate-General for Maritime Affairs and Fisheries 2023). Goal 14 aims to 'conserve and sustainably use the oceans, seas and marine resources for sustainable development'. (The Global Goals, n.d.)

The International Convention for the Prevention of Pollution from Ships, the 1978 Protocol MARPOL 73/78 and Annexes I and II (1983) deal with all forms of ship-generated marine pollutants (IMO, 2019). This is particularly important as oil spills from tankers such as *Torrey Canyon (1967), Amoco Cadiz (1978), Sea Empress (1996)* or *Exxon Valdez (1989)*, as well as smaller accidental spillages and day-to-day discharges of oil and chemicals into the sea, can have a lasting effect on wildlife. The effects of oil spills on whales and seals, as well as other wildlife were seen after the 1989 *Exxon Valdez* oil spill, when a Chevron Oil tanker released 11 million gallons of oil into Prince William Sound, Alaska.

Adam Nicholson (2021, pp. 313–321) explores the intertidal reaches, recounts the history of the 1967 Torrey Canyon Oil spill that dispersed highly toxic chemical dispersants. He explains that the spill meant 'Vast areas of seaweed were killed, along with the fish, crabs, winkles, topshells, mussels and barnacles that lived among them. The limpets in particular were poisoned and died in uncounted numbers'. This event had a damaging effect on the delicate balance in the intertidal zone, which enables it to function as a habitat for numerous species of animals.

In international terms, there are other regional agreements such as the Polar Code (International Code for Ships Operating in Polar Waters, 2017), which regulates the use of polar waters (see the Intergovernmental Oceanographic Commission), the United Nations Environment Programme, the Regional Seas Conventions, the Agreement on the Conservation of Small Cetaceans of the Baltic (UNEP, 2024b), Northeast Atlantic, Irish and North Seas (ASCOBANS, 2018) and the Convention for the Protection of the Marine Environment of the North-East Atlantic (OSPAR), including the Bergen Declaration (OSPAR, 2024).

The Global Programme of Action for the Protection of the Marine Environment from Land-based Activities (UNEP, n.d.) is important as marine ecosystems and habitats:

> are often the foci of tourism activity. For instance, less visually attractive habitats, such as mangroves and marshes, are often drained and used for resort construction. And since visitors generally want a view of the sea and easy access to the beach hotels tend to be sited close to the tide line. This can result in changes in natural sand movement and accretion, and lead to serious erosion. Other activities that are often associated with

> tourism development such as coast stabilisation and causeway construction and mariculture development can also have severe impacts. (Ceballos-Lascurain, 1996)

Marine Protected Areas (MPAs)

The marine environment (Schmidt et al., 2022) is protected at an international and national level through the development of Marine Protected Areas:

> In 1980 IUCN, with World Wildlife Fund (WWF) and UNEP, published the *World Conservation Strategy,* which emphasised the importance of marine environments and ecosystems in the goal of providing for conservation for sustainable development. In 1983 UNESCO organised the First World Biosphere Reserve Congress in Minsk, USSR (UNESCO, n.d.). At that meeting it was recognised that the Biosphere Reserve concept is potentially applicable to the marine environment and that an integrated, multiple use Marine Protected Areas can conform to all of the scientific, administrative and social principles that define a Biosphere Reserve under the UNESCO Man and the Biosphere (MAB) Programme. (Kelleher & Kenchington, 1991, pp. 3–5)

Biosphere reserves are 'learning places for sustainable development. They are sites for testing interdisciplinary approaches to understanding and managing changes and interactions between social and ecological systems, including conflict prevention and management of biodiversity' (UNESCO, n.d.). The Man and the Biosphere Programme 'aims to establish a scientific basis for enhancing the relationship between people and their environments' (UNESCO, n.d.).

Marine Protected Areas (MPAs) are established around the world using a wide range of legislative instruments (Kriegl et al., 2021; Suratman, 2022). They are areas of no specific size and operate to control potentially damaging human activities (Alger, 2021). There is an international call to classify 30% of national maritime space as MPAs by 2030 (Kriegl et al., 2021, p. 3) along with Other Effective Area-based Conservation Measures (OECMs). Currently, in the EU, MPAs operate as part of the Natura 2000 network, designated under the EU Birds and Habitats Directives and through complementary national designation (European Environment Agency, 2023) and the Marine Strategy Framework Directive (MSFD). Its 'aim is to achieve a good environmental status of the EU's marine waters and sustainably protect the resource base upon which marine-related economic and social activities depend'. This is intended to ensure that the 'ecosystem-based approach became a legally binding and operational principle for managing the EU's entire marine environment' (European Commission, n.d.). The EU has stated the desire to meet the 30/30 target of 30% protection by 2030 under the new biodiversity strategy (European Commission, 2022).

At the national level, in the UK, MPAs operate on much the same basis by creating areas that seek to restrict damaging human activity and protect habitats and the species within them and have listed conservation objectives to ensure healthy, functioning marine ecosystems. (Marine Management Organisation, 2023). The Fisheries Act 2020 introduced new powers enabling the Marine Management Organisation (MMO) to implement fisheries management measures in MPAs in English offshore waters. The first four offshore MPA by-laws were implemented in 2022 (Defra, 2024). There are three highly protected marine nature reserves, including Allonby Bay in the Irish Sea, Dolphin Head in the English Channel, and North East of Farnes Deep in the North Sea (Ashworth, 2023). There are also marine conservation zones designated under the Marine and Coastal Access Act 2009, such as in Studland in Dorset, where any harmful activities can be banned, including commercial and recreational fishing, dredging, construction and anchoring (Defra, 2023). The UK government wants to create several MPAs in areas beyond national jurisdiction within the Arctic Ocean (Foreign and Commonwealth Office, 2023).

The development of MPAs is important at both national and international levels as it brings a form of accountability to those who create stresses on marine life. Activities such as commercial fishing (Scholaert, 2023) can still put unintended stresses on protected marine life, which may be caught as by-catch or from becoming entangled in nets. Whilst the use of long drift-nets on the high seas is already the subject of a UN and EU ban (Regulation (EU) 2016/2336, Regulation (EU) 2022/1614), this needs to be strictly enforced.

Other pressures (JNCC, n.d.) include pollutants such as plastics and other debris, noise pollution (Bakker, 2023) and air pollution, shipping and war. There are also emerging potential stresses, such as the announcement by Norway that it may begin commercial mining on the seabed for lithium, scandium and cobalt (International Seabed Authority, 2024). This illustrates one of the challenges faced in protecting wildlife. Unfortunately, the desire to 'go green' can be complicated by the fact that essential raw materials might be found in places where extracting them may cause competing harm (Dolman et al., 2016). The desire to do positive things for the climate can lead to unfortunate and undesirable outcomes, which is likely to be a theme of discussion in the coming years.

However, overall, there appears to be a number of positive outcomes to support the creation of more sanctuaries and MPAs. There are calls for a new MPA to cover the area around Antarctica, and this is supported by the Commission for the Conservation of Antarctic Marine Living Resources, which regulates fishing in the Southern Ocean. Unfortunately, this development has stalled as the agreement of China and Russia is needed. This is important as the whales and super trawlers overlap at certain times of the year, potentially leading to bad outcomes for the whales (Fair, 2023). Canada became the first nation to unilaterally declare a marine protected area (Cyca et al., 2023). It is hoped that the High Seas Treaties will lead to the establishment of MPAs on a global level, but whatever way they come into existence, they all need effective management, adaptive governance and legitimacy (Schmidt et al., 2022) and be ecologically representative (Reisinger et al., 2022).

Marine animals are also protected under the Convention on Biological Diversity, the Bern Convention, the Ramsar Convention, the Bonn Convention, the UNESCO World Heritage Convention, as well as some regional conventions such as the OSPAR Convention. In terms of trade, CITES has recently put together guidance on shipping in relation to combating the illegal wildlife trade (World Shipping Council, n.d.). One of the problems with protecting marine mammals with CITES is that protection depends upon which Appendix it is on. Whilst these conventions provide some protection to all marine life (along with the law on fisheries management see Nakamura & Kuemlangan, 2023), there are specific protections for marine mammals, so for example, the International Whaling Commission (IWC) has research and conservation programmes for the conservation of the smaller whales, dolphins and porpoises (IWC, 2024).

In relation to marine mammals in the UK, the species-specific protection provided is generally inconsistent, as outlined in a government report on marine mammals, which found the current UK legal framework around the protection of marine mammals to be incoherent and not sufficient to effectively preserve these precious species. (House of Commons Environment, Food and Rural Affairs Committee, 2023, p. 17). This can be seen in relation to seals, where UK legislation appears to contradict government intentions. In 2023, the House of Commons Environment, Food and Rural Affairs Committee (2023) stated that both grey and common seals should be a nationally protected species. However, grey seals are not protected under Schedule 5 of the Wildlife and Countryside

Act, which means they have no greater protection than other marine animals. Being included in Schedule 5 would be helpful as the Act prohibits the intentional killing, injuring or taking of the species listed and prohibits their possession or trade. Perhaps a way forward is to pass specific legislation to specifically protect marine mammals, which would cover species such as the grey seal or any that need greater protection. In the United States, higher protection is given to marine mammals through the Marine Mammal Protection Act 1972 (House of Commons Environment, Food and Rural Affairs Committee, 2023).

One of the most iconic species on Earth, and particularly in the marine environment, is the whale, and it is the subject of its own legal protection framework.

Case study – the protection of whales

The killing of whales provides an example of one of the most shameful impacts of humans on wildlife. Whale numbers were reduced by approximately 80% before the moratorium on whaling was introduced in 1986 by the International Whaling Commission (IWC). The IWC has a significant place in the development of the international protection of whales, but the IWC has come under increasing pressure to re-introduce whaling.

History of whaling

Kempf and Phillips (1995, pp. 6–8) set out the history of whaling in some detail. They state that:

> The Basques began whaling in the 11th century, followed by the Dutch and English, and whaling then spread to the US. In the 19th century, whaling was revolutionised by steam-powered whaling boats and the exploding grenade that was attached to a harpoon. These factory ships killed more whales in four decades than had been killed in the previous four centuries. In 1925, the League of Nations recommended that the whaling industry should be regulated, to stop overhunting, and in 1930, the Bureau of International Whaling Statistics was set up by the International Council for the Exploration of the Sea. The first treaty on whales, the Convention for the Regulation of Whaling, was signed in 1931 by 22 nations; unfortunately, the largest whaling nations were not parties to the agreement and in that year 43,000 whales were hunted.

In 1946, one of the first international conventions with a specific conservation focus, the International Convention on Whaling, was brought into existence, and the International Whaling Commission (IWC) was set up to provide and oversee the legal framework for whaling. The IWC is responsible for the conservation and management of whales, including in more recent times, the stresses on whales and other marine creatures from climate change, the threats from commercial fishing and entanglement in nets, plastics and other debris, and from pollution and ocean noise (House of Commons Environment, Food and Rural Affairs Committee, 2023). The IWC also regulates whale watching and includes guidance in its strategic plan and whale watching handbook (IWC, n.d.).

Whales have long been a focus of public campaigns, such as the calls for a moratorium on whaling during the 1970s. The resulting moratorium on whaling by the IWC in 1986, is seen as a 'blueprint' for other campaigns by the World Wildlife Fund (WWF):

> Even though the true extent of the killing was not known at the time, public concern and anger at what was happening to the great whales was building up rapidly in many countries around the world, especially among WWF supporters. 'Saving the whales' came to symbolise the fast-growing concern for saving the whole planet from over-exploitation by humans. As Sir Peter Scott said in 1972 'If we cannot save the whales from extinction, we have little chance of saving mankind and the life-supplying biosphere.' (Kempf & Phillips, 1995, pp. 6–8)

The central method of whaling control, the moratorium on commercial whaling, was announced at the IWC meeting in July 1982 and came into effect in 1986. Previously, in 1979, the first whale sanctuary was created in the Indian Ocean, where commercial whaling was banned. In addition, the IWC membership expanded to include more nations with a conservation mindset (Kempf & Phillips, 1995, pp. 6–8). The moratorium strengthened as the first sanctuary was made permanent in 1992, when the IWC agreed by consensus that it should remain a sanctuary for an indefinite period. A second sanctuary in the Southern Ocean around Antarctica was adopted in 1994. There has also been a proposal for a sanctuary in the South Atlantic Ocean, but it has not yet received the required number of votes to become designated as a sanctuary by the IWC. At a national level, many countries have laws prohibiting whaling. In the UK, for example, whaling ended in 1963 and is prohibited within the UK's 200-mile fisheries limit. In addition, cetaceans are protected within territorial waters under the Wildlife and Countryside Act 1981.

Along with this, CITES' control of international trade is a crucial weapon in the effective enforcement of the moratorium. All whale species regulated by the IWC have been listed in CITES' Appendix I since 1986, and international trade in all whale products is prohibited between the parties to CITES. Under Article I, 'Introduction from the sea means transportation into a State of specimens of any species which were taken in the marine environment not under the jurisdiction of any State'. This covers 'marine areas beyond the areas subject to the sovereignty or sovereign rights of a state consistent with international law, as reflected in the United Nations Convention on the Law of the Sea' (CITES, n.d.). The problem with CITES is that whilst it covers the trade of endangered species, trade also occurs in other forms, with over "3,600 whales and dolphins held in captivity" (WDC, n.d.). Also, despite the best efforts of CITES, there have been recent examples of smuggling and illegal trade in whale meat involving Norway, Russia, Taiwan, the Republic of Korea (Lee et al., 2019) and Japan (McCurry, 2023).

How effective is international law in protecting whales?

The IWC is the major regulator of international whaling, although protection under CITES plays an important part in preventing trade in whales and derivative products. One of the problems with the regulation of whaling is that it is hard to estimate whale population numbers, although the IWC does publish estimates (IWC, 2024). This leads to it being difficult to say with any precision how effective current controls are, and this can depend upon what type of whaling is being undertaken. There are three different types of whaling; firstly, commercial whaling, which is banned completely under the moratorium; secondly, by special permits, which are known as scientific whaling and regulated by states, not the IWC (Article VIII of the Convention); and thirdly, subsistence or aboriginal whaling, which is regulated by the IWC.

In terms of commercial whaling, the moratorium has not been completely effective because some countries still undertake commercial whaling as there is no effective sanction to stop them. Norway still catches whales commercially under a formal objection lodged by the Norwegian Government when the moratorium was introduced. Iceland left the IWC in 1992 and rejoined in 2002 with a reservation to the moratorium (WDC n.d.) and now catches whales commercially. However, a report and investigation in 2023 led to Iceland suspending whaling as they were found to be engaging in methods that did not comply with their own Act on Animal Welfare (Tómas, 2023) However, this licence was reissued for 2024 (Lukiv, 2024). Norway and Iceland establish their own catch limits but must provide information on their catches and associated scientific data to the IWC. Japan left the IWC in 2019 and resumed commercial whaling the same year. Having left the IWC, Japan is no longer bound by the moratorium, but Japanese catches are reported to the IWC.

Before Japan left the IWC, it was frequently accused of killing whales for the commercial market using the special permits as part of the scientific exception (Newell, 2012), which kept the spotlight on Japan for many years at a political level. It has been argued that this meant it was easier to reinstate commercial whaling as it had never been completely stopped in the first place (IWC, 1995). Nussbaum and Nussbaum (2017) also argue that it is problematic that there is no firm definition of 'scientific' whaling and that no reasons need to be provided as to why whales need to be killed, and it is a 'screen for commercial whaling' (Nussbaum & Nussbaum, 2017, p. 362; and highlights the conflict arising from scientific work in this conflicted area (Singleton & Lidskog, 2018).

The IWC recognises and omits from the moratorium, indigenous or aboriginal subsistence whaling (IWC, 2024). Indigenous or aboriginal subsistence whaling is where communities need to kill whales for cultural and nutritional needs as an essential part of their diet in places such as Greenland in relation to the Inuit population (WDC, n.d.), Russia (Chukotka), St Vincent and the Grenadines (Bequia) and the United States (Alaska). The Makah Tribe of Washington State is also expressing interest in resuming subsistence whaling.

This form of subsistence whaling has long been an issue, and whilst this exception is seen as legitimate by many states, it caused controversy at the 1996 IWC annual meeting. This arose over an application by the Makah Indian Tribe of Washington State to obtain a quota of five grey whales. Aboriginal whaling is calculated on nutritional and cultural needs, and the Makah's application was based on the fact that they had hunted whales 70 years ago, and thus they had a whaling tradition. However, there was concern among groups such as the Whale and Dolphin Conservation Society (WDCS) that the tribe wanted to commercialise the hunt. The WDCS brought tribal elders to the meeting who opposed the resumption of hunting. The US government provided support to its resumption as it was prepared to adjust the definition of 'aboriginal whaling' from subsistence use to one including cultural tradition, which would allow the application to succeed. This is a concern as there are another 18 tribes in the US and Canada who wish to start whaling, leading to concerns that the change to the definition in this way could put many whales at risk (WDCS, 1995, pp. 6–7). These changes had not taken place at the time of writing (Breda, 2023) but the debate in North America shows the clash of interests between the rights of indigenous peoples and the welfare of whales (Larsson & Päiviö Sjaunja, 2021).

Some of these communities are having difficulties due to climate change, which is making other forms of fishing difficult leading to the collapse of fisheries, degradation, and loss of terrestrial habitats. This is exacerbated by overpopulation and poverty and that these communiities should be seen as 'integrated socio-environmental systems in need of holistic sustainability strategies to benefit both the whalers and the whales' (Fielding, 2022, pp. 1–2).

Whichever method of whaling takes place, there are concerns about how whales are killed, and many groups consider the methods of killing inhumane. Since the IWC was established, it has recognised that the harpooning of whales and killing them with explosive charges is a cruel method of hunting. In a Norwegian hunt in 1993, one whale was recorded as taking over 55 minutes to die by harpooning. Sir Sydney Frost (1978) concluded in his report to the Australian government on humane killing and whaling that ... 'there is a significant difference in the methods used for the killing of whales and the humane practices required by law for the slaughter of cattle, sheep and pigs. In abattoirs and most slaughterhouses the animal is stunned instantaneously and then immediately killed, dying whilst unconscious ….' (WDCS, 1995, pp. 8–9)

These concerns are recognised by the IWC (IWC, 2024), which set out a Welfare Action Plan in 2014. It also has a whale welfare assessment tool based on the five domains model (IWC, 2024). However, this does not cover the killing of whales by harpoon or the beaching of whales as occurs in the Faroe Islands (WDC, n.d.) and Taiji, Japan. Killing whales in these instances involves driving them onto beaches or into a cove, respectively, before killing them with blades whilst beached on land or in the sea (WDC, n.d.). Concerns about the welfare implications of killing whales are supported by claims that there needs to be an established and accepted set of animal welfare norms in international law. Scholtz (2017) argues that 'the recognition of humane killing as an expression of concern for the welfare of animals may ultimately constitute a phase in an incremental process towards the non-lethal utilisation of whales' (Scholtz, 2017, p. 19).

The future of whaling

The future of whales is closely linked to the success of the IWC in restricting whaling since 1986. The World Wildlife Fund (WWF) argues that the IWC has been fundamental in protecting whales and 'is the only international organisation with the authority to regulate for whale conservation worldwide. Without the IWC, there would be no international control of the whaling industry, no moratorium on commercial whaling, and no high seas sanctuaries' (Kempf & Phillips, 1995, pp. 22–24). Membership in the IWC remains the only real way to ensure that individual countries comply with the general consensus but this is an extremely fragile relationship, as shown by Japan's relatively recent withdrawal. It does seem to be important for countries to be encouraged to stay in the IWC and thereby be bound to its decisions. The IWC relies on diplomacy, a certain degree of compromise, and clearly a lot of work is needed to ensure that the convention is enforced adequately and that its provisions are not flouted so whale habitats continue to be protected.

If countries continue to defy the collective will of the IWC, it seems likely that a return to the public opinion-led pressure of the 1970s is more likely. In the modern world of social media, it is not difficult to see how this could become a diplomatic issue for the countries involved, both from their own population and those overseas. Whaling does not present a country in its best light as it is a brutal and upsetting process that is out of kilter with other methods of killing animals for food – and even those methods are controversial. If countries continue to defy the convention or leave it, it is important for the full weight of international opinion to be placed upon them to rejoin or comply with the requirements of the convention through trade sanctions. Shaming does not seem to have worked in the case of Japan (Kolmas, 2021), but there must be diplomatic pressure on countries to conform to international efforts to provide strong legal protection based on trust, accountability and legitimacy (Sand, 2017).

An alternative income stream may be one way to solve the clash between a community's economic needs and the welfare of whales (Fiori et al., 2019). Whale watching has become big business across the globe, which may in itself mean that the sight of whales being slaughtered would not be seen as acceptable. However, this is another brand of eco-tourism, which, as discussed above, brings with it concerns for the welfare of wildlife. Here, codes of good practice would seem to be the least that should be provided, as well as giving whales 'safe areas' or protecting the marine environment in which they live. This requirement aligns with the overall need to reassess whether there is adequate enforcement of the law that seeks to protect marine wildlife (Nurse, 2013), as well as the development of more marine protected areas and an expansion of marine rewilding (Rewilding Britain, 2024).

Conclusion

This chapter and the preceding chapter together examine the significant issues that wildlife is facing. How the law responds to these concerns can be examined from a legal, philosophical, ethical, social, ecological and practical approach. At the core of the wildlife issue is the distinction that is drawn by commentators such as Adam and Schaffner (2017) that 'International wildlife law addresses conservation and sustainable use issues requiring international cooperation, while animal law pursues humane treatment of the individual animal and moral considerations of wildlife well-being. Generally, conservation lawyers want to ensure that the species does not go extinct, while animal lawyers aim for the well-being of individuals of the species.' This creates a potential stumbling block for those seeking change as there may be different approaches to the same major issues we face in terms of cruelty, extinction, biodiversity loss and climate change. This can most starkly be seen in the case of zoos, where the issue of whether it is cruel to keep wild animals in captivity comes up against the concern to conserve species.

It is difficult to discuss the issues around wildlife protection in isolation, as the Earth is a whole ecosystem and every action we take has an impact (Hayes, 2024). The interconnectedness of our planet is clear in the case study of whales. They are important in environmental terms as they take carbon dioxide from the atmosphere when they die, whilst the waste from whales provides food for phytoplankton, tiny marine algae that, in turn, absorb carbon (Fair, 2023, p. 65). The trade in endangered species can also lead to the problems associated with invasive species, and these issues can move beyond the immediate confines of concern for individual animals into wider concerns around the protection of wildlife and ecosystems. An example is the trade in exotic species as pets, which can then escape and predate on indigenous wildlife. A stark example is the killing of Burmese pythons, not in Burma, but in the Everglades in the United States in a hunting contest. These are thought to have been introduced through the wild pet trade, but once they escaped into the wild, their numbers expanded and they have 'totally eliminated or killed over 90% of some local species, such as racoons, marsh rabbits and possums' (Matza, 2023).

The main framework we have for protecting the planet is international law, which Gilbert (2023, p. 690) argues operates from the viewpoint of seeing nature as a 'resource to be owned, traded, exploited or protected'. He argues this is due to 'underlying historical, political and structural reasons – from colonisation, economic interests, political and territorial disputes where nature has been used as proxy'. He suggests this does not have to be the case and that principles of the 'Rights of Nature' (RoN) could be introduced to provide parameters where people would have to work with nature.

International law has begun to recognise that the voices of indigenous and marginalised people (United Nations Department of Economic and Social Affairs Indigenous Peoples mandated areas Environment, n.d.) and countries need to be heard. This is a process that needs to continue alongside the provision of financial aid for communities and countries to be able to adapt to our changing world and the challenges they are facing, such as through the loss and damage fund that has been set up to support those countries particularly vulnerable to the effects of climate change (United Nations Environment Programme, 2024).

The need for participation (Lee, 2023), openness and consultation have long been an important requirement for accountability (Graham & Prosser, 1988). This is also the case for discussions around these 'super wicked' policy issues (Baldauf, (ed.) 2020; Levin et al., 2012), particularly climate change (Abate, 2015, 2016, 2019). 'Super wicked' policy issues are those that are defined as 'complex, involving multiple possible causes and internal dynamics that could not be assumed to be linear, and have very negative consequences for society if not addressed properly' (Peters & Tarpey, 2019, p. 385). The challenge posed by the climate emergency has led to increased worldwide cooperation, but international law has yet to adequately deal with that or the loss of biodiversity and extinctions (Burke, 2022; Trouwborst, 2015). It is vital that international law finds a way, as a stable regime based on transparency and accountability, to create trust and bring into line not only compliant parties but also those that are non-compliant with accepted norms (Sand, 2017, p. 27).

The protection of habitat is central, along with effective measures to protect the animals within it. However, the challenge is how this can be accomplished whilst recognising the interconnectedness of ecosystems and the practical problems of how to measure success by estimating the 'data on species-specific estimates for the total abundance (i.e., the number of individuals) of wild mammals' (Greenspoon et al., 2023, p. 1). The choices may be difficult to make, as some species may simply not be able to survive, and we may not be able to save them. There are some who maintain a distinctly optimistic outlook on this, including Myers (1979, p. 284):

> To end on a brighter note, a whole-hearted decision to accept the challenge of a disappearing species could have an important spin-off benefit. The effort could help to articulate the common interest of nations. After all, conservation of species can be presented as a less likely source of political friction than many other international problems. A strategy to conserve species might even encourage governments to adopt a more collective approach to other collective issues that confront their global community.

Some of this optimism has been realised with the Convention on Biological Diversity and the myriad of international, regional, and national laws that have been passed (Visseren-Hamakers, 2022). There is also cause for optimism based on studies about the success of the IUCN Red List of Threatened Species, which reveal that trends in species extinction risk would have been at least 20% worse in the absence of conservation action (IUCN, Nature 2030 Programme; Langhammer et al., 2024).

However, there are some stark facts that run counter to this optimism. The UNEP suggests, as have many others, that the planet is experiencing a dangerous decline in nature because of our activities – the largest loss of life since the dinosaurs. It is possible that 'One million plant and animal species are now threatened with extinction, many within the next few decades' (UNEP, 2022). It is easy for those of us in the Global North to look at the iconic species in countries in the Global South, such as elephants, and feel like more needs to be done when wildlife comes into conflict with human populations (Murphy, 2023). We, perhaps, ignore our own part in this when we book a flight to go on safari or travel the globe and so we must all be aware of our actions to minimise our environmental footprint during our time on Earth.

In terms of law and policy, whilst on the one hand it can be argued that its success has been to mitigate more widespread destruction, on the other it can be argued that it has failed to deliver effective conservation or protection of wildlife. In fact, as Sollund (2011, p. 448) suggests, the law can unintentionally legitimise exploitation, abuse and species decline rather than protecting animals. On a positive note, wildlife can recover if given the right conditions, but the question remains whether this can be achieved in time, given the pressure of the effects of climate change and other stressors.

There is clearly a need for better legal protection, expanding and connecting protected areas, including regenerative agriculture and rewilding, dedicated species recovery work (including reintroductions), as well as improving habitats. There is also a need to reduce pressures, such as habitat loss and hunting, including for those species that are already making a comeback (Ledger et al., 2022).

It seems likely that conservation will benefit most from conflict management approaches that have clear goals, recognise the values of others, and foster open collaboration between stakeholders, academics and policymakers to consider the evidence and trade-offs involved in negotiating a way forward that all parties can live with (Conservation Evidence, 2020; University of Cambridge, 2024). In addition, the monitoring and evaluation of management processes is needed to act as a feedback mechanism for improving outcomes (Redpath et al., 2013, p. 107). One example of this is seal conservation in the Moray Firth, where discussions between all relevant stakeholders were done on an equal footing. This resulted in a management plan acceptable to government advisers, ecologists and fishery stakeholders alike, even though some had previously been resistant to seal conservation (Redpath et al., 2013, p. 104).

However, there are clear gaps in both the coverage and success in terms of dealing with this crucial international issue, despite the use of new technology such as drones. A greater and more focused effort is required to improve biodiversity and habitat protection and regulate trade (UNEP, 2024). This is also the case at a national level (Wildlife Trusts, n.d.) a European level (Milica Predragovic et al. 2024) and international level where biodiversity is still falling in protected areas for a variety of reasons (Natural History Museum 2024). There is a need for a whole-system approach that recognises both the welfare requirements and the cruelty issues, as well as biodiversity and extinction concerns. There needs to be a rethinking of laws that assume a hierarchy of species that puts many wild animals at the bottom of the list (Wyatt, 2021). At a regional level, such as the EU, wildlife protection needs to be strengthened by ensuring it is applied in member states, along with improved funding and data collection, and increased activity to raise public and governmental consciousness

Other avenues to affect change are worthy of exploration. For example, the role of various types of legal mechanisms, such as those seen in Earth law jurisprudence (Dancer, 2024), the role of judges (Lucky, 2018) and domestic environmental courts (Angstadt, 2023). Others include the wider use of legal specialists, such as the Biodiversity Law Centre, which is supporting a case to protect South African penguins using the South African Constitution, an approach often used in environmental litigation that might have a place in increasing understanding and reforming wildlife law. Another suggestion is to use the template of human rights law to help reinforce compliance (Koh et al., 2022). Using human rights has worked previously in relation to the welfare of animals (Wilson, 2019) and for climate change litigation (*Urgenda Foundation (on behalf of 886 individuals)* v. *The State of the Netherlands (Ministry of Infrastructure and the Environment)* (2015), and in the case of *Verein Klimaseniorinnen Schweiz and others* v. *Switzerland* (2024)). Other mechanisms could be used, such as developing the crime of ecocide (Legge & Brooman, 2020). In addition, national or regional law-making bodies could criminalise more activities that are detrimental to the environment, and increase penalties to improve enforcement, as the EU has done by updating Directive 2008/99/EC in 2024.

There are concerns with how conventions are brought into being, which undermines their effectiveness (Burke, 2022). Some conventions assume the status quo of property ownership and human interests rather than applying a fundamentally different philosophy or ethics (Zimmerman et al., 2005, which are less anthropocentric in nature. Whilst animal-centred theories such as those formulated by Singer and Regan are at the forefront of animal ethics, other ethical theories could provide and maybe have provided a new wave of animal ethicists with a way forward (Offor, 2023). These include Aldo Leopold's land ethics theory, holistic environmental ethics and the problem of eco-fascism, ecofeminism (Hunnicutt, 2021), social justice, environmental continental philosophy and eco phenomenology, as well as political ecology (Zimmerman et al., 2004). There is also deep ecology (Naess, 1989) and the Gaia theory (Lovelock, 1995, 1995, 2007).

However, whilst it has been argued that environmental and animal welfare ethics have a lot in common, some argue that:

> ... these convergences are significant because it is precisely in virtue of their respective holism and individualism the ecological and animal welfare ethics are incommensurable at the level of theory and incompatible at the level of practice. The two are incommensurable at the level of theory because there does not appear to be any way to measure the primary value of animals on a welfare ethics against the differential value an ecological ethic assigns to them on the basis of their functional role in a community. This incommensurability is amplified by the practical intractability of the two causes, an intractability that stems from the fact that promoting the good of the whole ecological community often involves favouring and promoting the good of entities that are only of derivative value on a welfare ethic over the interests of the sentient or rights holding animals which are of primary value on a welfare ethic. (Campbell, 2018, p. 61)

Almiron (2019, p. 1119) argues that:

> ... a clever strategy, ... may be to maintain a pluralistic approach, very much adapted to the different targets we address, as well as to avoid ecological aims in conflict with animal ethics and include the animal ethical claim in order to keep consistency, authenticity, and expectancy high. That is, to rank high in our advocacy toolkit the claim that to harm other animals is simply ethically 'wrong', regardless how many other collateral benefits and reasons also justify stopping harming them, and that however this is argued, it needs regulation to implement it.

This chapter, alongside Chapter 7, has contended that the welfare of animals needs to be considered, at least on a practical level, with the ecological causes of harm to wildlife and that welfare and cruelty concerns cannot be seen in isolation from the impact that environmental stressors are having on wildlife. How welfare extends to wild animals has been considered by Sykes (2016), who argues that welfare and conservation should be seen as one principle – that of protecting non-humans and their habitats (an argument also developed by Kopnina & Washington, 2020). There are clearly difficulties at an ethical level in terms of the overall direction of travel for the ethics of animal and environmental responsibilities, but this is countered by Nijhuis (2021), who suggests that on a practical and species survival level, we need to show solidarity.

The question remains as to how the law can put these competing arguments into practice. Legal theory is being developed through the idea of environmental personhood (Rochford, 2024) and in relation to more holistic legal theories such as 'wild law' with contributors such as Cullinan (2011) who argue that we need an 'Earth jurisprudence' that recognises how the Earth functions alongside a recognition of the connections between people and nature.

> In recent years there has been a welcome global surge in the recognition of Earth jurisprudence, ranging from the United Nations' Harmony with Nature dialogues to the International Union for the Conservation of Nature (IUCN) and the African Commission for Human and Peoples' Rights, as well as a growing number of precedents recognising Earth-centred customary governance systems and the Rights of Nature. (Gaia Foundation; and see García Ruales et al., 2024)

These all recognise the interdependence of these issues and the need to fundamentally change the law to become more in tune with nature through 'eco-literacy' (Capra & Mattei, 2015), all of which are relevant to how Animal Law moves forward.

The human relationship with wild animals is problematic on both a practical and theoretical level. What can we, logically, do? And how far should we go in terms of the competing interests of other animals and humans affected by them? Law and science increasingly recognise animal sentience beyond what was previously attributed to them, including that of many wild animals, the great apes, dolphins, whales and many other mammals (Wandesforde-Smith & Hart, 2015). There are calls for legal personhood, or 'legal animalhood' (Castelló, 2022) for some non-domestic animals kept in captivity, which could be extended for the sake of consistency to all wild animals (Wyatt et al., 2020, 2022) and New Zealand and other Pacific Islands have signed a Treaty (known as He Whakaputanga Moana (a declaration of the sea and lakes) granting whales legal personhood (Guenzler, 2024). As White (2013) argues there is a need for "a single comprehensive international law instrument (p. 391). Frameworks have been suggested such as a Universal Declaration on Animal Welfare and there should be the further development and collaboration of countries through the World Organisation for Animal Health (WOAH) animal health standards and the One Health approach. An international convention on animal health and protection has also been proposed by the Global Animal Law Association (White, 2013; Nyilas, 2021). A rights-based approach such as RoN (Gilbert, 2023) may extend to some wildlife and there are increasing examples of nature being accorded rights which may also protect wildlife within that habitat.

The issue of whether animals feel pain is central to debates around necessary and unnecessary suffering, and the law has primarily been designed around these issues. With the increase in understanding of both pain and sentience, 'necessary suffering' of animals becomes more morally unjustifiable. Adam and Schaffner (2017, p. 16) argue there is the need for an 'ethic of compassion and morality to supplement, if not replace, the principle of sustainability and conservation that remains firmly entrenched in international wildlife policy'. This is certainly more in line with species-led animal ethics, which would not accept the use of wildlife just because it is sustainable, as its proponents would almost always consider the individual animal and its suffering at the heart of decision-making. It is probably true to say that the suffering of a whale would never be acceptable in commercial whaling, no matter how sustainable it became (Adam & Schaffner, 2017, p. 17).

In conclusion, how the law develops to protect wildlife on the planet is the most fundamental challenge of our time:

> Scientists, conservationists and the planet's liberal public do not seek to defend biodiversity (any more than they do whales) because of the potential material gains of our or future generations. They do so rather in tacit recognition of the values of intellectual inquiry, spiritual fulfilment and recreational satisfaction that the mere existence of biodiversity bestows. While in an economic sense biodiversity represents unimaginable wealth, in this ethical sense it is simply priceless. (International Council for Bird Preservation, 1992)

Given that we have lost 69% of species since 1970 (WWF Living Planet Report, 2022), how the law responds to these challenges will determine the future of wildlife, what is left for future generations of humankind to enjoy.

Conclusion

> The ideal welfare law applies to all sentient animals, is clearly written, includes failing to meet an animal's needs among the offences, is easy to amend in line with new scientific knowledge and ethics, has high legal status, which allows for prosecutions, has a clear enforcement responsibility, involves an enforcement body with sufficient power and funds, and includes education of the public and industry. (Wolfensohn, 2020)

In setting out the characteristics for the ideal animal welfare law, Wolfensohn's quote identifies the key challenges in Animal Law: the challenge of drafting legislation that is well written and has clear definitions and whose scope is wide enough to encompass all sentient animals; the challenge for the law to be flexible enough to adapt to new knowledge in the science of animal biology and behaviour and new ideas in our philosophical thinking about animals and where the balance lies between human and animal interests; the challenge of effective enforcement of the law which means having clear enforcement bodies with adequate funding who take animals seriously and allocate adequate time and resources to enforcing Animal Law; the challenge of biodiversity loss and climate change and the conflict between protecting individual animals from cruelty versus the wider concerns of conservation; the challenge of educating the public, and those living and working with animals, on our most up-to-date understanding of the needs of animals, how animals are currently treated in society (especially where we fail to meet those needs) and what the law can do to improve their lives.

This concluding chapter draws out the key themes identified in the preceding chapters: the sentience of animals; the legal concepts of cruelty and unnecessary suffering; the legal status of animals; the welfare versus rights debate; the link to the environment, especially the extinction of animals, the loss of biodiversity and climate change; the enforcement of the law; the role of protest in instigating legal reform; the need for education to ensure there is an informed debate about our treatment of animals, and the need for law reform. In the introduction, we identified the themes we saw as emerging in Animal Law, which create the most significant challenges for Animal Law. Here, we refine those themes into four areas we consider to be creating and forming the key challenges in Animal Law:

1. Challenges arising from our use of sentient animals.
2. Challenges in drafting and interpreting legislation.
3. Challenges in enforcing existing legislation to protect animals.
4. Challenges in creating better accountability and change in Animal Law, and the importance of law reform.

Challenges arising from our use of sentient animals

Sentience is the cornerstone of Animal Law. Without sentience, there would be no need for the legal protection of animals. It is because animals are sentient that they need to be legally protected and for their own benefit, not just for reasons that benefit humans or the environment. Since animals are capable of experiencing suffering and pain, it is ethically right that we should avoid, inflicting such suffering and pain. A key challenge is that our definitions of sentience continue to change as we make more discoveries about the experience and sentient capabilities of animals. What was acceptable in ethical theory at one time may become outdated by the weight of scientific evidence and observation. For example, at one stage 'suffering' of an animal in farming was defined in terms of direct harm and limited freedoms to move and access water, etc., whereas the development of law in recent times has recognised animals living a life according to that which is natural for their species.

In certain interactions with animals, we accept that pain and suffering are unavoidable; for example, in the UK, most companion animal dogs are given annual vaccinations by a vet. This will momentarily cause pain, discomfort and stress for the dog, but it is justifiable because it is for the dog's own benefit to be protected from the risk of future illness. Therefore, there may be times it is justifiable to cause an animal pain and suffering for the benefit of that animal. What about causing an animal pain and suffering or even death to benefit humans or other animals? Can this be justified? As discussed in Chapter 8, is it justifiable to cull an invasive species of animal in order to protect another species? In the UK, the native red squirrel is under threat from the non-native grey squirrel that was introduced into the country in the 19th century and rapidly spread and colonised much of mainland England. The law in the UK permits the culling of this invasive species to protect native flora and fauna.

What about causing an animal pain and suffering or death for human benefit? Is this justifiable? For example, is it ethical in the West to raise a pig on an intensive farm and kill it for food when there are plenty of healthy and nutritional alternatives to eating meat? These questions demonstrate how law and ethical theories are intertwined in the context of our relationship with animals. The level of protection for animals under the law depends on the underpinning assumptions of a society. For example, in the West, most people think it is justifiable to raise and kill a farmed animal for meat to feed humans or to carry out painful experiments on animals for medical research. Therefore, the level of legal protection given to animals will reflect the view that animals can be used for our benefit. In the West, this anthropocentric approach prevails, meaning that animals can be used as resources for humans, and in Chapter 1, we examined the history behind this approach, especially major influences such as the Ancient Greeks and religion. The legal protection a specific animal enjoys is dependent on the way in which humans use it rather than its biology or species. For example, a rabbit can be used by humans in many different ways – as food, for its fur, as a laboratory subject, as entertainment, as a companion animal, or it may be a wild rabbit – and in each case the legal protection for the individual rabbit varies depending on its use. This use-based approach to the legal protection of domestic and captive animals is prevalent across the globe and reflects our anthropocentric view of animals.

In Chapter 2, we saw the history of how the law has treated animals. We used the UK as a case study, but the underlying legal concepts that were examined in the chapter apply worldwide, especially the recognition of sentience in animals and the legal status of domestic and captive animals as property. Sentience and property status are the modern key themes in Animal Law. The theme of sentience illustrates the integral link between law, ethics and science and how each influences the other. As scientific research progresses and provides new evidence of animal sentience, ethics and law need to evolve to keep pace with new knowledge. In Chapter 2, the case study on cephalopods and decapods demonstrates this evolution, with new laws now protecting these species in some countries following the relatively recent recognition in science that they are sentient. However, in Chapter 6, we saw how the law does not yet go far enough to protect sentient invertebrates that are used as food, and plans for the world's first commercial octopus farm in Spain illustrate the challenge for law reform, which is a slow process and struggles to keep up with advances in scientific knowledge. Legislative changes usually take considerable time from inception to implementation, leaving some sentient animals vulnerable to suffering and exploitation.

Our modern relationship with animals is complex. In the West, we recognise animals as sentient and seek to protect them from pain and suffering, but we also want to be able to use animals as resources for human benefit even if that causes the animals such pain and suffering. Francione refers to this as our 'moral schizophrenia' (Francione, 2004). We shower love and affection on our companion animals while simultaneously causing immense suffering to billions of animals in intensive farms and laboratories. Religious, cultural and geographical factors dictate which animals we eat rather than the sentience or intelligence of the animal. For example, dogs and pigs are very similar with respect to their cognitive, emotional and social capacities, but most people in the West perceive one of these species as suitable companions and the other as food. Our moral schizophrenia towards animals is socially ingrained and linked with religion and culture. This makes it difficult to isolate and challenge our perception and treatment of certain species; for example, our treatment of pigs in intensive farming practices causes the animals pain and suffering but is socially acceptable in society. Wolfson highlights our inconsistency in our treatment of farm animals, observing that 'cruel practices are specifically allowed that would be illegal if practiced on domestic companion animals. Is this ethically and legally consistent?' (Wolfson, 1999, p. 24).

To answer this question, we need to understand the history and philosophy of our current relationship with animals within the context of law, which is the focus of Chapters 1, 2 and 3. These chapters helped us to understand our existing moral and legal treatment of animals and how it could change in the future.

Chapters 5 to 7 examined the key legal concept of 'unnecessary suffering', which seeks to manage our complex relationship with animals by prohibiting humans from causing suffering to animals that is unnecessary while allowing necessary suffering. While the book focuses on UK law, the theme of unnecessary suffering is prevalent in Animal Law worldwide. There are significant challenges with the concept of unnecessary suffering as a method of protecting animals as sentient beings from pain and suffering. Clearly suffering is a pre-requisite, and while it may be relatively easy to show that an animal has suffered physical harm, it is more difficult to prove mental suffering given the language barrier; an animal cannot tell us how it is feeling. Even more challenging is the question of necessity because it is essentially a subjective concept. Since causing an animal necessary suffering is generally permitted under the law, the question of necessity is vital. Who decides necessity? If it is shown that a pig suffers when it is raised on an intensive farm and is slaughtered at an abattoir, who decides whether that suffering is necessary or not? Clearly, a vegan will feel very differently about the necessity of that suffering compared to someone who eats meat. Ultimately it will be for the courts to decide the question of necessity in individual cases, but as we saw in the cases discussed in Chapters 5 and 6, restrictive interpretation of legislation by the courts can leave animals lacking adequate protection.

The legal status of domestic and captive animals as property is a central theme of Animal Law worldwide. The property status of animals permits us to use them as our resources, food and commodities, entertainment and as test subjects in laboratories. In most cases, this relationship is exploitative and detrimental to the animals. We can also keep them as companion animals, and for most animals, this can be a beneficial experience (although in Chapter 5, we explored situations when pet ownership is detrimental to animals; for example, the breeding of extreme traits in dogs, such as brachycephalic dogs).

A key contemporary debate in Animal Law is that of welfare versus rights, as discussed in Chapter 3. The welfare approach exists within the property paradigm, with law reform focusing on giving animals the best life possible within the parameters of how we use them; for example, ensuring they have a suitable environment and diet. In contrast to the welfare approach is the rights approach, which would require a significant shift in current thinking because it would abolish the existing property status of some animals and grant them legal personhood instead. Granting some animals fundamental legal rights, such as the right to life or bodily integrity (not to be enslaved) would mean they could not be used as resources for our benefit – we could not eat them or use them as test subjects in experiments. Depending on which animals are granted legal personhood, this shift in paradigms for our relationship with animals, from property to legal person, could have major implications for society, for example, by ending the eating of sentient animals as food.

Challenges in drafting and interpreting legislation

A key theme in Animal Law is the welfare versus rights debate, as discussed above and in Chapter 3. The current legal framework for protecting animals adopts a 'welfarist' approach that permits us to use animals as our resources but prohibits unnecessary suffering and, in some cases, takes positive action to promote their welfare. In recent years, there have been a few instances worldwide of animals being given fundamental legal rights; for example, in 2023, the City of Ojai in California amended its municipal code to grant elephants the legal right to bodily liberty within the city, but such instances are rare. Worldwide, most laws that seek to protect animals are welfare laws existing within the property paradigm. Therefore, it is important that welfare-based law adequately protects animals. It must be sufficiently comprehensive in scope and content and interpreted by the courts in a way that provides the best protection for animals within the confines of the wording used in the legislation. Comprehensive in scope means including all sentient animals within the protection of the law; for example, in England, the Animal Welfare Act 2006 needs to be amended to include sentient invertebrates. Comprehensive in content means ensuring protection given to animals is not diluted by wide exclusions and exemptions, such as in the US, where the 'customary farming practice' exemption excludes, from the criminal law, many farming practices that cause suffering to animals.

Chapters 5 and 6 identified the challenges presented by the courts' restrictive interpretation of animal welfare legislation that can leave animals at risk of suffering. For example, in the English case of *Patterson* v. *RSPCA* (2013), the court's interpretation of the legislation meant that a person disqualified from keeping animals could lawfully live in a house with many animals and even be alone in the house with them and not be in breach of their disqualification order. This restrictive interpretation of the legislation significantly dilutes the effectiveness of the law in protecting animals from those who are known to abuse them.

The challenge of enforcing legislation to protect animals

Enforcement in Animal Law continues to be an issue and is an emerging theme in several areas of law, as illustrated in this book. On paper, many regions, including the UK and the EU, seem to have strong legislation to protect the interests of animals, but without adequate enforcement, the law is undermined and loses the confidence of interest groups and the wider public. The level of protection and enforcement can depend on the use of the animals in question and societal views towards them (APGAW, 2022). For example, animals kept as companions are more visible in society, making it easier to report abuse to the relevant authorities. As a society, we tend to care more about their welfare, often treating them like family members. The level of suffering we deem necessary for them is low, compared to that of other groups, and enforcement on their behalf is stronger. For some animals, such as those used in farming or experimentation, their suffering is largely invisible, taking place behind closed doors. Society tends to accept a certain level of suffering for their use, and usually due to financial pressures (Nurse, 2014). The issue with enforcement is whether anyone is present to witness or report the animal suffering and whether that suffering is considered unnecessary and therefore unlawful.

In Chapters 5 and 6, in relation to domesticated and farmed animals, respectively, we explored how enforcement is mainly left to non-governmental organisations and charities that have no statutory powers of enforcement, or arms of government acting with ever-reducing funding to enact their statutory powers, such as local authorities. This is not unique to the UK, and this overall scenario for enforcement raises issues of concern. Without statutory powers, it is sometimes difficult for animal welfare organisations to ensure the law is enforced, though it must be noted that many do collaborate effectively with local authorities and statutory bodies. However, these organisations can also face scrutiny, as seen with the RSPCA in England, which encountered several challenges, forcing it to rethink how it operates. Without the vital work of the RSPCA, many animal welfare infringements would go unnoticed, and the laws would remain unenforced. There have been attempts, as outlined in Chapter 6, to incorporate technology into enforcement, such as the use of CCTV in slaughterhouses, and this has helped to reduce non-compliance with animal welfare regulations, but the overall effectiveness of this has been difficult to measure.

As discussed in Chapters 7 and 8, wildlife is protected by additional methods of enforcement due to significant powers held by the National Wildlife Crime Unit. However, limited resources mean they are hampered by a lack of inspectors across the country. Some police forces may have a Police and Wildlife Crime Officer, but not all, and they are often not solely focused on wildlife crimes within a force (Wellsmith, 2011). The enforcement of wildlife crime can also be politicised, such as with fox-hunting, which can disrupt legal interventions.

Animals used in experiments in the UK are subject to scrutiny by the national inspectorate and have dedicated resources from the Animals in Science Regulation Unit. Establishments are often inspected by the Home Office to ensure licence requirements are being adhered to. There have been no prosecutions; however, under the Animals (Scientific Procedures) Act 1986, there is evidence from undercover work of high non-compliance involving large numbers of animals and significant welfare concerns.

The crucial question is how to improve enforcement. Firstly, the evidence suggests that more funding is imperative to investigate potential animal welfare offences and support the enforcement of existing laws. Currently, the UK government does not provide a funding stream for the enforcement of these offences, and it is left to local authorities to fund from their general budget, which will have other financial pressures placed upon it. This appears to be a constant problem, which is heightened in times of national austerity, where animal welfare crime and enforcement issues are of low priority, meaning that issues go undetected or law enforcement is inadequately regulated. For example, in Chapter 6, reports by charities such as Animal Equality (2022) highlighted that the low level of inspections of farmed animals leads to hidden breaches of the law. The lack of funding for local authorities also sends a message that the central UK government does not take animal welfare matters seriously. Local authorities are left to prioritise other areas, and this can deflect attention away from the lack of central funding to leave the blame lying with local authorities – limited resources can only stretch so far.

Secondly, enforcement of animal health and welfare regulations is often left to different departments within local authorities, resulting in a piecemeal approach. Licensing activities, such as zoos and pet shops, may be with trading standards, whilst farming regulation is with environmental health. The inspectors in different departments may lack training in animal health and welfare, and this can result in welfare issues being missed. However, this is not always the case, and some excellent inspectors and local authorities are working to improve animal welfare. To ensure that standards are consistent and maintained across the country, a dedicated animal health and welfare inspectorate team is needed in each local authority; alternatively, work could be coordinated across several local authorities in close geographic proximity so that training and monitoring can receive better oversight.

Alternatively, charities and non-governmental organisations can be given greater statutory powers of enforcement. As discussed in Chapters 5 and 6, the RSPCA in England is attempting to gain statutory powers with the hope this will strengthen their investigative functions. Unfortunately, this might come at the cost of relinquishing their role in prosecutions, which would be handed over to the central Crown Prosecution Service (CPS), which does not have the same success rate. There is a risk that the CPS may not prioritise the prosecution of animal offences as it would have to be balanced directly against other crimes. A better course of action may be to maintain the functions of organisations such as the RSPCA, allowing them to continue with their role in investigations and enhancing them with more statutory powers to do this role more effectively.

The enforcement of animal protection laws needs improvement if it is to be fully effective. To do this requires a greater commitment from central government to help enforcement agencies, such as local authorities, to adequately carry out their enforcement functions. As Ellison (2017, p. 1) notes, the enforcement of 'animal welfare laws should not be a charity case'.

Challenges in law reform and how to change the law to protect animals better

Two clear themes emerged for us in relation to the challenge of law reform in Animal Law – the role of protests and campaigns and the role of education. Lobbying to change the law and highlighting cases where the law is not working or is being broken is an important part of holding to account those who make or enforce the law, for example campaigners want to ensure that public bodies use a new duty under s. 245 of the Levelling- up and Regeneration Act 2023 to 'seek to further' the aims of protecting landscapes when public bodies are making decisions that could have an impact on those landscapes. This is important for wildlife and this duty is seen as a game changer for those campaigning to protect wildlife and the natural landscape. Campaigners want to see guidance and regulations introduced to give the legislation more strength and will use judicial review to ensure that this duty is taken into account in decision making (Harvey, 2024). In addition, it is important to ensure that people are well-educated about the treatment of animals in society, especially where there is suffering and/ or exploitation. The World Animal Protection Index ranks a number of countries around the world in terms of the adequacy of their animal welfare legislation and policy. It provides a valuable educational resource and helps those lobbying for law reform to understand the effectiveness of laws worldwide (www.api.worldanimalprotection.org).

The role of protests and campaigns in law reform

The animal rights movement has used a variety of techniques to make its case heard. There are a large number of pressure groups advocating for domestic animals, such as the Cats Protection League, and for farming, organisations such as Compassion in World Farming. Some organisations advocate for specific animals, such as whales and dolphins, and there are conservation groups specifically for injured animals, or that campaign against specific practices, such as the League Against Cruel Sports. There are also wildlife organisations such as the Wildlife Trusts, as well as broader environmental groups such as Greenpeace, Friends of the Earth, and Extinction Rebellion (there is also an animal rebellion group), to name just a few (Richardson, 2020).

Robert Garner examines the effectiveness of direct action, such as demonstrations, in creating change:

> In political terms, it [can be] argued that a system of decision making which allows for what Singer calls a 'fair compromise' between competing interests does place constraints on disobeying the law. In reality, however, modern industrial societies can only provide mechanisms which approximate to this ideal of political equality. In the system of pressure group politics, powerful economic interests who benefit from using animals have considerable resources which seriously disadvantage the campaign for change. Although further research into the role of key exploiters is needed, a preliminary examination would suggest that the animal protection movement can make considerable progress through the mobilisation of public opinion. (Garner, 1993, p. 239)

This highlights the importance of educating the public about Animal Law and the treatment of animals in society so the public can make informed choices about what action, if any, to take to better protect animals (the role of education is considered in the section below).

However, we must now weigh the value of political protest against the increasing use of legislation to curb this activity (Chow, 2023). The Aarhus Convention states that peaceful environmental protest is a legitimate exercise of the public's right to participate in decision-making and that those engaged in it must be protected. However, a recent report by the UN Special Rapporteur on Environmental Defenders found that peaceful protesters involved in environmental activism increasingly faced repression (Forst, 2024). In the UK, there has been a plethora of legislation on public order from the Public Order Act 1986, the Police, Crime, Sentencing and Courts Act 2022 and the Public Order Act 2023, which have increasingly restricted and criminalised protest. For example, protesters blocking a road can now be liable for arrest for interfering with vital national infrastructure under the Public Order Act 2023. The courts now have a balancing act between the more restrictive public order legislation and the Human Rights Act 1998 (Cammiss et al., 2022; Chow, 2022):

> One may now discern two distinct judicial approaches to civil disobedience. One approach focuses on 'law and order', stressing legal compliance and the need to deter recidivism. The other recognises the social importance of civil disobedience within certain limits (for example, non-violence) and in this context seeks to balance protesters' rights to free expression and assembly and the right of others to be free from disruption caused by protest activities. (Chow, 2023, p. 929)

Direct action has often been used in relation to the peace movement, animal rights and environmental activism. However, direct action has become more difficult to defend in law as various defences have been withdrawn from protesters (Jegatheeswaran, 2024). This can be seen in relation to the defence of lawful excuse when causing criminal damage to property. In the case of *Attorney General's Reference on a Point of Law (No. 1 of 2023)* [2024], the court considered the defence of lawful excuse under the Criminal Damage Act 1971, s.5(2) which states that, 'where a person is charged with an offence of criminal damage, there is a lawful excuse for their actions if they believed that the property owner consented to the damage or would consent if they had known about the damage and its circumstances'. This belief in consent is a subjective test which permits an honest and genuine mistake to be made so that although a person's purpose may be dishonest, they will have a defence if their belief is honest. In the judgment it was stated that:

> 'It was not Parliament's intention in enacting s.5(2)(a) to give protesters free rein to publicise their cause through the criminal courts. By applying the normal principles of statutory construction, the merits, urgency or importance of any matter about which the defendant might be protesting did not constitute the circumstances of the damage for the purpose of s.5(2)(a)' (at paras 49–50). The court went onto state; 'A judge could withdraw a defence from a jury if no reasonable jury properly directed could reach a particular conclusion. They must exercise considerable caution before taking that step and should not substitute their decision for that of the jury when deciding to withdraw the defence.' (Attorney General's Reference (No. 1 of 2023) (para 64) (2024)

Given the importance of this defence to protesters, it will be interesting to see in future how the phrase 'no reasonable jury' is interpreted by judges when defendants attempt to use the defence. Jegatheeswaran (2024) argues that whilst this seems to curtail rather than remove the defence:

> [T]here is no denying it still forms part of a landscape of increasingly restricted rights to freedom of expression and freedom of assembly, and perhaps less obviously, the right to a fair trial.

There is evidence that both direct action and political protest can have an effect (Stephan & Chenoweth, 2008), as seen with the outcome of the campaign to save the whale. More recently, specific changes to the law have been made to reflect public concern about animal cruelty (Munro, 2005; Jacobsson & Lindblom, 2016), as in the campaign that led to the Animal Welfare (Service Animals) Act 2019 (Finn's Law) in England. Successful campaigning can also take place on social media and campaign sites where it is easy to click and support petitions, email political representatives, and to keep in touch with what is happening.

We might assume for a moment that all campaigning has resulted in improved conditions for animals and that animals are treated far better than before these groups began to campaign for their better treatment. It is true that some practices such as bear-baiting, bull-baiting, and the generally barbaric treatment of horses, cattle and other animals have been removed in most of the advanced industrialised nations of the world, but cruelty continues. Any claim that animals are now accorded greater respect and are 'better off' than they were two centuries ago is questionable. So, whilst the law has been used to prevent excesses of cruelty, such as fox-hunting in the UK, animal welfare laws permit us to use animals on a massive scale, for example, in farming, with a relatively guilt-free conscience. In terms of wild animals, as we have seen in Chapter 8, biological diversity is decreasing, and extinctions are increasing. Campaigning can work to slow down change, as can be seen in relation to the conflict around Europe and the UK over nature restoration laws and climate mitigation projects, and in relation to some farmers who see these changes as threatening their livelihoods and futures.

There are continuing questions raised as to whether animal rights advocates should adopt an 'all or nothing approach' and how, if at all, animal welfare issues relate to or coexist alongsideenvironmental issues. The history of 'green' politics in general is littered with instances of disagreements over what they should be campaigning for and what they should accept as a compromise, as political and pressure groups will always attract a mixture of hardliners and moderates. If the inevitability of internal conflict is accepted, then the next question for those within a pressure group is whether they are prepared to accept a compromise of their demands at a political level. In terms of the role of the law, Gruen (Adams et al., 2023) observes that there is a debate between reform and revolution, whether incremental or total change is necessary, whether there is abolition of cruel practices, or whether changes should be made to improve the welfare of animals. Gruen (Adams et al., 2023, p. 255) argues that this debate between these extremes should be 'interrupted' and suggests a 'third way' of 'non-reformist reforms'. Gruen quotes Gorz (1967, p. 259), who argues that some reforms can be made without compromising wider goals, and Gruen uses this to argue that 'transforming the social structures that harm so many is a fundamentally different project to reforming systems in order to make them less harmful or more efficient at doing good'. Gruen argues that people need to work in mutual aid and solidarity with humans and animals. Whilst not everyone will agree with Gruen's conclusions, the issues that are raised are important when thinking about the role and reform of Animal Law.

Considering these criticisms and the weight of evidence showing the inconsistencies of moral justification and practical application of the law, there are strong arguments that a review of the law relating to animals is necessary, particularly at the international level. As discussed in Chapter 8 do we base changes in the law on Rights of Nature (RoN) (Schmidt, 2022; Laitos, 2021), or see them as part of a wider development of Earth Jurisprudence? RoN may be used to reinterpret international law '... such as the precautionary approach, intergenerational equity, and stewardship ... to be reinterpreted and better aligned with the RoN movement. Their apparent anthropocentric orientation may be based more on how they are currently interpreted rather than anything inherent in the norms themselves' (Gilbert, 2023, p. 692). Any reform of international law also needs to consider the impact and interaction of laws on human rights and indigenous people (Giacomini, 2022; Gilbert, 2023; Offor, 2023; Washington et al., 2024).

There are obviously questions as to how changes to the law covering ecological or conservation concerns protect individual animals. In the past, there have been suggestions to introduce an international regime for animal rights (Peters, 2021) or an international body for animals (Moss, 1991). At a national level in the UK, a ministry or a minister for animals has been mooted (Jenkins, 1992). However, would this help resolve the issue, or would it isolate animals from the wider issues that affect them? Another way forward might be to impose a duty to consider the impact on animals on any policy development.

How the law is reformed depends upon whether it is individual animals you want to protect or the whole ecology of the world. To protect individual animals from cruelty and harm has often been the basis of Animal Law in the past, but increasingly there is a recognition that it needs to consider the impact of environmental harms and the climate emergency, and there has been a growth of innovative litigation in this area (UNEP, 2023). If the world is not habitable, then this will impact all of us, humans and animals. Climate change is the most pressing problem in the world today, and its effects are being felt globally. It reaches into all parts of our planet's life including food, water and habitat, and even whether species will exist at all – and this includes the human race. There is a need to look at issues holistically and to think long-term when formulating law and policy. This is problematic with short-term election cycles in democracies and may be even more challenging in autocratic countries and those where populism is rising, but life on Earth is dependent upon the law and politics reflecting this. How the law deals with these challenges will be fundamental to how life on the planet moves forward.

The role and importance of education

Education is key to the advancement of Animal Law, as ignorance of the potential suffering of animals may lead to an offence being committed. It is important to inform those who may transgress the law of both the harm done and the personal consequences of their actions, with the hope that it acts as a preventative measure. Education can shed light and hopefully prevent suffering before it occurs.

Animal Law interacts with many areas of law, including criminal, public, family, housing, and environmental law. Animal Law is worthy of educational processes, and any benefits for humans may be a collateral outcome. When we look to achieve justice for animals, it often becomes the case that humans are impacted too (Linzey, 2009). In Chapter 6, we saw how the intensive rearing of farmed animals can harm human health and welfare, and in Chapter 5, we explored how violence against animals in a domestic situation can contribute to violence against humans. We also saw the mental health benefits of living with companion animals and how the forced relinquishment of a companion animal can adversely affect human well-being. As we have seen in Chapter 8, extinctions and biodiversity loss also have serious negative impacts on humans. How we treat animals often directly feeds back into human life. You only need to consider the likely cause of the COVID-19 pandemic – it is believed that the virus transferred from wild animals to humans – to see how misdirected interaction with animals can severely impact human health (Schuck-Paim et al., 2023). Would this have occurred if the warning by scientists about the risks of animal-to-human virus transfer – in the public domain for some time – had been heeded?

We also know that there is a lack of public awareness of the law relating to animals. For example, Chapter 4 highlighted a public misconception about animals used in experiments, with a high proportion still believing that cosmetic testing is legal in the UK, though it has not been for some time. Putting in place measures to educate people would improve knowledge and awareness, particularly in schools where the reach of such education might be decisive and potentially adjust harmful behaviours. However, we note existing burdens on schools, the limited space in modern curricula, and the workloads of an already stretched teaching body, which again raises the issue of resourcing.

Scientific developments relating to animals, such as discoveries around sentience, are constantly emerging, but it can be hard for governments and the public to keep up with the current state of knowledge. New knowledge and awareness must be disseminated, as both can be a powerful tools in generating change by placing pressure on governments (Garner, 2006). Throughout this book, there are examples of laws introduced largely because of public support for change. Information and education provide the public with a strong and collective voice, but pressure groups provide the method to inform. The work of charities and non-governmental organisations in producing reports and going undercover to gather evidence, is vital to the cause, along with the effective use and cooperation of the media.

The number of undergraduate and postgraduate Animal Law courses in UK universities remains low compared with the overall number of law courses, and where they are offered, they appear as stand-alone modules or incorporated into other subjects (Dunn et al., 2022). This means that the majority of law students are not equipped with knowledge of Animal Law when they go into practice or into other professions, though it is likely they will come across some of these issues and perhaps encounter specialist animal lawyers and firms. For example, Chapter 5 outlined how pet custody disputes are becoming more prevalent, and those working in family law need to understand the legal issues involved in order to represent their client properly. As an antidote to this, the Cambridge Centre for Animal Rights Law is supporting the introduction of animal rights modules in universities in several countries, and this work will help to deliver more courses in Animal Law to match the significant progress in Animal Law education taking place in law schools in the United States.

Another theme throughout this book is the close connection between practical Animal Law and the ethical/philosophical debates that underpin it. This impacts the changing morality and, in turn, can lead to changes in the law to improve animal protection worldwide. The 'why' of Animal Law is a prime example of an area where there is a need to provide educational opportunities in the context of philosophical debate and theories. As lawyers progress through their careers and potentially join the judiciary, they may need to make decisions relating to animals and thus will benefit from being properly informed about the deep roots of Animal Law in philosophical discourse.

In Chapters 5 and 6, we examined how judicial decisions made in Animal Law cases can sometimes render the law practically ineffective (*Patterson* v. *RSPCA* [2013]). The court may be hesitant to disrupt the status quo and cause huge changes (*The King (on the application of The Humane League UK)* v. *Secretary of State for Environment, Food and Rural Affairs* [2023]). An education in Animal Law and the science informing it could benefit future practitioners and judges in their approach to Animal Law cases, which may be why there is so much attention given to the subject in the United States. However, law courses in the UK and elsewhere, in Australia for example, are currently being squeezed into delivering courses that recognise a narrow form of legal education, focused on employability into a specific profession, rather than for the wider importance of law in society. It has altered and fettered the more socio-legal forms of education, including Animal Law and made them much less diverse in coverage – skills rather than knowledge are in vogue and philosophical debate about the form and function of law in an area such as Animal Law is gradually being lost. It is hoped that other jurisdictions do not follow this path, and we strongly recommend that they adopt the growth approach taken in the United States (Brooman, 2017).

Overall, we are in no doubt that education about animals, including Animal Law, is needed at all levels of education. Knowledge and understanding are important, not just for those directly handling animals, such as vets, farmers, laboratory workers and slaughterhouse workers, where a good understanding of, and compliance with, existing animal welfare laws will significantly benefit animals, but also for the public, who are then equipped to lobby and campaign for law reform where it is needed. Non-governmental organisations and charities do a lot of work to educate the public on the problems animals face within our society and legal system, but their resources are limited. Governments can achieve deep-rooted and long-lasting change – if the will is there. We hope that in reading this book you found something that will help you to contribute to changing Animal Law wherever it is needed.

Cases

Arrington v. *Arrington*, 613 S.W. 2d 565 (Tex. Civ. App. 1981)

Attorney General's Reference (No. 1 of 2022) [2022] EWCA Crim 1259, [2023] K.B. 37, [2022] 9 WLUK 223

Attorney General's Reference on a Point of Law (No 1 of 2023) [2024] EWCA Crim 243.

Blades v Higgs 1865 11 HL Cas 621

Borwick Development Solutions Limited v. *Clear Water Fisheries Limited* [2020] EWCA Civ 578

BUAV v. *Newcastle University* [2010] *Appeal No.: EA/2010/006*

Case of Swans 1592 7 CO Rep

CASE OF VEREIN KLIMASENIORINNEN SCHWEIZ AND OTHERS v. *SWITZERLAND*, 53600/20 ECHR 09/04/2024

C G Fry and Son Ltd v. *Secretary of State for Levelling Up Housing and Communities* King's Bench Division (Administrative Court) [2023] EWHC 1622 (Admin) 30 Jun 2023.

Commission of the European Communities v. *Grand Duchy of Luxembourg* (1996), Case C-274/93, OJ 1996 I2079

DPP v. *Barry* [1989] Crim LR 645

DPP (Crown Prosecution Service CCU Southwest) v. *Anthony Wright*; and *The Queen on the Application of Maurice Scott, Peter Heard & Donald Summersgill* v. *Taunton Deane Magistrates Court* [2009] EWHC 105 (Admin)

Dred Scott v. *Sandford* [1856] 60 US (19 How) 393

Dyrebeskyttelsen Norge v. *Norsk Kennelklubb, Norsk Bulldog Klubb, og Norsk Cavalierklubb* HR-2023–1901-A, 10 October 2023

ET v. *Ministerstvo životního prostředí* (2022) Judgment of the Court (Fourth Chamber) of 8 September 2022. ET v Ministerstvo životního prostředí. Request for a preliminary ruling from the Nejvyšší správní soud. Reference for a preliminary ruling – Protection of species of wild fauna and flora by regulating trade therein – Regulation (EC) No 338/97 – Article 8(3)(d) – Concept of 'specimens of animal species that are born and bred in captivity' – Regulation (EC) No 865/2006 – Article 1(3) – Concept of 'breeding stock' – Article 54(2) – Establishment of the breeding stock – Controlled ancestry. Case C-659/20. ECLI identifier: ECLI:EU:C:2022:642

Ford v. *Wiley* [1889] 23 QBD 203

Gray and others v. *RSPCA* [2010] EW Misc 8 (EWCC)

Harris v. *Environment Agency* Queen's Bench Division (Administrative Court) [2022] EWHC 2264 (Admin) 6 Sep 2022.

Hedley Lomas (Ireland) Ltd v *Ministry of Agriculture, Fisheries and Food* Case C-5/94, ILEC 011 (CJEU 1996), 23rd May 1996

Hudnott v. *Campbell*, The Times, 27 June 1986

Humane League UK v. *Secretary of State for Environment, Food and Rural Affairs* [2024] EWCA Civ 1560

Juelfs v. *Gough*, 41 P.3d 593 (Alaska 2002).

Kirkland v. *Robinson (*1987) 1 JP 377

League Against Cruel Sports Ltd v. *Scott and Others* [1986] QB 240

Noah v. *The Attorney General* (HCJ 9232/01, 215)

Northern Ireland Badger Group and Wild Justice Application, 2023 NIKB 117.

Patterson v. *Royal Society for the Prevention of Cruelty to Animals (RSPCA)* [2013] EWHC 4531 (Admin)

Ploni v. *Plonit*, March 12 2004 (unpublished) in the Ramat Gan Family Court. FC 32405/01

R v. *Coventry Airport, ex p Phoenix Aviation* [1995] 3 All ER 37

R. (on the application of Wyatt) v. *Fareham BC* Court of Appeal (Civil Division) [2022] EWCA Civ

R v. *Secretary of State for the Environment, ex p Royal Society for the Protection of Birds (Port of Sheerness Ltd intervening)* (1996) The Times, 2 August (ECJ: Full Court)

R., ex parte Hedley Lomas (Ireland) Limited v. *Ministry of Agriculture, Fisheries and Food*, Final judgment, Case C-5/94, ILEC 011 (CJEU 1996), 23rd May 1996, Court of Justice of the European Union [CJEU]; European Court of Justice [ECJ]; European Court of Justice (Grand Chamber)

Raymond v. *Lachmann*, 695 N.Y.S.2d 308, 309 (N.Y. App. Div. 1999).

Roberts v. *Ruggerio* [1985] QBD 3 April 1985 (unreported)

Rowley v. *Murphy* [1964] 2 QB 43; [1964] 1 All ER 50, [1963] 3 WLR 1061, 128 JP 88

State of Hawaii v. *Kenneth Le Vasseur* [1980] 613 P.2d 1328

The King (on the application of The Humane League UK) v. *Secretary of State for Environment, Food and Rural Affairs* [2023] EWHC 1234 (Admin).

The King on the application of Cruelty Free International v. *Secretary of State for the Home Department* [2023] CA-2023–000967

The Queen v. *Ministry of Agriculture, Fisheries and Food, ex parte: Hedley Lomas (Ireland) Ltd* [1996] E.C.R. 1–2553

The Queen on the Application of Maurice Scott, Peter Heard & Donald Summersgill v. *Taunton Deane Magistrates Court* [2009] EWHC 105

Tilikum v. *Sea World Parks and Entertainment* [2012] CASE NO. 11cv2476 JM(WMC)

Urgenda Foundation (on behalf of 886 individuals) v. *The State of the Netherlands (Ministry of Infrastructure and the Environment),* First instance decision, HA ZA 13–1396, C/09/456689, ECLI:NL:RBDHA:2015:7145, ILDC 2456 (NL 2015), 24th June 2015, Netherlands; The Hague; District Court.

Wild Justice v. *Natural Resources Wales* [2021] EWHC 35 (Admin)

Bibliography

Abatc, R. (2015). *Climate Change impacts on ocean and coastal law*. Oxford University Press.

Abate, R. (2016). *Climate justice: Case studies in global and regional governance challenges*. ELI Press.

Abate, R. (2019). *Climate change and the voiceless: Protecting future generations, wildlife, and natural resources*. Cambridge University Press.

Adam, R., & Schaffner, J. (2017). International law and wildlife well-being: Moving from theory to action. *Journal of International Wildlife Law and Policy*, *20*(1), 1–17. https://doi.org/10.1080/13880292.2017.1315277

Adams, C. J., Crary, A., & Gruen, L. (2023). *The good it promises, the harm it does: Critical essays on effective altruism*. Oxford University Press.

Advocates for animals. (2021). *RSPCA Reviews Prosecutorial Role*. https://www.advocates-for-animals.com/post/rspca-reviews-prosecutorial-role-implications-for-animal-protection Retrieved May 25, 2023.

Agyepong-Parsons, J. (2020). Could brexit undermine the birds and habitats directives? https://www.endsreport.com/article/1672350/brexit-undermine-birds-habitats-directives#:~:text=The%20UK's%20exit%20from%20the,James%20Agyepong%2DParsons%20reports.&text=%E2%80%9CIn%20other%20words%2C%20the%20longer,have%20done%2C%E2%80%9D%20she%20said Retrieved May 14, 2024.

Alexander, P. (2023). How cats and dogs affect the climate – And what you can do about it. https://theconversation.com/how-cats-and-dogs-affect-the-climate-and-what-you-can-do-about-it-206812 Retrieved October 3, 2023.

Alexander, P., Berri, A., Moran, D., Reay, D., & Rounsevell, M. D. A. (2020). The global environmental paw print of pet food. *Global Environmental Change*, *65*, 102153. https://doi.org/10.1016/j.gloenvcha.2020.102153

Alger, J. (2021). *Conserving the oceans: The politics of large marine protected areas*. Oxford University Press.

Allen, D., Arathoon, J., & Selby-Fell, H. (2022). Experiences of dog theft and spatial practices of search/ing. *The Geographical Journal*, *188*(4), 518–533. https://doi.org/10.1111/geoj.12474

Allen, J., Doyle, D. M., McCorristine, S., & McMahon, A. (2020). De-extinction, regulation and nature conservation. *Journal of Environmental Law*, *32*(2), 309–322. https://doi.org/10.1093/jel/eqaa009

Allen, T., Murray, K. A., Zambrana-Torrelio, C., Morse, S. S., Rondinini, C., Di Marco, M., Breit, N., Olival, K.J., & Daszak, P. (2017). Global hotspots and correlates of emerging zoonotic diseases. *Nature Communications*, *8*(1), 1124. https://doi.org/10.1038/s41467-017-00923-8

Almiron, N. (2019). Greening animal defense? Examining whether appealing to climate change and the environment is an effective advocacy strategy to reduce oppression of nonhumans. *American Behavioral Scientist*, *63*(8), 1101–1119. https://doi.org/10.1177/0002764219830466

Alomar, M., Palaian, S., & Al-Tabakha, M. M. (2019). Pharmacovigilance in perspective: Drug withdrawals, data mining and policy implications. *F1000Research*, *8*, 2109. https://doi.org/10.12688/f1000research.21402.1

American Public Health Association, & Defra. (2018), Updated September 22, 2022. Policy paper: Animal health and welfare framework. https://www.gov.uk/government/publications/animal-health-and-welfare-framework-2018/animal-health-and-welfare-framework Retrieved August 3, 2023. *AP journal* (2024) Animal Protection Index: United Kingdom. https://api.worldanimalprotection.org/country/united-kingdom Retrieved March 13, 2024.

American Veterinary Medical Association (AVMA). (2023). Pet owners in San Francisco become pet guardians. https://www.avma.org/javma-news/2003–03–01/pet-owners-san-francisco-become-pet-guardians Retrieved October 3, 2023.

Andrew, A. (2021). From fringe to mainstream: How millions got a taste for going vegan. *Guardian*. Accessed via. https://www.theguardian.com/lifeandstyle/2021/oct/10/from-fringe-to-mainstream-how-millions-got-a-taste-for-going-vegan Retrieved March 6, 2024

Angling Trust. (2022). *Fishing Gets Us Talking Again*. Available at: 'Fishing gets us talking again' – Time to Talk Day 2022. anglingtrust.net Retrieved May 14, 2024

Angstadt, J. M. (2023). Can domestic environmental courts implement international environmental law? A framework for institutional analysis. *Transnational Environmental Law*, *12*(2), 318–342. https://doi.org/10.1017/S2047102523000092

Animal and Plant Agency. (2022). Bovine TB: Incidence of TB in cattle in licensed badger control areas in 2013 to 2021. http://www.gov.uk/government/publications/bovine-tb-incidence-of-tb-in-cattle-in-licensed-badger-control-areas-in-2013-to-2021 Retrieved May 14, 2024

Animals Australia. (2023). *Federal Judge Orders Live Cattle Export from Brazil to End*. https://animalsaustralia.org/our-work/government-and-policy/federal-judge-orders-live-cattle-export-from-brazil-to-end/ Retrieved October 16, 2024.

Animal Equality. (2022). *The enforcement problem.* https://animalequality.org.uk/app/uploads/2022/10/Report_The-Enforcement-Problem-in-the-UK.pdf Retrieved February 24, 2024.

Animal Equality. (2023). *The enforcement solution.* https://animalequality.org.uk/app/uploads/2023/02/The_Enforcement_Solution_Report.pdf Retrieved February 24, 2024.

Animal Procedures Committee. (1993). *Report of the Animal Procedures Committee for 1992.* HMSO.

Animal Procedures Committee. (1996). *Report of the Animal Procedures Committee for 1995.* HMSO.

Animal Procedures Committee. (2003). Review of cost–benefit assessment in the use of animals in research. https://assets.publishing.service.gov.uk/media/5a7b35a7e5274a319e77dc1d/cost-benefit-assessment.pdf Retrieved March 6, 2024.

Animal Procedures Committee. (2012). Reporting on Infringements: What should be included in the public domain. https://assets.publishing.service.gov.uk/media/5a7a4207ed915d1a6421c2de/reporting-infringements.pdf Retrieved March 6, 2024.

Animal protection index. (2023). https://api.worldanimalprotection.org/country/united-kingdom Retrieved February 1, 2024.

Anthony, J. (2020). Agriculture minister introduced "unlawful and invalid" pig welfare standards, judge rules. *Stuff News.* https://www.stuff.co.nz/business/farming/123392691/agriculture-minister-introduced-unlawful-and-invalid-pig-welfare-standards-judge-rules Retrieved March 26, 2024.

APG. (2020) All-Party Human Relevant Science Parliamentary Group. https://www.humanrelevantscience.org/wp-content/uploads/APPG-report-March-2022.pdf Retrieved March 13, 2024.

APGAW. (2022). Improving the effectiveness of animal welfare enforcement. https://apgaw.org/wp-content/uploads/2022/08/Improving-Animal-Welfare-Enforcement-Report.pdf Retrieved 8/5/2024.

Appleby, T., & Harrison, J. (2019). Taking the pulse of environmental and fisheries law: The common fisheries policy, the habitats directive, and brexit. *Journal of Environmental Law, 31*(3), 443–464. https://doi.org/10.1093/jel/eqy027

Aquinas, St. T. (1945). 13th century. Summa contra gentiles. In Pegis, A. *The Translator, Basic Writings of Saint Thomas Aquinas* (pp. 220–224). Random House.

Aristotle (1912). Politics. In W. Ellis (Ed.), *The Politics of Aristotle* (pp. 1252–1254). Dent.

Arluke, A. (1994). Managing emotions in an animal shelter. In A. Manning & J. Serpell (Eds.), *Animals and human society: Changing perspectives* (pp. 145–165). Routledge.

Armitage, D., Mbatha, P., Muhl, E.-K., Rice, W., & Sowman, M. (2020). Governance principles for community-centered conservation in the post-2020 global biodiversity framework. *Conservation Science and Practice*, *2*(2). https://doi.org/10.1111/csp2.160

Ashworth, A. (2023). UK creates three new 'highly protected' marine nature reserves in England. http://www.nhm.ac.uk/discover/news/2023/february/uk-creates-three-new-highly-protected-marine-nature-reserves-england.html Retrieved October 15, 2024.

Australian Sports Commission. (2015). Lessons to be learnt, for duty holders and the regulator, from reviews and for duty holders and the regulator, from reviews and investigations into non-compliance. https://assets.publishing.service.gov.uk/media/5a7efd58ed915d74e6227c01/ASClessonsToBeLearnt2Jul14.pdf Retrieved May 14, 2024.

Australian Sports Commission. (2021). Animals sentience committee: Terms or reference. https://data.parliament.uk/DepositedPapers/Files/DEP2022–0007/Animal_Sentience_Committee_Draft_Terms_of_Reference.pdf Retrieved March 13, 2024.

Backler, C. (2012). Cheale Meats animal abusers jailed. https://www.animalaid.org.uk/cheale-meats-animal-abusers-jailed/ Retrieved April 9, 2024.

Badgers Trust. (n.d.). Protection of badgers. http://www.badgertrust.org.uk/protection-of-badgers-act Retrieved May 14, 2024.

Bagniewska, J., & Macdonald, D. (2010). *Executive summary of the report Animal welfare, international development, biodiversity conservation – The road to peaceful coexistence*. Wildlife Communications Conservation Research Unit, Zoology Department, University of Oxford. Report commissioned by RSPCA International.

Baker et al. (2013). Rough trade: Animal welfare in the global wildlife trade. *BioScience*, *63*(12), 928–938. https://doi.org/10.1525/bio.2013.63.12.6

Bakker, K. (2023). *Noise pollution is a menace to humanity – And a deadly threat to animals*. The Guardian Life Insurance Company of America. https://www.theguardian.com/commentisfree/2023/jan/03/noise-pollution-is-a-menace-to-humanity-and-a-deadly-threat-to-animals Retrieved May 14, 2024.

Baldauf, C. (Ed.). (2020). *Participatory biodiversity conservation concepts, experiences, and perspectives* (1st ed.). Springer International Publishing.

Baran, B. E., Rogelberg, S. G., & Clausen, T. (2016). Rountinized killing of animals: Going beyond dirty work and prestige to understand the well-being of slaughterhouse workers. *Organization*, *23*(3), 351–369. https://doi.org/10.1177/1350508416629456

Barkham, P. (2024). Wolves are thriving again across Western Europe. *Is it time to bring them back to the UK? The Guardian*. https://www.theguardian.com/environment/2024/mar/10/derek-gow-the-rewilding-enthusiast-wants-to-bring-back-the-wolf

Barnes, S. (2018). *Rewild Yourself- 23 spellbinding ways to make nature more visible*. Simon & Schuster.

Barrett, M., & Fischer, B. (2023). Challenges in farmed insect welfare:

Beyond the question of sentience. *Animal Welfare*, *32*. https://doi.org/10.1017/awf.2022.5

Barrow, C. (2022). *The State of Britain's Hedgehogs*. http://www.britishhedgehogs.org.uk Retrieved May 14, 2024.

BASC. (2024). Quarry species and shooting seasons. https://basc.org.uk/quarry-species-and-shooting-seasons/ Retrieved May 14, 2024.

BBC News. (2017). Elderly people in struggle to keep pets in care homes, says charity. http://www.bbc.co.uk/news/av/uk-38553330/elderly-people-in-struggle-to-keep-pets-in-care-homes-says-charity Retrieved November 2, 2017.

BBC News. (2019). Boohoo warned over advertising real fur as fake. https://www.bbc.co.uk/news/newsbeat-46809757 Retrieved March 7, 2024.

BBC News. (2020). Confessions of a slaughterhouse worker. https://www.bbc.co.uk/news/stories-50986683 Retrieved March 7, 2024.

BBC News. (2024a). River Wye pollution leads chicken firm to be sued. https://www.bbc.co.uk/news/articles/c06l7e0edx2o Retrieved April 28, 2024.

BBC News. (2024b). Kidderminster woman pleads guilty to role in monkey torture network. https://www.bbc.co.uk/news/uk-england-hereford-worcester-68968718#:~:text=A%20British%20woman%20has%20pleaded,by%20the%20BBC%20Eye%20team. Retrieved May 18, 2024.

Beauchamp, T. L., & Morton, D. B. (2015). The upper limits of pain and suffering in animal research. *Cambridge Quarterly of Healthcare Ethics*, *24*(4), 431–447. https://doi.org/10.1017/S0963180115000092

Beck, A., & Katcher, A. (1996). *Between pets and people: The importance of animal companionship*. Purdue University Press.

Bedford, E. (2023). Expenditure on pets in the United Kingdom 2005–2022. https://www.statista.com/statistics/308266/consumer-spending-on-pets-and-related-products-in-the-united-kingdom-uk/ Retrieved March 13, 2024.

Beirnes, P. (1994). The law is an ass: Reading EP Evans' The medieval prosecution and capital punishment of animals. *Society and Animals*, *2*(1), 27–46. https://doi.org/10.1163/156853094X00063

Bell, S. et al. (2024). *Environmental Law* (10th ed.). Oxford University Press.

Bengston, C. (2012). The Leagues History with badgers. http://www.league.org.uk/media/filer_public/8e/7c/8e7c4c81-b90d-4bb7-b9d6–1724d43e27a7/leagues_history_with_badgers___league_against_cruel_sports.pdf Retrieved May 14, 2024.

Bhagwat, S. A. (2018). *Management of nonnative invasive species in the Anthropocene*. Elsevier.

Biodiversity Law Centre. http://www.biodiversitylaw.org Retrieved May 14, 2024.

Birch, J., Burn, C., Schnell, A., Browning, H., & Crump, A. (2021). Review of the evidence of sentience in cephalopod molluscs and decapod crustaceans. https://www.wellbeingintlstudiesrepository.org/af_gen/2/ Retrieved May 14, 2024.

Birdlife International. (n.d.). http://www.birdlife.org/?gad_source=1&gclid=EAIaIQobChMIvbzRn5T7hQMVrIxQBh30mAbnEAAYASAAEgKlZfD_BwE Retrieved May 14, 2024.

Birds International. (1990) [Annual report]. Birdlife International.

Bishop, P. (2012). Badgers and bovine tuberculosis: The relationship between law, policy and science: *Badger Trust v Welsh* ministers [2010] EWCA Civ 807. *Journal of Environmental Law*, *24*(1), 145–154. https://doi.org/10.1093/jel/eqs001

Blackstone, Sir W. (1794). *Commentaries on the laws of England* (12th ed.), *II*. T. Cadell.

Blattner, C. E. (2019). The recognition of animal sentience by the law. *Journal of Animal Ethics*, *9*(2), 121–136. https://doi.org/10.5406/janimalethics.9.2.0121

Blouin, D. D. (2013). Are dogs children, companions, or just animals? Understanding variations in People's orientations towards animals. *Anthrozoos*, *26*(2), 279–294. https://doi.org/10.2752/175303713X13636846944402

Blunt, W. (1976). *The ark in the park – The zoo in the nineteenth century*. Hamish Hamilton.

Bonas, S., McNicholas, J., & Collis, G. (2000). Pets in the network of family relationships: An empirical study. In A. Podberscek, E. Paul, & J. Serpell (Eds.), *Companion Animals and Us: Exploring the relationships between people and pets* (pp. 209–236). Cambridge University Press.

Borgelt, J., Dorber, M., Høiberg, M. A., & Verones, F. (2022). More than half of data deficient species predicted to be threatened by extinction. *Communications Biology*, *5*(1), 679. https://doi.org/10.1038/s42003-022-03638-9

Borkowski, A. (1994). *Textbook on roman law*. Blackstone Press.

Bostock, S. St C. (1993). *Zoos and animal rights*. Routledge.

Bouvard, V., Loomis, D., Guyton, K. Z., Grosse, Y., Ghissassi, F. E., Benbrahim-Tallaa, L., Guha, N., Mattock, H., Straif, K., & International Agency for Research on Cancer Monograph Working Group. (2015). Carcinogenicity of consumption of red and processed meat. *The Lancet. Oncology*, 16(16), 1599–1600. https://doi.org/10.1016/S1470-2045(15)00444-1

Bowring, J. (1859). *The works of Jeremy Bentham*. Vol 1: Bentham, J. 'The Principles of Modern Penal Law', *Part III*, Chapter XVI. William Tait. Edinburgh.

Boyle, A. E., & Redgwell, C. (2021). *Birnie, Boyle, and Redgwell's international law and the environment*. Oxford University Press.

Brambell, F. W. R. (1965). Report of the technical committee to enquire into the welfare of animals kept under intensive livestock husbandry systems. *The "Brambell Committee"*. (Command Rep. 2836). HMSO.

Brando, S., & Chapman, S. (2023). *Optimal wellbeing of ageing wild animals in human care*. Springer.

Braverman, I. (2012). *Zooland: The institution of captivity* (1st ed.). Stanford University Press.

Breda, I. (2023). makah tribe may soon exercise treaty right to hunt gray whales off wa coast. *Seattle Times*. http://www.seattletimes.com/seattle-news/environment/makah-tribe-may-soon-exercise-treaty-right-to-hunt-gray-whales-off-wa-coast/ Retrieved March 14, 2024.

British association promoting science and technology. (1994). *Animals and the advancement of science*. BAPST.

British Field Sports Society (BFSS). (n.d.). *Hunting the facts*. British and Foreign School Society.

British Veterinary Association. (2018). Brachycephalic dogs policy position. https://www.bva.co.uk/media/4231/bva-position-on-brachycephalic-dogs-full.pdf Retrieved March 13, 2024.

British Veterinary Association. (2023). BSAVA and BVZS. *Response to Defra Consultation*, 18 July 2023.

British Veterinary Association, & BSAVA. (2021). Position on the Dangerous Dogs Act (1991) and dog control. https://www.bva.co.uk/media/4115/full-position-bva-and-bsava-position-on-the-dda-and-dog-control.pdf Retrieved March 13, 2024.

Broom, D. M. (2009). Animal welfare and legislation. In F. J. M. Smulders & B. Algers (Eds.), *Welfare of production animals: Assessment and management of Risks 339–352*. Wageningen Academic Publishers.

Broom, D. M. (2011). A history of animal welfare science. *Acta Biotheoretica*, *59*(2), 121–137. https://doi.org/10.1007/s10441-011-9123-3

Broom, D. M. (2014). *Sentience and animal welfare*. CABI Publishing.

Broom, D. M. (2017). Animal welfare in the European Union—Study for the peti committee. *Directorate general for internal policies EU*.

Broom, D. M. (2018). Animal welfare and international trade. In J. Pan & S. Li (Eds.), *The key role of animal welfare science in the development of green agriculture* (pp. 8–21). Jilin Publishing.

Broom, D. M. (2019). Sentience. In C. Choe & J. (Eds.), *Encyclopedia of animal behaviour* (2nd ed.) (pp. 131–133). Elsevier Ltd.

Broom, D. M. (2022). Animal welfare concepts. In A. Knight, C. Phillips, & P. Sparks (Eds.), *Routledge handbook of animal welfare*. Routledge.

Brooman, S. (2017). Creatures, the academic lawyer and a socio-legal approach: Introducing animal law into the legal education curriculum. *Liverpool Law Review*, *38*(3), 243–257. https://doi.org/10.1007/s10991-017-9205-7

Brooman, S. (2018). Animal Sentience in UK Law: Does the new clause need claws? *UK Journal of Animal Law*, *2*(1), 21–31.

Brooman, S., & Legge, D. (1997). *Law relating to animals*. Cavendish Publishing.

Brooman, S., & Legge, D. (2023). Protection for cruelty for animals in Europe: An improving Picture? *UK Journal of Animal Law*, *7*(1), 1–13.

Brophy, B. (1971). In pursuit of a fantasy. In S. Godlovitch, R. Godlovitch, & J. Harris (Eds.), *Animals, Men and morals, 1971* (pp. 143–144). Victor Gollancz Ltd.

Broughton, R. K., Ramellini, S., Maziarz, M., & Pereira, P. F. (2022). The Red-billed Leiothrix (Leiothrix lutea): A new invasive species for Britain? *Ibis*, *164*(4), 1285–1294. https://doi.org/10.1111/ibi.13090 Accessed March 14, 2024.

Brown, C. (2015). Fish intelligence, sentience and ethics. *Animal Cognition*, *18*(1), 1–17. https://doi.org/10.1007/s10071-014-0761-0

Brown, L. (1989). *Cruelty to animals: The moral debt*. Macmillan.

Browning, H., & Veit, W. (2022, December). The sentience shift in animal research. *The New Bioethics*, *28*(4), 299–314. https://doi.org/10.1080/20502877.2022.2077681

Browning, H., and Veit, W. (2022) The sentience shift in animal research. *The New Bioethics* 28(4), 299–314.

Brumbaugh, R. (1978). Of man, animals, and morals: A brief history. In R. Morris & M. Fox (Eds.), *On the fifth Day*. Acropolis Books Ltd.

Buckland, W. (1932). *A textbook of roman law from Augustus to Justinian*. Cambridge University Press.

Bulsara, M., Wood, L., Giles-Corti, B., & Bosch, D. (2007). More than a furry companion: The ripple effect of companion animals on neighbourhood interactions and sense of community. *Society and Animals*, *15*(1), 43–56. https://doi.org/10.1163/156853007X169333

Burke, A. (2022). An architecture for a net zero world: Global climate governance beyond the epoch of failure. *Global Policy*, *13*(Suppl. 3), 24–37. https://doi.org/10.1111/1758-5899.13159

Burns, F. et al. (2023). State of nature 2023. *the State of Nature partnership*. http://www.stateofnature.org.uk Retrieved March 14, 2024

Burns, J. H., & Hart, H. (1970a). *Jeremy Bentham, an introduction to the principles of morals and legislation*. University of London Press.

Burns, J. H., & Hart, H. L. A. (1970b). *Jeremy Bentham, an introduction to the principles of morals and legislation*. University of London.

Burns et al. (2000). *Committee of Inquiry into hunting with dogs in England and Wales*. HMSO.

Büscher, B., Fletcher, R., Brockington, D., Sandbrook, C., Adams, W. M., Campbell, L., Corson, C., Dressler, W., Duffy, R., Gray, N., Holmes, G., Kelly, A., Lunstrum, E., Ramutsindela, M., & Shanker, K. (2017). Half-earth or whole earth? Radical ideas for conservation, and their implications. *Oryx*, *51*(3), 407–410. https://doi.org/10.1017/S0030605316001228

Byrne, R. (1985). *The thinking ape: Evolutionary origins of intelligence*. Oxford University Press.

Cahoone, L. (2009). Hunting as a moral good. *Environmental Values*, *18*(1), 67–89. https://doi.org/10.3197/096327109X404771

Conservation evidence 2020 and University of Cambridge 2024. http://www.zoo.cam.ac.uk/research/conservation-science/conservation-science Retrieved March 14, 2024.

Cammiss, S., Hayes, G., & Doherty, B. (2022). Necessity, non-violent direct activism, and the Stansted 15: Reasserting "Hoffmann's bargain". *The Modern Law Review*, *85*(6), 1515–1533. https://doi.org/10.1111/1468-2230.12715

Campbell, I. J. (2018). Animal welfare and environmental ethics: It's complicated. *Ethics and the Environment*, *23*(1), 49–69. https://doi.org/10.2979/ethicsenviro.23.1.04

Canham, J. (2022). Landmark progress towards stronger legal protections for fish. *UK Journal of Animal Law*, *6*(2), 21–26.

Capra, F., & Mattei, U. (2015). *The Ecology of law: Toward a legal system in tune with nature and community* (1st ed.). Berrett-Koehler Publishers.

Carbon Brief. (2024). COP16: More than 85% of countries miss UN deadline to submit nature pledges. www.carbonbrief.org/cop16-countries-miss-un-deadline-to-submit-nature-pledges/#:~:text=More%20than%2085%25%20of%20countries%20are%20set%20to%20miss%20the,Carbon%20Brief%20and%20the%20Guardian Retrieved October 29 2024.

Carew, K. (2023). *Beastly, a new history of animals and us*. Canongate Books.

Carruthers, P. (1992). *The animals issue*. Cambridge University Press.

Carson, G. (1972). *Men, beasts and gods*. Charles Scribner's & Sons.

Carson, H. (1917). The trial of animals and insects: A little known chapter of medieval jurisprudence. *American Philosophical Society Journal*, *56*, 410–415.

Carson, R. (1968). *Silent spring*. Penguin Books.

Carvalho, A. F., de Morais, I. O. B., & Souza, T. B. (2023). Profiting from cruelty: Digital content creators abuse animals worldwide to incur profit. *Biological Conservation*, *287*, 110321. https://doi.org/10.1016/j.biocon.2023.110321

Carvalho, C., Gaspar, A., Knight, A., & Vicente, L. (2018). Ethical and scientific pitfalls concerning laboratory research with non-human primates, and possible solutions. *Animals: An Open Access Journal from MDPI*, *9*(1), 12. https://doi.org/10.3390/ani9010012

Carver, S., Convery, I., Hawkins, S., Beyers, R., Eagle, A., Kun, Z., Van Maanen, E., Cao, Y., Fisher, M., Edwards, S. R., Nelson, C., Gann, G. D., Shurter, S., Aguilar, K., Andrade, A., Ripple, W. J., Davis, J., Sinclair, A., Bekoff, M., . . . Soulé, M. (2021). Guiding principles for rewilding. *Conservation Biology*, *35*(6), 1882–1893. https://doi.org/10.1111/cobi.13730

Compassion in World Farming (CIWF) (n.d.) https://www.ciwf.org.uk/farm-animals/pigs/pig-welfare/ Retrieved February 5, 2025.

Conservative animal welfare foundation and animal equality UK. (2018). *The Case for Regular Inspections and Mandatory CCTV in Fish Slaughterhouses*. https://animalequality.org.uk/app/uploads/2022/02/A.nimalEqualityUKCAWF_FishSlaughterReport_Jan22.pdf Retrieved March 4, 2024.

Cassidy, A. (2019). *Vermin, victims and disease: British debates over bovine tuberculosis and badgers* (1st ed.). Springer Nature.

Cassidy, E. S., West, P. C., Gerber, J. S., & Foley, J. A. (2013). Redefining agricultural yields: From tonnes to people nourished per hectare. *Environmental Research Letters*. University of Minnesota, *8*(3), 034015. https://doi.org/10.1088/1748-9326/8/3/034015

Castelló, P. P. (2022). A strategic proposal for legally protecting wild animals. *Journal of International Wildlife Law and Policy*, *25*(2), 103–134. https://doi.org/10.1080/13880292.2022.2103918

Castelló, P.P. (2022) A Strategic Proposal for Legally Protecting Wild Animals. *Journal of International Wildlife Law & Policy* 25(2), 103–134,

Caton, E. (2023). Imports of ivory from hippos and killer whales to be banned in the UK. Natural History Museum. http://www.nhm.ac.uk/discover/news/2023/may/imports-of-ivory-from-hippos-and-killer-whales-to-be-banned-in-the-uk.html Retrieved March 14, 2024.

Cats protection. (2019). *Purrfect landlords: A guide*. https://www.cats.org.uk/media/1571/purrfect-landlords-report.pdf Retrieved March 13, 2024.

Cawardine, M. (2016) What is the Ramsar Convention? *BBC Wildlife Magazine*. BBC. http://www.discoverwildlife.com/people/what-is-t.he-ramsar-convention-everything-you-need-to-know/ Retrieved March 14, 2024

Convention on Biological Diversity (CBD). (n.d.). National biodiversity strategies and action plans. CBD. http://www.cbd.int/nbsap/related-info/region-bsap Retrieved March 14, 2024.

Ceballos-Lascurain, H. (1996). *Tourism, eco-tourism and protected areas*. IV World Congress on National Parks and Protected Areas. International Union for Conservation of Nature.

Centre for Environment, Fisheries and Aquaculture Science. https://www.uea.ac.uk/climate/centre-for-environment-fisheries-and-aquaculture-science#:~:text=Cefas%20is%20an%20executive%20agency,security%20and%20support%20marine%20economies Retrieved March 4, 2024.

Challender, D. W. S., Cremona, P. J., Malsch, K., Robinson, J. E., Pavitt, A. T., Scott, J., Hoffmann, R., Joolia, A., Oldfield, T. E. E., Jenkins, R. K. B., Conde, D. A., Hilton-Taylor, C., & Hoffmann, M. (2023). Identifying species likely threatened by international trade on the IUCN Red List can inform CITES trade measures. *Nature Ecology and Evolution*, *7*(8), 1211–1220. https://doi.org/10.1038/s41559-023-02115-8

Channel Four. (1995). Do vampire bats have friends? *Equinox*, *20*.

Chapman, P. M. (1999). Does the precautionary principle have A role in ecological risk assessment? *Human and Ecological Risk Assessment*, *5*(5), 885–888. https://doi.org/10.1080/10807039991289176

Chapron, G., Epstein, Y., & López-Bao, J. V. (2019). A rights revolution for nature. *Science*, *363*(6434), 1392–1393. https://doi.org/10.1126/science.aav5601

Charles, N., & Davies, C. A. (2008). My family and other animals: Pets as kin. *Sociological Research Online*, *13*(5), 1–12.

Chow, P. Y. S. (2022). Reconsidering sentencing principles in cases of civil disobedience: '*Cuadrilla Bowland Ltd and others v Persons* Unknown and Others. *The Modern Law Review*, *85*(4), 1062–1070. https://doi.org/10.1111/1468-2230.12704

Chow, P. Y. S. (2023). The change in judicial practice in cases concerning civil disobedience protests and its constitutional significance. *The Modern Law Review*, *86*(4), 927–950. https://doi.org/10.1111/1468-2230.12787

Chriki, S., Ellies-Oury, M.-P., & Hocquette, J.-F. (2022). Is "cultured meat" a viable alternative to slaughtering animals and a good comprise between animal welfare and human expectations? *Animal Frontiers: The Review Magazine of Animal Agriculture*, *12*(1), 35–42. https://doi.org/10.1093/af/vfac002

CITES secretariat. (n.d.). http://www.cites.org/eng/disc/sec/index.php. Retrieved March 14, 2024

CITES (n.d.) E-Guidance_mgt_ivorystockpiles.pdf (cites.org) Retrieved October 14, 2024.

Clark, J. (1987). Public concerns for animals in research. *Laboratory Animal Science Special Issue*, January 1987, 120–121.

Clark, S. (1977). *The moral status of animals*. Oxford University Press.

Clark, S. (2011). Animals in classical and late antique philosophy. In T. Beachamp & R. Frey (Eds.), *The Oxford handbook of animal ethics* (pp. 35–60). Oxford University Press.

Clarke, S. (1977). *The moral status of animals*. Oxford University Press.

Clutton-Brock, J. (1994). The Unnatural World: Behavioural aspects of humans and animals in the process of Domestication. In A. Manning & J. A. Serpell (Eds.), *Animals and human society: Changing perspectives* (pp. 23–35). Routledge.

Coates, P. A. (2023). *Squirrel nation: Reds, greys and the meaning of home*. Reaktion Books.

Cochrane, A. (2013). Cosmozoopolis: The case against group-differentiated animal rights. *Law, Ethics and Philosophy*, 127–141.

Code of Practice for the Welfare of Privately Kept nonhuman Primates. (2013). https://www.gov.uk/government/publications/code-of-practice-for-the-welfare-of-privately-kept-non-human-primates Retrieved March 13, 2024.

Coe, J. B., Young, I., Lambert, K., Dysart, L., Nogueira Borden, L., &

Rajić, A. (2014). A scoping review of published research on relinquishment of companion animals. *Journal of Applied Animal Welfare Science*, *17*(3), 253–273. https://doi.org/10.1080/10888705.2014.899910

Council of Europe, Chart of signatures and ratifications of Treaty 125 (European Convention for the Protection of Pet Animals) as at 03/11/2 23. https://www.coc.int/cn/wcb/conventions/full-list?module=signatures-by-treaty&treatynum=125 Retrieved May 13, 2024.

Cohen, C. (1986). The case for the use of animals in biomedical research. *The New England Journal of Medicine*, *315*(14), 865–870. https://doi.org/10.1056/NEJM198610023151405

Cohn, J. P. (1991). Zoos as conservation leaders. *BioScience*, *41*(6), 375.

Colley, C., & Wasley, A. (2023). Suffering of gassed pigs laid bare in undercover footage from UK abattoir. *Guardian Newspaper*. https://www.theguardian.com/environment/2023/may/02/suffering-of-gassed-pigs-laid-bare-in-undercover-footage-from-uk-abattoir Retrieved May 13, 2024.

Colodner, D. C., & Bechert, U. (Eds.). (2023). Local flora and fauna conservation – A role for zoos, aquariums and Botanical Gardens. MDPI—Multidisciplinary Digital Publishing Institute.

Compassion in World Farming. (2009). Beyond factory farming: Sustainable solutions for animals. *People and the Planet*. https://www.compassioninfoodbusiness.com/media/3817096/beyond-factory-farming-report.pdf Retrieved March 6, 2024.

Compassion in World Farming. (2016). Millions of Animals Suffer as EU Live Exports repeatedly break the Law. https://www.ciwf.org.uk/media/press-releases-statements/2016/02/millions-of-animals-suffer-as-eu-live-exports-repeatedly-break-the-law Retrieved May 13, 2024.

Compassion in World Farming. (September 2017). Long-distance live transport: Common problems and practical solutions. https://www.ciwf.org.uk/research/live-transport/.

Compassion in World Farming. (2018). *Humane Slaughter: Atlantic salmon*. https://www.compassioninfoodbusiness.com/media/7434842/humane-slaughter-atlantic-salmon.pdf Retrieved February 24, 2024.

Compassion in World Farming. (n.d.-a). Farm animals: Chickens. https://www.ciwf.org.uk/farm-animals/chickens/ Retrieved March 7, 2024.

Compassion in World Farming. (n.d.-b). Pig welfare. https://www.ciwf.org.uk/farm-animals/pigs/pig-welfare/ Retrieved March 7, 2024.

Compassion in World Farming. (n.d.-c). Farm animals. https://www.ciwf.org.uk/farm-animals/ Retrieved March 7, 2024.

Convention on International Trade in Endangered Species of Wild Fauna and Flora. (n.d.). http://www.cites.org/eng Retrieved March 14, 2024.

Cook, E. A. J., de Glanville, W. A., Thomas, L. F., Kariuki, S., Bronsvoort, B. M. C., & Fèvre, E. M. (2017). Working conditions and public health

risks in slaughterhouses in western Kenya. *BMC Public Health*, *17*(1), 14. https://doi.org/10.1186/s12889-016-3923-y
Cooke, R. (1996). *Natures' place* (11, March). English Nature.
Copernicus. (n.d.). http://www.copernicus.eu/en.
Coplan, K. S., Green, S. D., & Fischer Kuh, K. (2021). *Climate change law: An introduction* (1st ed.). Edward Elgar Publishing Limited.
Cornford, R., Spooner, F., McRae, L., Purvis, A., & Freeman, R. (2023). Ongoing over-exploitation and delayed responses to environmental change highlight the urgency for action to promote vertebrate recoveries by 2030. *Proceedings. Biological Sciences*, *290*(1997), 20230464–20230464. https://doi.org/10.1098/rspb.2023.0464
Council of Europe. (2024a). Case File dashboard. http://www.coe.int/en/web/bern-convention/active-cases Retrieved March 14, 2024.
Council of Europe. (2024b). Emerald Network of Areas of Special Conservation Interest. http://www.coe.int/en/web/bern-convention/emerald-network Retrieved March 16, 2024.
Council of Europe. (n.d.). http://www.coe.int/en/web/portal Retrieved March 14, 2024.
Countryside Alliance. (2017). The RSPCA, bad governance and a shaky future for animal welfare. https://www.countryside-alliance.org/resources/news/the-rspca-bad-governance-and-a-shaky-future-for-a Retrieved May 13, 2024.
CPS. (2022a). Hare coursing. http://www.cps.gov.uk/legal-guidance/hare-coursng)0.1136/vr.m1350 Accessed March 14, 2024.
CPS. (2022b). Hare coursing. http://www.cps.gov.uk/legal-guidance/hare-coursing Retrieved March 14, 2024.
CPS. (n.d.). Hunting act 20024. http://www.cps.gov.uk/legal-guidance/hunting-act-2004.
Cravens, Z. M., & Boyles, J. G. (2019). Illuminating the physiological implications of artificial light on an insectivorous bat community. *Oecologia*, *189*(1), 69–77. https://doi.org/10.1007/s00442-018-4300-6
Crick, F. (2012). The Cambridge declaration on consciousness Memorial Conference. https://fcmconference.org/img/CambridgeDeclarationOnConsciousness.pdf. Retrieved April 21, 2024.
Croft-Cooke, R., & Cotes, P. (1976). *Circus a world history*. Elek.
Crowley, S. L., Hinchliffe, S., & McDonald, R. A. (2017). Conflict in invasive species management. *Frontiers in Ecology and the Environment*, *15*(3), 133–141. https://doi.org/10.1002/fee.1471
Cruelty Free international. (2015). *Cruelty Free International Slams Unacceptable Levels of Suffering in UK Laboratories*. https://crueltyfreeinternational.org/latest-news-and-updates/cruelty-free-international-slams-unacceptable-levels-animal-suffering-uk Retrieved May 13, 2024.
Cuerda, E., & Lopez-Munoz, F. (2013). Ethical considerations of the

human research: Syphilis experiments and denial of drug therapy. *Clinical and Experimental Pharmacology*, *3*(3).

Cullinan, C. (2011). *Wild law: A manifesto for earth justice* (2nd ed.). Green Books Book Company.

Cupp, Jr., R. L. (2013). Children, chimps, and rights: Arguments from "marginal" cases. *Arizona State Law Journal*, *45*, 1–52.

Cusato, E., & Jones, E. (2024). The'imbroglio'of ecocide: A political economic analysis. *Leiden Journal of International Law*, *37*(1), 42–61.

Cuthbert, R. N., Diagne, C., Haubrock, P. J., Turbelin, A. J., & Courchamp, F. (2022). Are the "100 of the world's worst" invasive species also the costliest? *Biological Invasions*, *24*(7), 1895–1904. https://doi.org/10.1007/s10530-021-02568-7

Cuthill, I. C. (2007). Ethical regulation and animal science: Why animal behaviour is not so special. *Animal Behaviour*, *74*(1), 15–22. https://doi.org/10.1016/j.anbehav.2007.04.003

Cyca, M. et al. (2023). We're tired of waiting: the First Nation that unilaterally declared a marine protected area. *The Guardian*. MPA. http://www.theguardian.com/environment/2023/may/03/canada-first-nation-that-unilaterally-declared-a-marine-protected-area#:~:text='My%20community%20basically%20said%2C%20%27,marine%20protected%20area%20 Retrieved March 14, 2024.

Daggett, H. (1792). The rights of animals: An oration. Delivered at the Commencement of Providence-College, September 7, 1791. David Frothingham.

Dancer, H. et al. (2024). *UK earth law judgments: Reimagining law for people and planet*. Hart Publishing.

Darnell, H. (2022). The protection of badgers: Where are we now? *UK Journal of Animal Law*, *6*(2), 27–36.

Darwin, C. (1871). *The descent of Man*. (1981 ed.). Princeton University Press.

Darwin, C. (1872). *The expression of the emotions in Man and animals* (1979 ed.), Friedman.

Davies, M. (2022). *EcoLaw: Legality, life, and the normativity of nature*. Routledge.

Davis, S. J. M., & Valla, F. R. (1978). Evidence for the domestication of the dog 12,000 years ago in Natufian of Israel. *Nature*, *276*(5688), 608–610. https://doi.org/10.1038/276608a0

Day, C. (2023). Judicial Review and nature cases in the UK: Current challenges and future opportunities. In A. L. R. Jackson (Ed.), *Nature law and policy in Europe*. Routledge.

de Vere, A. J., & Kuczaj, S. A. (2016). Where are we in the study of animal emotions? *Wiley Interdisciplinary Reviews. Cognitive Science*, *7*(5), 354–362. https://doi.org/10.1002/wcs.1399

Defra. (2018). Code of practice for the welfare of meat chickens and meat breeding chickens. https://assets.publishing.service.gov.uk/

media/5ab525afed915d78b9a45b0f/meat-chicken-code-march2018.pdf Retrieved May 13, 2024.

Defra. (2023a). The mandatory use of closed circuit television in slaughterhouses (England) *Regulations* 2018: Post Implementation Review. https://www.legislation.gov.uk/uksi/2018/556/pdfs/uksiod_20180556_en_001.pdf Retrieved March 4, 2024.

Defra. (2021a). The fur market in Great Britain. https://consult.defra.gov.uk/animal-welfare-in-trade/fur-market-in-great-britain/#:~:text=Overview,animals%20trapped%20for%20their%20fur. Retrieved March 5, 2024.

Defra. (2021a). *Our action plan for animal welfare*. Defra.

Defra. (2021b). Action plan for animal welfare. https://www.gov.uk/government/publications/action-plan-for-animal-welfare/action-plan-for-animal-welfare#foreword-by-the-secretary-of-state-for-environment-food-and-rural-affairs Retrieved March 5, 2024.

Defra. (2023a). http://www.gov.uk/government/organisations/department-for-environment-food-rural-affairs Retrieved March 14, 2024.

Defra. (2023b). Enforcement of animal health and welfare offences. https://consult.defra.gov.uk/animal-health-and-welfare/penalty-notices-for-ahw-offences-in-england/supporting_documents/Introducing%20penalty%20notices%20for%20animal%20health%20and%20welfare%20offences%20in%20England.pdf Retrieved March 4, 2024.

Defra. (2023c). Government sets our plans to ban the keeping of primates as pets. https://www.gov.uk/government/news/government-sets-out-proposals-to-ban-the-keeping-primates-as-pets Retrieved October 6, 2023.

Defra. (2024a). http://www.gov.uk/government/organisations/department-for-environment-food-rural-affairs.

Defra. (2024b). Government backs new pet abduction law in pet theft crackdown. https://www.gov.uk/government/news/government-backs-new-pet-abduction-law-in-pet-theft-crackdown Retrieved May 9, 2024.

Defra. (2024c). Government announces TB eradication strategy refresh to end the badger cull. https://deframedia.blog.gov.uk/2024/09/02/government-announces-tb-eradication-strategy-to-end-the-badger-cull/ Retrieved October 17 2024.

DeGrazia, D. (2016). Meat eating. In S. Armstrong & R. Botzler (Eds.), *The animal ethics reader* (3rd ed.) (pp. 245–251). Routledge.

Delon, N. (2019). Beyond the personhood paradigm. *ASEBL Journal*, *14*(1), 26–29.

DeMello, M. (2012). *Animals and Society: An introduction to Human-Animal Studies*. Columbia University Press.

Descartes, R. (1637). Discourse V. In Veitch, J. *The Translator*, Descartes,

R. (1912). A discourse on method, Everyman edition. *Dent, (London, UK), V*, 43–46.

Descartes, R. (1960). *The rationalists* (pp. 450–451). Dolphin Books.

Dhar, V. (2023). The paradigm shifts in artificial intelligence. https://doi.org/10.48550/arxiv.2308.02558

Diamond, J. (1991). *The rise and fall of the third chimpanzee.* Vintage Book Company.

Dias, B. F. S. (2020). The slow but steady progress in the implementation of the biodiversity agenda. http://www.iucn.org/news/world-commission-environmental-law/202007/slow-steady-progress-implementation-biodiversity-agenda Retrieved March 14, 2024.

Dillard, J. (2008). A slaughterhouse nightmare: Psychological harm suffered by slaughterhouse employees and the possibility of redress through legal reform. *Georgetown Journal on Poverty Law and Policy*, *15*, 391.

Directorate general for environment. (no date). *Natura* 2000. European Commission. http://www.environment.ec.europa.eu/topics/nature-and-biodiversity/natura-2000_en Retrieved May 16, 2024..

Doke, S. K., & Dhawale, S. C. (2015). Alternatives to animal testing: A review. *Saudi Pharmaceutical Journal*, *23*(3), 223–229. https://doi.org/10.1016/j.jsps.2013.11.002

Dolman, S. et al. (2016). Fulfilling EU laws to ensure marine mammal protection during marine renewable construction operations in Scotland. *Advances in Experimental Medicine and Biology*, *875*, 223–230. https://doi.org/10.1007/978–1-4939–2981–8_26

Dolman, S.J. et al. (2016). Fulfilling EU laws to ensure marine mammal protection during marine renewable construction operations in Scotland. *Effects of Noise on Aquatic Life II*, *875*, 223–230. https://doi.org/10.1007/978-1-4939-2981-8_26.

Donaldson, S., & Kymlicka, W. (2011). *Zoopolis: A political theory of animal rights*. Oxford University Press.

Dorset Wildlife Trust. (n.d.). Badgers and bovine tuberculosis. http://www.dorsetwildlifetrust.org.uk/things-do/actfornature/badgers-and-bovine-tuberculosis-btb Retrieved March 14, 2024.

Draper, C. (2011) The Zoo Licencing Act 1981 and the welfare of animals in uk zoos. *Journal of Animal Welfare Law*, March 2011.

Du Toit, L., & Kotzé, L. J. (2022). Reimagining international environmental law for the Anthropocene: An earth system law perspective. *Earth System Governance*, *11*, 100–132. https://doi.org/10.1016/j.esg.2022.100132

Dubois, S., Fenwick, N., Ryan, E. A., Baker, L., Baker, S. E., Beausoleil, N. J., Carter, S., Cartwright, B., Costa, F., Draper, C., Griffin, J., Grogan, A., Howald, G., Jones, B., Littin, K. E., Lombard, A. T., Mellor, D. J., Ramp, D., Schuppli, C. A., & Fraser, D. (2017). International consensus principles for ethical wildlife control. *Conservation Biology*, *31*(4), 753–760. https://doi.org/10.1111/cobi.12896

Dunn, R. (2019) For Fur's Sake. Can the UK ban imports of fur from other countries. *UK Journal of Animal Law, 3*(1), 42–49.

Dunn, R. (2021). Brexit: A boon or a curse for animals used in scientific procedures? *Animals: An Open Access Journal from MDPI, 11*(6), 1547. https://doi.org/10.3390/ani11061547

Dunn, R., & Jowitt, J. (2024). The animal sentience committee: Evolution or revolution in the legal recognition of animal sentience in the UK? In *Kotzmann*, J. and Rodriguez Ferrere, M.B. *The Legal Recognition of Animal Sentience: Principles, Approaches and Applications*. Hart Publishing.

Dunn, R., Rook, D., Sparks, P., & Mitchell, T. (2023). Teaching Animal Law in UK universities: The benefits, challenges and opportunities for growth. *The Law Teacher, 57*(1), 15–37. https://doi.org/10.1080/03069400.2022.2129333

Dunn, R. et al. (2023). Investigating the English public's awareness of the Bern Convention and their education on environmental issues and laws. *Legal* Studies, *43*(3), 402–424. https://doi.org/10.1017/lst.2022.37

Dunoff, J. et al. (2023). *International law: Norms, actors, process*. Aspen Publishers.

ECHA. (2024). European Chemicals Agency: Alternatives to animal testing under REACH. https://echa.europa.eu/animal-testing-under-reach Retrieved May 13, 2024

Edwards, R., & Marsh, F. (1978). *Reasonableness, murder and modern science*. 58 *Phi Kappa Phi Journal*, 24–29.

Efra. (2018). Fur trade in the UK [Summary]. https://publications.parliament.uk/pa/cm201719/cmselect/cmenvfru/823/82303.htm Retrieved March 4, 2024.

EIA. (2024). http://www.eia-international.org Retrieved March 14, 2024.

Eisen, J. (2019). Down on the farm: Status, exploitation, and agricultural exceptionalism. In C. E. Blattner, K. Coulter, & W. Kymlicka (Eds.), *Animal Labour: A new frontier of interspecies justice?* Oxford University Press.

Eisnitz, G. A. (2006). *Slaughterhouse: The shocking story of greed, neglect, and inhumane treatment inside the US meat industry*. Prometheus Books.

Ellison, P. C. (2017). Enforcing the animal cruelty laws should not be charity case. *Penn Undergraduate Law Journal, 4*(2), 1–11.

Enders-Slegers, M. (2000). The meaning of companion animals: Qualitative analysis of the life histories of elderly cat and dog owners. In A. Podberscek, E. Paul, & A. Serpell (Eds.), *Companion Animals and Us: Exploring the relationships between people and pets* (pp. 237–256). Cambridge University Press.

Engel, M., & Comstock, G. (Eds.). (2016). *The moral rights of animals*. Lexington Books.

Enticott, G., Donaldson, A., Lowe, P., Power, M., Proctor, A., & Wilkinson, K. (2011). The changing role of veterinary expertise in the food chain. *Philosophical Transactions of the Royal Society of London. Series*

B, Biological Sciences, *366*(1573), 1955–1965. https://doi.org/10.1098/rstb.2010.0408

Environmental Investigations Agency. (1994). *News*. EIA.

Epstein, Y., & Bernet Kempers, E. (2023). Animals and nature as rights holders in the European Union. *The Modern Law Review*, *86*(6), 1336–1357. https://doi.org/10.1111/1468-2230.12816

ESFA. (2020) Welfare of pigs at slaughter. *EFSA Journal*. European Food Safety Authority, *18*(6).

Espin, R. (2018). Reintroducing wildlife into the United Kingdom: Practical and welfare perspectives. *UK Journal of Animal Law*, *2*(2), 39–48.

Ethirajan, A. (2023). Sri Lanka's endangered elephants are dying at an unprecedented rate. *BBC News*. BBC. http://www.bbc.co.uk/news/world-asia-68090450 Retrieved March 14, 2024.

Eurogroup for Animal Welfare. (1994). *Analysis of major areas of concern for animal welfare in Europe*. Eurogroup for Animal Welfare.

Eurogroup for Animals. (2023a). Landmark ruling against unethical dog breeding in Norway. https://www.eurogroupforanimals.org/news/landmark-ruling-against-unethical-dog-breeding-norway Retrieved May 13, 2024.

Eurogroup for Animals. (2023b). Live animal exports might be banned in Brazil – Setting the scene for the kind of change we want to see in Europe. https://www.eurogroupforanimals.org/news/live-animal-exports-might-be-banned-brazil-setting-scene-kind-change-we-want-see-europe Retrieved May 13, 2024.

Eurogroup for Animals. (n.d.). http://www.eurogroupforanimals.org Retrieved March 14, 2024.

European Commission. (2017a). Commission staff working document. https://eur-lex.europa.eu/legal-content/EN/TXT/PDF/?uri=SWD:2017:353:REV1&from=EN Retrieved May 13, 2024.

European Commission. (2017b). Report from the Commission to the European Parliament, the Council, the European Economic and Social Committee and the Committee of the Regions in accordance with Article. *EU on the protection of animals used for scientific purposes*, *58* of Directive 2010/63. https://eur-lex.europa.eu/legal-content/EN/TXT/?qid=1510219889073&uri=COM:2017:631:FIN Retrieved May 13, 2024.

European Commission. (2024). Reports under Directive 2010/63. EU. https://environment.ec.europa.eu/topics/chemicals/animals-science_en Retrieved May 13, 2024.

European Commission. (n.d.). http://www.commission.europa.eu/index_en Retrieved March 14, 2024.

European Commission. Directorate-General for Maritime Affairs and Fisheries. (2023). http://www.commission.europa.eu/about-european-commission/departments-and-executive-agencies/maritime-affairs-and-fisheries_en Retrieved March 14, 2024.

European Communities. (November 25, 2013). Measures prohibiting the importation and marketing of seal products, panel [Report]. *WTO Docs WT/DS400/R, WT/DS401/R, WT/DS*400/R/Add1, WT/DS401/R/Add1 (European Commission. *Seal products (panel)*), Paragraphs 7.409, 7.420.

European Council. (1986). *Council Directive (86/609) of 24 November 1986 on the approximation of laws, regulations and administrative provisions of the Member States regarding the protection of animals used for experimental and other scientific purposes (OJ L358/1 p.p. 1–13)*. European Environment Agency. http://www.eea.europa.eu/en Retrieved March 14, 2024

European Council of the European Union. (n.d.). http://www.consilium.europa.eu/en/ Retrieved March 14, 2024.

European Environment Agency. (n.d,) www.eea.europa.eu/en Retrieved October 15 2024.

European Food Safety Authority (EFSA). (2020). Welfare of pigs at Slaughter. https://www.efsa.europa.eu/en/efsajournal/pub/6148.

European Parliament. (2002). *Report on Directive 86/609 on the protection of animals used for experimental and other scientific purposes*. https://www.europarl.europa.eu/doceo/document/A-5–2002–0387_EN.html Retrieved May 13, 2024.

European Union. (1997) [Protocol], *33* on the protection and welfare of animals. http://eur-lex.europa.eu/legal-content/EN/TXT/?uri=CELEX:12006E/PRO/33 Retrieved March 6, 2024.

European Union. (2023). *Commission proposes new rules to improve animal welfare* [Press release]. Brussels. https://ec.europa.eu/commission/presscorner/detail/en/ip_23_6251 Retrieved March 7, 2024.

Evans, E. P. (1907). The criminal prosecution and capital punishment of animals. *The American Law Register*. Faber & Faber, 55(5), 10–11. https://doi.org/10.2307/3307180. Reproduced with kind permission of Faber & Faber

Evans, M. (2023). RSPCA warns UK dog fighting on the rise and reveal hotspots. *The Northern Echo*. https://www.thenorthernecho.co.uk/news/national/uk-today/23657547.rspca-warns-uk-dog-fighting-rise-reveal-hotspots/.

Eves, D. (2006). *The Eves review: Review of the animal health and welfare delivery*.

Ewaso Lions (2024). http://www.ewasolions.org Retrieved March 14, 2024.

Fair, J. (2023). Whale conservation. *Science Focus*. BBC Magazine, 60–65.

Fairholme, E. G., & Pain, W. (1924). *A century of work for animals: The history of the RSPCA, 1824–1924*. John Murray.

Farm Animal Welfare Council. (2003). *Report on the welfare of farmed animals at slaughter or killing, Part 1: Red meat animals*. Defra Publications. https://assets.publishing.service.gov.uk/media/5a7ed35f40f0b62305b836b2/FAWC_report_on_the_welfare_of_farmed_animals_at_slaughter_or_killing_part_one_red_meat_animals.pdf Retrieved May 13, 2024.

Farm Animal Welfare Council. (2009). *Farm animal welfare in Great Britain: Past, present and future.*

Farmed Animal Welfare Committee. (2015a). Opinion on CCTV in slaughterhouses. https://assets.publishing.service.gov.uk/media/5a806a6be5274a2e87db9af6/Opinion_on_CCTV_in_slaughterhouses.pdf Retrieved March 4, 2024.

Farmed Animal Welfare Committee. (2015b). Opinion on the welfare of farmed fish. https://assets.publishing.service.gov.uk/media/5a7e2cd640f0b62302689a6a/Opinion_on_the_welfare_of_farmed_fish.pdf Retrieved March 4, 2024.

Fasel, R. N., & Butler, S. C. (2023). *Animal rights law.* Bloomsbury Publishing.

Fasoli, E., & McGlone, A. (2018). 'The Non-Compliance Mechanism Under the Aarhus Convention as 'Soft' enforcement of international environmental law: Not so soft after all. *Netherlands International Law Review, 65*(1), 27–53. https://doi.org/10.1007/s40802-018-0102-0 Accessed March 14, 2024.

Favre, D. (2010). Living property: A new status for animals within the legal system. *Marquette Law Review, 93*, 1021–1071.

Favre, D. (2021). *The future of animal law.* Edward Elgar Publishing Ltd.

Feber, R. E., Johnson, P. J., & Macdonald, D. W. (2020). Shooting pheasants for sport: What does the death of Cecil tell us? *People and Nature, 2*(1), 82–95. https://doi.org/10.1002/pan3.10068 Accessed March 14, 2024.

Feinberg, J. (2017). The rights of animals and unborn generations. In S. Vanderheiden (Ed.), *Environmental rights* (pp. 241–265). Routledge.

Ferguson, D. (2019). How the Victorians turned mere beasts into man's best friends. *The Guardian.* https://www.theguardian.com/lifeandstyle/2019/oct/19/pets-how-victorians-turned-beats-into-mans-best-friends Retrieved November 1, 2023.

Fielding, R. (2022). Whalers in "A post-whaling world": Sustainable conservation of marine mammals and sustainable development of whaling communities—With a case study from the eastern Caribbean. *Sustainability, 14*(14), 8782. https://doi.org/10.3390/su14148782

Fiori, L. *et al.* (2019) 'Effects of whale-based tourism in Vava'u, Kingdom of Tonga: Behavioural responses of humpback whales to vessel and swimming tourism activities', *PloS one,* 14(7), pp. e0219364–e0219364. https://doi.org/10.1371/journal.pone.0219364.

Finlayson, C. M., Fennessy, S., Grillas, P., & Kumar, R. (2022). Commemorating the 50th anniversary of the Ramsar Convention on Wetlands. *Marine and Freshwater Research, 73*(10), i–v. https://doi.org/10.1071/MF22161

Finnis, J. (1980). *Natural law and Natural Rights.* Clarendon Press.

Fischer, C. P., & Romero, L. M. (2019). Chronic captivity stress in wild animals is highly species-specific. *Conservation Physiology, 7*(1), coz093. https://doi.org/10.1093/conphys/coz093

Fitzgerald, A. J. (2007). 'They gave me a reason to live': The protective effects of companion animals on the suicidality of abused women. *Humanity and Society*, *31*(4), 355–378. https://doi.org/10.1177/016059760703100405

Fitzgerald, A. J., Kalof, L., & Dietz, T. (2009). Slaughterhouses and increased crime rates: An empirical analysis of the spillover from "the jungle" into the surrounding community. *Organization and Environment*, *22*(2), 158–184. https://doi.org/10.1177/1086026609338164

Fletcher, M.-S., Hamilton, R., Dressler, W., & Palmer, L. (2021). Indigenous knowledge and the shackles of wilderness. *Proceedings of the National Academy of Sciences of the United States of America*, *118*(40), e2022218118. https://doi.org/10.1073/pnas.2022218118

Flynn, C. (2000a). Battered women and their animal companions: Symbolic interaction between human and nonhuman animals. *Society and Animals*, *8*, 99–127. https://doi.org/10.1163/156853000511032.

Flynn, C. (2009). Women-battering, pet abuse, and human–animal relationships'. In A. Linzey (Ed.), *The link between animal abuse and human violence* (pp. 116–125). Sussex Academic Press.

Flynn, C. P. (2000b). Woman's best friend: Pet abuse and the role of companion animals in the lives of battered women. *Violence Against Women*, *6*(2), 162–177. https://doi.org/10.1177/10778010022181778

Food and Agriculture Organization of the United Nations. (2020). Global remote sensing survey. https://www.fao.org/3/cb7449en/cb7449en.pdf Retrieved March 4, 2024

Food Standards Agency. (2021) Business Committee Meeting: Animal Welfare Update. Available. https://www.food.gov.uk/sites/default/files/media/document/fsa-21-09-15-animal-welfare.pdf Retrieved March 4, 2024.

Foreign and Commonwealth Office. (2023). Looking North The UK and the artic. *The UK's Artic. Policy Framework, (London)*. http://www.gov.uk/government/publications/looking-north-the-uk-and-the-arctic/looking-north-the-uk-and-the-arctic-the-united-kingdoms-arctic-policy-framework. Retrieved May 23, 2024.

Foreman, D. (2004). *Rewilding North America: A vision for conservation in the 21st century* Island Press.

Forst, M. (2024). State repression of environmental protest and civil disobedience: A major threat to human rights and democracy. Available at: UNSR_EnvDefenders_Aarhus_Position_Paper_Civil_Disobedience_EN.pdf (unece.org) Retrieved March 14, 2024.

Fox, M., & Ray, M. (2019). No pets allowed? Companion animals, older people and residential care. *Medical Humanities*, *45*(2), 211–222. https://doi.org/10.1136/medhum-2019-011651

Franceschini, M. M. (2021). Legal personhood: The case of Chucho the Andean bear. *Journal of Animal Ethics*, *11*(1), 36–46. https://doi.org/10.5406/janimalethics.11.1.0036

Francione, G. (1996). *Rain without thunder: The ideology of the animal rights movement*. Temple University Press.

Francione, G. (2004). *Animals, property and the law*. Temple University Press.

Francione, G. (2015). *Animal rights: The abolitionist approach* p. 2015. Exempla Press.

Francione, G. L., & Charlton, A. E. (2017). Animal rights. In L. Kalof (Ed.), *The Oxford handbook of animal studies* (pp. 25–42). Oxford University Press.

Frank, D. M. (2021). Disagreement or denialism? "Invasive species denialism" and ethical disagreement in science. *Synthese*, *198*(Suppl. 25), 6085–6113. https://doi.org/10.1007/s11229-019-02259-w

Free, B. (2022). Time to end the fur trade in Britain. https://www.bornfree.org.uk/news/time-to-end-the-fur-trade-in-britain/ Retrieved April 29, 2024.

Free, B. (2024). Zoos – A matter of public trust. http://www.bornfree.org.uk/news/zoos-a-matter-of-public-trust. Retrieved May 19, 2024.

French, R. (1975). *Anti-vivisection and medical science in Victorian society*. Princeton University Press.

Frey, R. (1980). *Interests and rights: The case against animals*. Clarendon Press.

Friedmann, E., Katcher, A. H., Lynch, J. J., & Thomas, S. A. (1980). Animal companions and one-year survival of patients after discharge from a coronary unit. *Public Health Reports*, *95*(4), 307–312.

Friedmann, E., Thomas, S. A., & Eddy, T. (2000). Companion animals and human health: Physical and cardiovascular influences. In A. Podberscek, E. Paul, & J. Serpell (Eds.), *Companion Animals and Us: Exploring the relationships between people and pets* (pp. 125–142). Cambridge University Press.

Friedmann, E., Thomas, S. A., Son, H., Chapa, D., & Mccune, S. (2013). Pet's presence and owner's blood pressures during the daily lives of pet owners with pre-to-mild hypertension. *Anthrozoos*, *26*(4), 535–550. https://doi.org/10.2752/175303713X13795775536138

Friese, C., & Marris, C. (2014). Making De- extinction mundane? *PLOS Biology*, *12*(3), e1001825. https://doi.org/10.1371/journal.pbio.1001825

Fur Free Alliance. (2016). Real fur falsely sold as "faux fur" by 17 retailers. https://www.furfreealliance.com/real-fur-falsely-sold-faux-fur-17-retailers/. Retrieved March 4, 2024.

Fur Free Alliance. (n.d.).a) Fur Farming. Available at: https://www.furfreealliance.com/fur-farming/ Retrieved March 4, 2024.

Fur Free Alliance. (n.d.).b) Fur bans. Available at: https://www.furfreealliance.com/fur-bans/ (Retrieved March 4, 2024).

Gaget, E., Le Viol, I., Pavón-Jordán, D., Cazalis, V., Kerbiriou, C., Jiguet, F., Popoff, N., Dami, L., Mondain-Monval, J. Y., Defos du Rau, P., Abdou, W. A. I., Bozic, L., Dakki, M., Encarnação, V. M. F., Erciyas-Yavuz, K., Etayeb, K. S., Molina, B., Petkov, N.,

Uzunova, D., . . . Galewski, T. (2020). Assessing the effectiveness of the Ramsar Convention in preserving wintering waterbirds in the Mediterranean. *Biological Conservation, 243*. https://doi.org/10.1016/j.biocon.2020.108485

Gaget, E., Pavón-Jordán, D., Johnston, A., Lehikoinen, A., Hochachka, W. M., Sandercock, B. K., Soultan, A., Azafzaf, H., Bendjedda, N., Bino, T., Božič, L., Clausen, P., Dakki, M., Devos, K., Domsa, C., Encarnação, V., Erciyas-Yavuz, K., Faragó, S., Frost, T., . . . Brommer, J. E. (2021). Benefits of protected areas for nonbreeding waterbirds adjusting their distributions under climate warming. *Conservation Biology, 35*(3), 834–845. https://doi.org/10.1111/cobi.13648

Gaia Foundation. (n.d.). http:// www.gaiafoundation.org/areas-of-work/earth-jurisprudence/#:~:text=In%20recent%20years%20there%20has,a%20growing%20number%20of%20precedents Retrieved March 14, 2024.

Galvin, R. W. (1985). What rights for animals?: A modest proposal. *Pace Environmental Law Review, 2*(2), 245. https://doi.org/10.58948/0738-6206.1191

Gandy, M. (2022). An Arkansas parable for the Anthropocene. *Annals of the American Association of Geographers, 112*(2), 368–386. https://doi.org/10.1080/24694452.2021.1935692

García Pinillos, R., Appleby, M. C., Manteca, X., Scott-Park, F., Smith, C., & Velarde, A. (2016). One Welfare – A platform for improving human and animal welfare. *The Veterinary Record, 179*(16), 412–413. https://doi.org/10.1136/vr.i5470

García-Díaz, P., Cassey, P., Norbury, G., Lambin, X., Montti, L., Pizarro, J. C., Powell, P. A., Burslem, D. F. R. P., Cava, M., Damasceno, G., Fasola, L., Fidelis, A., Huerta, M. F., Langdon, B., Linardaki, E., Moyano, J., Núñez, M. A., Pauchard, A., Phimister, E., . . . Tomasevic, J. A. (2021). Management policies for invasive alien species: Addressing the impacts rather than the species. *BioScience, 71*(2), 174–185. https://doi.org/10.1093/biosci/biaa139

García Ruales, J. Hovden, K. Kopnina, H. Robertson, C.D. Schoukens, H. (2024) *Rights of nature in Europe encounters and visions*. Routledge.

Gardner, R., Gardner, B., & Van Cantfort, T. (1989). *Teaching sign language to chimpanzees*. State University of New York Press.

Garfield, S. (2020). *Dog's best friend: A brief history of an unbreakable bond*. Weidenfeld & Nicolson.

Garlick, S., Matthews, J., & Carter, J. (2011). Countering brutality to wildlife, relationism and ethics: Conservation, welfare and the "Ecoversity". *Animals (Basel), 1*(1), 161–175. https://doi.org/10.3390/ani1010161

Garner, R. (1993) *Animals, politics and morality*. Manchester University Press.

Garner, R. (2006). Animal welfare: Political defense. *Journal of Animal Law and Ethics, 1*, 161–174.

Gaveau, D.L.A. et al. (2016) Rapid conversions and avoided deforestation:

examining four decades of industrial plantation expansion in Borneo. *Scientific Reports*, *6*(1), 32017–32017. https://doi.org/10.1038/srep32017

Gayle, D. (2023). Private jet service for rich dog owners condemned by climate campaigners. The Guardian newspaper. https://www.theguardian.com/environment/2023/sep/30/private-jet-service-for-rich-dog-owners-condemned-by-climate-campaigners Retrieved October 3, 2023.

Gerber, P., Opio, C., & Steinfeld, H. (2008). Poultry production and the environment—A review. Animal Production and Health Division, Food and Agriculture Organization of the United Nations p. 3. http://www.fao.org/ag/againfo/home/events/bangkok2007/docs/part2/2_2.pdf Retrieved May 13, 2024.

Giacomini, G. (2022). *Indigenous peoples and climate justice : a critical analysis of international human rights law and governance* (1st edn) Springer International Publishing. https://doi.org/10.1007/978-3-031-09508-5

Giannoulopoulos, D. (2020). The Eurosceptic right and (our) human rights: The threat to the Human Rights Act and the European Convention on Human Rights is alive and well. *European Human Rights Law Review*, *2020*(3), 225–242.

Gibbons, M., Crump, A., Barrett, M., Sarlak, S., Birch, J., & Chittka, L. (2022). Can insects feel pain? A review of the neural and behavioural evidence. *Advances in Insect Physiology*, *63*, 155–229. https://doi.org/10.1016/bs.aiip.2022.10.001

Gilbert, J. (2023). Creating synergies between international law and rights of nature. *Transnational Environmental Law*, *12*(3), 671–692. https://doi.org/10.1017/S2047102523000195

Gill, M. (2023). Zoos are the opposite of educational they construct fictions about animals. *The Guardian*. http://www.theguardian.com/commentisfree/2023/oct/22/zoos-are-opposite-of-educational-they-construct-fictions-about-animals Retrieved March 14, 2024.

Giuffra, E., Kijas, J. M., Amarger, V., Carlborg, O., Jeon, J. T., & Andersson, L. (2000). The origin of the domestic pig: Independent domestication and subsequent introgression. *Genetics*, *154*(4), 1785–1791. https://doi.org/10.1093/genetics/154.4.1785

Global animal welfare index. (n.d.). http://www.globalanimallaw.org/database/index.html Retrieved March 14, 2024.

Gómez-Leal, R., Costa, A., Megías-Robles, A., Fernández-Berrocal, P., & Faria, L. (2021). Relationship between emotional intelligence and empathy towards humans and animals. *PeerJ*, *9*, e11274. https://doi.org/10.7717/peerj.11274

Goodier, M. (2023). Met Police dealing with at least one dangerous dog a day, figures show. *The Guardian*. https://www.theguardian.com/uk-news/2023/jun/04/met-police-dealing-with-at-least-one-dangerous-dog-a-day-figures-show Retrieved May 13, 2024.

Goodyer, J. (2022). Talking to Dr Andrew Terry. *Science Focus*. BBC December 2022 magazine (pp. 22–23). BBC.

Goulson, D. (2021). *Silent Earth- averting the insect apocalypse.* Johnathan Cape.

Graham, C., & Prosser, T. (1988). *Waiving the rules: The constitution under Thatcherism*. Open University Press.

Green, J., Schmidt-Burbach, J., & Elwin, A. (2023). Taking stock of wildlife farming: A global perspective. *Global Ecology and Conservation, 43*, e02452. https://doi.org/10.1016/j.gecco.2023.e02452

Greenspoon, L., Krieger, E., Sender, R., Rosenberg, Y., Bar-On, Y. M., Moran, U., Antman, T., Meiri, S., Roll, U., Noor, E., & Milo, R. (2023). The global biomass of wild mammals. *Proceedings of the National Academy of Sciences of the United States of America*. Proceedings of the National Academy of Sciences, *120*(10), e2204892120. https://doi.org/10.1073/pnas.2204892120

Greger, M. (2007). The human/animal interface: Emergence and resurgence of zoonotic infectious diseases. *Critical Reviews in Microbiology*, *33*(4), 243–299. https://doi.org/10.1080/10408410701647594

Griffin, E. (2007). *Blood sport: Hunting in Britain since 1066*. Yale University Press.

Grove, R. (2023). European Commission hits pause on fur farm ban in the EU. World animal protection. https://www.worldanimalprotection.org.uk/latest/blogs/unnecessary-pause-fur-ban/#:~:text=The%20European%20Commission%20has%20delayed Retrieved March 4, 2024.

Gržinić, G., Piotrowicz-Cieślak, A., Klimkowicz-Pawlas, A., Górny, R. L., Ławniczek-Wałczyk, A., Piechowicz, L., Olkowska, E., Potrykus, M., Tankiewicz, M., Krupka, M., Siebielec, G., & Wolska, L. (2023). Intensive poultry farming: A review of the impact on the environment and human health. *The Science of the Total Environment, 858*(3), 160014. https://doi.org/10.1016/j.scitotenv.2022.160014

Guenzler, J, (2024) Whales in Pacific countries gain rights of legal personhood. nit.com.au/18-04-2024/10902/whales-in-pacific-countries-gain-legal-personhood-now-humans-can-sue-on-behalf-of-them Accessed October 29 2024.

Gupta, G. S. (2019). Land degradation and challenges of food security. *Review of European Studies*, *11*(1), 63–72. https://doi.org/10.5539/res.v11n1p63

Hadley, J. (2011). Telling it like it is: A proposal to improve transparency in biomedical research. *Between the Species: An Online Journal for the Study of Philosophy and Animals*, *15*(1), 7. https://doi.org/10.15368/bts.2012v15n1.3

Hall, S., Dolling, L., Bristow, K., Fuller, T., & Mills, D. (2017). *Companion Animal Economics: The economic impact of companion animals in the UK*. CABI Publishing.

Halpin, D. (2023). Animal welfare charity takes Government to court over

Frankenchickens. *The Independent*. https://www.independent.co.uk/news/uk/crime/government-high-court-rspca-poet-benjamin-zephaniah-b2331673.html Retrieved May 13, 2024.

Hampson, J. (1987). Legislation: A practical solution to the vivisection dilemma. In N. Rupke (Ed.), *Vivisection in historical perspective*. Routledge.

Hance, J. (2023). Making tracks: How linking patches of wilderness is saving Borneo's wildlife. *The Guardian*. https://www.theguardian.com/environment/2023/jul/18/making-tracks-how-linking-patches-of-wilderness-saving-borneo-wildlife-aoe#:~:text=Making%20tracks%3A%20how%20linking%20patches%20of%20wilderness%20is%20saving%20Borneo's%20wildlife,-This%20article%20is&text=In%202011%2C%20the%20German,endangered%20species%20of%20wild%20cattle Accessed March 14, 2024.

Hancocks, D. (1995). Can zoos survive? *Animals International*, *51*, WSPA.

Hanlon, A. J., & Magalhães-Sant'Ana, M. (2016). Zoocentrism. In H. In ten Have (Ed.), *Encyclopedia of global bioethics* (pp. 1–10). Springer.

Hannah et al. (2019). *Biodiversity and climate change: Transforming the biosphere* L. Hannah & T. E. Lovejoy (Eds.). Yale University Press.

Hansard. (2013). *House of Commons Debate (29th January 2013) RSPCA Prosecutions*, *557*. https://hansard.parliament.uk/commons/2013–01–29/debates/13012938000001/RSPCA(Prosecutions) Retrieved May 14, 2024.

Hansard. (June 4, 2018) Fur. House of Commons debate. https://hansard.parliament.uk/commons/2018–06–04/debates/8F9B6212-E631–4151-ABA7-AED8560CBBEB/FurTrade Retrieved March 4, 2024.

Hansard. (2022). UK Parliament debate on Breed-specific legislation, Retrieved June 6, 2022. https://hansard.parliament.uk/commons/2022–06–06/debates/E7DC68B3-E1E5–449B-B922-F3333187C8FB/Breed-SpecificLegislation Retrieved March 4, 2024.

Hare, D., Ambarlı, H., Dickman, A. J., Dröge, E., Farhidinia, M. S., Johnson, P. J., Khanyari, M., Mandisodza-Chikerema, R., Montgomery, R. A., Sutherland, C., Webster, H., & Wijers, M. (2023). Trophy hunting is not one big thing. *Biodiversity and Conservation*, *32*(6), 2149–2153. https://doi.org/10.1007/s10531-023-02597-9

Hargreaves-Méndez, M. J., & Hötzel, M. J. (2023). A systematic review on whether regenerative agriculture improves animal welfare: A qualitative analysis with a One Welfare perspective. *Animal Welfare*, *32*, e36. https://doi.org/10.1017/awf.2023.28

Harker, R. M., Collis, G. M., & McNicholas, J. (2000). The influence of current relationships upon pet animal acquisition. In A. Podberscek, E. Paul, & J. A. Serpell (Eds.), *Companion Animals and Us: Exploring the relationships between people and pets* (pp. 189–208). Cambridge University Press.

Harris, S. (2022). *A review of the use of Snares in the UK.* National Anti-Snaring Campaign.

Harrison, A. (1968). *The law of Athens: The family and property*. Oxford University Press.

Harrison, J. (2023). Significant international environmental law developments: 2022–2023. *Journal of Environmental Law*, *35*(3), 467–479. https://doi.org/10.1093/jel/eqad028

Harrison, J. R., Roberts, D. L., & Hernandez-Castro, J. (2016). Assessing the extent and nature of wildlife trade on the dark web. *Conservation Biology*, *30*(4), 900–904. https://doi.org/10.1111/cobi.12707

Harrison, R. (1964). *Animal Machines: The new factory farming industry*. Vincent Stuart.

Harrop, S. (2006). Parliamentary process, opposition in the House of Lords and the Hunting Act 2004: *R (Jackson and Ors) v Attorney General* [2005] 3 WLR 733, House of Lords. *Environmental Law Review*, *8*(4), 299–304. https://doi.org/10.1350/enlr.2006.8.4.299

Harrop, S. R. (2005). The Hunting Act 2004 — Cruelty, countryside, conservation, culture or a class act? *Environmental Law Review*, *7*(3), 201–205. https://doi.org/10.1350/enlr.2005.7.3.201

Harvey, F. (2024). Essex car park to be test case for legislation to protect landscapes. *The Guardian*, 31 October 2024.

Hayes, N. (2024). *Wild service: Why nature needs you*. Bloomsbury Publishing.

Hetherington, D. A., Miller, D. R., Macleod, C. D., & Gorman, M. L. (2008). A potential habitat network for the Eurasian lynx Lynx lynx in Scotland. *Mammal Review*, *38*(4), 285–303. https://doi.org/10.1111/j.1365-2907.2008.00117.x

Held, S., Cooper, J. J., & Mendl, M. T. (2009). Advances in the study of cognition, behavioural priorities and emotions'. In J. N. Marchant-Forde (Ed.), *The welfare of pigs*. Springer Science & Business Media BV (pp. 47–94). https://doi.org/10.1007/978-1-4020-8909-1_3

Held, S., Mendl, M., Devereux, C., & Byrne, R. W. (2000). Social tactics of pigs in a competitive foraging task: The "informer forager" paradigm. *Animal Behaviour*, *59*(3), 569–576. https://doi.org/10.1006/anbe.1999.1322

Herzog, H. (2011). The impact of pets on human health and psychological well-being: Fact, fiction, or hypothesis? *Current Directions in Psychological Science*, *20*(4), 236–239. https://doi.org/10.1177/0963721411415220

Hill, R. (1961). *Both small and great beasts*. Universities Federation for Animal Welfare.

Hobson-West, P., & Davies, A. (2018). Societal sentience: Constructions of the public in animal research policy and practice. *Science, Technology and Human Values*, *43*(4), 671–693. https://doi.org/10.1177/0162243917736138

Hoenig, C. (2023). Augustine of Hippo on nonhuman animals. *Journal of Animal Ethics*, *13*(2), 122–134. https://doi.org/10.5406/21601267.13.2.03

Holdsworth, Sir W. (1973). *A history of English law* (2nd ed.), *VII*. Sweet & Maxwell. https://doi.org/10.2307/844513

Hollands, C. (1986). Animal experimentation. *The Lancet,* 5 July 1986.

Holmberg, T., & Ideland, M. (2012). Secrets and lies: "selective openness" in the apparatus of animal experimentation. *Public Understanding of Science, 21*(3), 354–368. https://doi.org/10.1177/0963662510372584

Holwerda, M. et al. (2021). *Essential EU climate law* (2nd ed.). Edward Elgar Publishing.

Home Office. (1986). Consultation on the review of section 24 of the Animals (Scientific Procedures) Act 1986. Home Office. https://assets.publishing.service.gov.uk/government/uploads/system/uploads/attachment_data/file/313410/Consultation_on_the_review_of_Section_24_of_ASPA.pdf Retrieved May 13, 2024.

Home Office. (1994). *Statistics of scientific procedures on living animals in Great Britain.* HMSO.

Home Office. (2012). Home Office. *Supplementary note on the transposition of Directive 2010/63/EU on the protection of animals used for scientific purposes.* OGL.

Home Office. (2014). Working to reduce the use of animals in scientific research. Department for Business Innovation and Skills and Department of Health. https://assets.publishing.service.gov.uk/media/5a7c79b1e5274a559005a1ee/bis-14–589-working-to-reduce-the-use-of_animals-in-research.pdf Retrieved May 13, 2024.

Home Office. (2017a). Animal testing: Compliance investigations by the Animals in Science Regulation Unit: Anonymised reports of substantial investigations by the Animals in Science Regulation Unit. https://www.gov.uk/government/publications/compliance-investigations-by-the-animals-in-science-regulation-unit#full-publication-update-history Retrieved May 13, 2024.

Home Office. (2017b). Review of animals in science committee. https://assets.publishing.service.gov.uk/media/5a74e42ded915d502d6cbd4d/2017–07–20_Triennial_Review_Of_HO_Science_NDPBs.pdf Retrieved May 13, 2024.

Home Office. (2022). Animals in science regulation unit. *Annual Reports,* 2019–2021. https://assets.publishing.service.gov.uk/media/6628f6d43b0122a378a7e596/6.8698_HO_Scientific_Procedures_ARA2019–21_REVISED_FINAL_v6a_WEB.pdf Retrieved May 13, 2024.

Home Office. (2023a). Nontechnical summaries granted in 2023: Projects granted under the Animals (Scientific Procedures) Act 1986 in 2023. https://www.gov.uk/government/publications/non-technical-summaries-granted-in-2023 Retrieved May 13, 2024.

Home Office. (2023a). *Statistics of scientific procedures on living animals, Great Britain, 2022.* https://www.gov.uk/government/statistics/statistics-of-scientific-procedures-on-living-animals-great-britain-2022/

statistics-of-scientific-procedures-on-living-animals-great-britain-2022 Retrieved May 13, 2024.

Home Office. (2024). Animals in science committee: About Us. https://www.gov.uk/government/organisations/animals-in-science-committee/about Retrieved May 13, 2024.

Hone, D. (2017). Why the world needs zoos. *The Guardian*, 8 March 2017.

Hooton, V. E. (2019). Slaughtered at the altar of free trade: Are WTO rules hindering the progression of animal welfare standards in agriculture. *Manchester Rev. L. Crime & Ethics*, *8*, 152.

Horrigan, L., Lawrence, R. S., & Walker, P. (2002). How sustainable agriculture can address the environmental and human harms of industrial agriculture. *Environmental Health Perspectives*, *110*(5), 445–456. https://doi.org/10.1289/ehp.02110445

Horton, H. (2023). Peak District deal to protect birds of prey ends as illegal killing continues. *The Guardian*. http://www.theguardian.com/environment/2023/apr/25/peak-district-protect-birds-prey-conservationists-raptor-species#:~:text=Illegal%20killings%20of%20birds%20of,prey%20populations%20in%20the%20park Retrieved May 14, 2024.

House of Commons. (1876). *Cruelty to Animals Bill (Friday, 11th August 1876)* p. 1151. Hansard.

House of Commons. (2012). Post-legislative scrutiny of the Freedom of the Freedom of Information Act 2000. https://publications.parliament.uk/pa/cm201213/cmselect/cmjust/96/96.pdf Retrieved May 13, 2024.

House of Commons. (2021a). HL deb 16 June 2021, *812*, *col 1900 (Lord Benyon)*.

House of Commons. (2021b). HL deb 16 June 2021, *812*, *col 1902 (Baroness Young of Old Scone); HC Deb 14 March 2022*, vol 710, col 691 (Jim McMahon MP)

House of Commons. (2022). HC deb 14 March 2022, *710*, *col 704 (Dr Neil Hudson MP)*.

House of Commons Environment, Food and Rural Affairs Committee. (2013–2014). *Primates as Pets. Eleventh report of session.*

House of Commons Environment, Food and Rural Affairs Committee Protecting Marine Mammals in the UK and . *Abroad Sixth Report of Session 2022–23 published 28th June 2023*. Available at: Protecting Marine Mammals in the UK and Abroad. parliament.uk Retrieved May 14, 2024.

House of Commons Environmental Audit Committee. (2021). The UK's footprint on global biodiversity Second Report of Session 2021–22. *House of Commons, London*. http://www.committees.parliament.uk/publications/7462/documents/78136/default/.

House of Lords. (1979). 25 October 1979. Hansard. https://hansard.parliament.uk/Lords/1979-10-25/

debates/c0b52c20-6946-48f2-9734-d69b894daf19/LaboratoryAnimalsprotectionBillHl Retrieved May 13, 2024.

Howard, J. (2017). Should we let pandas go extinct. *BBC science focus magazine*. BBC.

Howe, H., & Katamine, T. (2023). Using the law to address harmful conformation in dogs: Is a breed-specific breeding ban the answer ? *UK Journal of Animal Law.*

Howkins, A., & Merricks, L. (1995). Dewy-eyed veal calves. Live animal exports and middle-class opinion, 1980–1995. *Agricultural History Review, 48*(I), 85–103.

Hubrecht, R. C., & Carter, E. (2019). The 3Rs and humane experimental technique: Implementing change. *Animals: An Open Access Journal from MDPI, 9*(10), 754. https://doi.org/10.3390/ani9100754

Hughes, A., Auliya, M., Altherr, S., Scheffers, B., Janssen, J., Nijman, V., Shepherd, C. R., D'Cruze, N., Sy, E., & Edwards, D. P. (2023). Determining the sustainability of legal wildlife trade. *Journal of Environmental Management, 341*, 117987–117987. https://doi.org/10.1016/j.jenvman.2023.117987

Hughes, L. J., Morton, O., Scheffers, B. R., & Edwards, D. P. (2023). The ecological drivers and consequences of wildlife trade. *Biological Reviews of the Cambridge Philosophical Society, 98*(3), 775–791. https://doi.org/10.1111/brv.12929

Humane Society International. (n.d.). The fur trade. https://www.hsi.org/news-resources/fur-trade/ Retrieved March 4, 2024.

Humboldt, A. H. (1845–1862). *Kosmos: A sketch of a physical description of the universe.* Harpers and Brothers.

Hume, D. (1739). *A treatise of human nature.* Clarendon Press.

Humphreys, R. (2014). Argument from existence, blood-sports, and "sport-slaves". *Journal of Agricultural and Environmental Ethics, 27*(2), 331–345. https://doi.org/10.1007/s10806-013-9466-7

Hunnicutt, G. (2021). *Gender violence in ecofeminist perspective. Intersections of Animal Oppression, Patriarchy and Domination of the Earth.* Routledge, London.

Hunt Saboteurs. (n.d.). http://www.huntsabs.org.uk Retrieved May 14, 2024.

Hunt Saboteurs Association. (1992). *What's wrong with angling, Howl, Summer 1992.* Hunt Saboteurs Association.

Huss, R. J. (2003). Separation, custody and estate planning issues relating to companion animals. *University of Colorado Law Review, 74*, 181.

Hutchinson, A., Stephens-Griffin, N., & Wyatt, T. (2022). Speciesism and the wildlife trade: Who gets listed, downlisted and uplisted in cites? *International Journal for Crime, Justice and Social Democracy, 10*(3), 191–209. https://doi.org/10.5204/ijcjsd.1945

Hutton, V. E. (2015). Social Provisions of the Human-Animal Relationship amongst 30 people living with HIV in Australia. *Anthrozoos*, *28*(2), 199–214. https://doi.org/10.1080/08927936.2015.11435397

Hyde, W. W. (1916). The prosecution and punishment of animals and lifeless things in the Middle Ages and modern times. *University of Pennsylvania Law Review and American Law Register*, *64*(7), 696–730. https://doi.org/10.2307/3313677

Illegal Wildlife Challenge Fund. (2024). http://www.iwt.challengefund.org.uk Retrieved May 14, 2024.

Ingold, T. (1994). From trust to domination: An alternative history of human-animal relations. In A. Manning & J. A. Serpell (Eds.), *Animals and human society: Changing perspectives* (pp. 1–22). Routledge.

Intergovernmental Oceanographic Commission. (n.d.). http://www.ioc.unesco.org/en Retrieved May 14, 2024.

International Council for Bird Preservation. (1992). *Putting biodiversity on the map– priority areas for global conservation*. International Council for Bird Preservation.

International Council for the Exploration of the Sea. http://www.ices.dk/Pages/default.aspx Retrieved May 14, 2024.

International Maritime Organization (IMO). (n.d.). http://www.imo.org Retrieved May 14, 2024.

International Seabed Authority. (2024). http://www.isa.org.jm/sessions/29th-session-2024 Retrieved May 14, 2024.

International tribunal for the law of the sea. (2024). *Request for an advisory opinion submitted by the commission of Small Island states on climate change and international law*. http://www.itlos.org/fileadmin/itlos/documents/cases/31/Advisory_Opinion/C31_Adv_Op_21.05.2024_orig.pdf Retrieved May 22, 2024.

International Union for Conservation of Nature (IUCN). (2024). *The IUCN Red List of Threatened Species*. International Union for Conservation of Nature and Natural Resources. http://www.iucnredlist.org Retrieved May 16, 2024.

International Union for Conservation of Nature and Natural Resources. (n.d.). http://www.iucn.org Retrieved May 14, 2024.

International Whaling Commission (IWC). (2024) Available at: www.http://iwc.int/en Retrieved May 14, 2024.

IPBES. (2023). Summary for policymakers of the thematic assessment report on invasive alien species and their control of the intergovernmental science-policy platform on biodiversity and ecosystem services. *IPBES Secretariat, (Bonn, Germany)*. https://doi.org/10.5281/zenodo.7430692

Ipsos. (2018a). An exploration into diets around the world. https://www.ipsos.com/sites/default/files/ct/news/documents/2018–09/an_exploration_into_diets_around_the_world.pdf Retrieved April 9, 2024.

Ipsos. (2018b). Public attitudes to animal research in 2018. https://www.ipsos.com/sites/default/files/ct/news/

documents/2019-05/18-040753-01_ols_public_attitudes_to_animal_research_report_v3_191118_public.pdf Retrieved May 6, 2024.

Ironmonger, J. (2020). Concern over UK cattle slaughtered in Middle East. *BBC News*. https://www.bbc.co.uk/news/uk-54435029 Retrieved May 13, 2024.

Irvine, L. (2013a). *My dog always eats first: Homeless people and their animals*. Lynne Rienner Publishers.

Irvine, L. (2013b). Animals as lifechangers and lifesavers: Pets in the redemption narratives among homeless people. *Journal of Contemporary Ethnography*, *42*(1), 3–30. https://doi.org/10.1177/0891241612456550

Irvine, L., & Cilia, L. (2017). More-than-human families: Pets, people and practices in multispecies households. *Sociology Compass*, *11*(2). https://doi.org/10.1111/soc4.12455

Jacobsson, K., & Lindblom, J. (2016). *Animal rights activism* (1st ed.). Amsterdam University Press. Accessed May 14, 2024. https://doi.org/10.1515/9789048525485

Janssens, B., & Trouwborst, A. (2018). Rhinoceros conservation and international law: The role of wildlife treaties in averting megaherbivore extinction. *Journal of International Wildlife Law and Policy*, *21*(2–3), 146–189. https://doi.org/10.1080/13880292.2018.1483300

Jegatheesan, B., Ormerod, E., Graham, T. M., Stone, W., Power, E., Rook, D., & McCune, S. (2024). Pets and housing: A one health one welfare issue. In A. H. Fine, M. K. Mueller, Z. Y. Ng, A. M. Beck, & J. M. Peralta (Eds.), *The Routledge international handbook of human animal interactions and anthrozoology*. Routledge.

Jegatheeswaran, D. (2024). *Climate protests and juries – Defending criminal damage after the Ag's reference on consent*. One Pump Court.

Jenkins, H. E., Woodroffe, R., & Donnelly, C. A. (2010). The Duration of the effects of repeated widespread badger culling on cattle tuberculosis following the cessation of culling. *PLOS ONE*, *5*(2), e9090. https://doi.org/10.1371/journal.pone.0009090 Accessed May 14, 2024.

Jenkins, s. (1992). *Animal rights and human wrongs*. Lennard Publishing.

Jensen, E. (2014). Evaluating children's conservation biology learning at the zoo. *Conservation Biology*, *28*(4), 1004–1011. https://doi.org/10.1111/cobi.12263

JNCC. (n.d.). http://www.jncc.gov.uk Retrieved May 14, 2024.

Johannsen, K. (2020). *Wild Animals Ethics- The Moral and Political problem of Wild Animal Suffering*. Routledge.

Johannsen, K. (2022). Précis of wild animal ethics. *Philosophia*, *50*(3), 847–851. https://doi.org/10.1007/s11406-021-00423-6

Johnson. (2016). What did Boro mark of the flying Frankish brothers protest at Riverside? *Therapeutic Gazette*. https://www.gazettelive.co.uk/news/teesside-news/what-boro-make-flying-frankish-11252953 Retrieved May 13, 2024.

Johnson, J. (1801). *The Works of John Locke in Ten Volumes, Some thoughts concerning education*, vol. 9 (1693) (10th ed.). London.

Jones, J. (1956). *Law and legal theory of the Greeks*. Clarendon Press.

Jones, L. (2020). Veganism: Why is it on the up? *BBC News*. https://www.bbc.co.uk/news/business-44488051 Retrieved April 9, 2024.

Jones, S. (2023). Police in Spain and France break up international eel smuggling gang. *The Guardian*. http://www.theguardian.com/environment/2023/may/12/police-in-spain-and-france-break-up-international-eel-smuggling-gang Retrieved May 14, 2024

Jongman, E. C., Woodhouse, R., Rice, M., & Rault, J. L. (2021). Pre-slaughter factors linked to variation in responses to carbon dioxide gas stunning in pig abattoirs. *Animal*, *15*(2), 100134. https://doi.org/10.1016/j.animal.2020.100134

Jörgensen, S., Lindsjö, J., Weber, E. M., & Röcklinsberg, H. (2021). Reviewing the review: A pilot study of the ethical review process of animal research in Sweden. *Animals: An Open Access Journal from MDPI*, *11*(3), 708. https://doi.org/10.3390/ani11030708

Jordon, W. and Ormrod, S. (1978). *The last great wild beast show*. Constable and Co.

Jowitt, J. (2022). Some thoughts on the Animal Welfare (Sentience) Act 2022. https://ukconstitutionallaw.org/ Retrieved May 14, 2024.

Judge Lucky, J. A. (2018). Diversity in judgments: The role of the courts in promoting biodiversity. *Journal of International Wildlife Law and Policy*, *21*(1), 1–10. https://doi.org/10.1080/13880292.2018.1439702

Jurkus, E., Povilanskas, R., & Taminskas, J. (2022). Current trends and issues in research on biodiversity conservation and tourism sustainability. *Sustainability*, *14*(6), 3342. https://doi.org/10.3390/su14063342

Kant, I. (1780–81). (1963). Lectures on ethics – Duties towards animals and other spirits. In L. Infield (trans) (pp. 239–240). Harper & Row.

Kapitza, K., Zimmermann, H., Martín-López, B., & von Wehrden, H. (2019). Research on the social perception of invasive species: A systematic literature review. *NeoBiota*, *43*, 47–68. https://doi.org/10.3897/neobiota.43.31619

Kassam, A. (2023). A symbol of what humans shouldn't be doing: The new world of octopus farming. *The Guardian*. https://www.theguardian.com/environment/2023/jun/25/a-symbol-of-what-humans-shouldnt-be-doing-the-new-world-of-octopus-farming Retrieved May 13, 2024.

Kaylor, A. (2023). Alternatives to animal testing models in clinical and biomedical research. *PharmaNews. Intelligence*. https://pharmanewsintel.com/features/alternatives-to-animal-testing-models-in-clinical-and-biomedical-research. Retrieved May 13, 2024

Kean, H. (2000). *Animal Rights, political and social change in Britain since 1800*. Reaktion Books.

Kelleher, G., & Kenchington, R. (1991). *Guidelines for establishing marine protected areas*. International Union for Conservation of Nature.

Kempf, E., & Phillips, C. (1995). *Whales in the wild*. WWF Special Species Report. WWF Verlagsgesellschaft.

Kevany, S. (2021a). How nearly 3,000 cattle came to be stranded at sea for three months. *The Guardian*. https://www.theguardian.com/environment/2021/mar/31/how-nearly-3000-cattle-came-to-be-stranded-at-sea-for-three-months Retrieved May 13, 2024.

Kevany, S. (2021b). Live farm animal exports to mainland EU at a standstill post-Brexit. *The Guardian*. https://www.theguardian.com/environment/2021/feb/05/live-farm-animal-exports-to-mainland-eu-at-a-standstill-post-brexit Retrieved April 9, 2024.

Kevany, S. (2022). Avian flu has led to the killing of 140m farmed birds since last October. https://www.theguardian.com/environment/2022/dec/09/avian-flu-has-led-to-the-killing-of-140m-farmed-birds-since-last-october Retrieved October 28, 2024.

Kirby, C. (1933). The English game law system. *The American Historical Review*, *38*(2). https://doi.org/10.2307/1838294

Klabbers, J. (2023). *International law*. Cambridge University Press.

Knight, A., Phillips, C., & Sparks, P. (Eds.). (2022). *Routledge handbook of animal welfare* (1st ed.). Routledge. https://doi.org/10.4324/9781003182351

Koh, N. S., Ituarte-Lima, C., & Hahn, T. (2022). Mind the compliance gap: How insights from international human rights mechanisms can help to implement the convention on biological diversity. *Transnational Environmental Law*, *11*(1), 39–67. https://doi.org/10.1017/S2047102521000169

Kolbert, E. (2014). *The sixth extinction: An unnatural history*. Henry Holt, and Company.

Kolmaš, M. (2021). International pressure and Japanese withdrawal from the International Whaling Commission: When shaming fails. *Australian Journal of International Affairs*, *75*(2), 197–216. https://doi.org/10.1080/10357718.2020.1799936

Köndgen, S., Kühl, H., N'Goran, P. K., Walsh, P. D., Schenk, S., Ernst, N., Biek, R., Formenty, P., Mätz-Rensing, K., Schweiger, B., Junglen, S., Ellerbrok, H., Nitsche, A., Briese, T., Lipkin, W. I., Pauli, G., Boesch, C., & Leendertz, F. H. (2008). Pandemic human viruses cause decline of endangered great apes. *Current Biology*, *18*(4), 260–264. https://doi.org/10.1016/j.cub.2008.01.012

König, H. J., Kiffner, C., Kramer-Schadt, S., Fürst, C., Keuling, O., & Ford, A. T. (2020). Human–wildlife coexistence in a changing world. *Conservation Biology*, *34*(4), 786–794. https://doi.org/10.1111/cobi.13513

Kopnina, H., & Washington, H. (Eds.). (2020). *Conservation integrating social and ecological justice* (1st ed.). Springer International Publishing.

Kotzmann, J., & Pendergrast, N. (2019). Animal rights: Time to start unpacking what rights and for whom. *Hamline Law Review*. Mitchell, *46*, 157.

Kramer, L., & Badger, C. (2024). *Kramers EU environmental law*. Hart Publishing.

Kriebel, D., Tickner, J., Epstein, P., Lemons, J., Levins, R., Loechler, E. L., Quinn, M., Rudel, R., Schettler, T., & Stoto, M. (2001). The precautionary principle in environmental science. *Environmental Health Perspectives*, *109*(9), 871–876. https://doi.org/10.1289/ehp.01109871

Kriegl, M., Elías Ilosvay, X. E., von Dorrien, C., & Oesterwind, D. (2021). Marine protected areas: At the crossroads of nature conservation and fisheries management. *Frontiers in Marine Science*, *8*(67), 6264. https://doi.org/10.3389/fmars.2021.676264

Kymlicka, W. (2017). Social Membership: Animal law beyond the property/personhood impasse. *Dalhousie Law Journal*, 123–155.

La Mettrie, J. O. (1747). L'homme machine. In Thomson, *A, la Mettrie: "machine man" and other writings, (1996)*. Cambridge University Press.

Ladwig, B. (2014). Human rights and human animals. In *Human rights and human nature* (pp. 23–42). Springer. https://doi.org/10.1007/978-94-017-8672-0_3

LaFollette, H. (2011). Animal experimentation in biomedical research. In T. L. Beauchamp & R. G. Frey (Eds.), *The Oxford handbook of animal ethics*. Oxford University Press.

Laitos, J. G. (2021). *Rethinking environmental law: Why environmental laws should conform to the laws of nature* (1st ed.). Edward Elgar Publishing Limited. https://doi.org/10.4337/9781788976039

Lal, R. (2020). Regenerative agriculture for food and climate. *Journal of Soil and Water Conservation*, *75*(5), 123A–124A. https://doi.org/10.2489/jswc.2020.0620A

Lambert, H., Cornish, A., Elwin, A., & D'Cruze, N. (2022). A kettle of fish: A review of the scientific literature for evidence of fish sentience. *Animals (Basel)*, *12*(9), 1182. https://doi.org/10.3390/ani12091182

Langhammer, P. F., Bull, J. W., Bicknell, J. E., Oakley, J. L., Brown, M. H., Bruford, M. W., Butchart, S. H. M., Carr, J. A., Church, D., Cooney, R., Cutajar, S., Foden, W., Foster, M. N., Gascon, C., Geldmann, J., Genovesi, P., Hoffmann, M., Howard-McCombe, J., Lewis, T., . . . Brooks, T. M. (2024). The positive impact of conservation action. *Science*. American Association for the Advancement of Science, *384*(6694), 453–458. https://doi.org/10.1126/science.adj6598

Langton, T. E. S., Jones, M. W., & McGill, I. (2022). Analysis of the impact of badger culling on bovine tuberculosis in cattle in the high-risk area of England, 2009–2020. *The Veterinary Record*, 190(6), e1384. https://doi.org/10.1002/vetr.1384

Larsson, J., & Päiviö Sjaunja, E.-L. (2021). *Self-governance and Sami communities: Transitions in early modern natural resource management*. Springer Nature.

Laslett, P. (Ed.). (1988). *John Locke: Two treatises of government.* Cambridge University Press.

Lawrence, M. J., Stemberger, H. L. J., Zolderdo, A. J., Struthers, D. P., & Cooke, S. J. (2015). The effects of modern war and military activities on biodiversity and the environment. *Environmental Reviews*, *23*(4), 443–460. https://doi.org/10.1139/er-2015-0039

League Against Cruel Sports. (n.d.). The hunting act. http://www.league.org.uk/what-we-do/hunting/hunting-act/#:~:text=The%20Hunting%20Act%202004%20is,on%20dogs%20chasing%20wild%20mammals Retrieved May 14, 2024.

Leahy, M. (1991). *Against liberation: Putting animals in perspective.* Routledge.

Leaky, R., & Lewin, R. (1992). Origins reconsidered. In *Search of what makes U S human.* Abacus Books.

Learmonth, M. J. (2019). Dilemmas for natural living concepts of zoo animal welfare. *Animals (Basel)*, *9*(6), 318. https://doi.org/10.3390/ani9060318

Leavitt, E. (1978). *Animals and their legal rights.* Animal Welfare Institute.

Ledger et al. (2022). *Wildlife Comeback in Europe: Opportunities and challenges for species recovery. Final report to Rewilding Europe by the Zoological Society of London.* Birdlife International and European Bird Census Council. https://doi.org/10.13140/RG.2.2.24283.44324

Lee, M. (2023). The Aarhus Convention 1998 and the Environment Act 2021: Eroding public participation. *The Modern Law Review* The Aarhus Convention 1998 and the Environment Act, *86*(3), 756–784. https://doi.org/10.1111/1468-2230.12789

Lee, S.-M., Choi, Y.-Y., Min, M.-S., Lee, H., & Lee, M.-Y. (2019). Research Article Molecular species identification of whale meat in South Korean markets. *Genetics and Molecular Research*, *18*(2). https://doi.org/10.4238/gmr18171

Lees, A. C., Newton, I., & Balmford, A. (2013). Pheasants, buzzards, and trophic cascades. *Conservation Letters*, *6*(2), 141–144. https://doi.org/10.1111/j.1755-263X.2012.00301.x

Legge, D., & Brooman, S. (2020). Reflecting on 25 years of teaching animal law: Is it time for an international crime of animal ecocide? *The Liverpool Law Review*, *41*(2), 201–218. https://doi.org/10.1007/s10991-020-09253-0

Lercier, M. et al. (Eds.). (2024). Special issue: "animals in wars and disasters". *Global Journal of Animal Law*, *12*(1).

Levin, K., Cashore, B., Bernstein, S., & Auld, G. (2012). Overcoming the tragedy of super wicked problems: Constraining our future selves to ameliorate global climate change. *Policy Sciences*, *45*(2), 123–152. https://doi.org/10.1007/s11077-012-9151-0

Levitt, L., Hoffer, T. A., & Loper, A. B. (2016). Criminal histories of a subsample of animal cruelty offenders. *Aggression and Violent Behavior*, *30*, 48–58. https://doi.org/10.1016/j.avb.2016.05.002

Lewis, K. (2016). Brothers filmed throwing pet bulldog down the stairs spared jail. *The Independent.*

Lewis, S. A., & Parr, K. (2023). Deer culling in Britain: What's the problem and why are deer culled? BBC Countryfile. http://www.countryfile.com/wildlife/mammals/deer-culling-in-britain/ Retrieved May 14, 2024

Liebniz, G. (1710). Discourse on metaphysics. In J. Veitch, R. Elwes, & G. Montgomery (Eds.).

Link. (2023). http://www.nationallinkcoalition.org Retrieved May 14, 2024.

Linzey, A. (1979). Animals and Moral theology. In D. Paterson & R. Ryder (Eds.), *Animal rights – A symposium* (pp. 34–42). Centaur Publishing.

Linzey, A. (2009). *The link between animal abuse and human violence.* Liverpool University Press.

Littlewood Report. (1965). *Report of the departmental committee of experimentation on animals.* Cmnd 2641. HMSO.

Liu, G., David, B. T., Trawczynski, M., & Fessler, R. G. (2020). Advances in pluripotent stem cells: History, mechanisms, technologies, and applications. *Stem Cell Reviews and Reports, 16*(1), 3–32. https://doi.org/10.1007/s12015-019-09935-x

London Zoo. (2024). http://www.londonzoo.org/?gclsrc=aw.ds&gad_source=1&gclid=* Retrieved May 14, 2024.

Lorimer, J., & Driessen, C. (2016). From "nazi cows" to cosmopolitan "ecological engineers": Specifying Rewilding through a history of heck cattle. *Annals of the American Association of Geographers, 106*(3), 631–652. https://doi.org/10.1080/00045608.2015.1115332

Lovelock, J. (1995a). *Gaia- A new look at life on Earth.* Oxford University Press.

Lovelock, J. (1995b). *The ages of Gaia.* Oxford University Press.

Lovelock, J. (2007). *The revenge of Gaia.* Penguin Books Ltd.

Lowe, S. et al. (2000). 100 of the World's Worst Invasive Alien Species A selection from the Global Invasive Species Database. *The Invasive Species Specialist Group (ISSG) a specialist group of the Species Survival Commission (SSC) of the World Conservation Union (IUCN), 100.* http://www.issg.org/booklet.pd Retrieved May 14, 2024.

Lowther, J., Sellick, J., & Payne, S. (2018). Brexit: Implications for UK environmental law and policy. *The International Journal of Sustainability Policy and Practice, 14*(3), 1–15. https://doi.org/10.18848/2325-1166/CGP/v14i03/1-15

LSE. (2024). *Climate Change Laws of the World.* LSE. http://www.climate-laws.org Retrieved May 16, 2024.

Lucas, C. (2013). *RSPCA (Prosecutions)*, January 29, 557 p. cc195WH. Hansard.

Lucky, A (2018) Diversity in Judgments: The Role of the Courts in

Promoting Biodiversity. *Journal of International Wildlife Law & Policy* 21(1), 1–10.

Luskin, M. S., Albert, W. R., & Tobler, M. W. (2017). Sumatran tiger survival threatened by deforestation despite increasing densities in parks. *Nature Communications*, *8*(1), 1783. https://doi.org/10.1038/s41467-017-01656-4

Lukiv, J (2024) Iceland permits whale hunting amid sharp criticism. BBC News. www.bbc.co.uk/news/articles/c2ll8d00kzgo Retrieved October 22, 2024.

Luther, E. (2013). Tales of cruelty and belonging. In Search of an ethic for urban human-wildlife relations. *Animal Studies Journal*, *2*(1), 35–54.

Luyt, Z., & Van Der Merwe, P. (2022). The potential of frogging as an ecotourism product for South African National Parks. *Koedoe*, *64*(1), 1–11. https://doi.org/10.4102/koedoe.v64i1.1725

Pet Theft Taskforce Policy Paper. (2021). HM Government. https://www.gov.uk/government/publications/pet-theft-taskforce-report/pet-theft-taskforce-report.

Oxfam Research Report. (2015). Lives on the line: The human cost of cheap chicken. https://s3.amazonaws.com/oxfam-us/www/static/media/files/Lives_on_the_Line_Full_Report_Final.pdf. Retrieved April 9, 2024.

Maeler, A., & Tröhler, U. (1987). Animal experimentation from antiquity to the end of the eighteenth century: Attitudes and arguments. In N. Rupke (Ed.), *Vivisection in historical perspective* (pp. 15–16). Routledge.

Mahalwal, S., & Kabra, A. (2023). The slow violence of fortress conservation creates conditions for socially unjust "voluntary" relocation. *Biological Conservation*, *286*, 110264. https://doi.org/10.1016/j.biocon.2023.110264

Mancini, F. et al. (2023). *State of Nature 2023, the State of Nature Partnership*. http://www.stateofnature.org.uk Retrieved May 14, 2024.

Marchant, G. E. (2003). From general policy to legal rule: Aspirations and limitations of the precautionary principle. *Environmental Health Perspectives*, *111*(14), 1799–1803. https://doi.org/10.1289/ehp.6197

Marino, L., & Colvin, C. M. (2015). Thinking pigs: A comparative review of cognition, emotion and personality in Sus domesticus. *International Journal of Comparative Psychology*, *28*. https://doi.org/10.46867/ijcp.2015.28.00.04

Marshall, C. (2023). World's first octopus farm proposals alarm scientists. BBC. https://www.bbc.co.uk/news/science-environment-64814781 Retrieved May 14, 2024.

Martyn, M. (2023). The Truth about Pet Spending Statistics and how much pet owners spend on pet ownership. https://worldanimalfoundation.org/advocate/pet-spending-statistics/ Retrieved May 13, 2024.

Mason, J. (2017). *The Oxford handbook of animal studies*. Misotheory: Contempt for animals and nature, its origins, purposes, and Repurcusions. In Kalof. *Law and Education*. Oxford University Press.

Masson, J., & McCarthy, S. (1996). *When elephants weep: The emotional lives of animals*. Vintage Book Company.

Matfield, M. (1991). Animal research within an ethical framework, from a lecture given to the Parliamentary and Scientific Committee on 19 November 1991, (December 1991) 48 *Science in Parliament, 5*.

Matfield, M. (1996). Ten years of the Animals (Scientific Procedures) Act. *RDS news,* April 1996. Research Defence Society.

Matza, M. (2023). US snake hunters fight pythons big enough to devour gators. *BBC News*. London. http://www.bbc.co.uk/news/world-us-canada-66206671 Retrieved May 14, 2024.

Maulana, R. (2023). Architecture for wildlife: The possible solution to human-wildlife conflicts in Indonesia. IOP Conference Series: Earth and Environmental Science 6th International Conference on Eco Engineering Development, 2022(1) Rt-PA Rheza Maulana 2023 IOP Conf. Ser. Sci.1169, 012046DOI. https://doi.org/10.1088/1755-1315/1169/1/012046

Mayer, B. (2022). *International law obligations on climate change mitigation* (1st ed.). Oxford University Press.

McCulloch, S. (2022). Banning farrowing crates in the UK: Transitioning to free farrowing to meet the welfare needs of pigs. https://www.conservativeanimalwelfarefoundation.org/wp-content/uploads/2022/07/Banning-Farrowing-Crates-Report-Brochures-V6.pdf Retrieved May 13, 2024.

McCulloch, S. P. (2019a). Brexit and animal welfare impact assessment: Analysis of the threats Brexit poses to animal protection in the UK, EU and internationally. *Animals: An Open Access Journal from MDPI, 9*(3), 117. https://doi.org/10.3390/ani9030117

McCulloch, S. P. (2019b). Brexit and animal welfare impact assessment: Analysis of the opportunities Brexit presents for animal protection in the UK, EU, and internationally. *Animals: An Open Access Journal from MDPI, 9*(11), 877. https://doi.org/10.3390/ani9110877

McCurry, J. (2023). Whale meat on the menu as Japanese suppliers enlist influencers. *The Guardian*. http://www.theguardian.com/environment/2023/mar/23/whale-meat-on-the-menu-as-japanese-suppliers-try-to-tempt-tourists.

McDonald, S. E., Collins, E. A., Nicotera, N., Hageman, T. O., Ascione, F. R., Williams, J. H., & Graham-Bermann, S. A. (2015). Children's experiences of companion animal maltreatment in households characterized by intimate partner violence. *Child Abuse and Neglect, 50*, 116–127. https://doi.org/10.1016/j.chiabu.2015.10.005

McGubbin, M. (2023). *An atlas of endangered species*. Two Roads.

McKeown, P., & Dunn, R. A. (2021). A "Life-Style choice" or a philosophical belief? The argument for veganism and vegetarianism to be a protected philosophical belief and the position in England and Wales. *The Liverpool Law Review, 42*(2), 207–241. https://doi.org/10.1007/s10991-020-09273-w

McMahon, A., & Doyle, D. M. (2020). Patentability and de-extinct animals in Europe: The patented woolly mammoth? *Journal of Law and the Biosciences, 7*(1), G1–. https://doi.org/10.1093/jlb/lsaa017

McNicholas, J., Gilbey, A., Rennie, A., Ahmedzai, S., Dono, J.-A., & Ormerod, E. (2005). Pet ownership and human health: A brief review of evidence and issues. BMJ, 331(7527), 1252–1254. https://doi.org/10.1136/bmj.331.7527.1252.

Mellor, D. J. (2017). Operational details of the Five Domains Models and its key applications to the assessment and management of animal welfare. *Animals: An Open Access Journal from MDPI, 7*(8), 60. https://doi.org/10.3390/ani7080060

Mellor, D. J., & Reid, C. S. W. (1994). Concepts of animal well-being and predicting the impact of procedures on experimental animals. In *Improving the well-being of animals in the research environment; Australian and New Zealand council for the care of animals in research and teaching (ANZCCART): Glen Osmond, SA* (pp. 3–18). Australia.

Menache, S. (2000). Hunting and attachment to dogs in the PreModern Period. In A. Podberscek, E. Paul, & J. Serpell (Eds.), *Companion Animals and Us: Exploring the relationships between people and pets* (pp. 42–60). Cambridge University Press.

Mercury, L. (2022). https://www.leicestermercury.co.uk/news/leicester-news/police-dog-bo-retiring-hes-7094721 Retrieved May 14, 2024.

Merz, J. J., Barnard, P., Rees, W. E., Smith, D., Maroni, M., Rhodes, C. J., Dederer, J. H., Bajaj, N., Joy, M. K., Wiedmann, T., & Sutherland, R. (2023). World scientists' warning: The behavioural crisis driving ecological overshoot. *Science Progress, 106*(3), 368504231201372. https://doi.org/10.1177/00368504231201372

Met Office. (2023). What *do we mean by a climate tipping point*. Met Office. http://www.blog.metoffice.gov.uk/2023/09/11/what-do-we-mean-by-a-climate-tipping-point/ Retrieved May 14, 2024.

Michael, M. (2017). Animals as scientific objects'. In A. Kalof (Ed.), *The Oxford handbook of animal studies* (pp. 380–396). Oxford University Press.

Michener, L. H. (2015). Meating America's Demand: An analysis of the hidden costs of factory farming and alternate methods of food production. *Journal of Animal & Environmental Law, 7*(1), 145–185.

Midgley, M. (1983). *Animals and why they matter*. University of Georgia Press.

Milburn, J., & Van Goozen, S. (2021). Counting animals in war: First steps towards an inclusive just-war theory. *Social Theory and Practice, 47*(4), 657–685. https://doi.org/10.5840/soctheorpract2020123110

Miller, G. (2022). Livestock shipping strikes again: Death and cruelty on the high seas. *Freightwaves*. https://www.freightwaves.com/news/livestock-shipping-is-already-infamous-its-reputation-just-got-worse.

Mills, A. (2023). Meeting Lofty Aspirations? English national planning policy, international law, and climate change. Climate Law, 13(3–4), 163–187. https://doi.org/10.1163/18786561-bja10040

Minias, P. (2023). The effects of urban life on animal immunity: Adaptations and constraints. *The Science of the Total Environment*, *895*, 165085. https://doi.org/10.1016/j.scitotenv.2023.165085

Molesworth, W. (1994). *The collected works of Thomas hobbes*. Routledge/Thoemmes Press.

Monaghan, R., & da Silva, J. R. (2023). Militant animal rights activity: Terrorism, extremism or something else? *Studies in Conflict and Terrorism*, 1–16. https://doi.org/10.1080/1057610X.2023.2195066

Monbiot, G. (2023). Feeding the world without devouring the planet. *ReGenesis*. Penguin Books.

Moore, J. H. (1906). *The universal kinship* (1992 ed.). Centaur Publishing.

Moorhouse, T. P., Dahlsjö, C. A. L., Baker, S. E., D'Cruze, N. C., & Macdonald, D. W. (2015). The customer isn't always right-conservation and animal welfare implications of the increasing demand for wildlife tourism. *PLOS ONE*, *10*(10), e0138939. https://doi.org/10.1371/journal.pone.0138939

Moorhouse, T., D'Cruze, N. C., & Macdonald, D. W. (2017). Unethical use of wildlife in tourism: What's the problem, who is responsible, and what can be done? *Journal of Sustainable Tourism*, *25*(4), 505–516. https://doi.org/10.1080/09669582.2016.1223087

Mordue, T. (2009). Angling in modernity: A tour through society, nature and embodied passion. *Current Issues in Tourism*, *12*(5–6), 529–552. https://doi.org/10.1080/13683500903043244

Morell, V. (1997). The Origin of dogs: Running with the wolves. *Science*, *276*(5319), 1647–1648. https://doi.org/10.1126/science.276.5319.1647

Morelle, R., & Francis, A. (2024). World's first IVF rhino pregnancy'could save species. *BBC News*. http://www.bbc.co.uk/news/science-environment-68064432 Retrieved May 14, 2024

Moreno-Saiz, J. C., Albertos, B., Ruiz-Molero, E., & Mateo, R. G. (2021). The European Union can afford greater ambition in the conservation of its threatened plants. *Biological Conservation*, *261*. https://doi.org/10.1016/j.biocon.2021.109231

Moroșan, Ș., Pașca, A., & Leech, K. (2019). *Transparency and communication: Good Practice in Animal Research Communication*.

Morse, S. S., Mazet, J. A. K., Woolhouse, M., Parrish, C. R., Carroll, D., Karesh, W. B., Zambrana-Torrelio, C., Lipkin, W. I., & Daszak, P. (2012). Prediction and prevention of the next pandemic zoonosis. *The Lancet*, *380*(9857), 1956–1965. https://doi.org/10.1016/S0140-6736(12)61684-5

Morton, O., Scheffers, B. R., Haugaasen, T., & Edwards, D. P. (2022). Mixed protection of threatened species traded under CITES. *Current Biology*, *32*(5), 999–1009.e9. https://doi.org/10.1016/j.cub.2022.01.011

Morton, R., Hebart, M. L., & Whittaker, A. L. (2020). Explaining the gap between the ambitious goals and practical reality of animal welfare law enforcement: A review of the enforcement gap in Australia. *Animals: An Open Access Journal from MDPI*, *10*(3), 482. https://doi.org/10.3390/ani10030482

Moss, R. (1991). *Europe animal welfare concern and chaos?* Universities Federation for Animal Welfare.

Mubanga, M., Byberg, L., Nowak, C., Egenvall, A., Magnusson, P. K., Ingelsson, E., & Fall, T. (2017). Dog Ownership and the risk of cardiovascular disease and death – A nationwide cohort study. *Scientific Reports*, *7*(1), 15821. https://doi.org/10.1038/s41598-017-16118-6

Muller, S. M. (2018). Zombification, Social Death, and the Slaughterhouse: U.S. Industrial Practices of Livestock Slaughter. American Studies, 57(3), 81–101. https://doi.org/10.1353/ams.2018.0048.

Munro, L. (2005). *Confronting cruelty: Moral orthodoxy and the challenge of the animal rights movement* (1st ed.). BRILL.

Murphy, J. (2023). Elephant corridors: The busy trunk routes where locals take care to cross. *BBC News*. BBC. http://www.bbc.co.uk/news/science-environment-66317706 Retrieved May 14, 2024.

Murray, M. (2008). *Nature, red in tooth and claw: Theism and the problem of animal suffering*. Oxford University Press.

Myers, N. (1979). *The sinking ark*. Pergamon Press.

Næss, A. (1989). *Ecology, community and lifestyle: Outline of an ecosophy*. D. Rothenberg (Trans.). Cambridge University Press.

Nagtzaam, G. (2017). *From environmental action to ecoterrorism? Towards a process theory of environmental and animal rights oriented political violence*. Edward Elgar Publishing Limited.

Nakamura, J. N., & Kuemlangan, B. (2023). *Implementing the Convention on International Trade in Endangered Species of Wild Fauna and Flora (CITES) through national fisheries legal frameworks – A study and a guide* (2nd ed.). FAO Legal Guide No. 4. Food and Agriculture Organization. https://doi.org/10.4060/cc8051en

Nash, R. (1990). *American environmentalism: Readings in conservation history* (3rd ed.). McGraw-Hill.

Nash, R. (2001). *Wilderness and the American mind*. Yale Nota Bene.

Natali, M. (2023). A loophole in article VII of CITES: A case against annex I species breeding. *Journal of International Wildlife Law and Policy*, *26*(3), 209–221. https://doi.org/10.1080/13880292.2023.2291261

National Cancer Coalition. (1984). *Nature conservation in Great Britain*. Nature Publishing Conservancy Council.

National Gamekeepers Association. (n.d.). http://www.nationalgamekeepers.org.uk

Natural England. (2019). Wildlife management advice note. http://www.

assets.publishing.service.gov.uk/media/5f11bd67d3bf7f5badfe3d88/wml-gu02-animal-welfare-act-wildlife-managment.pdf Retrieved May 14, 2024.

Natural England. (n.d.). http://www.natural-england.org.uk Retrieved May 14, 2024.

Natural History Museum (2024) Towards 30 by 30: Balancing nature and people. www.nhm.ac.uk/content/dam/nhmwww/our-science/services/data/biodiversity-intactness-index/policy/30by30/towards-30by30-balancing-nature-and-people.pdf.

Nature Watch Foundation. (2017). Transparency and animal experiments: A case for repealing section 24 of the Animals (Scientific Procedures) Act, *1986*. https://naturewatch.org/files/uploads/Transparency_and_Animal_Experiments15.06.18.pdf Retrieved May 13, 2024.

Nautical Institute Department of Health. (2024). https://www.health-ni.gov.uk/articles/animal-scientific-procedures#:~:text=The%20Act%20requires%20a%20rigorous,care%20and%20welfare%20of%20animals. Retrieved May 13, 2024.

NAVS. (1986). Parliamentary briefing: The repeal of section 24 of the amended Animals (Scientific Procedures) Act 1986. Republished online 2014. National Anti-vivisection Society. https://www.navs.org.uk/downloads/navs_98f152e04e6643040c9a5c1aa1bcef03.pdf Retrieved May 13, 2024.

NAVS. (2013). Ministerial and parliamentary briefing of the Animals (Scientific Procedures) Act 1986. Prepared by NAVS, Retrieved August 2013. https://www.alaw.org.uk/wp-content/uploads/aspa-s24–190813-f2.pdf Retrieved May 13, 2024.

Naylor, M., & Astley, O. (2023) £60,000 seized from dealer who traded ivory from slaughtered elephants. *Derby Telegraph*. http://www.derbytelegraph.co.uk/news/derby-news/60000-seized-dealer-who-traded-6991070 Retrieved May 14, 2024.

NCad. (2016). *Transition to non-animal research: On opportunities for the phasing out of animal procedures and the stimulation of innovation without laboratory animals. Opinion of the Netherlands National Committee for the protection of animals used for scientific purposes*. https://www.ncadierproevenbeleid.nl/documenten/rapport/2016/12/15/ncad-opinion-transition-to-non-animal-research Retrieved May 13, 2024.

NC3Rs. (2015). *National centre for the replacement, refinement and reduction of animal research: Our vision 2015–2025*. https://nc3rs.org.uk/sites/default/files/2021–09/NC3Rs%20Our%20Vision%202015–2025.pdf Retrieved May 13, 2024.

New Scientist. (1997). *Space Monkeys* `were put at risk'. https://www.newscientist.com/article/mg15420800–800-space-monkeys-were-put-at-risk/ Retrieved May 13, 2024.

New Zealand Government. (2023). Exports of Livestock by sea have ended.

Ministry for Primary Industries. https://www.mpi.govt.nz/export/animals/live-animals-including-livestock/ Retrieved May 13, 2024.

Newell, M. (2012). The laws of whaling: Humane Society International Inc v Kyodo Senpaku Kaisha Ltd (2008). FCA 3 (15 January 2008). Southern Cross University Law Review. c, 15 (pp. 87–97).

Matthew, N. (2012). The laws of whaling: Humane Society International Inc v Kyodo Senpaku Kaisha Ltd (2008) FCA 3 (15 January 2008). *Southern Cross University Law Review*, *15*, 87–97.

Nicholson, A. (2021). *The sea is not made of water – life between the tides*. HarperCollins.

Nidditch, P. (Ed.). (1975). *John Locke: An essay on human understanding* (1689). Oxford University Press.

Nijhuis, M. (2021). *Beloved beasts: Fighting for life in an age of extinction* p. 60–. Bookmarks. Bookmarks Publications LLC.

No author. (2017). Zoo licensing system: "not fit for purpose". *The Veterinary Record*, *180*(21), 510–510. https://doi.org/10.1136/vr.j2532

Nobis, N. (2011). The harmful, nontherapeutic use of animals in research is morally wrong. *The American Journal of the Medical Sciences*, *342*(4), 297–304. https://doi.org/10.1097/MAJ.0b013e3182299421

Nozick, R. (1974). *Anarchy, state and utopia*. Blackwell Publishing.

Nurse, A. (2013). Privatising the green police: The role of NGOs in wildlife law enforcement. *Crime, Law and Social Change*, *59*(3), 305–318. https://doi.org/10.1007/s10611-013-9417-2

Nurse, A. (2016). Beyond the property debate: Animal welfare as a public good. *Contemporary Justice Review*, *19*(2), 174–187. https://doi.org/10.1080/10282580.2016.1169699

Nurse, A. (2017). Criminalising the right to hunt: European law perspectives on anti-hunting legislation. *Crime, Law and Social Change*, *67*(4), 383–399. https://doi.org/10.1007/s10611-016-9669-8

Nurse, A. (2019). A question of sentience: Brexit, animal welfare and animal protection law. *Journal of Animal & Environmental Law*, *10*(2), 32–59. https://doi.org/10.5565/rev/da.404

Nussbaum Wichert, R., & Nussbaum, M. C. (2017). Scientific whaling? The scientific research exception and the future of the International Whaling Commission. *Journal of Human Development and Capabilities*, *18*(3), 356–369. https://doi.org/10.1080/19452829.2017.1342386

Nyilas, F. (2021). CITES and animal welfare: The legal void for individual animal protection. *Global Journal of Animal Law*, *9*. ISSN 2341-8168. https://ojs.abo.fi/ojs/index.php/gjal/article/view/1720.

Office for Environmental Protection (OEP). (2024). http://www.theoep.org.uk/office-environmental-protection Retrieved May 14, 2024.

Offor, I. (2020). Animals and the impact of trade law and policy: A global animal law question. *Transnational Environmental Law*, *9*(2), 239–262. https://doi.org/10.1017/S2047102519000402

Offor, I. (2023). *Global animal law from the margins: International trade in animals and their bodies*. Taylor & Francis.
Offor, I., & Walter, J. (2017). The applicability of GATT article XX(a) to animal welfare. *UK Journal of Animal Law, 1*(1), 10–20.
O'Hare, R. (2019). Badger culling drives animals further afield increasing risk of TB spread. Imperial College London. http://www.imperial.ac.uk/news/193326/badger-culling-drives-animals-further-afield/ Retrieved May 14, 2024.
Okin, G. S. (2017). Environmental impacts of food consumption by dogs and cats. *PLOS ONE, 12*(8), e0181301. https://doi.org/10.1371/journal.pone.0181301
One Planet Sustainable Development Programme. (2021). http://www.unwto.org/sustainable-development/one-planet Retrieved May 14, 2024.
Oram, F., Kapar, M. D., Saharon, A. R., Elahan, H., Segaran, P., Poloi, S., Saidal, H., Abulani, A., Lackman, I., & Ancrenaz, M. (2022). 'Engaging the Enemy': Orangutan (Pongo pygmaeus morio) Conservation in Human Modified Environments in the Kinabatangan floodplain of Sabah, Malaysian Borneo. *International Journal of Primatology, 43*(6), 1067–1094. https://doi.org/10.1007/s10764-022-00288-w
O'Riordan, T., & Stoll-Kleemann, S. (2002) UN *Biodiversity. Sustainability and human communities: Protecting beyond the protected*. Cambridge University Press.
OSPAR. (2024). http://www.ospar.org Retrieved May 14, 2024.
O'Sullivan, S. (2006). Transparency and animal research regulation: An Australian case study. *Animal Liberation Philosophy and Policy Journal, 4*(1), 1–25.
Packer, R. M. A., O'Neill, D. G., Fletcher, F., & Farnworth, M. J. (2019). Great expectations, inconvenient truths, and the paradoxes of the dog-owner relationship for owners of brachycephalic dogs. *PLOS ONE, 14*(7), e0219918. https://doi.org/10.1371/journal.pone.0219918
Paemelaere, E. A. D., Mejía, A., Quintero, S., Hallett, M., Li, F., Wilson, A., Barnabas, H., Albert, A., Li, R., Baird, L., Pereira, G., & Melville, J. (2023). The road towards wildlife friendlier infrastructure: Mitigation planning through landscape-level priority settings and species connectivity frameworks. *Environmental Impact Assessment Review, 99*. https://doi.org/10.1016/j.eiar.2022.107010
Pallotta, N. (2017). Alaska legislature becomes first to require consideration of animals' interests in custody cases. *Animal legal defense fund*. https://aldf.org/article/alaska-legislature-becomes-first-to-require-consideration-of-animals-interests-in-custody-cases/ Retrieved May 14, 2024.
Papier, K., Fensom, G. K., Knuppel, A., Appleby, P. N., Tong, T. Y. N., Schmidt, J. A., Travis, R. C., Key, T. J., & Perez-Cornago, A. (2021). Meat consumption and risk of 25 common conditions: Outcome-wide

analyses in 475,000 men and women in the UK Biobank study. *BMC Medicine*, 19(1), 53. https://doi.org/10.1186/s12916-021-01922-9

Parliament. (2023) Debate on the import and sale of fur. House of Commons. https://researchbriefings.files.parliament.uk/documents/CDP-2023-0140/CDP-2023-0140.pdf Retrieved March 5, 2024.

Parliamentary Group for Animal Welfare. (n.d.). Wild animals. https://apgaw.org/wild-animals/ Retrieved May 14, 2024.

Paton, W. (1993). *Man and mouse* (2nd ed.). Oxford University Press.

Pepys, S. (1661). From Pepys' diary, number two, cited in Thomas, K. (1983). *Man and the natural world: Changing attitudes in England 1500–1800*. Allen Lane.

Pet Theft Taskforce (2021) Policy paper. https://assets.publishing.service.gov.uk/media/6130fa358fa8f5032d8d178f/Pet_Theft_Taskforce_Report_GOV.UK_PDF.pdf

PETA. (2024). Animal rights uncompromised: Catch-and-release fishing. http://www.peta.org/about-peta/why-peta/catch-and-release-fishing/ Retrieved May 14, 2024.

Peters, A. (2021). *Animals in international law*. Brill.

Peters, A. et al. (Eds.). (2022). *Animals in the international law of armed conflict*. Cambridge University Press.

Peters, B. G., & Tarpey, M. (2019). Are wicked problems really so wicked? Perceptions of policy problems. *Policy and Society*, *38*(2), 218–236. https://doi.org/10.1080/14494035.2019.1626595

Pew Commission. (2017). *Environmental impact of industrial farm animal production: A report of the pew commission on industrial farm animal production*. https://www.lclark.edu/live/files/6699-environmental-impact-of-industrial-farm-animal Retrieved March 5, 2024.

Pilcher, H. (2023). Back from the brink. *Science Focus*. BBC.

Pinillos, R. G., Appleby, M. C., Manteca, X., Scott-Park, F., Smith, C., & Velarde, A. (2016). One Welfare – A platform for improving human and animal welfare. *The Veterinary Record*, *179*(16), 412–413. https://doi.org/10.1136/vr.i5470

Plantlife. (n.d.). http://www.plantlife.org.uk Retrieved May 14, 2024.

Plato (*De Leg*, IX.12).

Platvoet, V. (2023). Wild things: Animal rights in EU conservation law. *Journal of International Wildlife Law and Policy*, *26*(2), 79–103. https://doi.org/10.1080/13880292.2023.2229628

Pound, P., & Blaug, R. (2016). Transparency and public involvement in animal research. *Alternatives to Laboratory Animals*, *44*(2), 167–173. https://doi.org/10.1177/026119291604400210

Power, E. (2008). Furry families: Making a human-dog family through home. *Social and Cultural Geography*, *9*(5), 535–555. https://doi.org/10.1080/14649360802217790

Pratschke, K. M. (2017). Current thinking about brachycephalic syndrome: More than just airways. *Veterinary Ireland Journal*, *5*(11), 536–542.

Predragovic, M., Assis, J., Sumaila, U. R., Gonçalves, J. M. S., Cvitanovic, C., & Horta e Costa, B. (2024). Up to 80% of threatened and commercial species across European marine protected areas face novel climates under high emission scenario. *Npj Ocean Sustainability*, *3*(1), 1–9. https://doi.org/10.1038/s44183-024-00068-4

Pressat. (2023). Lawyers welcome UN CRC's General Comment on child rights acknowledging the impact of both positive and negative interactions with animals. https://pressat.co.uk/releases/lawyers-welcome-un-crcs-general-comment-on-child-rights-acknowledging-the-impact-of-both-positive-and-negative-interactions-with-animals-9b7467683432b57487c6fdd0b2f84aff/ Retrieved May 14, 2024

Primatt, H. (1776). *The duty of Mercy.* (1992). Centaur Publishing.

Prisner-Levyne, Y. (2020). Trophy hunting, canned hunting, tiger farming, and the questionable relevance of the conservation narrative grounding international wildlife law. *Journal of International Wildlife Law and Policy*, *23*(4), 239–285. https://doi.org/10.1080/13880292.2E was020.1866236

Proctor, H. S., Carder, G., & Cornish, A. R. (2013). Searching for animal sentience: A systematic review of the scientific literature. *Animals: An Open Access Journal from MDPI*, *3*(3), 882–906. https://doi.org/10.3390/ani3030882

Purwoko, A., Kuswanda, W., Situmorang, R. O. P., Hutapea, F. J., Saputra, M. H., & Pasaribu, P. H. P. (2022). Orangutan ecotourism on Sumatra island: Current conditions and a call for further development. *Sustainability*, *14*(18), 11328. https://doi.org/10.3390/su141811328

Rachels, J. (1991). *Created from animals.* Oxford University Press.

Radford, M. (1996). Protecting wild mammals. *The New Law Journal*, *146*, 458.

Radford, M. (2001). *Animal welfare law in Britain.* Oxford University Press.

Radford, M. (2023). *Keynote Speech: Animal Sentience SLS Workshop*. Newcastle University (no date). http://www.ramsar.org Retrieved May 14, 2024.

Ramsey, S., Randour, M. L., Blaney, N., & Gupta, M. (2010). *Protecting Domestic Violence victims by Protecting their Pets. Juvenile and family justice today.* National Council of Juvenile and Family Court Judges.

Ratcliffe, R. (2024). Malaysia plans to give orangutans to countries that buy palm oil. *The Guardian.* https://www.theguardian.com/world/article/2024/may/09/malaysia-plans-give-orangutans-gifts-countries-buy-palm-oil.

Rawls, J. (1972). *A theory of justice.* Oxford University Press.

Rayburn, S. W., Anderson, S., & Sierra, J. J. (2020). Future thinking: A marketing perspective on reducing wildlife crime. *Psychology and Marketing*, *37*(12), 1643–1655. https://doi.org/10.1002/mar.21413

Reaka-Kudla et al. (1997). *Biodiversity II Understanding and protecting our biological Resources.* Joseph Henry Press.

Redpath, S. M., Young, J., Evely, A., Adams, W. M., Sutherland, W. J., Whitehouse, A., Amar, A., Lambert, R. A., Linnell, J. D. C., Watt, A., & Gutiérrez, R. J. (2013). Understanding and managing conservation conflicts. *Trends in Ecology and Evolution*, *28*(2), 100–109. https://doi.org/10.1016/j.tree.2012.08.021

Regan, T. (1980). Utilitarianism, vegetarianism, and animal rights. *Philosophy and Public Affairs*, *9*(4), 305–324.

Regan, T. (1982). *All that dwell therein*. University of California Press.

Regan, T. (1983). *The case for animal rights*. University of California Press.

Regan, T. (1985). The case for animals rights. In P. Singer (Ed.), *Defence of animals*. Blackwell Publishing.

Regan, T. (2008). The case for animal rights. In *Armstrong, S, and Bolzler, R. The Animal Ethics Reader* (2nd ed.) (pp. 19–23). Routledge.

Regan, T., & Singer, P. (Eds.). (1989). *Animal rights and human obligations* (2nd ed.). Prentice Hall.

Reid, C. (1994). Nature *Conservation law*. Sweet & Maxwell.

Reid, C. T. (2021). Mapping post-Brexit environmental law. *ERA Forum*, *21*(4), 655–665. https://doi.org/10.1007/s12027-020-00627-5

Reins, L., & Verschuuren, J. (2022). *Research handbook on climate change mitigation law* (2nd ed.). Edward Elgar Publishing.

Reisinger, R. R., Brooks, C. M., Raymond, B., Freer, J. J., Cotté, C., Xavier, J. C., Trathan, P. N., Bornemann, H., Charrassin, J.-B., Costa, D. P., Danis, B., Hückstädt, L., Jonsen, I. D., Lea, M.-A., Torres, L., Van de Putte, A., Wotherspoon, S., Friedlaender, A. S., Ropert-Coudert, Y., & Hindell, M. (2022). Predator-derived bioregions in the Southern Ocean: Characteristics, drivers and representation in marine protected areas. *Biological Conservation*, *272*, 109630. https://doi.org/10.1016/j.biocon.2022.109630

ResPublica. (2022). *UK Trade Policy and Animal Welfare*. https://www.respublica.org.uk/wp-content/uploads/2022/07/UK-Trade-Policy-Animal-Welfare.pdf Retrieved April 9, 2024

ReVista, Harvard University, 2023. Estrellita the Woolly Monkey and the Ecuadorian Constitutional Court: Animal Rights Through the Rights of Nature. Accessed at: https://revista.drclas.harvard.edu/estrellita-the-wooly-monkey-and-the-ecuadorian-constitutional-court-animal-rights-through-the-rights-of-nature/. (accessed 14 May 2024)

Rural sport. (n.d.). Arguments for hunting. Available at: e. http://www.ruralsports.co.uk/arguments-for-hunting.html Retrieved May 14, 2024.

Rewilding Britain (2024). http://www.rewildingbritain.org.uk/?gad_source=1&gclid=EAIaIQobChMI66qVu4P5hQMVKpVQBh3TiQHZEAAYASAAEgK-tfD_BwE Retrieved May 14, 2024.

Royal Commission (1876). *Report of the royal commission on the practice of subjecting live animals to experiments for scientific purposes*. HMSO.

Senedd Cymru/Welsh Parliament. (2021) Finally ban the manufacture,

sale and use of animal snares in Wales. https://business.senedd.wales/documents/s116299/Research%20brief.pdf Retrieved May 14, 2024.
Rhys, E. (1913). *The ethics of Spinoza and de Emendatione.* Dent.
Richards, J. F. (2014). *The world hunt: An environmental history of the commodification of animals.* University of California Press.
Richardson, B. J. (2020). *From student strikes to the extinction rebellion: New protest movements shaping our future* (1st ed.). Edward Elgar Publishing.
Richardson, J., Lockhart, C., Pongolini, S., Karesh, W. B., Baylis, M., Goldberg, T., Slingenbergh, J., Gale, P., Venturini, T., Catchpole, M., de Balogh, K., Pautasso, M., Broglia, A., Berthe, F., Schans, J., & Poppy, G. (2016). Drivers for emerging issues in animal and plant health. *EFSA Journal. European Food Safety Authority*, *14*(Suppl. 1), e00512–n/a. https://doi.org/10.2903/j.efsa.2016.s0512
Rigal, S., Dakos, V., Alonso, H., Auniņš, A., Benkő, Z., Brotons, L., Chodkiewicz, T., Chylarecki, P., de Carli, E., Del Moral, J. C., Domşa, C., Escandell, V., Fontaine, B., Foppen, R., Gregory, R., Harris, S., Herrando, S., Husby, M., Ieronymidou, C., . . . Devictor, V. (2023). Farmland practices are driving bird population decline across Europe. *Proceedings of the National Academy of Sciences of the United States of America.* Proceedings of the National Academy of Sciences, *120*(21), e2216573120. https://doi.org/10.1073/pnas.2216573120
Ripple, W. J., Wolf, C., Gregg, J. W., Rockström, J., Newsome, T. M., Law, B. E., Marques, L., Lenton, T. M., Xu, C., Huq, S., Simons, L., & King, S. D. A. (2023). The 2023 state of the climate report: Entering uncharted territory. *BioScience*, 73(12), 841–850. https://doi.org/10.1093/biosci/biad080
Ritvo, H. (1994). Animals in Nineteenth-Century Britain: Complicated attitudes and competing categories. In A. Manning & J. A. Serpell (Eds.), *Animals and human society: Changing perspectives* (pp. 106–126). Routledge.
Robertson, I. (2015). *Animals, welfare and the law: Fundamental principles for critical assessment.* Routledge.
Rochford, F. (2024). *Environmental personhood: New trajectories in law* (1st ed.). Routledge. https://doi.org/10.4324/9781003388272
Rodd, R. (1990). *Biology, ethics and animals.* Clarendon Press.
Rodman, J. (1977). The liberation of nature. *Inquiry*, *20*(1–4), 83–131. https://doi.org/10.1080/00201747708601834
Rodríguez Goyes, D. (2021). Contending philosophical foundations in international wildlife law: A discourse analysis of cites and the Bern convention. *Revista Catalana de Dret Ambiental* [Preprint], 12(1). https://doi.org/10.17345/RCDA3051
Roelcke, V. (2004). Nazi medicine and research on human beings. *The Lancet*, *364*(Suppl. 1), s6–s7. https://doi.org/10.1016/S0140-6736(04)17619-8
Rohr, J. R., Barrett, C. B., Civitello, D. J., Craft, M. E., Delius, B., DeLeo, G. A., Hudson, P. J., Jouanard, N., Nguyen, K. H., Ostfeld, R. S., Remais, J. V., Riveau, G., Sokolow, S. H., & Tilman, D. (2019).

Emerging human infectious diseases and the links to global food production. *Nature Sustainability*, *2*(6), 445–456. https://doi.org/10.1038/s41893-019-0293-3

Rollin, B. (1995). *Farm animal welfare: Social, bioethical, and research issues*. Iowa State University Press.

Rollin, B. E. (2017). The ethics of animal research. In A. Kalof (Ed.), *The Oxford handbook of animal studies* (pp. 345–363). Oxford University Press.

Rolo, E. A., Oliveira, A. R., Dourado, C. G., Farinha, A., Rebelo, M. T., & Dias, D. (2013). Identification of sarcosaprophagous Diptera species through DNA barcoding in wildlife forensics. *Forensic Science International*, *228*(1–3), 160–164. https://doi.org/10.1016/j.forsciint.2013.02.038

Rook, D. (2014). Who gets Charlie? The emergence of pet custody disputes in family law: Adapting theoretical tools from Child Law. *International Journal of Law, Policy and the Family*, *28*(2), 177–193. https://doi.org/10.1093/lawfam/ebu004

Rook, D. (2018). For the Love of Darcie: Recognising the Human–Companion Animal Relationship in Housing Law and Policy. *Liverpool Law Review*, *39*(1–2), 29–46. https://doi.org/10.1007/s10991-018-9209-y

Rook, D., & Jegatheesan, B. (2024). 'No Pet' covenants and the law: A harm assessment approach to regulating companion animals in rental housing across the world. *Liverpool Law Review*.

Rook, D., Legge, D., & Browning, H. (2023). Sentient food? – The legal protection of sentient invertebrates in food production in England. *The UK journal of animal law*.

Rowan, A. (1984). *Of mice, models and men*. State University of New York Press.

Rowan, A. N., D'Silva, J. M., Duncan, I. J. H., & Palmer, N. (2021). Animal sentience: History, science, and politics. *Animal Sentience*, *6*(31). https://doi.org/10.51291/2377-7478.1697

Royal Society for the Prevention of Cruelty to Animals. (1995). *Animal life*. Royal Society for the Prevention of Cruelty to Animals.

Royal Society for the Prevention of Cruelty to Animals. (2014). Do you give a monkey's: The need for a ban on pet primates. https://www.rspca.org.uk/documents/1494939/7712578/Do+you+give+a+monkey%27s.pdf/6872c3ae-8bbd-9dd4-f26d-eb48fc8bbbee?t=1553169391718.

Royal Society for the Prevention of Cruelty to Animals. (2019). RSPCA prosecutions annual report. https://www.rspca.org.uk/documents/1494939/7712578/Prosecutions+Annual+Report+2019+%28PDF+1.83MB%29.pdf/5a5a3644-ea97–606e-cce1–373159a0a7c6?t=1583770854006 Retrieved May 13, 2024.

Royal Society for the Prevention of Cruelty to Animals. (2020a) Eat. Sit. Suffer. Repeat. The life of a typical meat chicken. https://www.rspca.org.uk/webContent/staticImages/BroilerCampaign/EatSitSufferRepeat.pdf.

Royal Society for the Prevention of Cruelty to Animals. (2020b). 2021–2030 strategy summary: Together for animal welfare. https://www.rspca.org.uk/whatwedo/strategy Retrieved May 13, 2024.
Royal Society for the Prevention of Cruelty to Animals. (2021). Getting justice for animals. https://www.rspca.org.uk/whatwedo/strategy/prosecution Retrieved April 9, 2024.
Royal Society for the Prevention of Cruelty to Animals. (n.d.). Key issues surrounding the welfare of farmed fish. https://www.rspca.org.uk/adviceandwelfare/farm/fish/keyissues Retrieved February 24, 2024.
Royal Society for the Prevention of Cruelty to Animals. (n.d.). Animal fighting. http://www.rspca.org.uk/whatwedo/endcruelty/investigatingcruelty/organised/animalfighting#:~:text=Animal%20fighting%20-%20such%20as%20dog,day%20across%20England%20and%20Wales. Retrieved May 14, 2024
Royal Society for the Prevention of Cruelty to Animals. (n.d.). Badgers. http://www.rspca.org.uk/adviceandwelfare/wildlife/badgers/law Retrieved May 14, 2024.
Royal Society for the Protection of Birds. (n.d.). Game bird Shooting laws and impact. http://www.rspb.org.uk/helping-nature/what-we-do/influence-government-and-business/game-bird-shooting-laws-and-impact Retrieved May 14, 2024.
Rushby, K. M. (2023). Rhinos return to Zimbabwe and a new kind of safari starts to take shape. *The Guardian*. http://www.theguardian.com/travel/2023/may/15/rhinos-return-to-zimbabwe-and-a-new-kind-of-safari-starts-to-take-shape Retrieved May 14, 2024.
Russell, W. M. S., & Burch, R. L. (1959). *The principles of humane experimental technique*. Methuen, and Co. Ltd.
Russill, C. (2015). Climate change tipping points: Origins, precursors, and debates. *WIREs Climate Change*, *6*(4), 427–434. https://doi.org/10.1002/wcc.344
Ryder, R. (1981). British legislation and proposals for reform. In D. Sperlinger (Ed.), *Animals in research: New perspectives in animal experimentation* (pp. 11–38). John Wiley.
Ryder, R. (1983). *Victims of science* (2nd ed.). Centaur Publishing.
Ryder, R. (1989). *Animal revolution*. Blackwell Publishing.
Salt, H. (1915). *Animals' rights: Considered in relation to social progress*. Bell & Sons.
Salvatori, V., Donfrancesco, V., Trouwborst, A., Boitani, L., Linnell, J. D. C., Alvares, F., Åkesson, M., Balys, V., Blanco, J. C., Chiriac, S., Cirovic, D., Groff, C., Guinot-Ghestem, M., Huber, D., Kojola, I., Kusak, J., Kutal, M., Iliopulos, Y., Ionescu, O., . . . Ciucci, P. (2020). European agreements for nature conservation need to explicitly address wolf-dog hybridization. *Biological Conservation, 248*. https://doi.org/10.1016/j.biocon.2020.108525
Sample, I. (2023). Britons urged not to buy exotic pets "on a whim" amid

welfare concerns. *The Guardian*. https://www.theguardian.com/lifeandstyle/2023/feb/16/britons-urged-not-buy-exotic-pets-whim-welfare-concerns Retrieved May 13, 2024.

Sand, P. H. (2017). International protection of endangered species in the face of wildlife trade: Whither conservation diplomacy? *Asia Pacific Journal of Environmental Law*, *20*(1), 5–27. https://doi.org/10.4337/apjel.2017.01.01

Sandin, P. (1999). Dimensions of the precautionary principle. *Human and Ecological Risk Assessment*, *5*(5), 889–907. https://doi.org/10.1080/10807039991289185

Sandler, R. (2020). The ethics of genetic engineering and gene drives in conservation. *Conservation Biology*, *34*(2), 378–385. https://doi.org/10.1111/cobi.13407

Sandler, R. L. (2012). *The ethics of species: An introduction* (pp. xii–xii). Cambridge University Press. https://doi.org/10.1017/CBO9781139151221.

Saraiva, J. L., Arechavala-Lopez, P., & Sneddon, L. U. (2022). Farming fish. In A. Knight, C. Phillips, & P. Sparks (Eds.), *Routledge handbook of animal welfare* (pp. 115–127). Routledge.

Sarkar, A. R. (2023). South Korea to ban divisive practice of eating dog meat, ruling party says. *Independent*. https://www.independent.co.uk/asia/east-asia/south-korea-dog-meat-ban-b2449066.html Retrieved May 13, 2024.

Satz, A. (2009). Animals as vulnerable subjects: Beyond interest convergence, hierarchy and property. *Animal Law*, *16*, 65–122.

Saunders, T. (1970). *Plato: The laws*. Penguin Books.

Scarborough, P., Clark, M., Cobiac, L., Papier, K., Knuppel, A., Lynch, J., Harrington, R., Key, T., & Springmann, M. (2023). Vegans, vegetarians, fish-eaters and meat-eaters in the UK show discrepant environmental impacts. *Nature Food*, *4*(7), 565–574. https://doi.org/10.1038/s43016-023-00795-w

Schaffner, J. (2011). *An introduction to animals and the law*. Palgrave Macmillan.

Schapper, A., Hoffmann, C., & Lee, P. (2022a). Procedural rights for nature–a pathway to sustainable decarbonisation? *Third World Quarterly*, *43*(5), 1197–1216. https://doi.org/10.1080/01436597.2022.2057293

Schapper, A. et al. (2022b). Mainstreaming the animal in biodiversity governance: Broadening the moral and legal community to nonhumans. Cambridge University Press.

Scherr, S. J., & Yadav, S. (1996). Land degradation in the developing world: Implications for food, agriculture, and the environment to 2020. *Food, Agriculture, and the Environment* Discussion Paper 14.

Schmidt, D. N., Pieraccini, M., & Evans, L. (2022). Marine protected areas in the context of climate change: Key challenges for coastal social-ecological systems. *Philosophical Transactions of the Royal Society of London. Series B, Biological Sciences*, *377*(1854), 20210131–. https://doi.org/10.1098/rstb.2021.0131

Scholaert, F. (2023). EPRS. European Parliamentary Research Service Members' Research Service PE 747.917 – Retrieved June 2023. http://www.europarl.europa.eu/RegData/etudes/BRIE/2023/747917/EPRS_BRI(2023)747917_EN.pdf Retrieved May 14, 2024

Scholtz, W. (2017). Killing them softly? Animal welfare and the inhumanity of whale killing. *Journal of International Wildlife Law and Policy*, *20*(1), 18–37. https://doi.org/10.1080/13880292.2017.1309865

Schopenhauer, A. (1819). The world as will and idea. In. In (6th ed.), 1909 R. Haldane & J. Kemp (trans), *2* (pp. 480–481). Kegan Paul, Trench and Trübner.

Schreefel, L., Schulte, R. P. O., De Boer, I. J. M., Schrijver, A. P., & Van Zanten, H. H. E. (2020). Regenerative agriculture–the soil is the base. *Global Food Security*, *26*, 100404. https://doi.org/10.1016/j.gfs.2020.100404

Schuck-Paim, C., Alonso, W. J., & Slywitch, E. (2023). Animal welfare and human health. In A. Knight, C. Phillips, & P. Sparks (Eds.), *Routledge handbook of animal welfare* (pp. 321–335). Routledge.

Schweitzer, A. (1923). *Civilisation and ethics*. A & C Black Ltd.

Scott, A. J. (2021). *Improving Strategic Planning for Nature Conservation, report to Planning Advisory Service, Pas. London*. http://www.local.gov.uk/pas/plan-making/strategic-plans/strategic-planning-research-paper-improving-strategic-planning#_ftn1.

Scruton, R. (1996). *Animal rights and wrongs*. Demos.

Scully, M. (2011). *Dominion: The Power of Man, the suffering of animals and the call to mercy*. Souvenir Press.

Secretariat of the Convention on Biological Diversity. (2020). http://www.cbd.int/secretariat Retrieved May 14, 2024.

Sellheim, N., & Schumacher, J. (2022). Increasing the Effectiveness of the Bonn Convention on the Conservation of Migratory Species. *Journal of International Wildlife Law and Policy*, *25*(4), 367–383. https://doi.org/10.1080/13880292.2022.2153461

Serpell, J. A. (2000). Creatures of the unconscious: Companion animals as mediators. In A. Podberscek, E. Paul, & J. A. Serpell (Eds.), *Companion Animals and Us: Exploring the relationships between people and pets* (pp. 108–124). Cambridge University Press.

Serpell, J. A., & Paul, E. (1994). Pets and the Development of positive attitudes to animals. In A. Manning & J. A. Serpell (Eds.), *Animals and human society: Changing perspectives* (pp. 127–144). Routledge.

Seymour, M., & Connelly, S. (2023). Regenerative agriculture and a more-than-human ethic of care: A relational approach to understanding transformation. *Agriculture and Human Values*, *40*(1), 231–244. https://doi.org/10.1007/s10460-022-10350-1

Shapiro, G. (2019). Response to Shawn Thompson on "Supporting ape rights: finding the right fit between science and the law". *ASEBL Journal*, *14*(1), 25–26.

Sharpe, R. (1988). *The cruel deception: The use of animals in medical research.* Thorsons Publishers.

Shaw, G. (1949) in Bowker, G. (Ed.). *Shaw on vivisection.* George Allen & Unwin.

Shaw, P., Ogada, D., Dunn, L., Buij, R., Amar, A., Garbett, R., Herremans, M., Virani, M. Z., Kendall, C. J., Crocs, B. M., Odino, M., Kapila, S., Wairasho, P., Rutz, C., Botha, A., Gallo-Orsi, U., Murn, C., Maude, G., & Thomsett, S. (2024). African savanna raptors show evidence of widespread population collapse and a growing dependence on protected areas. *Nature Ecology and Evolution*, 8(1), 45–56. https://doi.org/10.1038/s41559-023-02236-0

Shea, S. et al. (2022). Supply and Demand: The EU's role in the global shark trade. Stichting IFAW (International Fund for Animal Welfare). http://www.ifaw.org/international/resources/eu-role-global-shark-trade.

Shir-Vertesh, D. (2012). 'Flexible Personhood': Loving animals as family members in Israel. *American Anthropologist*, *114*(3), 420–432. https://doi.org/10.1111/j.1548-1433.2012.01443.x

Shoard, M. (1997) *This land is our land.* Gaia Books.

Shore, E. R., Petersen, C. L., & Douglas, D. K. (2003). Moving as a reason for pet relinquishment: A closer look. *Journal of Applied Animal Welfare Science*, *6*(1), 39–52. https://doi.org/10.1207/S15327604JAWS0601_04

Shotton, J. (July 2023). Sad snakes and geckos with bone disease – We vets see the dark side of the UK's exotic pet boom. *The Guardian.* http://www.theguardian.com/commentisfree/2023/jul/03/snakes-geckos-vet-dark-side-uk-exotic-pet-boom.

Siddique, H. (2022). Consequences "dire" if Human Rights Act ditched, more than 50 groups warn. *The Guardian*, Retrieved May 9, 2022. https://www.theguardian.com/law/2022/may/09/consequences-dire-human-rights-act-ditched-northern-ireland-boris-johnson, Retrieved May 4, 2024.

Sigsgaard, T., & Balmes, J. (2017). Environmental effects of intensive livestock farming. *American Journal of Respiratory and Critical Care Medicine*, *196*(9), 1092–1093. https://doi.org/10.1164/rccm.201706-1075ED

Silva, E. B., & Smart, C. (1999). *The new family?* SAGE.

Silverstein, H. (1996). *Unleashing rights: Law, meaning, and the animal rights movement.* University of Michigan Press.

Simberloff, D. (2013). *Invasive species: What everyone needs to know.* Oxford University Press.

Simonds, C. H. (2023). Ethical veganism as moral phenomenology: Engaging Buddhism with animal ethics. *Journal of Animal Ethics*, *13*(1), 48–60. https://doi.org/10.5406/21601267.13.1.06

Sindhøj, E., Lindahl, C., & Bark, L. (2021). Review: Potential alternatives to high-concentration carbon dioxide stunning of pigs at slaughter. *Animal*, *15*(3), 100164. https://doi.org/10.1016/j.animal.2020.100164

Singer, P. (1975). *Animal liberation* (3rd ed.). Pimlico.

Singer, P. (1980). Utilitarianism and vegetarianism. *Philosophy and Public Affairs*, *9*, 325–337.

Singer, P. (1991). To do or not to do. In R. Baird & S. Rosenbaum (Eds.), *Animal experimentation: The moral issues*. Prometheus Books.

Singer, P. (2015). *Animal liberation*. Random House.

Singleton, B. E., & Lidskog, R. (2018). Science, red in tooth and claw: Whaling, purity, pollution and institutions in marine mammal scientists' boundary work. *Environment and Planning E*, *1*(1–2), 165–185. https://doi.org/10.1177/2514848618768213

Slabbert, M. (2004). Prosecuting animals in medieval Europe: Possible explanations. *Fundamina: A Journal of Legal History*, *10*, 159–179.

Slawson, N. (2021). Brighton cat killer jailed for five years. *The Guardian*. https://www.theguardian.com/uk-news/2021/jul/30/brighton-cat-killer-steve-bouquet-jailed-for-five-years Retrieved December 9, 2023.

Smith, J., & Boyd, K. (1991). *Lives in the balance: The ethics of using animals in biomedical research*. Oxford University Press.

Smith, M. J., Benítez-Díaz, H., Clemente-Muñoz, M. Á., Donaldson, J., Hutton, J. M., Noel McGough, H., Medellin, R. A., Morgan, D. H. W., O'Criodain, C., Oldfield, T. E. E., Schippmann, U., & Williams, R. J. (2011). Assessing the impacts of international trade on CITES-listed species: Current practices and opportunities for scientific research. *Biological Conservation*, *144*(1), 82–91. https://doi.org/10.1016/j.biocon.2010.10.018

Sollund, R. (2011). Expressions of speciesism: The effects of keeping companion animals on animal abuse, animal trafficking and species decline. *Crime, Law and Social Change*, *55*(5), 437–451. https://doi.org/10.1007/s10611-011-9296-3

Sollund, R. (2020). Wildlife management, species injustice and ecocide in the Anthropocene. *Critical Criminology*, *28*(3), 351–369. https://doi.org/10.1007/s10612-019-09469-1

Sollund, R. (2022). Wildlife trade and law enforcement: A proposal for a remodeling of CITES incorporating species justice, eco-justice, and environmental justice. *International Journal of Offender Therapy and Comparative Criminology*, *66*(9), 1017–1035. https://doi.org/10.1177/0306624X221099492

Spark, G. B. (2014). Protecting wild animals from unnecessary suffering. *Journal of Environmental Law*, *26*(3), 473–494. https://doi.org/10.1093/jel/equ023

Sparks, P., & Brooman, S. (2017). Brexit: A new dawn for animals used in research, of a threat to the "most stringent regulatory system in the world"? *The UK Journal of Animal Law*, *1*(2), 1–10.

Spee, L. B., Hazel, S. J., Dal Grande, E., Boardman, W. S. J., & Chaber, A.-L. (2019). Endangered exotic pets on social media in the Middle East: Presence and impact. *Animals (Basel)*, *9*(8), 480. https://doi.org/10.3390/ani9080480

Springmann, M., Clark, M., Mason-D'Croz, D., Wiebe, K., Bodirsky, B. L., Lassaletta, L., de Vries, W., Vermeulen, S. J., Herrero, M., Carlson, K. M., Jonell, M., Troell, M., DeClerck, F., Gordon, L. J., Zurayk, R., Scarborough, P., Rayner, M., Loken, B., Fanzo, J., . . . Willett, W. (2018). Options for keeping the food system within environmental limits. *Nature, 562*(7728), 519–525. https://doi.org/10.1038/s41586-018-0594-0

Stamp-Dawkins, M. (1980). *Animal suffering*. Chapman & Hall.

Stanton, M. M., Tzatzalos, E., Donne, M., Kolundzic, N., Helgason, I., & Ilic, D. (2019). Prospects for the use of induced pluripotent stem cells in animal conservation and environmental protection. *Stem Cells Translational Medicine, 8*(1), 7–13. https://doi.org/10.1002/sctm.18-0047

Stavisky, J., Brennan, M. L., Downes, M., & Dean, R. (2012). Demographics and economic burden of un-owned cats and dogs in the UK: Results of a 2010 census. *BMC Veterinary Research*, *8*, 163. https://doi.org/10.1186/1746-6148-8-163

Steinfeld, H., Gerber, P. J., & Wassenaar, T. (2006). *Livestock's long shadow: Environmental issues and options (UN Food & Agriculture Organization).*

Stephan, M. J., & Chenoweth, E. (2008). Why civil resistance works: The strategic logic of nonviolent conflict. *International Security*, *33*(1), 7–44. https://doi.org/10.1162/isec.2008.33.1.7

Stone, A. (2023). Frances Power Cobbe and the philosophy of anti-vivisection. *Journal of Animal Ethics*, *13*(1), 21–30. https://doi.org/10.5406/21601267.13.1.04

Strassburg, B. B. N., Iribarrem, A., Beyer, H. L., Cordeiro, C. L., Crouzeilles, R., Jakovac, C. C., Braga Junqueira, A., Lacerda, E., Latawiec, A. E., Balmford, A., Brooks, T. M., Butchart, S. H. M., Chazdon, R. L., Erb, K.-H., Brancalion, P., Buchanan, G., Cooper, D., Díaz, S., Donald, P. F., . . . Visconti, P. (2020). Global priority areas for ecosystem restoration. *Nature, 586*(7831), 724–729. https://doi.org/10.1038/s41586-020-2784-9

Stringham, O. C., Maher, J., Lassaline, C. R., Wood, L., Moncayo, S., Toomes, A., Heinrich, S., Watters, F., Drake, C., Chekunov, S., Hill, K. G. W., Decary-Hetu, D., Mitchell, L., Ross, J. V., & Cassey, P. (2023). The dark web trades wildlife, but mostly for use as drugs. *People and Nature, 5*(3), 999–1009. https://doi.org/10.1002/pan3.10469

Stuart, C., & Stuart, T. (1996). *Africa's vanishing wildlife*. Sawn Hill Press.

Stucki, S. (2020). Towards a theory of legal animal rights: Simple and fundamental rights. *Oxford Journal of Legal Studies*, *40*(3), 533–560. https://doi.org/10.1093/ojls/gqaa007

Sugiarto, W. (2023). Impact of wildlife crossing structures on wildlife–vehicle collisions. *Transportation Research Record*, *2677*(2), 670–685. https://doi.org/10.1177/03611981221108158

Summers, J., & Gough, A. (2018). *Non-state actors and international obligations: Creation, evolution and enforcement*. Brill.

Sunstein, C., & Nussbaum, M. (Eds.). (2004). *Animal rights: Current debates and new directions*. Oxford University Press.

Suratman, M. N. (Ed.). (2022). *Protected Area Management: Recent advances*. IntechOpen.

Suzuki, K. K., Oka, T., & Yasuda, M. (2022). Spatiotemporal changes in antlerless proportion of culled sika deer in relation to deer density. *Journal of Forestry Research*, *33*(3), 1095–1101. https://doi.org/10.1007/s11676-021-01405-w

Swann, S. (2023). How undercover sting outwitted pangolin traffickers. *BBC News*. http://www.bbc.co.uk/news/world-africa-66375281 Retrieved May 14, 2024.

Sykes, K. (2016). Globalization and the animal turn: How international trade law contributes to global norms of animal protection. *Transnational Environmental Law*, *5*(1), 55–79. Available at. https://doi.org/10.1017/S2047102516000054

Sykes, K. (2021). *Animal welfare and international trade law: The impact of the WTO seal case*. Edward Elgar Publishing.

Taylor, K., & Alvarez, L. R. (2019). An estimate of the number of animals used for scientific purposes worldwide in 2015. *Alternatives to Laboratory Animals*, *47*(5–6), 196–213. https://doi.org/10.1177/0261192919899853

The Convention on Biological Diversity. (n.d.). http://www.cbd.int Retrieved May 14, 2024.

The Global Goals. (n.d.). http://www.globalgoals.org/take-action/?gad_source=1&gclid=EAIaIQobChMIu_vt7vb4hQMVb4hQBh3IUg_PEAAYASAAEgIlwvD_BwE Retrieved May 14, 2024.

The New York declaration on animal consciousness. (2024). Google. https://sites.google.com/nyu.edu/nydeclaration/declaration Retrieved 21/4/2024.

The Humane League. (2021a). UK public backs calls for stronger fish welfare laws. https://thehumaneleague.org.uk/article/uk-public-backs-calls-for-stronger-fish-welfare-laws?utm_source=thehumaneleagueuk&utm_medium=blog Retrieved March 4, 2024.

The Humane League. (2021b). Governments fail to inspect fish welfare at slaughter. https://thehumaneleague.org.uk/article/governments-fail-to-inspect-fish-welfare-at-slaughter Retrieved March 4, 2024.

USDA report. (2023). *New Zealand sheep production and trends*. https://fas.usda.gov/data/new-zealand-new-zealand-sheep-production-and-trends

Understanding Animal Research. (2020). *Public attitudes to animal research under Covid-19*. https://www.understandinganimalresearch.org.uk/application/files/2016/5226/6731/attitudes_to_animal_research_under_covid-19_final.pdf Retrieved May 6, 2024.

Takenaka, C. S., Alves de Souza, C. N., & Momo, C. (2023). Case studies and technical aspects of the forensic necropsy of exhumed companion animals. *Forensic Science International*, *345*, 111624. https://doi.org/10.1016/j.forsciint.2023.111624

Tapper, J (2024) Adverts for `cruel` elephant rides still rising despite new law, says charity. The Guardian. https://www.theguardian.com/world/2024/oct/20/adverts-cruel-elephant-rides-uk-law-legislation-unethical-animal-tourism#:~:text=Duncan%20McNair%2C%20a%20barrister%20who,record%201%2C220%20that%20advertised%20in Retrieved October 29 2024

Tatum, J. (1988). On the ineffectiveness of Canadian animal care committees. *Psychiatry* [ETA bulletin], Fall 1988 (pp. 3–5).

Taylor, I. (2016). Using first nations systems thinking to operationalize sustainable development. In A. Masys (Ed.), *Applications of systems thinking and soft operations research in managing complexity. Advanced sciences and technologies for security applications*, 307–322. Springer. https://doi.org/10.1007/978-3-319-21106-0_14

The Animals (Scientific Procedures) Act. (1986). A fact sheet produced in 1992. British Union for the Abolition of Vivisection.

Thomas, D. (2005). Laboratory animals and the art of empathy. *Journal of Medical Ethics*, *31*(4), 197–202. https://doi.org/10.1136/jme.2003.006387

Thomas, D. (2017). Freedom of information and animal experiments: A case study. *UK J. Animal Law*, *1*, 28.

Thomas, D. (2022). Improving the law for animals: A campaigning Lawyer's perspective. *The Liverpool Law Review*, *43*(1), 107–121. https://doi.org/10.1007/s10991-022-09293-8

Thomas, K. (1983a). *Man and the natural world: Changing attitudes in England 1500–1800*. Allen Lane, London.

Thomas, R.H. (1983b). *The politics of hunting*. Gower Publishing.

Thompson, B. S. (2022). Ecotourism anywhere? The lure of ecotourism and the need to scrutinize the potential competitiveness of ecotourism developments. *Tourism Management*, *92*, 104568. https://doi.org/10.1016/j.tourman.2022.104568

Thompson, S. (2019). Supporting ape rights: Finding the right fit between science and the law. *ASEBL Journal*, *14*(1), 3–24.

Timperley, J. S. (2021). Rewilding: Can it save our wildlife and temper climate change? *Science focus magazine*. BBC.

Toepfer, G. (2019). On the impossibility and dispensability of defining "biodiversity". In E. Casetta, J. Marques da Silva, & D. Vecchi (Eds.), *From assessing to conserving biodiversity: Conceptual and practical challenges* (1st ed.) (pp. 341–351). Springer. Nature Publishing. https://doi.org/10.1007/978-3-030-10991-2_16

Tómas, R. (2023). No whaling this summer: Minister halts fin whale hunting. Iceland review. Iceland. http://www.icelandreview.com/news/

no-whaling-this-summer-minister-halts-fin-whale-hunting/ Retrieved May 14, 2024.

Tree, I., & Burrell, C. (2023). *The book of wilding*. Bloomsbury Publishing.

Trouwborst, A. (2015). Global large carnivore conservation and international law. *Biodiversity and Conservation*, *24*(7), 1567–1588. https://doi.org/10.1007/s10531-015-0894-8

Trouwborst, A. (2020) *Obligations of Bern Convention parties regarding the conservation of candidate and adopted Emerald Network sites: A legal analysis*. Elsevier.

Trouwborst, A., & Somsen, H. (2020). Domestic cats (Felis catus) and European nature conservation law—Applying the EU birds and habitats directives to a significant but neglected threat to wildlife. *Journal of Environmental Law*, *32*(3), 391–415. https://doi.org/10.1093/jel/eqz035

Tucker, G. M. (2022). *Divergence of environmental policy post Brexit: A comparison of biodiversity targets emerging in the EU and UK* [Report]. Institute for European Environmental Policy. http://www.ieep.eu/publications/ieep-uk-a-comparison-of-biodiversity-targets-emerging-in-the-eu-and-uk-post-brexit/ Retrieved May 14, 2024.

Tulloch, J. S. P., Owczarczak-Garstecka, S. C., Fleming, K. M., Vivancos, R., & Westgarth, C. (2021). English hospital episode data analysis (1998–2018) reveal that the rise in dog bite hospital admissions is driven by adult cases. *Scientific Reports*, *11*(1), 1767. https://doi.org/10.1038/s41598-021-81527-7

Turner, E. S. (1992). *All heaven in a rage* (2nd ed.). Centaur Publishing.

Tyson, E. (2021). Enforcing the Zoo Licensing Act 1981. In *Licensing laws and animal welfare. The Palgrave Macmillan animal ethics series*, 107–148. Palgrave Macmillan. https://doi.org/10.1007/978-3-030-50042-9_6

UK Centre for Animal Law. (2023) the_uk_centre_for_animal_law_a_law_and_the_focus_on_animal_law_group_the_foal_group_respond_to_the_governments_announcement_that_it_intends_to_add_the_american_xl_bulldog_to_the_list_of_banned_breeds_under_the_dange.pdf. mcusercontent.com Retrieved October 3, 2023.

UK Centre for Animal Law and Wildlife and Countryside Link. (2023). A review of Brexit: Getting the best Brexit deal for animals. https://www.alaw.org.uk/wp-content/uploads/2023/06/BDFA-Brexit-Review-June-2023.pdf Retrieved April 9, 2024.

UK Government. (2012). *Consultation on the options for transposition of European Directive 2010/63. EU on the protection of animals used for scientific purposes: Summary report and government response*. https://assets.publishing.service.gov.uk/media/5a7ac5e140f0b66a2fc02b55/gvt_response.pdf (assessed 9 April 2024).

UK Government. (2014). Code of practice for the housing and care of animals bred, supplied or used for scientific purposes. https://www.gov.uk/government/publications/code-of-practice-for-the-housing-and-care-of-animals-bred-supplied-or-used-for-scientific-purposes#:~:text=The%20code%20of%20practice%20 sets,may%20comply%20with%20those%20requirements Retrieved April, 9 2024.

UK Government. (2024). Rod fishing laws. http://www.gov.uk/guidance/national-rod-fishing-byelaws-for-england-freshwater-fishing-with-a-rod-and-line.

UK Pet Food (2024). UK Pet Population survey. https://www.ukpetfood.org/information-centre/statistics/uk-pet-population.html Retrieved May 13, 2024.

UN Environment Programme. (2020). Preventing the Next Pandemic: Zoonotic diseases and how to break the chain of transmission. https://www.unep.org/resources/report/preventing-future-zoonotic-disease-outbreaks-protecting-environment-animals-and Retrieved April 9, 2024.

UN General Assembly. (1948). 10 December 1948. *Universal Declaration of Human Rights, 217a,* (III). https://www.refworld.org/docid/3ae6b3712c.html Retrieved May 4, 2024.

United Nations Department of Economic and Social Affairs Indigenous Peoples mandated areas Environment. (n.d.). United Nations Educational, Scientific and Cultural Organization. United Nations Educational, Scientific and Cultural Organization (no date). http://www.ocial.desa.un.org/issues/indigenous-peoples/unpfii-mandated-areas-environment. http://www.unesco.org/en Retrieved May 14, 2024.

United Nations Department of Economic and Social Affairs. (2022). The Sustainable Development Goals Report 2022. https://doi.org/10.18356/9789210018098c019

Ungoed-Thomas, J. (2023). Premature death of 80m chickens raises concerns over UK's fast-growing breeds. *Guardian.* https://www.theguardian.com/world/2023/nov/11/premature-death-of-80m-chickens-raises-concerns-over-uks-fast-growing-breeds Retrieved May 14, 2024

United Nations. (2006). *Livestock's long shadow – environmental issues and options.* Food and Agriculture Organization, United Nations.

United Nations. (2013a). Tackling climate change through livestock: A global assessment of emissions and mitigation opportunities. Food and Agriculture Organization, United Nations. https://openknowledge.fao.org/server/api/core/bitstreams/e1afd815–5a76–4b88-beac-fb9bc0e92001/content.

United Nations (2013b) Global governance and governance of the global commons in the global partnership for development beyond 2015 www.un.org/en/development/desa/policy/untaskteam_undf/thinkpieces/24_thinkpiece_global_governance.pdf.

United Nations (UN). (n.d.). http://www.un.org Retrieved May 14, 2024.

United Nations Committee on the Rights of the Child. (2023). CRC/C/GC/26: *General comment, 26 on children's rights and the environment with a special focus on climate change.* https://www.ohchr.org/en/documents/general-comments-and-recommendations/crccgc26-general-comment-no-26-2023-childrens-rights Retrieved May 14, 2024.

United Nations Environment Programme (UNEP). (2023). *Global climate litigation report: 2023 status review.* Nairobi.

United Nations Environment Programme (UNEP). (2024a). Publications and data. http://www.unep.org/publications-data Retrieved May 16, 2024.

United Nations Environment Programme (UNEP). (2024b). Regional Seas related Multilateral Environmental Agreements (MEAs). http://www.unep.org/explore-topics/oceans-seas/what-we-do/working-regional-seas/partners/regional-seas-related#:~:text=Regional%20Seas%20related%20Multilateral%20Environmental%20Agreements%20(MEAs)&text=The%20Regional%20Seas%20Conventions%20and,MEAs)%20dealing%20with%20marine%20issues Accessed May 16, 2024.

United Nations Environment Programme (UNEP). (n.d.). http://www.unep.org Retrieved May 14, 2024.

United Nations Office on Drugs and Crime (UNODC). (2021). *Wildlife and forest crime analytic toolkit report: United Kingdom of Great Britain and Northern Ireland.* http://www.unodc.org/documents/Wildlife/UK_Toolkit_Report.pdf Retrieved May 14, 2024.

UNODC. (n.d.). www.unodc.org/unodc/frontpage/2023/April/viet-nam-customs-seize-seven-tons-of-smuggled-ivory.html Retrieved May 14, 2024.

Van der Meer, L., Kasdan, I., & Galvin, J. (2018). The importance of evidence, animal-based measures, and the rule of law to ensure good animal welfare. *Aquatic Mammals*, *44*(2), 142–149. https://doi.org/10.1578/AM.44.2.2018.142

Van Huis, A. (2021). Welfare of farmed insects. *Journal of Insects as Food and Feed*, *7*(5), 573–584. https://doi.org/10.3920/JIFF2020.0061

van Uhm, D., South, N., & Wyatt, T. (2021). Connections between trades and trafficking in wildlife and drugs. *Trends in Organized Crime*, *24*(4), 425–446. https://doi.org/10.1007/s12117-021-09416-z

Veterinary Record. (2020). The Badger cull figures have been condemned as 'appalling'. *Veterinary Record*, *186*(13), 402–404.

Vettese, T. (2023). Want to truly have empathy for animals? Stop owning pets. *The Guardian.* https://www.theguardian.com/commentisfree/2023/feb/04/want-to-truly-have-empathy-for-animals-stop-owning-pets#:~:text=Pets%20are%20not%20always%20passive,presently%20endangering%20200%20species%20worldwide Retrieved May 14, 2024.

Victor, K., & Barnard, A. (2016). Slaughtering for a living: A Hermeneutic phenomenological perspective on the well-being of slaughterhouse employees. *International Journal of Qualitative Studies on Health and Well-Being, 11*, 30266. https://doi.org/10.3402/qhw.v11.30266

Višak, T., & Garner, R. (Eds.). (2016). *The ethics of killing animals*. Oxford University Press.

Visseren-Hamakers, I. J. (2022). *Transforming biodiversity governance* I. J. Visseren-Hamakers & M. T. J. Kok (Eds.). Cambridge University Press.

Wadiwel, D. (2002). Cows and sovereignty: Biopolitics and care life. *Borderlands e-Journal, 1*(2).

Wandesforde-Smith, G., & Hart, L. A. (2015). Exploring the borderlands between wild and non-wild animals: Wildlife law and policy in transition. *Journal of International Wildlife Law and Policy, 18*(4), 269–275. https://doi.org/10.1080/13880292.2015.1111708

Warwick, C., Steedman, C., Jessop, M., Arena, P., Pilny, A., & Nicholas, E. (2018). Exotic pet suitability: Understanding some problems and using a labeling system to aid animal welfare, environment, and consumer protection. *Journal of Veterinary Behavior, 26*, 17–26. https://doi.org/10.1016/j.jveb.2018.03.015

Washington, H., Piccolo, J. J., Kopnina, H., & O'Leary Simpson, F. (2024). Ecological and social justice should proceed hand-in-hand in conservation. *Biological Conservation, 290*, 110456. https://doi.org/10.1016/j.biocon.2024.110456

Wathes, C. (2010). Guarding the welfare of farm animals. *The Veterinary Record*, 167(15), 583–584. https://doi.org/10.1136/vr.c4785

Watters, F., Stringham, O., Shepherd, C. R., & Cassey, P. (2022). The U.S. market for imported wildlife not listed in the CITES multilateral treaty. *Conservation Biology, 36*(6), e13978-n/a. https://doi.org/10.1111/cobi.13978

WDCS. (1995). *IWC whale and dolphin conservation* [Report]. WDCS Bath.

Weber, E.J.W. and Barron, E.S. (2023) Coloniality and Indigenous ways of knowing at the edges: Emplacing Earth kin in conservation communities. *New Zealand Geographer, 79*(2), 132–137. https://doi.org/10.1111/nzg.12367

Webster, J., & Margerison, J. (2022). *Management and welfare of farm animals: The UFAW farm handbook* (6th ed.). John Wiley & Sons Ltd.

Weisberg, Z. (2019). The problem with the personhood argument. *ASEBL Journal, 14*(1), 33–36.

Weiss, R. (1974). The provisions of social relationships. In Z. Rubin (Ed.), *Doing unto others* (pp. 17–26). Prentice Hall.

Wellsmith, M. (2011). Wildlife crime: The problems of enforcement. *European Journal on Criminal Policy and Research, 17*(2), 125–148. https://doi.org/10.1007/s10610-011-9140-4

Whale and Dolphin Conservation (WDC). (n.d.). http://www.uk.whales.org/support/adopt/?gad_source=1&gclid=EAIaIQobChMIjZTSsf_4hQMVCphQBh1-XA1REAAYASAAEgLbifD_BwE Fate of orcas in captivity - Whale & Dolphin Conservation USA (whales.org). http://

www.uk.whales.org/support/adopt/?gad_source=1&gclid=EAIaIQobChMIjZTSsf_4hQMVCphQBh1-XA1REAAYASAAEgLbifD_BwE Retrieved May 14, 2024.

White, R. (1991). Beastly questions. In R. Baird & S. Rosenblum (Eds.), *Animal experimentation: The moral issues*. Prometheus Books.

White, S. (2013). Into the void: International law and the protection of animal welfare. *Global Policy*, *4*(4), 391–398. https://doi.org/10.1111/1758-5899.12076

Wienhues, A., Baard, P., Donoso, A., & Oksanen, M. (2023). The ethics of species extinctions. *Cambridge Prisms: Extinction*, *1*, e23. https://doi.org/10.1017/ext.2023.21

Wierucka, K., Hatten, C. E., Murphy, D., Allcock, J. A., Andersson, A. A., Bojan, J. W., Kong, T. C., Kwok, J. K., Lam, J. Y., Ma, C. H., Phalke, S., Tilley, H. B., Wang, R. S., Wang, Y., Webster, S. J., Mumby, H. S., & Dingle, C. (2023). Human-wildlife interactions in urban Asia. *Global Ecology and Conservation*, *46*. https://doi.org/10.1016/j.gecco.2023.e02596

Wildlife and Countryside Link. (2021). http://www.wcl.org.uk Retrieved May 14, 2024.

Wildlife Trust of India. (2021). http://www.wti.org.in/projects/right-of-passage-national-elephant-corridors-project/ Retrieved May 14, 2024.

Wildlife Trusts. (n.d.). http://www.wildlifetrusts.org Retrieved May 14, 2024.

Willcock, S., Cooper, G. S., Addy, J., & Dearing, J. A. (2003). Earlier collapse of Anthropocene ecosystems driven by multiple faster and noisier drivers. *Nature Sustainability*, 6(11), 1331–1342. https://doi.org/10.1038/s41893-023-01157-x

Wills, J. (2018). A nation of animal lovers? The case for a general animal killing offence in UK law. *King's Law Journal*, *29*(3), 407–436. https://doi.org/10.1080/09615768.2018.1555026

Wills, J. (2020). Animal rights, legal personhood and cognitive capacity: Addressing "levelling-down" concerns. *Journal of Human Rights and the Environment*, *11*(2), 199–223. https://doi.org/10.4337/jhre.2020.02.03

Wilson, A. (2019a). Animal Law in South Africa: Until the lions have their own lawyers, the law will continue to protect the hunter. dA. *Derecho Animal* (Forum of Animal Law Studies) 10(1), 35–58.

Wilson, A. P. (2019b). (NON)HUMAN(IMAL) RIGHTS: DISMANTLING THE SEPARATENESS IN LAW AND POLICY. *Society Register*, *3*(3). Available at SSRN. https://ssrn.com/abstract=3636994 Retrieved May 14, 2024, 39–65. https://doi.org/10.14746/sr.2019.3.3.03

Wilson, E.O. (2019c) *Biodiversity and climate change: transforming the biosphere*. L. Hannah and T.E. Lovejoy (Eds.). Yale University Press. https://doi.org/10.12987/9780300241198

Wilson, E. (1992). *The diversity of life*. Penguin.

Wise, S. M. (2018). The struggle for the legal rights of nonhuman animals begins-the experience of The Nonhuman Rights Project in New York and Connecticut. *Animal Law*, *25*.

Wolfensohn, S. (2020). Too cute to kill? The need for objective measurements of quality of life. *Animals: An Open Access Journal from MDPI*, *10*(6), 1054. https://doi.org/10.3390/ani10061054

Wolfson, & Sullivan. (2004). Foxes in the hen house: Animals, agribusiness and the law. In Sunstein & Nussbaum (Eds.), *Animal rights*. Oxford University Press.

Wolfson, D. (1999). McLibel. *Animal Law*, *5*, 21.

Wood, D., Buesching, C., & Newman, C. (2022). Failing badger protection. *Oryx*, *56*(2), 170–170. https://doi.org/10.1017/S0030605321001782

Wood, L., Martin, K., Christian, H., Houghton, S., Kawachi, I., Vallesi, S., & McCune, S. (2017). Social capital and pet ownership – A tale of four cities. *SSM – Population Health*, *3*, 442–447. https://doi.org/10.1016/j.ssmph.2017.05.002

Woodford, P. (2019). Response to Shawn Thompson on "Supporting ape rights: finding the right fit between science and the law". *ASEBL Journal*, *14*(1), 38–41.

Wooler, S. (2014). The independent review of the prosecution activity of the Royal Society for the Prevention of Cruelty to Animal. https://www.rspca.org.uk/webContent/staticImages/Downloads/WoolerReviewFinalSept2014.pdf Retrieved May 14, 2024.

World animal protection. (2020). *Why is it cruel to keep wild animals as pets?* http://www.worldanimalprotection.org/blogs/why-it-cruel-keep-wild-animals-pets#:~:text=They%20often%20lack%20adequate%20shelter,a%20life%20in%20the%20wild Retrieved May 14, 2024.

World Health Organization. (2023a). Ongoing avian influenza outbreaks in animals pose risk to humans. https://www.who.int/news/item/12–07–2023-ongoing-avian-influenza-outbreaks-in-animals-pose-risk-to-humans Retrieved April 9, 2024.

World Health Organization. (2023b). One health global. https://www.who.int/health-topics/one-health#tab=tab_1 Retrieved April 9, 2024.

World Shipping Council. (n.d.). Protecting wildlife. http://www.worldshipping.org/protectingwildlife Retrieved May 16, 2024.

World Society for the Protection of Animals/Born Free Foundation. (1994). The zoo inquiry, *WSPA?* Born Free Foundation.

World Trade Organization. (2014) European Communities – Measures Prohibiting the Importation and Marketing of Seal Products. https://www.wto.org/english/tratop_e/dispu_e/cases_e/ds401_e.htm Retrieved March 5, 2024.

World Wildlife Fund (WWF). (2022). *Living planet report*. Gland. http://www.wwf.org.uk/our-reports/living-planet-report-2022

WWF (2024) *Living planet report 2024 – a system in peril*. Gland.

World Wildlife Fund. (n.d.). http://www.support.wwf.org.uk Retrieved May 14, 2024.

Wulf, A. (2015). *The invention of nature: The adventures of Alexander von Humboldt, the lost hero of science (UK). The invention of nature: Alexander von Humboldt's New World (USA).* John Murray (Hodder & Stoughton).

Wyatt, T. (2021). *Is CITES protecting wildlife? Assessing implementation and compliance*. Routledge.

Wyatt, T., Maher, J., Allen, D., Clarke, N., & Rook, D. (2022). The welfare of wildlife: An interdisciplinary analysis of harm in the legal and illegal wildlife trades and possible ways forward. *Crime, Law, and Social Change*, *77*(1), 69–89. https://doi.org/10.1007/s10611-021-09984-9

Wyatt, T., van Uhm, D., & Nurse, A. (2020). Differentiating criminal networks in the illegal wildlife trade: Organized, corporate and disorganized crime. *Trends in Organized Crime*, *23*(4), 350–366. https://doi.org/10.1007/s12117-020-09385-9

Wynne-Tyson, E. (1965). *Porphyry on abstinence from animal food*. Centaur Publishing.

Xiong, L., Shah, F., & Wu, W. (2022). Environmental and socio-economic performance of intensive farming systems with varying agricultural resource for maize production. *The Science of the Total Environment*, *850*, 158030. https://doi.org/10.1016/j.scitotenv.2022.158030

Yong, E. (2022). *An immense world: how animal sense reveal the hidden realms around us*. Random House.

YouGov. (2020). YouGov/HIS survey results. https://docs.cdn.yougov.com/5r7ryfdp97/HSI_FurRegulation_200305_w.pdf Retrieved March 4, 2024.

Zahar, A. (2023). Agricultural exceptionalism in the climate change treaties. *Transnational Environmental Law*, *12*(1), 42–70. https://doi.org/10.1017/S2047102522000437

Zhao, J., Wan, W., Yu, K., Lemey, P., Pettersson, J. H.-O., Bi, Y., Lu, M., Li, X., Chen, Z., Zheng, M., Yan, G., Dai, J., Li, Y., Haerheng, A., He, N., Tu, C., Suchard, M. A., Holmes, E. C., He, W.-T., & Su, S. (2024). Farmed fur animals harbour viruses with zoonotic spillover potential. *Nature*, *634*(8032), 228–233. https://doi.org/10.1038/s41586-024-07901-3

Zimmerman, M. E. et al. (2005). *Environmental philosophy: From animal rights to radical ecology* (4th edn). Pearson Education.

Zu Ermgassen, S. O. S. E., Maron, M., Corlet Walker, C. M., Gordon, A., Simmonds, J. S., Strange, N., Robertson, M., & Bull, J. W. (2020). The hidden biodiversity risks of increasing flexibility in biodiversity offset trades. *Biological Conservation*, *252*. https://doi.org/10.1016/j.biocon.2020.108861 Retrieved May 14, 2024.

Index

More from www.5mbooks.com

9781910455807
Sep 2017
320p
PB
£39.95
$65.00
€48.00

A Practical Approach to Animal Welfare Law 2nd Edition

Noël Sweeney

A Practical Approach to Animal Welfare Law is designed to be informative and interesting to a broad, lay audience and covers all aspects of the Animal Welfare Act 2006 and the Dangerous Dogs Act 1991 as they affect animals in our care.

9781910455685
May 2017
552p
PB
£39.95
$65.00
€48.00

Veterinary Ethics

Navigating Tough Cases

Edited by Siobhan Mullan and Anne Quain

Veterinary Ethics presents a range of ethical scenarios that veterinarians and other allied animal health professionals may face in practice. The scenarios discussed are not only exceptional cases with potentially significant consequences, but often less dramatic everyday situations.

9781789180497
May 2019
160p
PB
£24.95
$39.95
€29.95

Animals, Ethics and Us

A Veterinary's View of Human-Animal Interactions

Madeleine Campbell

Bringing a wealth of veterinary knowledge and experience, the author aims to present a scientific and ethically sound perspective of the position of animals in modern society to a broad readership.

9781789180084
Dec 2018
320p
PB
£24.95
$39.95
€29.95

Animal Welfare Science, Husbandry and Ethics

The Evolving Story of Our Relationship with Farm Animals

Mark Fisher

This book explores the development of the symbiotic relationship of man and non-human animals as the result of a long intertwined history of biological, social and cultural needs.

Case Studies in Ecohealth

Examining the Interaction between Animals and their Environment

Edited by Susan Cork and Doug Whiteside

A fascinating examination of the impacts on animals of environmental change, using the effects on animals at the frontier of ecological disturbance as sentinels for what is happening to our planet. The scope of the book is global, spanning environments from the tropics to the Arctic regions. Encompassing the lives and behaviours of different animals in different habitats gives this book a majestic breadth, presenting a true picture of ecology of the Earth right now.

Apr 2024 | ISBN 9781789182408
£45 | $70 | €55 | 380p PB

9781789181180
9781789181821
Nov 2021
700p
HB/Special Ed
£85 / £125
$135 / $195
€100 / €150

The History of Veterinary Medicine and the Animal-Human Relationship

Bruce Vivash Jones

This comprehensive book is an exploration of the history of veterinary medicine from the ancient world to the present as well as an examination of the development of man's relationship with animals.

9781910455555
Nov 2016
398p
PB
£39.95
$65.00
€48.00

One Health Case Studies

Addressing Complex Problems in a Changing World

Edited by Susan Cork

This textbook discusses complex concepts in One Health, such as preparedness planning, national level governance, interagency co-operation, climate change, human activity in sensitive ecosystems, and the global food trade and food safety.